Artistic and scientific

taxidermy and modelling

A manual of instruction in the methods of preserving

and reproducing the correct form of all natural objects,

including a chapter on the modelling of foliage

Montagu Browne

Alpha Editions

This edition published in 2019

ISBN : 9789353925710

Design and Setting By
Alpha Editions
email - alphaedis@gmail.com

ARTISTIC AND SCIENTIFIC
TAXIDERMY AND MODELLING

A MANUAL OF INSTRUCTION IN THE METHODS OF PRE-
SERVING AND REPRODUCING THE CORRECT
FORM OF ALL NATURAL OBJECTS
INCLUDING A CHAPTER ON
THE MODELLING OF
FOLIAGE

BY

MONTAGU BROWNE, F.G.S., F.Z.S., ETC.

CURATOR OF THE LEICESTER CORPORATION MUSEUM AND ART GALLERY;
AUTHOR OF 'PRACTICAL TAXIDERMY,' 'THE VERTEBRATE ANIMALS OF LEICESTERSHIRE
AND RUTLAND,' ETC.

WITH 22 FULL-PAGE ILLUSTRATIONS AND 11 ILLUSTRATIONS IN TEXT

LONDON
ADAM AND CHARLES BLACK
1896

TO

Sir William Henry Flower,

K.C.B., D.C.L., LL.D., Sc.D., F.R.S., ETC.,

DIRECTOR OF THE BRITISH MUSEUM (NATURAL HISTORY),

THIS VOLUME IS,

BY PERMISSION, DEDICATED

AS A TRIBUTE OF GRATEFUL FRIENDSHIP AND ESTEEM, AND

IN RECOGNITION OF HIS SYMPATHY WITH

ALL WHICH TENDS TO ELEVATE

THE ARTS OF TAXIDERMY AND MODELLING, AND THE STATUS

OF MUSEUMS GENERALLY.

PREFACE

SOME years have elapsed since the publication of a work from my pen entitled *Practical Taxidermy*, which, despite its elementary character, has—judging from numberless letters received from all quarters of the globe—been of some service to its readers.

Since that time, the gratifying strides made by taxidermists towards a better understanding of their art, and by museum authorities towards a more scientific exposition of natural objects, have emboldened me to describe methods of taxidermy and modelling not yet published, most of which are, indeed, absolutely novel, and at present confined to the Leicester Museum.

Although many of the processes described are somewhat advanced and necessarily technical, yet, as the old methods of work have been re-described, corrected, and have had new light thrown upon them, the learner is easily led from the known to the unknown, the stages being so defined that he need not be alarmed at the magnitude of the task set him. Moreover, the writer is always ready, as of old, to render any further assistance to his readers if, when they write, a properly addressed envelope for reply be enclosed.

At the outset, it was intended to devote a somewhat lengthy chapter to a consideration of the aims of the scientific museum of the future (contrasted with the past and present), and to a review of all that is noteworthy in the management and arrangement of museums at home and abroad. So much material has accumulated, however, as to forbid its inclusion within the present pages, which are therefore restricted to a description of methods of Taxidermy and Modelling, leaving wider considerations of matters connected with museums to be dealt with in a future work.

MONTAGU BROWNE.

CORPORATION MUSEUM AND ART GALLERY,
LEICESTER, *February* 1896.

ERRATUM

Page 46, line 3, *for* subsequently, *read* previously.

CONTENTS

CHAPTER I

CHAPTER II

CHAPTER III

CHAPTER IV

CHAPTER V

CHAPTER VI

CHAPTER VII

CHAPTER VIII

CHAPTER IX

CHAPTER X

ILLUSTRATIONS

PRINTED SEPARATELY FROM THE TEXT

ILLUSTRATIONS

PRINTED IN THE TEXT

CHAPTER I

INTRODUCTION—THE ORIGIN AND PROGRESS OF TAXIDERMY

THE origin of taxidermy as a purely decorative art is involved in some obscurity, although the name itself, derived from the Greek—τάξις, order, arrangement, or preparation, and δέρμα, skin—plainly reveals its first intention. No doubt the preparation of skins for practical utility dates from the very earliest times. In the rude flint "knives" and "scrapers" found in such caves as those of the Dordogne and many other places, there is abundant evidence that pleistocene man knew how to flay and dress skins in some manner. It is manifestly clear that he could not have existed as a contemporary of animals such as the mammoth, woolly rhinoceros, bear, and numberless other beasts specially protected from the cold, without clothing of some kind, and, before the discovery of the art of weaving, the most obvious expedient was to convert to his own purposes the skins of the animals he trapped or otherwise overcame. As skins, to be worn at all, whether with the fur inside or out, must be softened in some manner, there is no reason to doubt that, either by scraping, and rubbing with earth, roots, or wood-ashes, or by a ley, he ultimately succeeded in the "preparation of skins," and thus became the first "taxidermist."

We may even presume that the earliest man—whose
existence is only known by the imperishable flint weapons he
fashioned, and by the stains of his cave-fires—not only flayed
the various wild animals he overcame with his stone and
wooden implements for the sake of the clothing they afforded
him, but, perhaps, inflated or stuffed some of their skins with
grasses as "stales" or decoys, or used the skins as coverings
when stalking animals of the same species, and he may certainly
have used skins for many other purposes, and have prepared
them also, as savages of later days have done and still do.

From these long-vanished peoples to the Egyptians and
Mexicans, with their methods of tanning the skins and embalming the bodies of their dead, and of cats, dogs, various
birds, and so on, is an easy step, and they were, probably, the
first "animal preservers," testimonies of whose work satisfactorily performed are to be found in many museums.

Dr. Shufeldt, of the United States National Museum, considers that the supposed gorillas mentioned by the Carthaginian
navigator Hanno, B.C. 500, as having been killed and flayed
in Africa and afterwards conveyed to Carthage, where "they
were preserved for many generations, are, no doubt, the
Gorgones described by Pliny."[1]

Supposing these to have been preserved merely as flat skins,
this would only mark the well-known fact that the ancients
were perfectly well acquainted with tanning ; indeed, this is an
art which every savage must know, to say nothing of such a
civilised people as the Carthaginians ; but if they, however
roughly, attempted to set up the skins, that would be indeed
the dawn of taxidermy as we understand the meaning of the
word.

Little is known of the beginnings of the practice of the "stuffing"
or "setting-up" of animals for ornament or for scientific purposes ;

[1] *Rep. Smithsonian Institution* for 1892, p. 370.

and it is highly probable, from what we gather from old works of travel or natural history, that the art is not more than some three hundred years old. It was practised in England towards the end of the seventeenth century, as is proved by the Sloane collection, which in 1725 formed the nucleus of the collection of natural history now lodged in the galleries at South Kensington.[1]

This assumption as to the three hundred years' limit derives some corroboration from another statement made by Dr. Shufeldt, who writes : [2]—

Probably, as Mr. Goode informs me, the oldest museum specimen in existence is a rhinoceros still preserved in the Royal Museum of Vertebrates in Florence. This was for a long time a feature of the Medicean Museum in Florence, and was originally mounted for the museum of Ulysses Aldrovandus in Bologna. It dates from the sixteenth century.

Davie also says [3] :—

It is told that the first attempt to stuff birds was when the Hollanders in the early part of the sixteenth century began their commercial intercourse with the East Indies.

A nobleman brought back to Amsterdam a large collection of live tropical birds and placed them in an aviary, which was heated to the proper temperature by a furnace. It happened that the attendant one night before retiring carelessly left the door of the furnace open, thereby allowing the smoke to escape, which suffocated the birds. The nobleman beholding the destruction of his large collection, which was the pride of the city, began to devise means for the preservation of the dead birds. To this end the best chemists of Amsterdam were called in for consultation, and it was decided to skin the birds and fill their skins with the spices of the Indies for their preservation. This was done, and they were then wired and mounted to represent life. For many years they were the hobby of the nobleman and the pride of the inhabitants.

[1] *Encyclopædia Britannica*, 9th ed., vol. xxiii. p. 89.
[2] *Rep. Smithsonian Institution* for 1892, footnote to p. 371.
[3] *Methods in the Art of Taxidermy*, Historical Introduction, pp. ii., iii.

Again, he says : [1]—

The oldest work in my collection is a *Natural History* published at Paris by the Royal Academy in 1687, on the dissection of various animals.   In this work mention is made of the fact that the Hollanders were the first to bring into Europe live specimens and skins of the cassowary and a number of other strange birds which they secured on their first voyages (1517) to the Indian archipelago.   These were stuffed at Amsterdam.

It must be conceded that to the writings of educated naturalists, who were often medical men, we owe the genesis of the present methods of mounting animals.   So far, however, as can be at present ascertained, one of the earliest writers upon, and exponents of, this delightful art was Réaumur, who, in 1748, published a treatise on preserving skins of birds.   From that date onward, the growing importance of the subject has continuously produced a large mass of literature relating to it, of which a bibliography—by no means complete, owing to the difficulty of exhaustively cataloguing various treatises scattered in the pages of current literature,—will be found at the end of this volume.   Of the works there enumerated, some are written by practical men for practical men and beginners ; very few, less than can be counted on the fingers of one hand, by educated men who were also workers ; the great majority are mere compilations.

There is no doubt that some of the works mentioned in the bibliography, especially those written by such men as the Abbé Manesse, Waterton, and Captain Thomas Brown, gave a great impetus to taxidermy ; but unfortunately, although those writers knew enough to be dissatisfied with their own and others' work, yet their processes were, except in rare instances (to be considered later), founded upon ancient methods which had no definite rules, but left almost everything to the fancy

[1] *Methods in the Art of Taxidermy,* Historical Introduction, p. iv.

of the "stuffer"—(*empailleur*, objects being formerly stuffed with straw),—who was, as now, usually an uneducated person working by "rule of thumb"; hence one can sympathise with, and fully endorse, the lament of Waterton, who writes :[1]—

Twenty years have now rolled away since I first began to examine the specimens of zoology in our museums. As the system of preparation is founded in error, nothing but deformity, distortion, and disproportion, will be the result of the best intentions and utmost exertions of the workman. Canova's education, taste, and genius enabled him to present to the world statues so correct and beautiful that they are worthy of universal admiration. Had a common stonecutter tried his hand upon the block out of which these statues were sculptured, what a lamentable want of symmetry and fine countenance there would have been. Now, when we reflect that the preserved specimens in our museums and private collections are always done upon a wrong principle, and generally by low and illiterate people, whose daily bread depends upon the shortness of time in which they can get through their work, and whose opposition to the true way of preparing specimens can only be surpassed by their obstinacy in adhering to the old method; can we any longer wonder at their want of success; or hope to see a single specimen produced that will be worth looking at?

Again, he continues :[2]—

Were you to pay as much attention to birds as the sculptor does to the human frame, you would immediately see, on entering a museum, that the specimens are not well done.

This remark will not be thought severe when you reflect that that which once was a bird has probably been stretched, stuffed, stiffened, and wired by the hand of a common clown. Consider likewise how the plumage must have been disordered by too much stretching or drying, and perhaps sullied, or at least deranged, by the pressure of a coarse and heavy hand—plumage which, ere life had fled from within it, was accustomed to be touched by nothing rougher than the dew of heaven, and the pure and gentle breath of air.

[1] *Wanderings in South America* (edited by Rev. J. G. Wood, 1893, p. 333).
[2] *Ibid.*, p. 335.

Captain Thomas Brown was the next who saw the matter in the same light; he writes : [1]—

Although considerable advances have been made of late years in the art of taxidermy, it is still far from perfection.   This is to be attributed, in a great measure, to the education of the persons who practise this art; for among all I have met with employed in the preservation of animals, none have had the advantage of anatomical study, which is quite indispensable to the perfection of stuffing.   One or two individuals, it is true, have attended to the structure of the skeleton of man, and a few of the more common animals, but this is far from the information which they ought to possess; for nothing short of a general and extensive knowledge of comparative anatomy can qualify them sufficiently for an art which is so comprehensive and varied in its application.

These observations are particularly applicable to quadrupeds and reptiles, for what are even the best stuffed specimens of the first museums in the world compared to the living subject ?   Nothing better than deformed and glaringly artificial productions, devoid of all the grace and beautifully turned points of living nature.   A knowledge of drawing and modelling are also indispensable qualifications, to enable the stuffer to place his subject in a position both natural and striking.   It is the too frequent practice for the stuffer to set about preserving the animal without having determined in what attitude he is to place it, so that it will appear to most advantage, and be in character with the ordinary habits of the creature.   This he leaves to the last efforts of finishing his work, and, consequently, its proportions and character are likely to be devoid of all appearance of animation.

The first thing, therefore, to be attended to in all great national natural history establishments, is to choose young persons who are yet in their boyhood, to be instructed in this art, most important to science. Their studies should be commenced by deep attention to drawing, model-ling, anatomy, and chemistry, while they, at the same time, proceed with the practical part of their art.   Every opportunity of examining the habits and actions of the living subject should be embraced, and its attitudes and general aspect carefully noted.   Without strict attention to these points, so manifestly obvious, the art of preserving

[1] *Taxidermist's Manual*, pp. 2-4, last reprint.

animals *never will* attain that degree of perfection which its importance demands. On the other hand, if this art is pursued in the manner here recommended, artists may be produced who will fulfil the objects of their profession with honour to themselves and advantage to their country. Would any person expect to arrive at eminence as a sculptor if he were unacquainted with the established preliminaries of his art, namely, drawing and anatomy? The thing is so self-evident, that I am only surprised it has not long ago been acted upon. Upwards of twelve years have elapsed since I pointed out these facts to the Professor of Natural History in the University of Edinburgh, but things continue as they were before that time.

In the ninth edition of the *Encyclopædia Britannica* (vol. xxiii. pp. 89, 90), the present writer briefly sketched the future of taxidermy thus :—

A new school of taxidermy, with new methods, whose aim is to combine knowledge of anatomy and modelling with taxidermic technique, is now coming to the front, and the next generation will discard all processes of " stuffing " in favour of modelling. . . . This . . . indicates the future of the art, the hope of which lies in the better education of taxidermists as designers, artists, and modellers.

Commenting on this, Dr. Shufeldt says :[1]—

Not only should they be better instructed in designing, in art, and in modelling, but, what is quite as important, they should be trained especially in the power of correct observation in animal morphology, and in other matters which will be enumerated further along.

At pages 380-382 the following valuable remarks occur :—

To be a scientific taxidermist requires, or should require, in the first instance, a very thorough education, quite equal to that given by our best colleges. He should have a complete training in biology, with especial emphasis having been placed upon his studies in comparative morphology, so as to be familiar, as far as possible, with the vertebrate skeleton and topographical anatomy, to include more particularly the study of the superficial muscles of vertebrates. He should have such

[1] *Rep. Smithsonian Institution* for 1892, pp. 375, 376.

a conception of physics as to be able to decide upon the possible and the impossible in animal postures. In a way, he should be a good artist, be enabled to use the photographic camera, and make intelligent sketches of animals of all kinds and their natural haunts. He should be fully abreast of the times in all taxidermic technique *per se*, and possess fine mechanical skill.

As full a knowledge as can be attained of the habits of animals from personal observations should be added, as well as a constitutional desire to become familiar through current literature with all advances made from time to time in his art, and a healthy ambition to ever utilise them and improve upon the same.

So far as human ability is concerned, were I at this moment called upon to decide as to the relative merits of the talent required to paint a life-sized elephant, to sculpture one in stone, or to properly preserve one in a natural position and colour so that it would safely resist the ravages of time and all else that might injure it, I should not hesitate a moment in rendering an opinion, for I should say it lay with the scientific taxidermic artist. Mind you, when I do thus decide, I have had in my lifetime, with specimens of smaller animals, experience with all. At the best, however, the difference is but of very small degree, and yet the taxidermist, in a way, should be master of both the art of the painter and the art of the sculptor, for frequently he has to use the brush with great fidelity to nature, and the time is fast coming on when he must be able to build up, in clay at least, the entire forms of the larger animals which he aims to preserve.

Next, it may be asked, why a collegiate education? Simply because I believe a man in any calling is a better man in every way for having received the four years' training which a university gives him. And surely neither the taxidermist, nor the artist, nor the sculptor offers any exception to the rule. Moreover, everything that the skilled taxidermist would acquire in a college course would materially assist him in his profession in his subsequent career. Whatever may have been written, and whatever may have been said on the broad question of the college man *versus* the self-made man, it has been my experience that the kind of men that bring our country the most desirable recognition from other nations are those who have received a liberal education. A taxidermist should be a good general biologist, and he should pay especial attention to the habits of all animals in nature; the geographical ranges of faunæ; breeding habits; the peculiar habits indulged in by various kinds of animals; their natural resorts during times of feeding, amusement, or conducting their young. Plants of all kinds should with scrupulous care be studied from the taxidermist's standpoint, as well as the localities where they grow, nature of surfaces of the ground, and all else presented on the part of field, ocean, stream, and forest. Nothing should escape his constant study of such matters, and, above all else, he should cultivate the faculty of patience. An impatient man, it may be safely said, can never attain to the highest position the art has in its power of giving him.

In comparative morphology, as I have said, he should devote a great deal of time to the skeleton and to topographical anatomy. The study of the skeleton is of the very highest importance, as without a knowledge of it there is no hope at all of a man being a perfect taxidermist in all its varied departments. Normal movements of the articulations and the *ligaments* that control them should receive most careful consideration, and no opportunity lost to study such matters scientifically upon all kinds of animal cadavers. Special drawings made by the taxidermist should record special points observed and worked out—the possibilities in normal movements and postures as exhibited by the osseous system. In its entirety, however, this cannot be fully appreciated without a full knowledge of the muscular system, for there are possible movements that the skeleton, when cleaned and dried, is capable of making, which, in life, become impossible from the operation of muscles and tendons. So myology must be systematically studied *pari passu* with the subject of skeletology, and with the aim constantly in view of acquiring a clear insight into the normal postures of animals.

This leads to the consideration of the question of correct form, and to acquire that requires prolonged research and study upon the entire subject of topographical anatomy. Muscles extended; muscles contracted; muscles at rest; contours formed by the normal deposit of adipose tissue, contours formed by parts of the skeleton that are merely subcutaneous; contours formed by the presence of glands of all kinds, of sesamoidal bones, cartilages, and every other structure that may in any way affect the normal contour of an animal. To this must be added the careful study of all external characters proper, as the hair and analogous parts, throughout the animal kingdom—the eyes and their surroundings, the nasal structures, the mouth of all vertebrates and invertebrates. Indeed, there is not a point properly falling within the range of topographical anatomy in its very widest sense that should be beneath the special notice of the taxidermist.

Colours of parts should also receive marked attention; and the taxidermist should keep a notebook devoted to that one branch alone. Never should an opportunity be lost to record by actual painted sketches the colours of every external anatomical character presented on the part of any animal whatsoever. Zoology itself would be far freer from gross errors of the colour descriptions of animals were naturalists, as a rule, more careful in such matters. This is markedly the case in ichthyology and in the naked skin-tracts of mammals and birds. We, then, are naturally led to the question of drawing and painting; and no one will doubt the necessity of a taxidermist being more or less proficient in all these branches. But none of them will be of any service to him unless the power be supplemented by the more important faculty of being a correct observer, and to be a correct observer is to see and appreciate things as they really exist. Taxidermists should have a knowledge of not only making correct sketches of all kinds of animals and their haunts and of plants and colouring them correctly, but they should be enabled to use such instruments as are demanded in making reduced drawings correctly from large subjects. Colouring in oil is also of great value in restoring the tints in some cases on the skins of preserved animals, and the student in this art should constantly aim to cultivate his sense of colour-appreciation, and of the matching of all the various shades.

While agreeing most thoroughly and heartily with the main propositions concerned, there are yet two matters upon which opinions may differ: one is the value of amateur photography, and what may be called eccentric photography—such as some of Muybridge's productions; the other is a collegiate education.

To take the first: amateur photography of animals is usually a great mistake, especially if the ubiquitous " Kodaker " is not an artist. Some of the photographs from living birds in Dr. Shufeldt's own work bear out this contention, especially those taken from the living domestic fowls, whose strained and inartistic attitudes are, if natural, at least those resulting from fright, and not those which any one but a photographer, anxious to take a "snap shot" at any risk, would perpetuate. Quite as incorrect is it to write, as Dr. Shufeldt does at page 383 :—

By the use of the camera the taxidermist can secure subjects that the unaided eye and pencil can never give him, and these are all kinds of animals in rapid motion, and they may be obtained, after a due amount of practice, by the use of the photographic camera. One has but to study the superb series of photographs obtained through the indefatigable Eadwuard Muybridge to appreciate my meaning here.

It may be asked : Would any taxidermist attempt to reproduce "animals in rapid motion" as shown by instantaneous photography ? Is it not yet fully understood that taxidermic representation of objects stands upon a level with pictorial art, and that to represent, by either method, attitudes, fixed by the lightning flash of the eye of the camera, which are invisible to the eye of man, is false in theory and in practice?

There are men, however—but they are professional photographers, with a wide knowledge of the limited resources of their art—who represent animals in natural and graceful positions, and we need go no farther than instancing the beautiful pictures of Gambier Bolton and of Captain Hayes, from which any learned taxidermist might derive inspiration.

The vexed and very delicate question of a university career for taxidermists is, perhaps, a little difficult to decide. It would be a distinct gain could one be sure that, having had the advantages of a scientific training in a university, such students would indeed rest content to embrace a profession where a capacity for a certain amount of hard work, unfashionably long hours, great technical skill, and some energy would enable them to lead a useful and honourable life.

Well-educated and of wide and far-reaching knowledge taxidermists should be, but of equal importance to them, and indeed to all curators of museums, are an accurate perception of form and colour, a sound grounding in anatomy, a great love of order, and, lastly, a familiarity, gained in the field, of the habits of animals. The absence of these qualifications explains the undoubted fact that there are dozens of ill-educated men who never should have become taxidermists or curators, and, on the other hand, there are likewise dozens of university men filling posts in museums in various countries, whose business habits and attainments as curators are *nil*, and to them, probably, is due the general and unfortunate conception of an ordinary museum as a place where everything is very dry, very inartistic, and very neglected.

One thing is abundantly plain : that taxidermists and also curators are of " no account " unless they realise form and lines of beauty, and have a good anatomical grounding and considerable aptitude. Colour, of course, is of high importance, but colour-sense is of no avail without sense of form, and this ignorance of the first principle in art is painfully evidenced every day. Who does not know the lovely colour-schemes and fine colour-perception revealed in Giacomelli's birds? Yet neither the artist nor the thousands of people who look at the reproductions of his works appear to be aware that the *forms* are those of the ignorant bird-stuffer ;—crooked-backed, all awry, and with eyes starting from their heads, these birds, so perfect in colour, are disgraceful in form, and in those obviously taken from life the drawing is but little better.

In the Royal Academy may constantly be seen such defects of drawing when artists are dealing with animal life, or what is called still life. In 1892 a study was exhibited in which an owl figured ; the painting was simply perfect and learned—but the bird ! A ragged, moth-eaten old specimen, stuffed by some incompetent hand; and the artist, as artists constantly do, failed to recognise the utter atrocity of the lines of form. No longer ago than 8th December 1894, there appeared on page 3 of the Supplement to the *Graphic* an article on "Modern Falconry," illustrated by a woodcut called by courtesy "A Peregrine Falcon," but which might well have represented, and perhaps did, a female sparrow-hawk; at all events, the drawing was made from an exceedingly ill-stuffed and very ragged hawk of the most pronounced "bird-stuffer's" type.

If artists blunder in this way, slavishly copying ill-matured creations, taxidermists should use every endeavour to more thoroughly and conscientiously grapple with the difficulties which surround them; until they do, they mislead artists who are "form-blind," and they live in a fool's paradise themselves. When they are thoroughly trained, and appreciate the niceties of contour and the "lines of beauty," they may spare their more scientific friends—who may not, however, be artists—the trouble and annoyance of publishing a work which, projected to do them and their country honour, has resulted in merely showing up their ignorance, or their disregard, of the most elementary principles of their art.

Indeed, such instances as the above show that taxidermy is an art but little understood and appreciated even by its votaries and critics, and probably, although of growing importance, no real progress will be made until educated youths are specially trained by artists and cultured men of wide knowledge. Coming to a consideration of the nations who have contributed most to the artistic side of taxidermy, there is no doubt that the Italians, French, and Germans were the pioneers in this, and probably some of the oldest groups now extant would be those mentioned by Dr. Shufeldt[1] on the authority of Professor Brown Goode :—

[1] *Rep. Smithsonian Institution* for 1892, footnote, p. 407.

The mounting of animals in picturesque and lifelike groups in the midst of accessories taken from their natural haunts appears to have been first attempted by Professor Paolo Savi in the early part of the present century.   In the museum of the University of Pisa nearly one hundred of these are still preserved.   One of these, a group of starlings upon the head of a dead sheep, is as fine as anything since produced anywhere ; and a pair of boar hounds attacking a boar is, for action, the best piece of mammal mounting I have ever seen. The collection is a wonderful one, and is still perfectly preserved.

The great Exhibition of 1851, which marked an era in English taxidermy, showed some notable groups executed by H. Ploucquet, of Stuttgart, who, apart from the comic groups and those serio-comic ones such as illustrated the fable of " Reinecke the Fox," contributed such large studies as a stag caught by five hounds, a wild boar set upon by three hounds, a goshawk attacking a large owl, and so on.[1]   Soon after this date, the English and others bestirred themselves, and Edwin Ward produced his " Lion and Tiger Struggle " ; John Wallace, " A Horseman attacked by Tigers " ; and Jules Verreaux, " An Arab Courier attacked by Lions " ; whilst a host of other " Lion and Tiger Struggles " and " Tiger and Leopard Struggles " were produced by inferior men.   In 1871 a fine group, " The Combat " (of Red Deer), was executed and exhibited by Rowland Ward, and to him, and to his whole family, taxidermists are indebted for many and notable applications of little-known methods, and for improvements in others, especially in those dealing with the larger mammals, until the culminating point was reached in the largest group ever attempted, viz. " The Trophy of Kooch Behar," or " The Jungle," exhibited at the Colonial and Indian Exhibition of 1886, which occupied a great space.   Probably it was considered that, in a large trophy such as this, detail was hardly

[1] The greater part of this collection is still exhibited at the Crystal Palace, Sydenham.

necessary, the correct pose and arrangement only of the subjects being aimed at; otherwise a critical observer might take exception to the fact that the tigers nearest the entrance were ill-managed about the heads—the tongues, thickly painted and exhibiting no papillæ, being apparently made of slabs of some material, probably clay (see p. 139), and the other parts of the mouths being somewhat shrivelled and destitute of palatal ridges and of large muscles around the teeth; but, whilst the mouths generally were bad, and the noses and the modelling and arrangement of the eyelids not good, the eyes themselves were excellent. Indeed, taking the mammals as a whole, with the exception of the eyes, the faults of the ordinary taxidermist were apparent, and the impression they left was, that there was too much paint and putty, and too little artistic modelling by proper methods.

Museum authorities never looked very cordially upon such large groups, nor, indeed, upon anything of a pictorial nature, and probably the first to take up the pictorial mounting of birds was the small museum of Ludlow, sometime about 1870, and the groups were arranged by one or the other of the Shaws—excellent taxidermists—of Shrewsbury.

About this time, a private museum of British birds was founded at the Dyke Road, Brighton, by Mr. E. T. Booth—a well-to-do sporting naturalist since deceased,—which created a considerable impression. No scientific principles were involved in the arrangement, only the truths of nature imitated by art. The setting-up of the birds — all collected by the owner, assisted by his wife—was of nearly uniform excellence, and the accessories were almost uniquely managed. Such things as robins in a woodyard, with chopper, chopping-block, glove, and backed up by posts and ivy; kingfishers with surroundings copied from a small sluice in Shoreham harbour, the broken posts and half-rotted hatch with seaweeds and a piece of rope;

and other subjects, being remarkably fine, whilst the "rock-work," nearly all of carefully moulded paper, was an exact transcript of the rocks of the original haunts of the birds, and was coloured with care and elegance.[1]

Then followed Leicester ; and the idea of using modelled foliage as accessories to the groups of birds and their nests is said to have originated in that town, and was taken up soon afterwards by the British Museum, and later by the American Government Museums. There is no doubt that such groups mark a great epoch in taxidermic work, and consequently in the progress and increasing popularity of museums generally, where formerly anything of the kind was rigidly tabooed. To the enlightened reign of Sir William Flower at the South Kensington Natural History Museum is due the development of the special groups illustrating albinism, melanism, and protective selection, and of the splendid Index collections.

In America, according to Mr. Hornaday, the group system was not well received, and the first group—to which, it may be hoped, Plate XVII.[2] does not do justice—was refused in 1879, as were several others afterwards, by the Government Museums. Three years later the group was, however, accepted by the National Museum, and in 1888 the largest museum group known—that of American bisons, three adults and young, enclosed in a single case,[3] with numerous accessories—was finished. Since that time others as large and important have been executed, and probably at the present date their groups far surpass ours in extent and size, though not in handling ; for America, the most progressive of all nations, is curiously behind the age in taxidermic knowledge : all their essays and books upon the subject abundantly prove this, and when their latest writer[4] is content to give

---

[1] This fine collection is now the property of the Brighton Corporation.
[2] *Taxidermy*, p. 231.   [3] *Rep. Smithsonian Institution* for 1887, Plate I.
[4] Shufeldt, *Rep. Smithsonian Institution* for 1892, pp. 369-436.

unqualified praise to such very unnatural and unskilled work as that shown on Plates XXXIX., XLVI., L., LVI., LVII., LVIII., LXI., LXII., LXV., LXXIII., XC. (Figs. 1 and 2), and many others—all of which, excepting XLV., LXIV., LXVIII., LXXVIII., and LXXIX., fall very far short of even an average standard,—there seems but little hope of improvement in birds at least. Some of their larger mammals, however, are better, and some, such as those shown on Plates LIV., LV., LXXX., LXXXII., LXXXIII., and LXXXV., approach perfection. Their most regrettable failure may be due to the fact that, as amongst ourselves, there are but few really artistic and learned men who have taken up taxidermy, and that the great institutions, owing to their policy, do not avail themselves of the best and latest knowledge, but rely in many cases upon unskilled workmen.

On the other hand, in models of fishes and reptiles, and of invertebrates especially, the Americans appear to have achieved great success, and in this and in their modelled foliage—the latter executed by English artists, however—they can easily surpass the British Museum.

Probably the future and hope of taxidermy will be the welding of the educated artist, designer, modeller, sculptor, biologist, and naturalist ; and the two last are by no means synonymous terms, as some might suppose. When this happens—and there is no reason why all these attributes should not be combined in one individual—taxidermy will become an exact science relieved, as painting is at present, by poetic inspirations.

At one time there was a hope that, by a fusion of interests amongst professional taxidermists, better methods of work might be evolved, which would benefit not only themselves but also the public at large. Accordingly, some of the leading men of America formed a national society at Rochester, N.Y., on 12th

March 1880, and this, which was called "The Society of American Taxidermists," was the first society of the kind, and should have done great things not only for American taxidermy, but for that of the world. Its first annual exhibition was held from 14th to 18th December 1880, when medals and certificates were granted to various members for work exhibited. Two other annual exhibitions were also held, which do not appear, however, to have been successes financially, although numbers of "pieces" were exhibited. The first annual report was issued in 1881, the second in 1882, and the third in 1883, and contained—especially the last—some capital papers (mentioned in the bibliography), notably one by the President, Mr. Frederic A. Lucas.[1] After that time the Society ceased to exist, whether from want of funds, from professional jealousy, or from the apathy of the public is unknown, but in any case its disappearance is regrettable.

One word of caution is necessary : in these pages will frequently appear references to work executed in the Leicester Museum ; it must not be supposed, however, that all is excellent or approaching perfection, for there is a great quantity of taxidermic work which is very defective, and the want of courage is often regretted which allowed these old and ill-mounted specimens to be retained, and to be patched up instead of burned ; fortunately, however, as fresh specimens are procured, they replace those which are unsatisfactory.

Finally, the object of the following pages is to pave the way for such a happy combination of qualities in the taxidermist as has been previously sketched, and if the methods and instructions are explicit enough to do this, that object will have been attained.

[1] " The Scope and Needs of Taxidermy," Address of the President, Frederic A. Lucas, *Third Annual Report of the Society of American Taxidermists*, 1882-83, pp. 51-58.

CHAPTER II

ALTHOUGH the tools absolutely necessary for skinning and setting up any animal are not many, yet there are quite a number which the artistic exponent of taxidermy will discover he wants and cannot do very well without. Such ordinary tools as saws, planes, brace and bits, set-square, chisels, gimlets, brad-awls, hammer, spokeshave, and chopper are not taken into consideration, these being tools which are almost necessities, and which every one can handle more or less (often less) dexterously. In the latter case he must call in the friendly carpenter. It may be urged, perhaps, that there are some tools figured upon Plate I. which are homely enough, such as the rule, knives, and scissors, but they are not quite so common as they look, being specialised for certain work.

Taking the rule first—which is unnumbered, and primarily placed in its position as a means of readily determining the size of each and every tool shown,—it will be observed (or would be were the scale of reproduction large enough) to be a steel rule, on the right-hand half of which is marked the ordinary British measure of twelve inches to the foot; this side is marked " London." On the other side, marked " Paris," are the metre and its divisions, and, as Science usually recognises these, this side will be found of use for many purposes. Most English works of reference give measurements in tenths of an inch, and therefore, if engraved with these, such a rule, costing but a trifle, is cheap and good.

No. 1 knife, as will be seen by reference to the rule, is eight inches in entire length, and about three-quarters of an inch wide in the blade. It is of a handy size and shape for skinning the larger animals, and for a variety of other purposes. No. 2 is of a different shape, but is equally useful, and comes in handily to supplement the other. No. 3 is too long for most purposes, but is figured to show that from this is made, by snapping and grinding the blade, the handy little knife No. 4, which is the one most useful in skinning birds and small mammals, and for "trimming and splitting" (see Chap. V.). All of these knives are cheap and strong, having polished hardwood handles riveted to the "tang" of the blade—a most necessary quality in any knife, but especially in one used for taxidermic purposes. No. 5 was originally an artist's double-edged eraser, with a handle of steel in one piece with the blade, but it has now one edge ground flat, and so makes a still smaller and handy scalpel-like knife. Its cost being but little, and its strength undoubted, it is a favourite instrument, although its handle is rather too thin, as is also that of the ordinary scalpel, No. 6, which has a bone handle, and is only figured in deference to the views of some taxidermists, who find it useful for small things.

No. 7, the spoon-shaped instrument, is the eye and brain scoop or extractor—a tool which may save the beginner some trouble in preventing the bursting of a bird's eyeballs, but which he will learn to discard in time, practice enabling him to pick out the eyes and extract the brains with the blade of his knife, or with the end of the tool No. 16.

No. 8 is a strong but not large pair of shears, much stronger and more efficient than ordinary scissors of the same size, and is required for cutting through the bones of the neck, wings, and legs of birds, dividing cartilage generally, and for many other purposes explained in these pages. No. 9 is a pair of long-shanked scissors, the blades of which are not merely truncated but are extended outwards in lobes, and are extremely useful where sharper points might penetrate and do some damage to a tender skin or delicate organ.

No. 10 is a generally useful and almost indispensable tool, the bell-hanger's or gas-fitter's pliers or side nippers, in which the end is made for grasping wire or metal ; just below is a roughened concavity for laying hold of a screw head or a gas-burner, then a flat plane—the " side nippers "—for cutting wire of moderate thickness, and lastly, just by the figure 10 on the right-hand side, a semicircular opening which, when the handles are closed sharply, makes a powerful nipper quite strong enough to shear through wire as large as the opening will admit. No. 11 is a pair of cutting-nippers, small and of French make, far superior, unfortunately, to those made in England, by reason of its fine temper, adjustable screw, and wider bows ; it is a watch-maker's tool, and is most useful for cutting through fine wires and entomological or other pins, which the larger nippers may be too heavy to manage delicately. No. 12 is the ordinary large pair of " nippers," useful, in a variety of ways, for large work, and also for such a purpose as snapping through thin or small pieces of rock when " developing." No. 13 is another watchmaker's tool, very handy at times, whose cutting-edges are at an oblique angle with the plane of the tool. No. 14 is a most useful adjunct to the series—a pair of spatulate, round-nosed feather-pliers, used for laying hold of the feathers of birds and coaxing them into proper position when twisted or otherwise refractory. No. 15 is a pair of fine, extra long-nosed pliers, useful especially for getting at or twisting together wires when articulating skeletons of small animals.

No. 16 is a " stuffer " or " crowder " made out of a piece of brass wire beaten flat at one end, nicked with a triangular file and the points rounded, the other end being fixed within a handle. It is used for pushing tow or other materials into the necks and bodies of small animals. No. 17 is a larger form made out of one piece of stout brass wire turned around at the bottom to form a handle.

No. 18 is the necessary pair of calipers for taking the diameters of solid bodies, and is therefore useful for getting the approximate sizes of the bodies of small animals, when skinned out, for reproduction in tow or modelling-materials. This shaped caliper will also, in many cases, take the place of the dividers.

No. 19 is a cheap "mop" brush made of some soft hair, useful for stroking a bird's feathers into place before "cottoning."

No. 20 is a steel wire pointed, with one end fixed within a handle ; it is used to drill the long bones of small animals. No. 21 is a longer and thicker steel wire, the upper end of which is flattened and to be inserted in a brace or drill-stock, the lower end being broadened as an ordinary drill for larger bones. Sets of various sizes of these can be made at little cost.

No. 22 is the ordinary "twist drill" of American origin. It is figured as being the best form of tool with which to bore rapidly and safely through large or thick bones, either length-wise or at any angle. The lower end is to be inserted into the stock of the brace.

No. 23 is a three-cornered "skin-needle," which, used with a sail-maker's "palm" (not figured), will go rapidly through the thickest skin and save previous boring with an awl. No. 24 is a skin-needle in a handle, which makes a most efficient piercing instrument.

No. 25 is a steel handle, with a universal chuck-head which screws up, and takes, and holds, any drilling instrument in its jaws, from a large brad-awl to a fine needle, and is therefore very useful for drilling the finer bones of animals, especially those of fishes.

Nos. 26 and 27 are crooked awls, fine and stout. The fine one is used for arranging the feathers of birds, and the eyelids of all animals over the artificial eyes, and so on. The larger one is used for the same purposes with larger animals, and also makes a very efficient undercutting tool for fine channelling in plaster work.

No. 28 is an ordinary three-cornered file introduced here merely to show that, if the learner commences with one file only, this is the best shape and size to get until he can procure others.

Nos. 29 to 36 are plasterers' modelling-tools. They are usually made double-ended, and of the length of blade shown in No. 33. When like this, however, they are for " sleeking," and using upon clay and with plaster in modelling, being set at all angles for this purpose ; but required, as they often are, for cutting and carving dry plaster, or plaster just set, and for many other purposes, they will be found of the greatest service if ground down to where the steel is stiff and thicker, and sharpened to the same angles as those to which they were originally set, as shown by all those figured except No. 33.

Nos. 36 to 39 are ordinary wood-carving tools, but, being stout, gouge-like, and cranked at various angles as well as V-shaped, they serve most admirably for cutting out and relieving orbits, nostrils, lips, and other parts in dry plaster models.

There are, of course, many other tools briefly hinted at, and other shapes of many of those figured, which the advanced modeller will acquire as he progresses, but the beginner may limit himself to a very few, and these may be particularised as the saw, hammer, chisel, brad-awl, gimlet, rule, and screwdriver, amongst ordinary tools, and, of those figured, Nos. 1, 4, 7, 9, 10, 16 or 17, 19, 26, and 28. With these he will manage very well, but will feel the want of others as he becomes more expert.

The materials absolutely required are tow, wadding, hemp, needles and thread, clay, wire of different sizes—those for small objects being at first sufficient, ranging, say, between Nos. 24 and 15,—pins, pieces of thin card, pieces of wood, nails, screws, preservatives (Formulæ 57 and 59), and artificial eyes.

Whatever tools are procured, let them be of the best shape and quality, remembering that whilst an experienced performer may do well with poor tools, an inferior or unskilled one is severely handicapped by them.

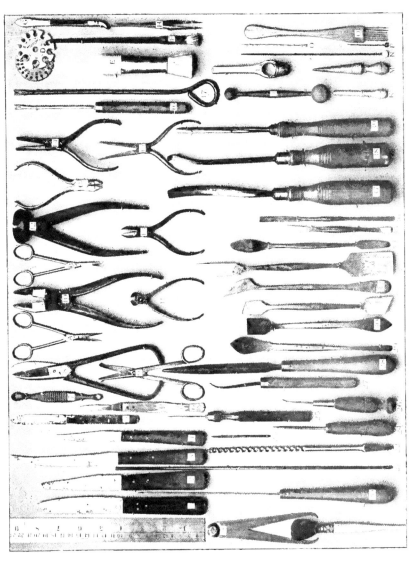

TOOLS USED IN TAXIDERMY AND MODELLING.

CHAPTER III

IN a number of the formulæ which follow, there are certain
rules to be observed prior to the actual preservation of the
subject, as a whole, in some liquid ; but in many instances it is
only necessary to steep it in some medium, which is a sufficient
preservative for a certain time.   These may be called preservatives of the first class, and are to be found in Division
I. of this chapter.   Others require the removal of the flesh
of the subject, so that the skin merely may be preserved,
and these are preservatives of the second class, and are to be
found in Division II.

DIVISION I

NARCOTISING, KILLING, AND PRESERVATIVE MEDIUMS,
WITH DIRECTIONS FOR THEIR USE

Undoubtedly one of the first things to be considered, after
having procured a specimen, is the method to be adopted in
quickly and efficiently narcotising, killing, or preserving it, as
the case may be.   Various methods for the treatment of the
vertebrata are described hereafter, but the treatment of the
invertebrata is quite a different matter, and has been made a
special study by many biologists ; but perhaps the most

generally accepted article upon the subject is one by the eminent *savant* at the Naples Station, Salvatore Lo Bianco,[1] from whose pages most of the following methods in this division, and some formulæ, have been compiled by the present writer, and will be found indispensable when dealing with animals which are so sensitive and alert that even the quickest methods of killing fail to fix them properly; in such cases slow narcotisation—of which the animal operated upon is unaware—is resorted to, by using such anæsthetics as chloroform, either as a vapour or as a liquid, nicotin, tobacco-smoke, and deprivation of air, also by other methods described in the following pages. The secret of success in all is the capability of taking infinite pains and adhering exactly to the instructions given. So with the sudden killing of large and small organisms; these are either paralysed, or killed at once by rapidly flooding them with some lethal fluid, or placed in others which cause them to more slowly die extended. In addition to such acids or mixtures as are indicated, fresh water, cold or hot, but especially the latter, are used to kill marine and some other organisms, and the application of dry heat is sometimes successful. It must not be supposed, however, that all methods of narcotising and killing animals are to be found in this work; a selection of those most useful is given, and

---

[1] "Metodi usati nella Stazione Zoologica per la conservazione degli animali marini," *Mittheilungen aus der Zoologischen Station zu Neapel*, ix. Band, iii. Heft, s. 435-474, 1890. Also "Méthodes en usage à la Station Zoologique de Naples pour la Conservation des Animaux Marins," par Salvatore Lo Bianco, *Bulletin Scientifique de la France et de la Belgique*, Tome xxiii., 4ième Sér., 2ième Vol., 1891, pp. 100-147. Also a comprehensive abstract of the preceding, entitled "Methods for the Preservation of Marine Organisms employed at the Naples Zoological Station," by Professor Playfair M'Murrich, *American Naturalist*, xxiv. 1890, pp. 856-865, and *Journal of the Royal Microscopical Society*, 1891, pp. 133-140. Also a *résumé*, "The Preservation of Marine Animals for Zoological Purposes," by J. T. Cunningham, M.A., *The Essex Naturalist*, July and August 1892, pp. 118-129. Also *The Microtomist's Vademecum*, by Arthur Bolles Lee, third edition, 1893 (see Formulæ (§) 12, 18, 811-813, 835, 838, 841, 845, 849, 851, 854, 855). See also De Castellarnau, *La Estacion Zoolog. de Napoles*, Madrid, 1885.

every order of the Invertebrata is represented.   For further details the reader is referred to the complete article by Lo Bianco mentioned in the foregoing footnote, and also to another author mentioned therein—Mr. Arthur Bolles Lee— to whom the present writer is much indebted for some other formulæ compiled from his invaluable manual.

Alcohol.—Amongst the preservatives of the first class, and amid the numberless preservatives to be found recommended in the pages of various manuals, there is nothing which at all compares with, or is so commonly used as a *general* preserva- tive, as pure alcohol, or rather alcohol of good quality.   At Naples, says Lo Bianco, it is considered indispensable, and is used in various strengths.

Probably the best definition of the various strengths and properties of alcohol is that given by Mr. Arthur Bolles Lee in his *Microtomist's Vade-mecum*, pp. 467, 468.   This, which is too valuable to abbreviate, is as follows :—

Absolute Alcohol.—The so-called "absolute alcohol" of commerce is generally of about 98 per cent. strength.

This grade is *not* necessary for ordinary work.

95 per cent. Alcohol.—This is the average strength of the common strong commercial alcohol, which ranges in general from 94 per cent. to 96 per cent. according to temperature.   The strength of this, or of the following, should be determined by means of an areometer (Gay-Lussac's being very convenient), so as to form a starting-point for the following mixtures.

This is the usual grade for dehydrating before clearing.   It is the highest grade that should be used for dehydrating celloidin sections.

90 per cent. Alcohol.—Made approximately by taking 100 vols. 95 per cent. alcohol, and 5.5 vols. water.

This is the usual strength of the strongest commercial *methylated spirit*, which (if free from mineral naphtha) may be taken instead of pure alcohol for common work.   If naphtha be present the alcohol becomes turbid on the addition of water.   Oil of bergamot will clear from this grade.

85 per cent. Alcohol.—Made by taking 100 vols. 90 per cent. alcohol, and 6.5 vols. water.

Rectified spirit B.P. is a little weaker than this, viz. 84.5 per cent.

70 per cent. Alcohol.—Made of 100 vols. 90 per cent. alcohol or methylated spirit, and 31 vols. water ; or 100 vols. 85 per cent. alcohol, and 23 vols. water.

Only exceptionally powerful clearers, such as anilin oil, will clear from this grade. This is the proper grade in general for preserving organisms and tissues in; higher grades should not generally be used unless it is desired to harden. This is the proper grade for washing out borax-carmine stains, corrosive sublimate after fixing, etc.

50 per cent. Alcohol.—Made by taking 100 vols. 90 per cent. alcohol, and 84.7 vols. water ; or 100 vols. 70 per cent. alcohol, and 41.7 vols. water.

This is the strength of *proof spirit.*

'One-third Alcohol.'—Made by taking 1 vol. of 90 per cent. alcohol and 2 vols. water.

Absolute Alcohol.—This is too strong for ordinary purposes, but has, says Lee, many advantages : it preserves the structure of nuclei (which no other strength of alcohol does), and is one of the most penetrating of all fixing agents, killing and hardening "with such rapidity that structures have not time to get deformed in the process by the energetic dehydration that unavoidably takes place ; " and although it is difficult to pre-serve its strength owing to the rapidity with which it hydrates upon exposure to the air, yet this is partly obviated, says Fol, by keeping a little quicklime in it, which also has the effect of neutralising the acidity often found in commercial alcohols. Mr. Lee mentions that the suspension of strips of gelatin in ordinary alcohol is said to render it absolute. Ranvier's system, however, is to treat 95 per cent. alcohol with cupric sul-phate, calcined, which, after being well agitated, is allowed to settle for a day or two, then filtered and treated afresh, and this is repeated until the addition of cupric sulphate fails to colour the alcohol, or until, upon a drop of turpentine being mixed with a drop of the treated alcohol, the microscope reveals no particles of water as an admixture.

It is said also (see Hamilton's *Pathology*, p. 54) that, although methylated spirit is not absolute alcohol, it may be made so " by the addition of a little dry carbonate of potash."

" Sea-stars" such as *Brisinga*, which readily cast or break their arms, are fixed by immersing them rapidly in absolute alcohol (Lo Bianco, p. 458).

1.—Absolute Alcohol and Sea-water (Lo Bianco, p. 443)

Alcohol (absolute)	. .	5 parts
Sea-water . .	. .	100 ,,

The worm-like Hemichordate vertebrate,[1] *Balanoglossus*, has been narcotised in a well-extended position by this means.

This is also used for narcotising and killing the Lamellibranch mollusca with their valves open. They should be left in it from six to twelve or more hours, according to circumstances, and, when opened, a wedge of wood should be placed between the valves. Certain other molluscs, such as " limpets," " ear-shells," etc., are fixed extended in like manner, but none should be transferred into the 70 per cent. alcohol until quite dead, otherwise contraction is liable to take place.

90 per cent. Alcohol.—*Amphioxus*, one of the Protochordata,[2] which, although a lowly vertebrate, is not, as Lo Bianco puts it (p. 473), to be classed with the fishes, is easily fixed and killed with the buccal cirrhus extended in—

2.—Alcoholised Sea-water

Alcohol (90 per cent.) .	.	10 parts
Sea-water .	.	90 ,,

[1] See *Amphioxus and the Ancestry of the Vertebrates*, by Arthur Willey, B.Sc.
[2] *Ibid.*

When death is brought about, which happens in a few minutes, the animal is placed in alcohol of 50 per cent. brought by degrees to 70 per cent.

Rectified Alcohol.—Lo Bianco states that rectified alcohol— ' to which distilled water may be added, in certain proportions, without affecting its limpidity or giving a precipitate—is to be preferred for the fixing and preservation of delicate and transparent organisms.

Soft and gelatinous organisms are, when fixed by any liquid whatever, afterwards preserved at Naples in alcohol, and the method adopted is first to allow them to remain from two to six hours in alcohol of 35 or 50 per cent., according to the degree of firmness of the subject, and afterwards to transfer them into alcohol of 60 per cent. followed by 70 per cent., or at once into that of 70 per cent., which is the definitive strength.

When the removal of a fragile animal from spirit of one strength to that of another would be likely to damage it, the spirit itself may be changed by means of a syphon without disturbing the subject.

It is necessary for the complete preservation of the subject that the 70 per cent. alcohol should be changed once after twelve to twenty-four hours, and, if the subject is thick, changed again after two days.

75 per cent. Alcohol.—In the Leicester Museum a somewhat greater strength than usual, viz. 75 per cent. of methyl-alcohol made as follows, has been proved of the greatest service :—

3.—**Alcohol** (M.B.).   For preservation of Fishes and Invertebrates.
   Take—
      Methyl-alcohol (methylated spirit), 90 per cent.   100 parts
      Water, distilled   20   „
or by the 1000 cubic centimetre measure—
      Methyl-alcohol, 90 per cent.   .   .   .   1000 cc.
      Water, distilled   200   „

Mix thoroughly, and, as heat is evolved by this mixing, let it stand for some hours (*i.e.* all night) to cool and precipitate. Afterwards filter through ordinary grey filter-paper (preferably doubled), and it will be brilliantly clear and clean, and may then be used. This is the method adopted in the Leicester Museum, and (so far) with the best results as a preservative, but of course it does not preserve the natural colours for any length of time.

70 per cent. Alcohol.—This is, as will be seen by Mr. Lee's most useful table, made by taking 100 volumes of 90 per cent. alcohol or methyl-alcohol and 31 volumes of water; but Dall's method for getting a 70 per cent. alcohol in a rough-and-ready manner is as follows:[1]—"The 70 per cent. alcohol is readily made with a sufficient approximation to accuracy by remembering that by adding nearly four-tenths of its volume of water to the ordinary 95 to 97 per cent. alcohol of commerce, an alcohol percentage of 70 is reached. Thus with an ordinary foot-rule the operator can mix his alcohols in cylindrical jars, thus :—

"Stand the jar upon the table, place the rule by the side of it with the scale next the glass, then pour in alcohol till some arbitrarily chosen tenth division of the rule outside is reached by the surface of the spirit, then add water to the spirit to the amount of nearly four more similar divisions of the rule, when the requisite dilution of 70 per cent. approximately is reached."

At Naples, as now in many other museums, 70 per cent. alcohol is the strength commonly used for definitive preservation of most organisms, and ordinary alcohol may, even if it has been used and become charged with organic matter thereby, be redistilled and neutralised by the addition of lime should it prove acid, or of hydrochloric acid should it, on the other hand, be alkaline.

[1] *Instructions for collecting Mollusks*, etc., 1892, pp. 44, 45, *Rep. Smithsonian Inst.*

Organisms of a certain degree of firmness are plunged at once into 70 per cent. alcohol, which is changed as stated. It happens occasionally, although rarely, that, even after these necessary changes, the alcohol becomes coloured again ; hence it is necessary to change it often.

When an organism is not sufficiently penetrated by alcohol, it is necessary to shake the vessel containing it, to prevent the formation of a body of weak alcohol in any position which would cause the subject to break up.

On the other hand, alcohol of a greater strength than 70 per cent. does not preserve so well in the majority of cases, as it often ends by becoming cloudy, and long immersion in such has a tendency to cause the subject to become tender or to break up.

Not only is alcohol of a lethal character, killing rapidly or slowly as diluted, but it is, as these pages will show, used as an anæsthetic.

The greater number of the sponges may be fixed by merely plunging them at once into alcohol of 70 per cent., and renewing it after twenty-four hours.

Numbers of the Crustacea are well preserved in alcohol ranging from 70 to 90 per cent.

Such "Feather-stars" as *Antedon (Comatula) rosacea*, Lo Bianco (p. 458) plunges at once into alcohol of 70 per cent. *A. phalangium*, however, breaks in this strength, and therefore must be fixed and killed in alcohol of 90 per cent.

Edwardsia, a genus of "sea-anemone," is narcotised slowly by adding, little by little, alcohol of 70 per cent. to the sea-water in which it lies extended, and is then killed with a *hot* saturated solution of bichromate of mercury.

The curious molluscs *Doris* and *Chromodoris* are narcotised in exactly the same manner, and are killed by plunging them into concentrated acetic acid or boiling bichloride of mercury (Formula 16).

Good results depend entirely upon complete insensibility before killing, and this is tested by touching the tentacles, or branchial appendages, with a needle (Lo Bianco, pp. 450 and 468).

Such Radiolarians as *Aulacanthidæ* and the *Acanthometræ* are, says Lo Bianco (p. 444), plunged directly into alcohol of 50 per cent., and after some hours into that of 70 per cent.

Such oceanic Hydrozoa as *Physophora*, *Agalma*, and *Halistemma* are hardened immediately in alcohol of 35 per cent., and after two hours are placed in alcohol of 70 per cent. (Lo Bianco, p. 455).

The common "starfishes" are prepared, says Lo Bianco (p. 458), with their ambulacral feet extended, by causing them to die in alcohol of 20 to 30 per cent., arranging them in the vessel with their ambulacral area uppermost.

One-third Alcohol.—This, says Mr. Lee, is useful for fixing, but care should be taken that 90 per cent. alcohol only is used, and objects may not be left longer than twenty-four hours in this mixture, or maceration takes place ; its chief use, therefore, is for extemporaneous and dissociation preparations. It is known as Ranvier's alcohol, "alcohol au tiers," "Drittelalcohol," or "Ranviersche Alcohol dilutus," and "alcool al terzo."

Alcohol and Glycerin.—Mixtures of these fluids have been used for many purposes, and Mr. Lee considers them valuable for delicate objects, especially when it is necessary to bring them from weak into strong glycerin ; he regards the following as one of the best, and preferable to alcohol in which to retain objects already fixed, until required for dissection or other purposes.

4.—Calberla's Liquid

Alcohol	
Glycerin	Equal parts
Water	

Two others strongly recommended by him differ in the first instance by one more part of water being added, and in the other by the further addition of two more parts of alcohol.

The following mixtures will also be found most useful for the purposes noted :—

5.—Jäger's Liquid (quoted from Vogt and Yung's *Traité d'Anat. comp. prat.*, p. 16)

Alcohol .	1 part
Glycerin	1 „
Sea-water	10 parts

6.—Alcohol and Glycerin (M.B.).   For Fishes and Cephalopods.

Methyl-alcohol, 70 per cent.	4 parts
Glycerin	1 part

7.—Alcohol and Glycerin (M.B.).   For the preservation of Cartilage.

Methyl-alcohol, 90 per cent.	1 oz.
Glycerin	1 lb.

8.—Alcohol and Chloral Hydrate (M.B.).   For the preservation of Cartilage.

Methyl-alcohol, 90 per cent.	1 oz.
Glycerin	1 lb.
Chloral hydrate .	1 oz.

Both of the preceding are used for the preservation of cartilage. Such objects as the cartilaginous skull of *Acipenser*, after being washed and steeped in a saturated solution of common salt, are placed in Formula 7 for six months or even more. They are then taken out, drained, and afterwards steeped for a week in Formula 8, drained again, dried with blotting-paper, allowed to remain, protected from dust but exposed to the air, from six to twelve hours, and finally varnished with the clearest and whitest varnish (French) to be procured. By this means many cartilaginous subjects have been prepared, and placed upon tablets as dry but unshrivelled specimens for the

Leicester Museum. Glycerin is, as these pages will show, one of the most useful of liquids to the advanced modeller ; it not only retards fermentation and decomposition remarkably, but, combining readily with either water or alcohol, is used in modelling-compositions as well as preservatives ; it is valuable also for brushing over the eyes, nose, and lips of mammals, and the bills and legs of birds, to keep them fresh and damp during modelling. Further, a small quantity added to the pastes or "cures" retards the drying of skins, which is often an advantage. It is also of great service to keep the fins of fishes damp, before and after casting.

Alcohol and Bichloride of Mercury.—The most perfect preservatives are probably those which contain with alcohol a certain percentage of bichloride of mercury, which has almost, if not quite, superseded carbolic acid in hospitals for antiseptic purposes, one part in a thousand being sufficient to prevent or kill disease germs and fungoid growths ; but it will be better for the taxidermist's purpose if he accepts the proportion of one part in five hundred.

Whenever these preparations are used for skins, etc., they should be applied with a brush, and invertebrate animals which have been killed in it should be lifted out with a piece of wood or with wooden forceps, the greatest care being necessary in all cases that this deadly poison does not come into contact with the fingers. When skins known to be charged with it are beaten out, the men should be warned to cover the mouth and nostrils, to prevent the inhalation of the poisonous dust. The same remark applies to arsenic also, but probably in a less degree.

9.—**Alcoholic Solution of Mercury,** one part in 1000.

For preventing and arresting mildew, and for external use upon skins.

Methyl-alcohol, 90-95 per cent.	.	1 pint
Bichloride of mercury	.	.	10 grains

10.—Alcoholic Solution of Mercury, one part in 500.

For preventing and arresting mildew, and for external use upon skins.

Methyl-alcohol, 90 per cent. .	1 pint
Bichloride of mercury	. 20 grains

11.—Alcoholic Solution of Mercury (M.B.)

For preventing and arresting mildew, and for external use upon skins.

Methyl-alcohol, 90 per cent.	1 pint
Bichloride of mercury . .	50 grains = $2\frac{1}{2}$ scruples

No. 10 will be found very useful to prevent mould from appearing in the water of the tanks containing non-alcoholic preparations, the various strengths of bichromate preservatives being singularly liable to fungoid growths, which spread over the tanks as leathery masses. This fungus, and another also, attacked the water in which the preparations were decolorising (see p. 55) in the Leicester Museum ; but the addition of one part in 500, or a few drops of a saturated solution, of bichloride of mercury has been effectual, even in warm weather, to prevent the formation of any fungoid growths.

Nos. 10 and 11, the latter for very badly infested skins, will be found very useful for brushing over the feathers, beak, and legs of any rare bird, to protect them from the attacks of insects ; and No. 10 is also a certain cure for all specimens which, in damp situations, are found to have "little white insects" (*acari*) running nimbly over them. The spirit soon evaporates, leaving no apparent trace of the contained mercury, which not only kills mites and insects at once, but prevents others, and mildew, ever appearing afterwards. It is useful also as a bath for dried insects (*i.e.* entomological specimens) which are affected either by mites or mould.

For valuable birds'-skins and for butterflies it will be found better to use sulphuric ether as a substitute for alcohol, the former, although much more expensive, evaporating so much more rapidly, which, when delicate butterflies are plunged therein, is of some importance. It is an effectual remedy for " mites " infesting dried insects.

12.—Ether and Bichloride of Mercury (M.B.)

Pure sulphuric ether	1 pint
Bichloride of mercury	10 grains

13.—Alcohol and Chromic Acid (Lo Bianco, p. 443)

Alcohol (70 per cent.)	} Equal parts
Chromic acid (1 per cent.)	

This is used by Lo Bianco to kill an octopod, *Scæurgus* (*Octopus*) *tetracirrhus*, which, after twenty minutes, should be passed into alcohol alone of 70 per cent.

14.—Alcohol and Hydrochloric Acid (Lo Bianco, p. 443)

Alcohol (50 per cent.) . . .	100 parts
Hydrochloric acid (concentrated) . .	5 ,,

Fecundated and transparent eggs of fishes may be preserved by leaving them for some minutes in the above mixture, and passing them afterwards into alcohol.

15.—Alcohol and Iodine (Lo Bianco, p. 443)

Alcohol (35 per cent. or 70 per cent.) . .	100 parts
Alcoholic tincture of iodine . .	2 or 5 parts

Such Radiolaria as species of the genus *Sphærozoum* and *Collozoum* are fixed in the 35 per cent. solution by being left from fifteen minutes to about an hour, care being taken to agitate the liquid, otherwise, in resting too long at the bottom of the vessel, the animals become flattened. Afterwards they should be transferred to alcohol of 35 per cent. for two hours, next to alcohol of 50 per cent., and, twelve hours afterwards, into alcohol of 70 per cent., which must be renewed after twenty-four hours.

Rectified Naphtha for Snakes and Frogs.—This has been used in the Leicester Museum for preserving small mammals and reptiles, frogs and fishes, which it certainly does for some years, but renders them very hard, and, except in the cases of frogs and snakes, ultimately breaks up their tissues in the same manner as weak alcohol ; within five years, however, the specimens, as evidenced by some young hedgehogs lately examined, are—although stained of a curious yellow colour—tough and leathery, and more fitted for " setting-up " than if preserved in some other media.

Bichloride of Mercury (*Corrosive Sublimate*). — Corrosive sublimate, says Mr. Lee (p. 32), " is stated in the books to be soluble in about sixteen parts of cold and three of boiling water. It will probably be found that the aqueous solution contains about 5 per cent. of the sublimate at the temperature of the laboratory. It is more soluble in alcohol than in water, and still more so in ether. Its solubility in all these menstrua is augmented by the addition of hydrochloric acid, ammonious chloride, or camphor. With sodium chloride it forms a more easily soluble double salt ; hence sea-water may dissolve as much as 15 per cent., and hence the composition of the liquid of Lang."

The following series of preservatives, which have no alcohol as their base, will be found of great use, and some of them of permanent value :—

16.—Bichloride of Mercury

Saturated solution (boiling) (Lo Bianco)

This is used at the Naples Station to kill, in a satisfactory manner, colonies of the Infusorian *Zoothamnium*, and, amongst the Actinozoa or "sea-anemones," *Heliactis, Sagartia dohrnii, Paranthus, Corynactis,* and small examples of *Aiptasia* are killed in like manner, but these should be left to harden for some minutes in chromic acid of $\frac{1}{2}$ per cent. before being placed in the 70 per cent. alcohol.

Hydroid polyps are, with rare exceptions, killed with the same reagent at a time when the polyps are completely extended, which is effected by placing them in fresh sea-water. After flooding the animals with the hot mercury, they should be turned into a porcelain dish containing spring-water, and left therein for five minutes to cool and wash them, after which they should be transferred into weak alcohol, followed, as usual, by other strengths up to 70 per cent. (Lo Bianco, p. 451).

Embryos of dog-fishes and sharks are well fixed, says Lo Bianco (p. 474), in a saturated solution of bichloride of mercury, being left therein from five to fifteen minutes, and afterwards well washed in the iodised alcohol (Formula 15), and, unless required solely for histological purposes, they are put in weak spirit, increased up to 70 per cent. Teleostean fishes with a silvery skin, such as *Trachypterus*, are fixed and treated in like manner, but leaving out the iodised alcohol.

17.—Bichloride of Mercury and Sea-water

Lo Bianco remarks (p. 445) that, with a saturated solution in sea-water, he has obtained the best results with some of the Protozoa as microscopical preparations, and instances amongst them *Trichophrya salparum*.

It has been stated that solutions of bichloride of mercury, either made with hot fresh or sea-water, or applied hot to certain objects, especially plants, have more effect than made or used cold ; if made or applied hot, however, care must be taken not to inhale the vapour, and no metal must be used either in their preparation or application. Earthenware vessels and wooden or bone instruments alone must be used.

18.—Bichloride of Mercury and Acetic Acid (Lo Bianco, p. 443)

Bichloride of mercury (saturated solution) . . 100 parts
Acetic acid (concentrated) . . . . 50 ,,

"Sea-anemones" such as *Actinia equina* and *A. cari* are fixed by the above mixture (boiling), followed by chromic acid of $\frac{1}{2}$ per cent.

Such Hydrozoa as *Eleutheria* (*Clavatella*), *Cladonema*, *Podocoryne*, and allied forms are killed by flooding them with the above mixture.

A "Portuguese man of war" (*Physalia caravella*) is treated in the following manner :—Primarily, the tentacles must not be touched with the fingers, or the flesh will be badly stung. It should be grasped by the pneumatophore and placed in a tall and large cylinder containing sea-water, allowed to remain until the tentacles are fully extended, and then flooded with the above mixture, in the proportions of one quarter to the volume of sea-water in which the *Physalia* rests. When dead it should be transported (by the means indicated above) into another preparation jar containing chromic acid of $\frac{1}{2}$ per cent. followed in about twenty minutes by immersion in alcohol of 50 per cent., and finally in that of 70 per cent. (Lo Bianco, p. 456).

19.—Bichloride of Mercury and Chromic Acid (Lo Bianco, p. 443)

Bichloride of mercury (saturated solution) .	100 parts
Chromic acid (1 per cent.) .	50 ,,

Amongst the Hydromedusæ large colonies of *Tubularia* and *Pennaria* are killed by this mixture, which is added in equal proportion to the volume of sea-water in which the polyps lie extended. After a few minutes they are transferred to weak alcohol, followed as usual by strengths leading up to 70 per cent.

20.—Pyroligneous Acid Mixture (Lo Bianco, p. 457)

Bichloride of mercury (saturated solution) .	
Pyroligneous acid (concentrated) . .	Equal parts
Chromic acid ($\frac{1}{2}$ per cent.) . .	

This is specially indicated by Lo Bianco as a fixative for *Callianira*, one of the Ctenophora, unless fixed by the chromosmic mixture (Formula 39).

21.—**Bichloride of Mercury and Sulphate of Copper** (Lo Bianco, p. 443)

Bichloride of mercury (saturated solution) . .	10 parts
Sulphate of copper (10 per cent. solution) .	100 ,,

Such Hydromedusæ as *Eucope*, *Gastroblasta*, and *Obelia* are fixed by the above, and after two minutes they should be washed in fresh water until all trace of the precipitate has disappeared.

Amongst the " worms," the Chætognatha are nicely fixed also by this reagent.

22.—"**Goadby's Fluids** (*Micro. Dict.*, art. ' Preservation ')

" 1st *Fluid*—

Bay salt (coarse sea-salt)	4 oz.
Alum	2 ,,
Corrosive sublimate . .	2 grains
Boiling water	1 quart

" This is found to be ' too strong ' for most purposes, and therefore the following is recommended for general purposes :—

23.—

" 2nd *Fluid*—

Bay salt .	4 oz.
Alum . . .	2 ,,
Corrosive sublimate . .	4 grains
Water	2 quarts

" ' Schultze recommends it for preserving *Medusæ*, *Echinodermata*, Annelid larvæ, *Entomostraca*, *Polythalamia*, and *Polycystina*, and advises the use of glycerin afterwards to produce transparence.' " [1]

It is said that, where carbonate of lime is found in the

[1] *Microtomist's Vade-mecum*, pp. 238, 239.

preparations, the alum must be dispensed with, and in this case the bay salt is doubled upon the 1st Fluid, and more salt should be added for marine animals.

Mr. Lee gives Owen's Fluid with the remark that it is "said to be very useful for the preservation of soft-bodied animals," but Lo Bianco (p. 440) expressly states that this and also Goadby's Fluids are of no avail for the preservation of gelatinous organisms, shrinking and deforming them completely, and, although Goadby's Fluids are universally quoted for general preservative purposes, yet they have always appeared to the writer to be more suited for the preservation of certain plants and some lowly organisms.

24.—Bichloride of Mercury and Alum (Boitard, p. 49).   For Small Mammals.

Bichloride of mercury	.	.	12 grammes
Alum .	.	.	100 ,,
Common salt .	.	115 ,,
Rain-water	.	.	1 litre

The following, it will be seen, is a modification of the above (Trois, cf. Packard, ex. Riley, *Directions for Collecting and Preserving Insects*, p. 94, 1892, *Report, Smithsonian Institution*).

25.—Preservative for Larvæ

Bichloride of mercury	.	.	18 centigrammes
Alum .	.	.	55 grammes
Common salt .	.	2.35 ,,
Water (boiling) .	.	.	5 litres

Allow the liquid to cool and add 50 grains of carbolic acid, and filter after standing five or six days.

In all of the foregoing the difficulty of getting bichloride of mercury to dissolve in water is apparently underestimated, and although it is also remarkably difficult of solution even in absolute alcohol, it readily yields to a saturated solution of sal ammoniac, half an ounce of which is quite sufficient to dissolve several ounces of it. The following will be found of service, and is probably an improvement upon Goadby's Nos. 1 and 2 :—

26.—Bichloride of Mercury and Potassium Nitrate (M.B.)
For Fishes, etc.

Bichloride of mercury . .	4 grains
Potassium nitrate (nitre or saltpetre) .	2 oz.
Alum	1 ,,
Sal ammoniac .	$\frac{1}{4}$,,
Water (boiling)	1 quart

Dissolve the mercury with the sal ammoniac before adding the others, and cool and filter before using.

27.—Preservative for Algæ (M.B.)

Borax . .	$\frac{1}{2}$ oz.
Alum . . .	$\frac{1}{2}$,,
Bichromate of potassa .	$\frac{1}{16}$,, (= 28 grains)
Sodium chloride (common salt) . .	2 ,,
Bichloride of mercury (saturated solution)	4 drops
Water (warm) . . .	2 gals.

Allow to cool, and filter before using.

Preserves the colour of seaweeds exactly and toughens the specimens, and has been found valuable for preserving, for a lengthened time, the colours of fleshy leaves of plants —a great advantage when modelling from them. Another, simpler in constitution but not *quite* so good, is—

28.—Preservative for Algæ (M.B.)

Nitre	2 oz.
Bichloride of mercury (saturated solution)	1 drop
Water (warm) . . .	1 quart

Allow the mixture to cool, and filter as before.

29.—Cupric Sulphate (Lo Bianco, p. 442)

Cupric sulphate (sulphate of copper) .	5 or 10 parts
Water (boiling) . .	95 or 90 ,,

This may be used alone, or in combination with bichloride of mercury (see Formula 16), to kill and fix larvæ and delicate organisms, which should afterwards, however, be well washed many times in water until it shows no trace of colour, otherwise crystals will form within the tissues and render the objects opaque.

Chloral Hydrate.—This is one of the most useful reagents employed at the Naples Station, and is used in such small proportions as follow :—

30.—Hydrate of Chloral Solution (Lo Bianco, pp. 442, 443)

Chloral hydrate (ordinary) . 2 parts
Sea-water . . . . 998 ,,
    or weaker by making it a 1 per thousand solution.

When such "sea-anemones," says Lo Bianco (p. 448), as *Heliactis bellis, Bunodes gemmaceus,* and *B. rigidus* are well extended in sea-water, remove from the vessel containing them two-thirds of the water, and substitute a 2 per thousand solution of hydrate of chloral. After two minutes remove some of the liquid, leaving sufficient to just cover the animals, which are then killed by flooding them with a cold saturated solution of bichloride of mercury, afterwards followed, of course, in the usual manner, by the preservative alcohols.

Amongst the "worms," the Nemerteans appear to have given Lo Bianco the most trouble, and it was only after reiterated experiments that he succeeded in narcotising such forms as *Carinella, Cerebratulus, Drepanophorus, Nemertes, Polia,* etc., well extended in a 1 per thousand solution of hydrate of chloral in sea-water, in which they remained from six to twelve hours, being subsequently hardened in a small long zinc box covered with wax on the bottom. Such Nemerteans as were insufficiently narcotised soon regained their vitality upon being placed again in fresh sea-water.

Amongst the Cephalopoda, Lo Bianco (p. 469) has found that small octopods are readily narcotised by a 2 per thousand solution, followed by their immediate immersion in alcohol, and although occasionally they contract and hide their bodies with their arms, yet after death it is easy to place them in a natural position.

Small Decapods are managed in like manner, with the intervention of alcoholised sea-water (Formula 2) between the chloral hydrate and definitive alcohol.

Some of the Ascidians, such as *Molgula, Polycarpa, Rhopalea,* and *Chevreulius* (*Rhodosoma*), are left for twelve hours in a 1 per thousand solution to narcotise them, then killed by the chrom-acetic mixture (Formula 38), and after that hardened for a short time in a 1 per cent. solution of chromic acid.

The advantages of these solutions are, that they narcotise various animals, and also that if, after a certain time, an animal does not assume the position desired, it is possible to revive it by replacing it in sea-water, after which it can be re-narcotised in a more favourable position. They are also used for fixing and killing the animals composing colonies of *Serpulæ* and *Madreporia.*

Formol or Formalin (= 40 per cent. formic aldehyd and 60 per cent. water).—This is valuable as an antiseptic, and is also used—usually in the following proportion—as a preservative :—

31.—Solution for various Preservative Purposes

Formol	.	.	5 parts
Water (distilled)			95 „

This is said to preserve perfectly the form and colours of animals ; it has, however, been tried for some fishes, invertebrata, and marine algæ in the Leicester Museum, and, although apparently a first-class preservative, it discharged the natural colours at once. It is now being tried with other subjects, and although it, like many other fluids, preserves reptiles without much change, yet its chief and most valuable property appears to be that of efficiently preserving objects subsequently treated with potassium bichromate. Specimens of fishes, etc., preserved by this salt, having been decolorised, as subsequently stated, by lengthy and constant soaking in water, have been transferred into a 5 per cent. solution of formol without any appreciable change or the formation of any precipitate. A few months only having elapsed, it is, taking into consideration its chemical instability, not possible to say more in its favour at present, nor is it known as yet how it would behave with soft or gelatinous invertebrata ; it is stated, however, that the following organisms are well preserved by formol[1] in the strengths given therewith :—Protozoa, in a 6 per cent. solution ; the larger Medusæ, Rotifera, and some of the fleshy Polyzoa, 5 per cent. ; some of the Crustacea, 8 per cent. ; Mollusca, 5 per cent. ; Cephalopoda, 4 per cent. ; Tunicata, 6 per cent. ; *Amphioxus*, Dogfishes, etc., 4 per cent.

Acetic Acid.—This is known to Lo Bianco (p. 441) as a most penetrative fixing reagent, and it kills rapidly many contractile organisms, but in some cases should be used in its concentrated form. It certainly, however, failed to fix rapidly enough—although it killed—some extended snails which the writer experimented upon. Needless to say, subjects must not be left long under its influence.

Medusæ, such as *Olindias müllerii*, are, says Lo Bianco, fixed with the above acid, and immediately transferred into chromic acid of 1 per cent., where, with small pliers, their marginal tentacles are displayed before being placed in alcohol.

Large " sea-cucumbers "—*Holothuria* and *Stichopus*,—when their buccal tentacles are fully extended, should be seized with

---

[1] See "The Use of Formalin as a Preservative Medium for Marine Animals," by James Hornell, *Natural Science*, vol. vii. (No. 46), pp. 416-420.

forceps or the fingers a little below the tentacles, lifted out of the sea-water, and the anterior portion plunged immediately into concentrated acetic acid contained in a deepish vessel. At the same time another person should inject with a syringe and cannula, by way of the anal aperture, alcohol of 90 per cent., this being done without the exertion of too much force, lest the body of the animal be unduly distended. After death the anal aperture is closed with a plug of cork or wadding, and the animal is immersed in alcohol of 70 per cent. The injection should be repeated at all subsequent renewals of alcohol (Lo Bianco, p. 459).

32.—Lactic Acid Solution

Lactic acid	1 part
Sea-water . . .	999 parts

This, says Lo Bianco (p. 442), is used to fix larvæ and small gelatinous organisms.

Carbolic Acid.—This is, especially in hot countries, indispensable to the taxidermist. Calvert was the chief, if not the only, maker of the pure preparation, which is sold in half-pound or one-pound bottles, in a solid crystalline state as if it were frozen. It should be of an ice-like whiteness, but is often pink, and in that state is said to be just as efficacious. When wanted for use, it must be dissolved by placing the bottle, *without* the stopper, in boiling water, and, a sufficient quantity being melted out, it must be diluted by the addition of many times its own weight of water. This preparation is of the greatest possible value in hot weather, for washing the fly-blown throats, etc., of birds or mammals required for taxidermic purposes.

A preparation of extreme strength and efficacy, for pickling the tongues or painting the noses of animals before or after skinning, is made by pouring diluted acid upon burnt alum or pure tannin, and shaking the whole well together. Two useful strengths of this are given :—

33.—Carbolic Wash for Mammals (M.B.)

Glacial carbolic acid	2 oz.
Burnt alum or pure tannin	1 oz.
Water (warm)	1 pint

34.—Carbolic Wash for Birds (M.B.)

Glacial carbolic acid	1 oz.
Water (warm)	1 pint

Shake before using.

Occasionally, collections of heads and skins are found to be infested with insects, and in such a case the best and most effectual mode of treatment is to plunge them completely into a mixture prepared as follows :—

35.—Carbolic Wash for Large Subjects

Carbolic acid	4 oz.
Bichloride of mercury	1 ,,
Sal ammoniac	$\frac{1}{4}$,,
Pure tannin	4 ,,
Water (hot)	4 gals.

This preparation—which is probably more efficacious if used hot, though less healthy to the operator—should be mixed and applied in some out-of-the-way place, care being taken not to allow the poisonous and acrid mixture to touch the skin of the hands.

Although so deadly and dangerous if used carelessly, yet there is no real need to inhale the fumes whilst hot, or to touch it either hot or cold, if reasonable precautions be taken ; and there is no doubt whatever as to its extreme efficacy when used as directed.

Osmic Acid.—This is usually rapid in its action as a fixative with most organisms, and is indispensable for many, but its use is attended with several inconveniences, one of the chief being that its vapours are doubtless injurious to some persons at any rate, causing irritation of the mucous tissues. It appears to be readily decomposed by dust, in presence of which it becomes brown or blackens rapidly, whilst it also renders fragile any organism which may be left in any of its solutions for even a comparatively short time. Washing freely with water before placing the subject in alcohol is the best method of obviating some of its disadvantages.

It has been added by Lo Bianco to sea-water containing certain Radiolaria, in the proportion of a few drops at 1 per cent., taking care, however, to wash the specimens well before transferring them to the definite alcohol ; and with this acid he has obtained the best results with *Acineta fœtida*.

36.—Kleinenberg's Liquid (Lo Bianco, p. 441)

Picric acid (saturated solution)	.	. 100 parts
Sulphuric acid (concentrated) .	.	. 2 ,,
Filter and add water (distilled)	.	. 300 ,,

This liquid, according to Lo Bianco, was one of the first employed at the Naples Station for the preservation of marine organisms, but, owing to its chemical composition, has been found of little service excepting for histological research and for the fixing of certain Protozoa (Gregarinidæ), which should remain therein for about an hour before their transference into weak alcohol.

Chromic Acid.—Lo Bianco remarks (pp. 440, 441) that, after alcohol, this acid is one of the most useful reagents, and serves to kill and harden gelatinous and soft organisms, but they must only rest for a limited time under its influence, otherwise it gives an ugly colour and renders them fragile. All subjects killed or hardened by it should be well washed in spring-water. It is best employed as a mixture with osmic,

4

acetic, and picric acids, bichloride of mercury, and with common or distilled water, rarely with sea-water, and is not recommended to be used with alcohol for many reasons.

Such sponges as the Halisarcidæ are fixed extended if left for half an hour in a 1 per cent. solution, which is used also as a secondary or hardening fluid.

The "sea-grapes"—egg clusters of such Cephalopods as *Sepia*—are fixed in a ½ per cent. solution, and in the course of an hour removed to weak alcohol, brought up gradually to 70 per cent.; but those which are contained in one common gelatinous envelope, after fixation by the acid, are placed definitively in 50 per cent. alcohol.

37.—Chromic and Acetic Acids (No. 1) (Lo Bianco, p. 443)

Chromic acid (1 per cent.)	.	.	.	100 parts
Acetic acid (concentrated)	.	.	.	5 ,,

Ascidians, such as the chains of young, and solitary forms, of *Salpa maxima* and *S. pinnata*, chains of young forms of *S. bicaudata*, the two adult forms of *S. fusiformis* and *democratica-mucronata* are fixed by the above for ten minutes, and then passed directly into weak alcohol, brought up gradually to 70 per cent.

38.—Chromic and Acetic Acids (No. 2) (Lo Bianco, p. 443)

Acetic acid (concentrated)	.	.	.	100 parts
Chromic acid (1 per cent.)	.	.	.	10 ,,

Some of the Alcyonaria are fixed by plunging them rapidly into the above, and suspending them as soon as dead in a preparation-jar containing weak alcohol, in such a manner that the polyps do not touch the sides; and if the polyps remain well extended, their transference into stronger alcohols, until 70 per cent. is reached, is made gradually. If, however, bubbles of air form in the weak alcohol and adhere to the polyps, which they tend to distort, a gentle tap or two upon the vessel will disperse them.

Some of the Pennatulidæ are, says Lo Bianco (p. 447), when extended, seized by the naked base and plunged very rapidly into a deep preparation-jar containing the foregoing mixture ; after a few seconds they are transferred to a porcelain pan containing alcohol of 50 per cent. Then, with a syringe and fine cannula, alcohol of 70 per cent. is injected through a small hole made in the basal extremity. To ensure the penetration of the alcohol, the tentacles are inflated, and, to prevent the alcohol escaping, a ligature is tied around.

Luidia (one of the " star-fishes ") is turned into a pan with a little sea-water, and, when the feet are displayed, flooded with the mixture. Immediately afterwards the animal is brought into weak alcohol, followed as usual by strengths leading up to 70 per cent.

Echinoids ("sea-urchins ") are killed with their ambulacral feet extended, by being placed in a little sea-water and flooded with the mixture. The transference into weak alcohol must be made immediately, otherwise the acid will attack the calcareous test of the animal.

39.—Chromic and Osmic Acid (Lo Bianco, p. 443)

Chromic acid (1 per cent.)	.	.	. 100 parts
Osmic acid (1 per cent.)	.	.	. 2 ,,

Of the Trachymedusæ, such forms as *Rhopalonema, Cunina, Æginota, Æginopsis, Liriope,* and *Carmarina* are fixed by the above liquid in five to twenty minutes, according to their size, afterwards washed in spring-water, and passed gradually into the full strength of alcohol.

Amongst the Ctenophora, *Beröe ovata, Hormiphora, Callianira, Lampetia, Euchlora,* and young examples of *Cestus, Eucharis,* and *Bolina* are narcotised and killed also by this liquid, lying in it, however, from fifteen to sixty minutes, according to size, but treated afterwards with the usual strengths of alcohol.

40.—Chromic and Picric Acid (Lo Bianco, p. 443)

Chromic acid (1 per cent.) . . . } Equal
Kleinenberg's liquid (Formula 36) . . } parts

Anemonia sulcata (*Anthea cereus*) is said by Lo Bianco (p. 448) to be the most easy to prepare. After being well extended in running water, it is killed by the above mixture in equal volume to the water in which it rests. Only sufficient water is left in the vessel to just cover the anemone, and the mixture is rapidly thrown in. After five or ten minutes, when the animal is dead, its base is detached from the vessel, and it is then transported into one containing chromic acid at $\frac{1}{2}$ per cent. In this it is suspended by its base from one or more hooks, and its tentacles naturally disposed. In half an hour it is placed in weak alcohol, followed as usual up to 70 per cent., in which it should be displayed in a proper manner.

Potassium Bichromate.—As Mr. Lee justly observes (p. 48), this is one of the most important of all hardening agents. In effect it is much slower than chromic acid, but there is no comparison in the manner in which it toughens the tissues, without rendering them brittle, under prolonged reaction. For work such as is detailed in *The Microtomist's Vade-Mecum*, weak solutions of from 2 to 5 per cent. are usually employed, these being gradually increased from one strength to the other; and the hardening of a sheep's eye, spinal cord, and brain take respectively three weeks, three to six weeks, and from three to six months.

The best-known and most generally used solution is that classical reagent known as—

41.—Müller's Fluid

Potassium bichromate (bichromate of potash) . 2-2½ parts or 45 grammes
Sodium sulphate (sulphate of soda)   .   .   1 part ,, 20   ,,
Water   .   .   .   .   100 parts ,, 2 litres

Lee remarks that this does not seem to be so much used of late years, simple bichromate solutions having taken its place, but that the superiority of Müller's Fluid is not illusory, owing to the formation in it of some proportion of free chromic acid.

42.—Potassium Bichromate Solution

Potassium bichromate .   .   .   .   5 parts
Distilled water .   .   .   .   . 95 ,,

This is stated by Lo Bianco to slowly harden some gelatinous animals without rendering them fragile, which is not the case with chromic acid. The abundant precipitate which it gives, however, when the objects are placed in alcohol is not a recommendation, but probably this may be obviated by after-treatment (see pp. 46, 54, and 55).

All varieties of Müller's solution have, as their chief base, the invaluable bichromate of potassa—invaluable, because experience has proved its efficiency in every manner possible, and in the Leicester Museum it is in daily use for a variety of subjects. In a former work it was noted that two "topers"— dog-fishes of six feet in length—were preserved in bichromate of potassa, the proportions then given being far in excess of what was needed. That was on 13th September 1882 ; one was cast from about two years afterwards, and made a good mould, and the other remains in a tub out of doors to present date, darker in colour, owing to the excess of bichromate, but yet pliable and fresh, and this after a period of more than thirteen years ! A conclusive proof of the value of this salt.

Since then, several specimens of the rare Dipnoid fish *Ceratodus forsteri* have reached the Museum from Australia, perfectly preserved in the fluid of the proportions following. The agent who sent them "washed his hands" of the responsibility, never having used anything but spirits, which, of course, shrivels specimens considerably. However, after treatment as described, they are now, after a lapse of three years, quite fresh, pliable, and with little loss of their original colour. Some are in an open tank with water, one is in weak spirits, and some dissections of the cartilaginous skull and the appendicular skeleton are in water, all perfectly unchanged and well preserved.

Although not recommended for mammals, it will yet preserve them very well, and, in cases where the fur is not white nor black, the colour will not be materially affected. A small opossum was perfectly preserved for some months in the fluid, and was successfully set up afterwards ; and a white rat, treated as an experiment, was not so much affected, after the colour had been discharged, as would be imagined.

Indeed there is no limit to its uses, and no *préparateur* should be without the following :—

43.—Fluid for preserving Reptiles, Amphibians, Fishes, and Invertebrates (M.B.)

Bichromate of potassa	$\frac{1}{2}$ oz.
Salt	$\frac{1}{4}$,,
Water	1 gal.

Pound up the crystals and mix well before using. Lay the specimen in a strong solution of salt—say two pounds to one gallon of water—for about an hour to remove the blood, etc., and then, having thoroughly cleansed it, place it in the above preservative for a week in the dark ; at the end of that time, change the liquid for fresh, and let the subject remain therein for some considerable time, say a month, sometimes longer, when it will be found to be stained of a yellowish colour. This staining has hitherto been regarded as an insuperable disadvantage, but if the specimen be removed from the solution and placed in clean cold water, constantly changed, the stain will gradually disappear without in any way interfering with the preservation, and this in spite of the fact that Lee says: " Bichromate objects have an ugly yellow colour which cannot be removed by soaking in water." Subsequently, however, he writes (p. 473) :—

" *Sulphurous Acid as a Bleaching Agent.*—Professor Gilson writes me that alcoholic solution of sulphurous anhydride (SO_2) is very convenient for the rapid decoloration of bichromate objects. A few drops suffice."

Further, it is stated that decolorisation takes place by washing the subject for a few minutes in chloral hydrate of 1 per cent., but probably this treatment may have a deleterious effect upon the tissues. Lo Bianco states that decolorisation is effected also by the addition of a few drops of concentrated sulphuric acid to the alcohol in which the specimens rest, which is practically the same as Professor Gilson's formula.

All subjects, during the process of hardening in this liquid, should be kept in the dark for some time, and the solution changed if it becomes offensive or charged with blood. Although it is stated by Fol (*vide* Lee) to be worthless for the preservation of mammalian embryos, yet it is most efficient for the preservation of brains, if properly injected and the usual precautions taken.

It must be borne in mind, however, that both the preservative and the water used subsequently are peculiarly liable to become mildewed, and to prevent this it is necessary to add bichloride of mercury in the proportion given in Formula 10. In a former work, the author recommended the addition of a few drops of carbolic acid (C_6H_5HO)—known also as phenol, phenic acid, phenic alcohol, and hydrate of phenyl,—but, unless used in so great a quantity as to shrivel the specimens, it is of no avail against the mildew. Examine the water from day to day, and, when coloured by the bichromate, throw away, and add fresh water with the same proportion of mercury as before. After about a month the water will scarcely be tinted at all, and will not require to be changed so frequently; nevertheless, it must be watched, and changed as occasion requires, and the subject afterwards preserved definitively (see Formol, p. 46).

This formula possesses a decided advantage over alcohol, inasmuch as it toughens and preserves the specimen equally well, *without causing the slightest shrinkage* or objectionable hardening, and, managed as directed, little loss of original colour takes place.

Alum.—This is one of the oldest substances known to the naturalist preparator, and although, to the taxidermist, its use is somewhat limited as a preservative, yet for certain purposes nothing can take its place. To the biologist it is said, although superseded by many other things, to be of service for the preservation of Medusæ, and Lee, quoting Pagenstecher, writes:—"Take two parts of common salt and one of alum, and make a strong solution. Throw the animals into it alive, and leave them there for twenty-four to forty-eight hours. Preserve in weak alcohol. A saturated solution of alum in sea-water preserves very well the forms of *Salpidæ, Medusæ, Ctenophora,* and other pelagic animals. It constitutes a preservative medium in which the objects may remain till wanted."

44.—Hardening and Preserving Solution (M.B.)

Alum . . . . . . } Equal
Nitre (saltpetre) . . . . } parts

Make as a saturated solution with hot water, and allow to cool before use.

Borax and Boracic Acid.—A preparation of borax is sold by the Patent Borax Company, who claim special preservative qualities for it, and say that it is also of value in the tanning of hides.

45.—Boracic Acid Solution

Boracic acid	1 part
Saturated solution of saltpetre . . .	50 parts

This preparation is said to preserve flesh ; *not*, however, if this has been salted, as salt destroys or nullifies the action of the acid phosphates.

46.—Preservative (provisional) for Larvæ (M.B.)

Boracic acid	1 grain
Water	$\frac{1}{2}$ pint

It is not claimed that this will preserve the colours for any length of time, but it preserves the greens and reds of naked larvæ for a sufficient time (a week or so) for models, etc., to be coloured therefrom.

47.—Messrs. Medlock and Bailey's Formula

Bisulphite of lime	1 gal.
Common salt	$\frac{1}{4}$ pint
Water	2-4 gals.

It is claimed for this that it will preserve large masses of flesh and fish for some considerable time.

Sodium Chloride (Common Salt).—This, either as bay salt or the ordinary table-salt, is, it need hardly be stated, of paramount importance to the taxidermist who wishes to preserve bodies of various small animals for a certain time, until they can be properly treated, and it is shown in these pages to be, in combination with other things, an efficient preservative.

48.—Saline Solution

Common salt	10 parts
Water . . .	90 ,,

This is given by Lo Bianco at the conclusion of his article (see footnote, p. 26) as being of service for the preservation of dog-fishes, and even of large sharks intended for skeletonising, or of their skin, and he says it is only necessary to remove the intestines and plunge the animal into the liquid, where it may remain, and will be preserved for some months.

So small a proportion as 10 per cent. has not been tried by the present writer, but a saturated solution, or rubbing the fish with a quantity, of salt has been attended with success.

49.—Saline Solution (M.B.)

Common salt	4 oz.
Water	1 gal.

50.—Preservative (provisional) for Flowers and Fruits (M.B.)

Glycerin . . . . . ⎫	Equal
Saline solution, Formula 49 . . . ⎭	parts

This mixture, after many trials of useless formulæ stated to perfectly preserve colours of plants, has given the best results. It is not yet claimed that it will preserve such objects for any prolonged period, but it preserves the form and colours of leaves, flowers, and fruit unchanged for a short time—an immense boon, seeing that a plant is often required for some weeks as a copy for modelling from.

In introducing the subject of insecticides, it may be as well to note that no atmospheric poison save cyanide of potassium, chloroform, and a few others, none of which can be used with safety except in small quantities and in close vessels, will ever inconvenience a moth- or beetle-larva, or cause it to leave off eating. Perhaps crude creosote or rough carbolic acid, naphthaline, or white carbon may be partial deterrents; but their odour is so penetrating, so sickening, and so doubtfully healthy, that probably the remedy (if remedy it be, which is far from certain) is worse than the affliction. Stoving with sulphur is not to be thought of for one moment in museum matters, as, when thoroughly done, it removes the colour from nearly all natural objects.

Such substances as camphor, tobacco, pepper, Russian leather (*i.e.* leather dressed with oil of birch), Russian tallow, fumes of turpentine or benzoline, and a dozen other " scents," are of as much use as would be a label " Please don't touch." Contact with a lethal fluid or substance is *the only* remedy, and safeguarding all specimens by constant supervision the only preventive.

One substance, however, is certain in its effects, although limited in application, and that is—

Insect Powder.—This, which is, when genuine, made from the flowers of the Russian tansy, is certainly a deterrent, if not actually a lethal agent, and whether the smell attracts and the fine dust smothers the insects, or whether it repels, or whether it is really toxic in its effects, is very hard to discover. Probably, however, it acts mechanically in some way, as dead moths and other insects are frequently found around skins it is protecting. There is no doubt that it is valuable, and it should be kept in all drawers containing skins, and may, in the case of delicately plumaged birds, be placed as a layer underneath paper on which the skins rest. It is apparently harmless, except to persons subject to " hay fever."

Sprinkling inside a newly-made skin is the best method, but when worked up in the preservative paste, or made as a wash for the inside of skins, as follows, it is doubtfully efficacious.

51.—Insecticide (M.B.)

Insect powder (best)	4 oz.
Hot water	1 quart

Bisulphide of Carbon (Riley, *Directions for Collecting and Preserving Insects*, p. 110).—It is said, " If the collection is found to be infested with insect pests, it may be renovated by pouring a little bisulphide of carbon into the boxes and closing them at once. This substance evaporates rapidly and will destroy all insect life, and does not injure specimens or pins nor stain the boxes. If infested specimens are received, these should be enclosed in a tight box and treated with bisulphide of carbon before being added to the general collection, and it is always well for those who are receiving pinned specimens by exchange or otherwise to keep a quarantine box of this kind on hand."

Cyanide of Potassium.—This has the same effect as the preceding, but it stains the cases, and the fumes it gives off are more deleterious, added to which it cannot be used with safety in bulk, and its use is limited to the killing of most Arthropoda and some small vertebrates (*e.g.* frogs and mice), by its inclusion with them in an air-tight jar or bottle.

Chloroform.—This is, when used with discretion, the best means of painlessly killing the Vertebrata ; owing, however, to its causing a stiffening of the wing-membranes of the Insecta, it is not so valuable for killing them as is cyanide of potassium made up in a " killing-bottle."

Lee has seen large Medusæ completely narcotised in an hour or so, in full extension, by squirting, with a fine pipette or syringe, liquid chloroform, a very small quantity at a time, into the sea-water containing the animals. It does not, how-ever, appear to succeed with the Actiniæ.

Nicotin.—Sometimes, says Lee, quoting Andres, the follow-ing is employed :—

52.—Nicotin Solution

Nicotin	.	.	.	.	1 gramme
Sea-water	.	.	.	.	1 litre

" The animal to be anæsthetised is placed in a jar contain-ing half a litre of sea-water, and the solution of nicotin is gradually conducted into the jar by means of a thread acting as a siphon. The thread ought to be of such a thickness as to be capable of carrying over the whole of the solution of nicotin in twenty-four hours."

A method of narcotisation by means of tobacco-smoke is thus described by Lo Bianco (pp. 449, 450) :—

Such a sea-anemone as *Adamsia rondeletii*, found upon shells tenanted by the large hermit-crab, is narcotised in the following manner. The object on which the anemone is fixed is suspended by a string from a small piece of wood supported upon the edges of a vessel containing sea-water. The animal is thus maintained perfectly extended without its tentacles touching the sides before commencing operations. One or many of these vessels are placed within a pan half filled with water, and this is covered with a bell-glass, which fits within the pan with its edges under water, so contrived, however, as to allow a tube to pass under from the outside, curved in such a manner as to come above the water of the pan. Through this, strong tobacco smoke is blown by means of a special apparatus until the bell-glass is filled with thick heavy fumes, the air being allowed to escape through a second tube, curved in the form of U, which is also passed beneath the edge of the bell-glass. To regulate the duration of narcotisation it is necessary to make the first fumigation towards the evening. Little by little the fumes commence to dissipate, and the water commences to absorb the narcotic, and the animals extend for the most part their crown of tentacles. Three hours afterwards a second fumigation is made, and the whole is left until the following morning, when the glass cover is removed with care, and the tentacles are touched with a needle to note their state of sensibility. If they contract, a third fumigation is made, and the tentacles are tried again with the needle after some two hours. When insensibility sets in, a small open tube containing some cubic centimetres of chloroform is placed in the water, and the cover is replaced, leaving the subjects exposed for from two to three hours to the fumes of the chloroform. Finally, the animals are killed by the chrom-acetic mixture No. 2 (Formula 38), hardened in ½ per cent. solution of chromic acid, followed as usual by alcohol, in which they are suspended.

By this singular method, probably derived from Hertwig (*Die Actinien*), Lo Bianco has obtained the most perfect results.

Hot and Cold Fresh Water.—"An excellent plan," says Lee, "for preparing many marine animals is to kill them in *hot fresh* water. Some of the larger Nemertians are better preserved by this method than by any other.

"Marine Animals are sometimes successfully killed by simply putting them into fresh water." This often induces them to extend the retractile parts, *e.g.* the Sipunculidæ.

"*Warm Water* will sometimes serve to immobilise and even kill both marine and fresh-water organisms."

These methods have been adopted, with fairly satisfactory results, in the laboratory of the Leicester Museum, with the terrestrial mollusca, slugs and snails often dying well extended even in cold water if air be excluded; but sometimes this fails, as does also warm water, owing, no doubt, to the difficulty of just hitting on the right temperature and knowing when to stop adding more and hotter water. Objects so killed have been subsequently hardened in bichromate solution (Formula 42), and casts have been successfully taken from them.

Probably, however, the best results may be obtained by placing the terrestrial gastropods, says Lee, "into a jar quite full of water that has been deprived of air by boiling, and hermetically closed. After from twelve to twenty-four hours, the animals are generally found dead and extended. The effect is obtained somewhat quicker if a little tobacco be added to the water." Fresh-water gastropods are, says Dall, quoting Professor Jno. Ryder (*Bulletin U.S.A.*, No. 39, p. 43), caused to die extended in the same manner, and hardened in alcohol of increasing strengths.

Turpentine.—Although turpentine is of little or no value as a preservative if used alone, yet it is a powerful insecticide, and may be used with advantage to kill the larvæ of moths and beetles in all skins, and even to clean others ; but its greasiness is such that, after it has done its work—and half an hour would suffice for this,—it must be removed from the specimen by the benzoline and plaster treatment (see p. 168).

Benzoline.—This most useful liquid is, needless to say, to be treated with care, and not brought too near to gas or fire-flame. In addition to its almost priceless value as a cleanser of nearly everything, it will *preserve* beetles for a considerable time—certainly a year—by immersion, and will also readily free them from grease. Moths and butterflies it also frees from grease, kills mites upon them, and only in very rare instances spoils them—some delicate greens and blues being affected.

What is, perhaps, of equal importance, is its property of preserving animal tissue for a certain time, and birds may be kept for a month in benzoline, and frogs have been kept for several months without much deterioration. As a means of preserving such objects for a *short* time, until the taxidermist can take them out to be skinned and set up, it has advantages over spirit in its clearness, cheapness, and the facility with which it is procured in out-of-the-way places. It is, of course, more dangerous in bulk, if kept at all exposed, than ordinary spirits ; but if a proper vessel is provided, such as those used for the latter at biological stations, there is no more danger than attaches to keeping a few gallons in a can for ordinary purposes.

It is of great value as an insecticide, especially in positions and with subjects where turpentine is objectionable ; for instance, in the Leicester Museum, whenever any suspicious traces of insects appear in the large wall-cases, where the specimen cannot be readily removed or cleaned after the use of turpentine, a copious spray of benzoline is directed upon all the objects in that case, and over all the rockwork, grasses, and mosses ; for it must not be supposed that fur and feathers are the only abiding-places of museum enemies ; they lurk, often for a number of years unsuspected, within the crevices of the rockwork, and within peat and mosses, by which, indeed, they are often introduced. Hence all natural grasses and mosses used as accessories should be plunged either into turpentine or benzoline, and dried in the air for a short time afterwards.

DIVISION II

PRESERVATIVES OF THE SECOND CLASS—SOAPS, POWDERS, ETC.

These are preservatives which are subsidiary to previous treatment—the removal of the flesh of the animal,—and may be gathered together under the comprehensive and suggestive title of " cures "—the " stuffer's " term for all preservative soaps, powders, and washes to be applied to the skin of any animal after the removal of the body.

The earliest known and used, and the most objectionable, are " cures " which have arsenical bases, and in a former work by the present author the ill effects of arsenic upon the human subject, and its uselessness save as an efficient drier, were pointed out, and the evidence *pro* and *con* gone into fully, and the opinion of Waterton was given, who wrote :—" It is dangerous to the operator and inefficient as a preservative." Since that time the evidence has been accumulating, and not in favour of arsenic, and no amount of assertions, such as that

" So-and-so has used arsenic for a great number of years, and has used it dry, *dusting* it on," will ever convince any sane person that arsenic is harmless, nay, a laudable article of diet. It is astonishing to find Mr. Hornaday, one of the chief taxidermists of America, writing as follows: [1] —

Arsenical soap is by all odds the safest poison that can possibly be used. It gives off no poisonous fumes whatsoever, its presence in the mouth, nose, or eyes is always detected instantly, and the worst that it ever does is to get into a cut or under the ends of the finger-nails of the careless taxidermist, and make a festering sore which is well in a few days—a purely local ill.

Dry arsenic is more injurious. It sometimes poisons the fingers of a careless operator, and if it is inhaled in the form of dust, the effect may be serious. A few persons are very susceptible to the effects of dry arsenic, others are not. If the blood is in a healthy condition, there is little to fear from it, except through carelessness. I have used, all told, probably more than a hundred and fifty pounds of arsenic in various forms, and never had an hour's illness in consequence, nor anything more serious than a sore finger.

On the other hand, in a less pretentious but exceedingly useful manual by another American taxidermist, are to be found the following sensible remarks by one who is frank enough to confess his former mistake: [2]—

Taxidermists for many years have made use of arsenic in some form as a preservative ; and in the first edition of my *Naturalists' Guide*, I recommended the use of it dry, stating that I did not think it injurious if not actually eaten. I have, however, since had abundant cause to change my opinion in this respect, and now pronounce it a dangerous poison. Not one person in fifty can handle the requisite quantity of arsenic necessary to preserve specimens for any length of time, without feeling the effects of it. For a long time I was poisoned by it, but attributed it to the noxious gases arising from birds that had been kept too long. It is possible that the poison from arsenic with which

[1] *Taxidermy and Zoological Collecting*, pp. 344, 345.
[2] *Manual of Taxidermy*, by C. J. Maynard, p. 44.

my system was filled might have been affected by these gases causing it to develop itself, but I do not think that the gas itself is especially injurious, as I have never been poisoned since I discontinued the use of arsenic.

The Rev. Mr. Housman [1] also gives his opinion, based on experience, of the uselessness of arsenic.

One has but to observe the cracked nails, soreness of the mucous membrane of the nose and lips, ulcers, feverish coughs and colds, chronic bronchitis, and partial or complete paralysis of the good old-fashioned "stuffer" who "always cures with arsenic," to be convinced of the harmful properties of the drug, to which, indeed, except when used medicinally, any doctor will testify.

Whilst being made, and whilst cooling, the arsenical preparations are always liable to give off injurious fumes, and when dry they are always ready to give off poisonous dust at the slightest provocation ; and as to arsenic being a finer preservative against the attacks of insects than anything known, how comes it that there is not a "stuffer" from the highest to the lowest in England, the Continent, or America who can truthfully say that his arsenical paste ever has kept, or ever will keep, the larvæ of moths or beetles from tearing his work to pieces *if not looked at* from time to time, or if put away in some dark corner?   If arsenic be so efficient a preservative, why this anxiety to protect the already supposed-to-be completely protected specimens by fumes of camphor, carbolic acid, creosote, albo-carbon, and various nostrums ?

The real truth—and it would be well that all museum curators and others should know it—is, that an absolutely "uncured" specimen would be more likely to escape if well dried and put in full light, than would an arsenically treated specimen if put in some dark corner or in a cupboard and neglected.   That is the whole gist of the matter—efficient

[1] *The Story of our Museum*, etc., p. 37.

treatment with some rapidly drying preservative, more LIGHT, and looking over the specimens now and then.

For the preservation of mammals, arsenical paste is quite useless, causing the hair to "sweat" from the skin, and not allowing the operator to stretch it without injury when modelling ; added to which, it is quite impossible to thoroughly relax such a skin by soaking in water, which is the *sine quâ non* of a first-class preservative. To sum up, arsenic is only a drier of tissue—a quality shared by many other things,—and merely sun-dried and earth-cured skins are often better preserved than many "cured" by the most elaborate arsenical soaps. Indeed, the writer possesses at the present moment a raven's head—a trophy of correct rifle-shooting—which was, after skinning, merely rubbed in with chalk and dried in a foreign sun, and which is now, after an interval of thirty years, quite firm and untouched by insects, although it has never been under glass.

Let a few additional facts be noted. Since 1884 the whole of the zoological collections in the Leicester Museum have been remodelled, and, in taking down the old specimens and dusting them out, the men were constantly affected with feverish colds, sore throats, and other symptoms of arsenical poisoning, and much milk was drunk by the doctor's orders. Some hundreds of birds—old specimens undoubtedly "cured" with arsenic— were badly "moth-eaten" [1] and infested with larvæ. All the groups executed by various London and provincial taxidermists, and certainly "cured" by some arsenical preparation, were burned because infested with larvæ both of moth and beetle ; and quite lately a bird of paradise under a glass shade, executed ten years ago by a man who presumably used arsenic, was eaten up !

---

[1] For the benefit of the unlearned in such matters, it may be stated that the moths themselves do not feed upon fur or feathers ; it is their larvæ (grubs) which do, but still, on the principle of "no moth no larvæ," it is the proper thing to kill all *small* moths flitting about a house or museum.

There are now in the museum hundreds of specimens more than there were in 1884 ; the old ones have been treated by a bichloride of mercury spray (see p. 36), and the new ones have been preserved by the non-poisonous but efficient formula No. 57 ; and during the past ten years perhaps not more than twenty specimens have suffered destruction from museum pests, and no camphor, albo-carbon, or other supposed deterrent has been used in the cases or drawers.

Since that time it has come to the knowledge of the writer that three men (and perhaps many others) have died from preventible causes connected with arsenic. In one case, coming under his own observation, the man was warned and advised to use the non-poisonous preservative ; but he said he " had always been used to cure with arsenic—especially dry— and believed in it " ! Yet that man's specimens were quite as much eaten up as any other stuffer's ; and, although the stuffers never own it, they know it to their cost and to that of their customers ; but so great is the Anglo-Saxon spirit in the midst of defeat, that they stick to the ways of their fathers rather than be guided by " new-fangled " (*i.e.* scientific) principles.

The following useless and dangerous arsenical preparations are given, not because there is any need to do so, but in the hope that those foolish enough to use them may live to see the error of their ways. The inventor of the first was one Bécœur, whose formula now following has been copied by every writer upon taxidermy :—

53.—"**Bécœur's Arsenical Soap** (Swainson, *Taxidermy*, 1840, p. 28, and others)

Camphor	5 oz.
Powdered arsenic	2 lb.
White soap	2 ,,
Salt of tartar	12 oz.
Lime in powder (or powdered chalk) . .	4 ,,

" Cut the soap into small slices as thin as possible ; put them into a pot over a gentle fire with very little water, stirring it often with a wooden spoon ; when dissolved, add the salts of tartar and powdered chalk : take it off the fire, add the arsenic, and stir the whole gently : lastly, put in the camphor, which must first be pounded in a mortar with a little spirits of wine. When the whole is properly mixed together, it will have the consistence of paste. It may be preserved in tin or earthenware pots well closed, and cautiously labelled. When wanted for use, it must be diluted with a little cold water to the consistence of clear broth : the pot may be covered with a lid of pasteboard, having a hole for the passage of the brush by which the liquor is applied."

The next is described by its inventor as follows :—

54.—"Swainson's Arseniated Soap (*The Naturalists' Guide*, p. 63, and *Taxidermy*, p. 28)

Arsenic	1 oz.
White soap	1 ,,
Carbonate of potash	1 drachm
Distilled water	6 drachms
Camphor	2 ,,

" This mixture should be kept in small tin boxes : when it is to be used, moisten a camel's-hair pencil with any kind of spirituous liquor, and with it make a lather from the soap, which is to be applied to the inner surface of all parts of the skin, and also to such bones as may not be removed."

One must, nevertheless, admire Swainson, who, in an age which could by no means do without arsenic in one form or another, was courageous enough to pen the following lines, which should have brought some inventor into the field, to replace by a harmless preparation the unfortunate invention of Bécœur, whose soap taxidermists of all nations have used, without giving themselves the trouble to inquire, " Is it more hurtful to the user than to the creatures it is intended to destroy ? " He says :—

Great care, however, must be taken in using this, as well as all other similar compositions.   If the least particle gets between the skin and the nail, and is not immediately removed, it separates both much lower down than their natural limits, creates great pain, and renders the fingers very tender.   We should therefore recommend the operator to wash his hands and clean his nails immediately after he has finished applying it to his specimens.

On the other hand, in a translation of a French work,[1] the author says, in speaking of M. Nicholas :—

Like the Abbé Manesse, he renounces poisons as dangerous to the preparers, and insufficient to avert the destructive effects of insects on zoological collections.   He pretends that by his soapy pomatum and tanning liquor, stuffed animals are preserved a long time.   The drugs which compose his preparations do not injure those who use them. We allow that this is not the case with the metallic soap, and supposing M. Nicholas's preservative equally efficacious, we should certainly give it the preference, but we have tried it without success.   We are therefore obliged to retain the arsenical soap : M. Dufresne has employed it for forty years, and has never been inconvenienced by it.   We may also instance Le Vaillant, Mangé, Desmoulins, and especially Bécœur, for no one in France has mounted so many birds as the latter.

Again : [2]—

It is necessary to use the oil of turpentine for the exterior of large *quadrupeds* and *fish ;* first, because the metallic soap cannot penetrate ; and secondly, because prudence does not allow us to employ it on the surface of any animal, not even on the parts free from hair.

In a footnote to this the author says :—

M. Dufresne means the exterior surface *only*, which is so much handled in the stuffing as to make it too dangerous to anoint it with

[1] Bowdich (*i.e.* Dufresne), *Taxidermy*, p. 11.
[2] *Op. cit.*, pp. 13, 14.

his soap; and I observe that the artists in the Zoological Laboratory at Paris carefully bend or turn down the points of the various wires, after they have inserted them (as they easily straighten them again with the fingers, if requisite), lest, by pricking their fingers, the arsenic might do them serious injury. M. Valenciennes, however, assures me that it is indispensably necessary for the traveller to anoint the naked parts of the legs of birds killed in hot climates.

It will be seen by this that the author, without intending it, deals what should have been a death-blow to arsenic, for M. Nicholas and the Abbé Manesse were educated and clever taxidermists; and the fact of Dufresne not being successful tells nothing, for we may see men at the present day unsuccessful in the preservation of anything by *any* medium, whilst others are successful with chalk alone ; and with regard to the user of arsenical soap for forty years, or the user of large quantities, not being injured by it, it is well known that there are men so constituted that it is impossible to injure them in any other way than with a sledge- or steam-hammer.

One of the most dangerous soaps is to be found in a little book professedly written by a well-known professional taxidermist, who may not, however, be the author of what he calls "the best known preservative for skins of all kinds," which is the following :—

55.—"**Arsenical and Mercurial Soap** (Gardner, *Bird, Quadruped, and Fish Preserving*, first edition, N.D., p. 9)

Arsenic	6 oz.
Corrosive sublimate . . .	3 ,,
Yellow soap	2 ,,
Camphor	1 ,,
Spirits of wine . . .	$\frac{1}{2}$ pint."

To say nothing of the danger of putting upon a fire, however "slow," such inflammable substances as camphor and spirits of wine in a "pipkin," the using of a "preservative" composed of nearly half poisons—and *such* poisons !—would be rather more risky than usual, and more useless.

As a variation from arsenical soaps, there have been men rash enough to advise the use of arsenical *powders.* The following was invented by Bullock, and is to be found in every compilation of taxidermy.

By an unconscious irony, it is quoted as—

56.—" Bullock's Preservative (!) **Powder** (Swainson, *Taxidermy*, p. 29, and others)

Arsenic .	.	.	.	.	.	1 lb.
Burnt alum	.	.	.	.	.	1 ,,
Tanner's bark	.	.	.	.	.	2 lbs.
Camphor .	.	.	.	.	.	$\frac{1}{2}$ lb.
Tincture of musk .	.	.	.		.	$\frac{1}{2}$ oz.

" Mix the whole thoroughly, and after reducing it to a powder, pass it through a sieve. Keep in close tin canisters. This powder is more particularly adapted to fill up incisions made in the naked parts of quadrupeds and the skulls of large birds."

It seems to be very generally imagined that all moths, or, rather, their larvæ, eat the *skins.* This is a fallacy in the majority of instances, the parts attacked being the *feathers,* not the skin.

Let it be once thoroughly grasped that no poison except bichloride of mercury—which is extremely dangerous to handle when made as a solution or paste, as is usually the case—is of any avail or protection against the irrepressible maggot, and common sense — should that rare quality abide with the ordinary taxidermist—will dictate the disuse of the dangerous and useless arsenical, and the substitution of an innocent and quickly drying, soap. Let it be grasped also that no claim is made that the following will resist the attacks of insects, any more than will the various arsenical preparations in use. All that is claimed is, that it is a more efficient drier and toughener of skin, and that it is quite as efficacious as arsenic when insects are considered. It is said that insects object to musk, and whether this be so or not, the addition of that powerful drug gives a lasting and pleasant perfume, which overpowers any other odours which may cling to the skin, and is therefore added for that purpose.

57.—Non-poisonous Preservative Soap (M.B.)

Whiting or chalk	$1\frac{1}{2}$ lbs.
White Windsor soap (common curd soap) .	$\frac{1}{2}$ lb.
Chloride of lime	$\frac{1}{2}$ oz.
Tincture of musk	$\frac{1}{2}$,,

Boil the soap and whiting together in about a pint of water until the soap is dissolved. Pound the chloride of lime finely and stir into the mixture whilst hot, taking care, however, not to inhale the fumes ; when cool add the musk.

Numberless people are now using this soap, and, for the benefit of those who imagine that the lime " burns " the skins, it is only necessary to point to the fact that skins prepared with this preservative relax in a perfect manner, by any method, after the lapse of many years, whereas skins cured with arsenic will often drop to pieces under the simplest methods. Nor does the lime unduly corrode the wires, unless the soap is used with an excess of water, which is incorrect ; the paste, to do its work efficiently, should be moistened, if dry, with a little methylated spirit, and applied of the consistence of thick cream. If quite dried up and hard, it will be necessary some-times to add a very little warm water ; but in our climate this seldom happens, unless, of course, a large quantity is made and stored, or exposed to the air for any length of time. Formerly it was recommended to keep it in tins ; but, as even the slightest damp rusts and corrodes tin, it has been found much more economical and convenient to keep it in closely-stoppered bottles or jars, and put a little out from this store into a galli-pot when wanted.

This preservative has been used for many years in the Leicester Museum, and the immunity from insects now enjoyed is not altogether attributed to its agency, but to methodical principles and to insistence upon light.

Many letters arrive, unsolicited, from all parts of the world, in praise of this formula.

Powders come next as preservatives, or rather driers of skin ; but, being astringents, they often dry the skin so rapidly as to render them practically useless, if much time be taken in shaping the specimen. They are, however, exceedingly useful to supplement pastes or soaps for drying up quickly what flesh may be left upon the tail, skull, or between the radius and ulna of the wings of large birds, or around the tail, feet, etc., of mammals. Some of them also will allow a skin treated by their means to be efficiently relaxed ; the following is one of these, and has been tried upon large specimens with a more than ordinary measure of success :—

58.—Non-poisonous Preservative Powder (M.B.)

Pure tannin	.	.	.	.	.	1 oz.
Red pepper	.		.	.	.	1 ,,
Camphor .	.	.	.	.		1 ,,
Alum (burnt)	.	.	.	.	.	8 ,,

Pound and thoroughly mix, and keep in stoppered bottles or canisters.

Although the preceding powder is quite admissible and efficacious for small mammals and most birds, it will not penetrate large skins and sufficiently fix the fur or hair, but can be highly recommended—insect-powder likewise—as an efficient substitute for snuff !

Some years ago, the writer was fortunate enough to stumble upon burnt alum, which is unaffected by heat or damp, as a substitute for the more than useless crude alum, and the following preparation has been of the greatest service to thousands, both abroad and at home, who have had occasion to "cure" the skins of mammals. It perfectly fixes the hair to the skin, even when first applied, and afterwards nothing can disturb the hair, which is tightened in an extraordinary manner. It is also perfectly staunch under the severest test of relaxing, and is altogether to be relied upon, as is testified by the many letters received upon the subject.

.59.—Preservative for Mammals (M.B.)

Alum (burnt)	4 parts
Saltpetre	1 part

It should be well rubbed into the skin, inside and out, particularly upon the eyelids, nose, lips, ears, and so on, and may be applied before skinning the specimen, should this not be so fresh as could be desired. A mixture made of the above proportions, with the addition of hot water and a little bichromate of potassa, makes a very fine bath in which to plunge a thick or slightly tainted skin.

Notwithstanding the almost universal approbation which this simple preservative has evoked, and in spite of the fact that it has been copied (usually without acknowledgment) in the pages of many treatises on taxidermy, correspondents often write complaining of efflorescence or mould appearing upon the skins cured by its means. The answers to these are, that mildew forms—(1) if the skins are not perfectly freed from fat; (2) if the specimen is cased before having been properly dried; or (3) if the case rests against a damp wall or is in a thoroughly damp situation, which would be quite sufficient to ruin anything else. In the first event,

the mildew would be the result of unskilfulness or carelessness on the part of the operator, and nothing can be done.
In the second event, the case must be opened, the mildew
removed, and the subject left until properly dried.   In the
third event, the same treatment must be followed, and the
case, of course, removed to a dry position.

If crystals or efflorescence form, however, it would point
to the belief that ordinary alum had been used instead of the
alum ustum of the formula, or that more saltpetre had been
used than was directed ; and the efflorescence must be removed
with warm water until no more appears, and when dry the
eyes, nose, and mouth of the specimen where it appeared must
be brushed with a little olive oil.   Thus the only blame in the
matter rests with the operator, and *not* with the formula.

Finally, the advice now repeated and insisted upon is, that
the skins of all taxidermic specimens should be treated with a
non-poisonous preservative (Formula 57 or 59), and that, when
quite finished and dried, and before being cased, they should
have a thorough dressing with one of the liquid preservatives,
Formula 10 or 11, over the feathers, bills, and legs of birds,
and over the whole of the fur and bare parts of mammals,
after which nothing—not even the *Dermestes* beetles—can
possibly feed upon them, and the *handling* of any poisonous
substance is thereby obviated.

All subjects should be as fresh as possible before preservation
by *any* method, but, if at all stale, they may often be saved by
steeping in either of the preservatives, Formula 3 or 31.

Blow-flies occasionally give trouble in hot weather, and all
specimens should be protected from them ; the brushing over
of the mouth, and eyes, and soft parts generally with the
preservative Formula 34 will prevent any damage, and it is
also an advantage if the specimens be enclosed, pending the
setting-up, in a light wooden framework covered with muslin,

the whole fitting upon a wooden bottom, around which strips are fixed to keep the framework tight and prevent insects from crawling under it. For strength and convenience of stacking, these frames may have a fixed wooden top.

DIVISION III

MODELLING-COMPOSITIONS, CEMENTS, AND VARIOUS GENERAL FORMULÆ

The following formulæ are accessory to the foregoing, and are chiefly modelling-compositions for introduction under the skin of an animal, together with cements, pastes, and various formulæ not previously considered, but which are often of great importance, and, indeed, in some cases indispensable. The first is—

Clay

Although the artist in plastic materials has usually the advantage of being able to take a cast directly from the specimen itself, yet it sometimes happens that it is desirable to copy certain objects by the eye alone, and for this purpose there are but three materials which are adapted for rapid and satisfactory working : these are clay, wax, and guttapercha, placed in their order of value, and, indeed, of the three, clay is far in advance of the others, whilst guttapercha is of little value for this particular purpose. Plaster of Paris—an indispensable accessory to modelling—is fully considered in processes described in these pages.

Modelling-clay or pipe-clay (for there is no need to use terra-cotta) is to be purchased cheaply from many wholesale merchants who supply sculptors, and also, but at very much higher rates, from artists' colourmen. It should be as white as can be procured, so that light and shade fall pleasantly upon it when being modelled, and should be smooth and not gritty—a condition easily ascertained by pressing it between the finger and thumb. If purchased in the dry state, it should be beaten up and kneaded with just sufficient water (and in some cases with very thin flour paste) to make it rather stiffer than putty, and may be kept damp from day to day by being covered with a wetted cloth.

The accessory materials are a board, and, usually, a cross of wood of varying size on which to build the clay should the subject to be copied be large, although for smaller things the clay may—if not used as a solid mass—have for its core some tightly bound tow or paper. The tools are those figured as Nos. 26, 27, and 29 to 39 (Plate II.), a knife, a stiff brush, a pair of calipers and dividers for measuring.

The object to be copied, being placed in front of the artist, is measured first for its greatest length and width, and a rough mass of clay, of the same length and breadth, is fixed upon the core of wood ; more and finer measurements are taken, and clay is added or subtracted to suit these requirements, the various tools coming into work as matters progress.

No detailed instructions as to how this or that is to be executed can be given, such work being entirely a matter of correct measurements, fine judgment, and an educated eye and hand acting together—accomplishments which come wholly and solely with experience ; so much so, that a skilful modeller will manage with the most unlikely materials. As a proof of this, there is in the Leicester Museum a grinning and grotesque head, as a large ornament to the model in paper, etc., of a dilapidated belfry-window (see Frontispiece), which was made in a few minutes—eyes and eyelids, bulbous nose, grinning mouth and teeth, all the features in fact—from glued wool !

The usefulness of knowing how to model is constantly demonstrated, and many examples are given. Sometimes it is an advantage to cover clay models with pasted tissue-paper to prevent cracking.

For rough or large work, modelling-clay is very well replaced by common fire-clay, or even by the common clays of the fields, some of those known to geologists as lias clays being the most tenacious and useful.

For insertion within the skins of animals, to assist the modelling of the head and limbs and so on, clay is, though somewhat heavy, exceedingly useful, and in connection with this it may be as well to point out to Mr. Hornaday,[1] who claims to have " discovered its value " in 1880, that the English taxidermists used it for these purposes long before the American, and, if *they* did not discover it, there is every probability that the foreign (*i.e.* European) taxidermists used it long ago.

Of modelling-wax it is only necessary to state that, being rather expensive either to buy or to make, its use is limited to small objects or to the representation of parts. The same may be said of guttapercha; this latter is, however, by no means a good medium in which to work.

Modelling-Compositions which in a short time become extremely hard

Hamilton (*Pathology*, p. 719) says, " Where a very strong substance is required in constructing a model, gilder's putty may be found useful. It has the following composition :—

60.—Gilder's Putty

Resin	1 lb.
Glue	1 ,,
Boiled linseed-oil . . .	2 gills
Precipitated chalk, a sufficiency.	

"The glue must first be thoroughly soaked in water and melted. The resin is to be dissolved in the boiled linseed-oil, and the

---

[1] *Taxidermy and Zoological Collecting*, pp. 112, 113.

two are then mixed.   They are subsequently stirred into precipitated chalk, so as to make the mixture of putty-like consistence."

For another—

Take linseed-oil and heat in a water-bath over a slow
fire ; add finely levigated whiting until the mass becomes of
the consistence of a pudding.   Next take some hot strong
glue and stir in whiting until it is as a thick paste ; mix
thoroughly and add to the other compound, heat the whole,
and blend with it a small quantity of Venice turpentine.
When melted together, add sufficient fine plaster to make
the whole mass, when stirred together, a stiff putty.   If at
all brittle at this stage, add more glue.   Put a little out on
a cold iron plate and work it together with a knife ; when
cooling, knead it with the fingers previously dipped in fine
plaster, and, if at all oily so that it wets the fingers, knead in
more fine plaster until it becomes, if properly made, like tough
dough or putty and of a nice consistence.   If this trial be all
right, work up with plaster what is left in the vessel into
pieces about the size of a large walnut, using it as made ; if,
however, more is made than can be rapidly used, and it should
cool and set, place each piece in a water bath, or dip it into
hot water, which does very well if quickly managed, and it will
become soft again and fit for use, and may be kept soft for
some considerable time by rolling it in a little glycerine, which
does not affect its ultimate hardness.

The exact proportions appear to be :—

61.—Modelling-Composition (M.B.)

Linseed-oil (heated) .	.	.	4 oz. (by measure)
Whiting (levigated) .	.	.	14 ,, (,, weight)
Glue (liquid)	.	.	10 ,, (,, measure)
Whiting .	.	.	8 ,, (,, weight)
Venice turpentine .	.	.	1 ,, (,, ,,)
Plaster .	.	.	2 ,, (,, ,,)

This composition is of the highest value for modelling under the skin inside the lips, eyes, and noses of mammals, as it hardens soon, but is amenable to working with warm fingers or a warm iron for alterations, and is valuable in sticking closely to the skin, and not coming away or getting out of shape in parts already modelled, when additions are required. Its lightness and rapidity of drying make it a first-class substitute for clay, which has not those qualities, and it is only rivalled, and not surpassed, in the only good quality possessed by clay—facility of handling.

62.—Plaster Putty (M.B.)

Best " S.F." (superfine) plaster of Paris . .	4 oz.
Boiled oil	1 „

Mix together until of the substance of ordinary putty; it is then easily worked between the fingers, and can be used for many purposes, especially for introducing under skins and for filling up cracks in various things (*i.e.* models). It ultimately dries exceedingly hard.

Plaster of Paris may also be mixed with weak glue as a water putty, but must be used at once, as it dries rapidly.

WAX COMPOSITIONS

White Wax

Madras wax, which is rather expensive, takes tube and dry colours without the purity of either being affected, but, although indispensable for the modelling of foliage (see Chap. IX.), it need only be used for the legs and bills of birds when delicate tints are required. For ordinary purposes of this kind, and for modelling in general, it may be replaced by any of the commoner, coarser waxes which follow.

6

Beeswax

Ordinary beeswax will, if warmed by fire-heat or warm water, or melted, do for many things without further preparation, but modelling-waxes of great service are as follow :—

63.—Modelling-Wax (M.B.)

Common beeswax	.	.	.	. 4 oz.
Resin (finely pulverised)	.	.		. 2 ,,
Plaster of Paris	.	.	.	. $\frac{1}{2}$,,
Red ochre (powder)	.	.	.	. 2 ,,

This is an ordinary dark red modelling-wax, is tough and pliable, works well with the fingers, and unites readily without showing joins.

64.—Modelling-Wax (M.B.)

Common beeswax	.	.	.	. 4 oz.
Resin (finely pulverised)	.	.	.	. 2 ,,
Whiting	.	.	.	. 1 ,,
Plaster of Paris	.	.	.	. $\frac{1}{2}$,,
Vermilion (powder)	.	.	.	. 1 ,,

This is a fine, bright red modelling-wax, rather hard and tough, and would do as the groundwork for the representation of blood.

65.—Modelling-Wax (M.B.)

Common beeswax	.	.	.	. 4 oz.
Resin (finely pulverised)	.	.	.	. 2 ,,
Plaster of Paris	.	.	.	. $\frac{1}{2}$,,
Flake white (powder)	.	.	.	. 2 ,,
Vermilion (powder)	.	.	.	. $\frac{1}{2}$,,

This is of a fine red, lighter in colour than the preceding, very good for brightly coloured flesh, and works beautifully by pressure upon moulds, etc.

66.—Modelling-Wax (M.B.)

Common beeswax	.	.	4 oz.
Resin (finely pulverised)	.	.	1 ,,
Plaster of Paris	.	.	1 ,,
Flake white (powder)	.	.	1 ,,
Vermilion (powder)	.	.	$\frac{1}{4}$,,
Ultramarine blue (powder)	.	.	5 grains

This is a fine wax, of a good colour for palates and tongues, tough and elastic, and works well by pressure.

67.—Tempered Wax (M.B.)

Common beeswax	.	.	1 oz.
Resin (finely pulverised)	.	.	$\frac{1}{4}$,,

This and the three following, for the bills and legs of birds, to be applied, hot, with a brush.

68.—Tempered Wax (M.B.)

Common beeswax	.	.	1 oz.
Resin (finely pulverised)	.	.	$\frac{1}{8}$,,

This is a little harder, and perhaps better, than the preceding.

69.—Tempered Wax (M.B.)

Common beeswax	.	1 oz.
Gum-arabic	.	$\frac{1}{4}$,,

70.—Tempered Wax (M.B.)

Common beeswax	.	.	1 oz.
Gum-arabic	.	.	$\frac{1}{8}$,,

The substitution of gum-arabic for resin improves the colour, but makes the wax "shorter."

Japan Wax

Beeswax, being rather expensive, is replaced for some purposes by Japan wax, which is exceedingly cheap—no more, indeed, than sixpence per pound. The following are found of use :—

71.—Japan Modelling-Wax (M.B.)

Japan wax	2 oz.
Plaster of Paris	1 ,,

Can be coloured by the addition of dry or tube-colours, and the addition of plaster takes out the greasy nature, whilst keeping the colour beautifully pure. It dries very hard, and, for subjects where hardness is not desirable, may be replaced by—

72.—Japan Modelling-Wax (M.B.)

Japan wax	10 oz.
Whiting	8 ,,
Madras white wax (common)	4 ,,
Tallow	1 ,,
Plaster of Paris	1 ,,
Canada balsam	$\frac{1}{2}$,,

This is rather soft and greasy, owing to the tallow and balsam, but is sometimes useful for modelling under the skins of mammals. It has also been used for modelling the long stems of the Flowering Rush (p. 359).

73.—Japan Modelling-Wax (M.B.)

Japan wax	$2\frac{1}{4}$ oz.
Madras white wax (common)	1 ,,
Plaster of Paris	1 ,,
Tallow	$\frac{1}{2}$,,
Canada balsam	$\frac{1}{4}$,,

A soft bright wax, useful, when coloured pink, for making up the mouths of mammals.

74.—Japan Modelling-Wax (M.B.)

Japan wax	$2\frac{1}{4}$ oz.
Madras white wax (common)	1 ,,
Plaster of Paris	1 ,,
Resin (finely pulverised)	1 ,,
Tallow	$\frac{1}{2}$,,

This is a fine, soft, strong wax, and, if vermilion be added, is of a light reddish-brown (owing to the resin). It is very useful for common work under skins and for other modelling, and was used very successfully for modelling the long stems of the Flowering Rush (see p. 359), for which purpose it was even better suited than Formula 72, being both softer and tougher.

75.—M. Peron's "Lithocolle" (Boitard, *Naturaliste Préparateur*, p. 251)
For fixing-in Glass Stoppers.

> Common resin well pulverised
> Red ochre in powder
> Yellow wax
> Essence of turpentine

Dissolve the wax and resin, stir well and add the ochre gradually; when the mixture has boiled for seven or eight minutes, *remove from the fire* and add the turpentine—the instructions given, and repeated in every other book, to add this *over the fire* and to continue boiling, being highly dangerous.

The proportions may be varied according to the brittleness or elasticity desired in the "lithocolle."

76.—Guttapercha Composition (M.B.)

Brown guttapercha	.	.	.	.	1 oz.
Beeswax .	.	.	.	.	. 2 „

Cut the guttapercha small, and heat the ingredients together in a water bath.

This is a most valuable waterproof composition for making up parts of the mouth or palate, or for setting eyes firmly in their orbits, or for getting a "squeeze," as, although it is hard when cold, it will readily knead up between moderately warm fingers, and reset quite hard. It may also be used, when warm, for smearing stoppers.

It should be remembered that, for actual india-rubber, *coal*-naphtha is a solvent. *Pure* Para rubber should be used. Sometimes turpentine will act as a solvent for this—*with heat.*

Dr. J. W. Williams, editor of *The Naturalist's Monthly*, kindly communicated the following :—

77.—Luting for Stoppers

"Indiarubber, *old* . . . . 5 parts
Asphalt . . . . . . 4 „

"Melt together and apply hot, the edges of the cover being previously ground, dipped in hot water, and well dried."

The following has been found of great value in the Leicester Museum :—

78.—Shellac Composition (M.B.)

Best shellac . . . ` . . I oz.
Rectified naphtha . . . . . 4 „
Digest in a water bath.

With this, if not used too thick, very large and weighty fossils or masses of rock may be joined, and will remain permanently joined. When it becomes too thick, dilute with naphtha, which will also remove any stains of shellac from the fossil.

Symington's Cement (Hamilton, *Pathology*, p. 53).—"Evaporate gold-size until it becomes considerably thicker than is natural and add red lead to make into a paste. Dries in a week and effectually fixes glass in which is spirit."

79.—Lead Putty

Red lead . . . .⎫
White lead . . . .⎬ Equal parts

Boiled oil—A sufficient quantity to be added to make a stiff putty when beaten up.

Useful for repairing leaks in tanks, etc.

80.—Ordinary Putty

Linseed-oil
Whiting

beaten into a stiff mass, but more cheaply bought ready-made.

"*Marine Glue.*[1]—Found in commerce. Carpenter says the best is that known as G K 4.

"It is soluble in ether, naphtha, or solution of potash. Its use is for attaching glass cells to slides, and for all cases in which it is desired to cement glass to glass.

"Receipts for preparing it may be found in Beale, p. 49, or in Cooley's *Cyclopædia.*"

81.—A Nice Delicate Glue for mounting Ferns and Seaweeds, and a good strong cement for China—will bear considerable rough usage.

Gum-arabic	.	.	.	.	5 parts
White sugar	.	.		.	3 ,,
Starch	.	.	.	.	2 ,,

Add a very little water, and boil until thick and white.[2]

82.—A Fine Paste (M.B.)

Best flour	.		.	.	2 oz.
Water	.	.	.	.	8 ,,
Essence of cloves	.	.	.	.	$\frac{1}{4}$,,

Put part of the water into a basin, and dust in the flour, so stirring it meanwhile with a spoon or spatula as to remove any lumpiness. When worked up as a smooth cream, add the remainder of the water, boil for a few minutes, and turn out into a jar and add the oil of cloves.

The above is useful for any purpose where cleanness is a desideratum, but, where strength is the chief requirement, finely powdered resin may be added, which, however, detracts from the cleanness. Shoemakers' paste, which is still stronger, and therefore useful for joining paper models, etc., is made with rye-flour and resin. In this case, the addition of alum keeps the paste sweet and strengthens it.

[1] *Microtomist's Vade-mecum*, Lee, pp. 254, 255.
[2] *Home Notes*, vol. v. (1895), p. 28.

83.—Starch Paste

Take some white starch and stir into it just enough cold water to make a smooth thick paste. Add to this sufficient *boiling* water to convert it into a stiff *clear* paste, stirring all the time to prevent lumps forming.

This is extremely useful for any clean paper work, especially for mounting photographs, as paper can be pasted upon cardboard by this medium without wrinkles. The front surface of the paper having been first wetted, the back should be pasted and laid evenly upon the cardboard, and the whole pressed and dried between blotting-paper.

LIST OF OIL-, WATER-, AND POWDER-COLOURS REQUIRED
FOR THE VARIOUS PROCESSES GIVEN IN THIS BOOK

The following list comprises all the pigments required, whether for the colouring of bills and legs of birds, soft parts of animals generally, or for models of fishes, etc., invertebrates, modelled foliage and flowers, diagrams, skies and backs of cases, rockwork, ferns and grasses, or for actual pictorial painting.

As a general rule, it may be considered that the common powder-colours (*italicized*) to be bought cheaply at so much a pound at the oil- and colour-merchants' (*not artists'* oilmen) are suitable only for large breadths of sky when expense is an object, and for the colouring of quantities of grasses, ferns, and rockwork; they are not permanent in oil nor in water.

The fine powder-colours—some very expensive—are to be purchased only of the artists' oil- and colour-makers (*i.e.* Winsor and Newton; Roberson; Lechertier, Barbe, et Cie.; Rowney, etc., who have agents in every town), and are only to be used as directed for flower- and foliage-modelling.

The artists' *moist* water-colours, either in *pans* or *tubes* (*not cakes*), supplement the fine powder-colours for the same purpose, and are also used for diagram-making and other artistic purposes.

The artists' oil-colours in tubes supplement both, but are useful in a much less degree, for the above purposes ; they are indispensable for the legs and bills of birds, soft parts generally of all animals, colouring of models of fishes, reptiles, and invertebrates, skulls, etc., for index collections, small or delicate dried ferns or grasses, and small masses of rockwork. All except the common powder-colours are absolutely permanent, *i.e.* unchangeable either by the action of direct or transmitted light, impure atmosphere (resisting one charged with sulphuretted hydrogen, etc.), or by mixture one with the other, or with flake white. The only colours which require partial safeguarding are the madders, which must not be mixed with flake white but with zinc white to be absolutely permanent, nor must they be mixed with any of the ochres, nor, indeed, with any colour which, like these, contains iron, nor with any colours containing lead.[1]

The properties of pigments have been studied for many years in the management of the Leicester Museum, and, before the writer went into this subject thoroughly, the changes of colour were remarkable under the influence of direct light, and of town atmosphere sometimes charged with deleterious gases. For instance, the changes in the colours of certain elements of the skulls exhibited in the index collection were noteworthy. The pre-maxilla, coloured formerly in a fairly permanent blue mixed with *chrome yellow* (a lead pigment), although at first a fine green colour, blackened rapidly. The maxilla, coloured with chrome yellow, also blackened to an ugly dirty yellow. The frontal, a pale lavender made by mixing permanent blue with

---

[1] For further and interesting details of the properties of colours, consult Field's *Chromatography* (last edition) : Winsor and Newton.

crimson lake (a fine but very fugitive colour now superseded by alizarin, which is coarser but permanent) and flake white, faded to a bluish drab.

It will be seen by this that, although "permanent blue" (an impure ultramarine) was used, it was killed by the fugitive colour, which, in turn, was killed by the lead white; and in this and all similar instances the fact must be thoroughly grasped, that a "permanent" colour is only *permanent per se*, or when mixed with other permanent colours, and is fugitive when mixed with any fugitive colour, although there are some which "hold up" for a certain time a colour known to be fugitive.

As a general rule it must be remembered that one pigment unmixed is absolute purity; two mixed are permissible and agreeable; three mixed are less pure and border on grey or brown; and four mixed are dirty, or perilously near to black; also that, the less mixing or "worrying" pigments undergo, the greater the purity of the combinations.

In these pages, a *colour* in the abstract is spoken of as a "hue"; when mixed with white it is a "tint"; whilst "tone" is relative light and shade, without reference to tint or hue.

PERMANENT OIL-, WATER-, AND POWDER-COLOURS, WITH PRICES

	Oil Tubes.	Moist Water. Half Pans or Tubes.	Powder-Colours. Fine. Per oz.	Powder-Colours. Common. Per lb.
Blacks—				
Blue Black . .	...	...	...	$2\frac{1}{2}$d.
Ivory Black . .	4d.	6d.	1s.	...
Lamp Black . .	...	...	...	$3\frac{1}{2}$d.
Blues and Violets—				
Cobalt . . .	1s.	1s.	6s.	...
Lime Blue . .	...	...	...	4d.

PERMANENT OIL-, WATER-, AND POWDER-COLOURS, WITH PRICES
(continued)

	Oil Tubes.	Moist Water. Half Pans or Tubes.	Powder-Colours. Fine. Per oz.	Powder-Colours. Common. Per lb.
Blues and Violets—				
Permanent Blue .	4d.	...	2s.	...
Permanent Mauve .	1s.	1s.	...	...
Permanent Violet .	1s.	1s.	...	...
Prussian Blue . .	...	...	2s.	2s. 4d.
French or Brilliant Ultramarine[1] . .	1s.	...	6s.	...
Ultramarine (common)	...	...	...	9d.
Browns—				
Burnt Umber . .	4d.	6d.	1s.	5d.
Caledonian Brown .	4d.	...	1s.	...
Vandyke Brown .	4d.	6d.	1s.	7d.
Citrons—				
Raw Umber . .	4d.	6d.	1s.	...
Verona Brown .	4d.	...	...	...
Greens—				
Emerald Green . .	4d.	...	...	...
Oxide of Chromium .	1s.	1s.	6s.	...
Terre Verte .	4d.	6d.	1s.	...
Viridian . . .	1s.	1s.	6s.	...
Green (Chrome, etc.) .	...	...	...	4d.
Reds and Russets—				
Alizarin Crimson .	6d.	...	...	...
Burnt Sienna . .	4d.	6d.	1s.	...
Chinese Vermilion .	6d.	6d.	1s. per pkt.	...
French Vermilion .	6d.	6d.	...	...
Indian Red . .	4d.	...	1s.	...
Mars Violet . .	1s.	...	9s.	...
Rose Madder . .	1s.	1s. 6d.	16s.	...

[1] This quality is quite good enough for every purpose, although the very finest quality is eight guineas per ounce, ranging downwards to a few shillings.

PERMANENT OIL-, WATER-, AND POWDER-COLOURS, WITH PRICES
(*continued*)

	Oil Tubes.	Moist Water. Half Pans or Tubes.	Powder-Colours. Fine. Per oz.	Powder-Colours. Common. Per lb.
Reds and Russets—				
Rubens Madder . .	6d.	9d.	12s.	...
Scarlet Madder . .	1s.	1s. 6d.	12s.	...
Terra Rosa . .	4d.	...	1s.	...
Venetian Red . .	4d.	...	1s.	2d.
Vermilion (*common*) .	...	...	...	2s. 7d.
White—				
Chinese White . .	...	6d.	1s.	...
Flake White .	4d.	...	6d.	3½d.
Zinc White . .	4d.	...	6d.	...
Yellows and Oranges—				
Aureolin . . .	1s. 6d.	1s. 6d.	8s.	...
Aurora Yellow . .	2s.	1s. 6d.	8s.	...
Brown Ochre . .	4d.	6d.	1s.	...
Cadmium Orange .	1s. 6d.	1s.	6s.	...
Chrome Yellow . .	...	...	...	9d.
Lemon Chrome . .	...	...	...	9d.
Lemon Yellow (deep) .	4d.	...	6s.	...
Orient Yellow . .	...	...	...	...
Oxford Ochre . .	4d.	...	...	...
Permanent Yellow .	4d.	...	...	...
Yellow Ochre . .	...	6d.	1s.	2d.
Roberson's Medium .	1s.	...	...	...

Of the foregoing list, it may be remarked that Lamp Black,
although permanent, is of so sooty and dense a nature as to be
useful for "rockwork" only.

Prussian Blue, though given as a powder-colour, is not
permanent; it is only fairly permanent when rubbed in dry,
but in oil or water it blackens in light and regains its colour

in the dark——a property of very doubtful value, and one not to be easily taken advantage of.

Emerald Green is too " rank " a colour to be used by the unskilled, but is valuable sometimes, and, indeed, not to be replaced by any combination of pigments ; it, however, unites with certain reds to form lovely greys of great tone-value.

Indian Red is another " rank " but useful colour, to be used with care as being surcharged with iron.

Terra Rosa is a finer preparation of Light Red, which it supersedes.

Zinc White has less body, and is more difficult to work with in oil than Flake White, although the fine powder is indispensable in flower-tinting, as it is, in its well-known form of Chinese White, for flower-painting.

Oxford Ochre replaces Yellow Ochre, of which it is a finer preparation.

The makers of the fine powder - colours will supply half ounces of any of those marked one shilling per ounce, and as small a quantity as an eighth of an ounce of all the extra colours ; one or two of the best makers, however, supply all colours in bottles of varying sizes, but at a uniform price of sixpence each.

OILS AND VARNISHES

These, if wanted for any of the finer pigments, had better be obtained from the artists' colourmen, and although they have for sale almost colourless oils, such as the nut- and poppy-oils, yet there is nothing better for the finer work described in these pages than rectified linseed - oil and turpentine of the best quality, mastic varnish, and the medium previously mentioned. For ordinary work, however, the ordinary linseed- and boiled oils, turpentine, and " paper varnish " — an inferior kind of mastic,—with still commoner varnishes for the roughest " rock-work," will be the only qualities necessary.

A first-rate medium, which should always be kept ready-made, and which will be found most useful for mixing with pigments with which to touch the legs and bills of birds—if unwaxed,—is

84.—Medium for Oil-Colours (M.B.)

Paper-varnish	.	.	.	.	1 part
Turpentine	.	.	.	.	5 parts

This gives just sufficient " quality " without any objectionable shininess, and will be found very useful when colouring fishes or the models of such, ferns, grasses, small pieces of " rockwork," and, indeed, for most purposes.

" Flatness," *i.e.* absence of gloss, is gained in two ways, namely, by leaving out oils and varnishes and using only turpentine, or by introducing those media into the colours and subsequently " flatting " with turpentine, by this means obviating the objectionable cracking which inevitably takes place when turpentine alone is used. *Extreme* flatness is gained by the use of benzoline, as a medium, with the tube oil-colours, but this probably causes cracks to appear in time.

CHAPTER IV

THE COLLECTING OF MAMMALS, BIRDS, AND OTHER VERTEBRATES, AND INVERTEBRATES, BY VARIOUS METHODS

To give even a tenth of the methods employed in the chase and procuring of the various animals which are fit subjects for the atelier of the ordinary taxidermist, or advanced artist, would fill a work much larger than the present, and therefore but a slight sketch can be given of the means adopted by the naturalist-collector, either in this or in any other country.

Taking the mammals first, it will be obvious that the larger foreign ones are collected by means of pitfalls, dead-falls, and other special methods in the cases of savage nations not fully supplied with firearms, but that the greater number procured by sportsmen and collectors all the world over are killed by arms of precision. It is not necessary here to enter into the respective merits of single- or double-barrelled rifles, of large or small bores, of "Express," "Paradox," and the thousand-and-one other breechloaders now placed upon the sporting markets of the world ; for a consideration of all these and many minor matters important to the "big-game" hunter, the reader is referred to current numbers of the *Field*, the American journal *Forest and Stream*, to some foreign periodicals, and to numberless works on shooting by such hunters as the late Sir Samuel Baker, C. J. Anderson, F. C. Selous, and many others, and particularly to those on *Big-game*

Shooting,[1] which no intending sportsman or collector abroad should be without, and in which are summarised all the technicalities of the art, past and present.

Perhaps it may be as well to point out that there is no one gun which will do *everything*, in spite of the ingenious combinations sold to intending sportsmen and emigrants, which, if the " Paradox " be excepted, are usually like other " combination " implements—more easily sold than used. A " battery," suited to the animals to be shot and to the man who is to use it, is a *sine quâ non*, as no one dreams of using, say, a double 4-bore elephant-gun upon deer. Even in England, where the wild animals to be shot with a rifle are limited to three—the red deer, the rabbit, and the rook,—two rifles of different calibre are necessary, unless, indeed, the ingenious " Morris tube " be used as a converter of a large-bored rifle to a lesser.

The " bagging " of foreign mammals, having a vast literature of its own, need not be further discussed, and the mammals of Britain, if the whales and other cetaceans (sometimes shot !) be excepted, are so few that their methods of capture are well known.

There are special methods of trapping known to many gamekeepers ; and some treatises there are which may be studied with advantage by the amateur trapper ;[2] usually, however, the traps are the ordinary steel ones, " figure of 4's," other dead-falls, various box-traps, and sometimes poison— which seems a villainous way of destroying animals, and should be made penal.

It is pleasing to find that the Hon. Gerald Lascelles considers the dead-fall and the box-trap humane, and decries the

---

[1] The Badminton Library, *Big-Game Shooting*, vols. i. and ii., by Clive Phillipps-Wolley.

[2] *The Game-preserver's Manual*, by Captain Darwin (" High Elms ") ; *Practical Trapping*, by W. Carnegie ; *Shooting* (*Field and Covert*), Badminton Library.

use of that most cruel of all traps, the common steel-toothed one.[1]

Birds

The literature dealing with the trapping or collecting of birds is, as may be supposed, much more extensive than that of mammals, and there are other books than those quoted which may with advantage be consulted.

Crows, which are difficult of approach, are said, both by " High Elms " (*op. cit.*) and the Hon. Gerald Lascelles (*op. cit.*), to be attracted near a concealed gunner by a tethered cat, or by a roughly-stuffed cat's skin, at either of which they will swoop, and in the nesting season, when they do a great deal of damage to game and young lambs, they will even go to greater lengths, as recounted by " High Elms " (p. 87) :—

To show how easily carrion crows may be deceived during the nesting time, I may here mention a very ridiculous imitation of a cat that was constructed by the under-keeper before alluded to, and used by him with great success last May. He cut the sleeve off an old worn-out shirt, stuffed it full of hay, and tied a string round the wrist at about six inches from the end. He filled that end also with hay, and tied it again. One of the ladies in his establishment then, by his direction, sewed a few black patches on different parts of the body, and two black buttons made capital eyes. The whole apparatus (being such a domestic cat as Guy Fawkes would doubtless have possessed) was then tied to a stick, and placed leaning against the tree in which a carrion crow had a nest and young ones. The keeper then hid himself, and he said it was quite ridiculous to observe the way in which the old birds attacked our friend " Dummy " on their visit to the nest. The long and short of it all was, that he killed them both without any difficulty.

The simplest method of decoying birds, and one which some fowlers both at home and abroad are expert in, is that of whistling birds nearer to the gun by the lips alone : such birds

---

[1] *Shooting (Field and Covert)*, Badminton Library, pp. 287-289.

as redshanks and other fen- or shore-birds can be successfully
"called" to the gun. The next simplest is assisting the
natural whistle by an artificial one.

This calling of birds is capable of extension to many
species, and there are whistles made which imitate their call
and decoy them to the gun. Such are curlew- and plover-
whistles, one variety of which will call both birds by modulating
the tones in stopping or leaving open the hole in the bell-
shaped part, and this remark applies also to the wood-pigeon-
call—a large pear-shaped whistle, by which a wonderfully good
imitation of the cuckoo's note is also obtained. The duck-call
—a trumpet-shaped instrument—may also be modified to the
exasperating cry of the landrail.

In Italy and Greece, where such birds as thrushes are not
despised for the table, great quantities are shot by the fowler
taking up his position in the groves during the time of the
autumnal migration, and hiding himself the while he skilfully
imitates the full song of the thrush, which the incoming birds
hear, and mistake for that of one which has arrived [in advance
of the main body. Usually made of silver, these whistles are
formed of a concave and a convex disk of metal soldered at
the edges, and with a hole in the centre. It is quite astonishing
what a perfect imitation it is in the mouth of an expert, who
alternately inspires and expires the breath whilst modulating the notes. So with the lark-whistle and others, whilst
the so-called "Punch-call"—two pieces of tin tied together,
with tape between them—is an absurdly good call for the
wryneck.

Steel traps, barbarous enough for mammals, are worse for
birds, which they usually catch by the legs, and these, if not
broken at once, subsequently break by the flutterings of the
poor things. No one but a savage should use them.

Dead-falls are of no use for collecting birds, as a flattened-out and crushed specimen is by no means desirable for taxidermic purposes.

Snares, either of wire or some other strong material, are best left to the imagination and to poachers, whose vested interest in such things must not be rudely disturbed, but small springes of horsehair are frequently used in all countries for taking small birds. Sir Ralph Payne - Gallwey has fully described in one of his works[1] a method of netting plover on flight, and in one of the volumes of the Badminton Library he briefly refers to this under the heading of " Plovers and Sand-pipers " :[2]—

They are netted in thousands in Ireland by a few men who make a living thereby, keeping secret the working details of their appliances. We have known them take in one fall of the net over one hundred plover, both green and golden, and as many as a thousand during a week.

This netting of plover is a fascinating sport, as the birds are taken on the wing. The net, previously laid flat on the ground, springs up just as the wild birds swoop down over the stuffed decoys. The trigger line that frees the net from its catches is pulled by the fowler as he lies concealed a hundred or more yards off. The net and operator must be quick as thought in action, or not a bird will be taken. The mode of working the net is easily learnt, and can be applied by any sportsman whose lands are frequented by plover, to the benefit of both his pocket and his table.

From the men who work these nets, from duck decoy-men, and from ordinary birdcatchers, good specimens may often be obtained ; but there is no doubt that by the blow-pipe, by which some few experts manage to kill small birds, and especially by the gun, which nearly every one can use with more or less success, will the greater number of specimens be procured. In Britain, and, indeed, in most parts of Europe, the battery need

[1] *The Fowler in Ireland.*
[2] *Shooting (Moor and Marsh)*, fourth edition (1893), pp. 203, 204.

not be large.   A strong rifle, calibre about ·450, for deer and
so on ; a small, light, single rifle, about ·320, for rabbits, rooks,
etc. ; a strong, hard-shooting 12-bore, C.F. bored for long paper
cartridges or Kynoch's brass "Perfects"; and a double ·410
collector's gun for small birds : with these four guns the collector
is well set up, but all must be, though not necessarily very
expensive, yet of sound quality and undeniable power.   The
question of the exact patterns must be left to the discretion
of each sportsman ; but, if only one 12-bore is procured, let it
be hammerless and a cylinder, in addition to being bored to *kill*
up to *fifty yards* with a long cartridge.   For a cylinder to be
made to do this is not a hard task for any good gunmaker,
and is within the writer's experience, who, having a full-choked
gun, had it altered to a cylinder, with the result that the proportion of kills to misses or "featherings," in strong or fast-
flying birds, was exactly reversed, both man and gun shooting
better and stronger, and the kills between forty and fifty yards
being certainties with the increased charge when well on the
bird.   Needless to say that a very light gun will not take these
heavy charges without "kicking," which, if not dangerous to
the gun, is certainly not conducive to clean killing by the
sportsman, whilst the strongly-built gun will not only take its
maximum charge without flinching, but will take the ordinary
paper cartridges with smaller charges for ordinary purposes.

The same gunmaker (Clarke, of Leicester), who so successfully and carefully rebored the 12-bore, makes the double C.F.
·410 collector's gun—a handy little weapon, which, though it
will kill a rabbit if the right place be hit, takes so small a charge
as not to damage little birds.

If, however, the collector lives on the coast, or has the
necessary time and money at disposal, his "battery" will no
doubt be augmented by the punt-gun with the necessary gun-
ning-punt, and by these means he will, as Sir Ralph Payne-

Gallwey and many others have done, get some rarities now and then not to be got otherwise. In addition to the works previously mentioned, there are quite a number which deal with shore-shooting and wild-fowl gunning.[1]

Decoy-birds, whether artificial or natural, are great aids to the collector armed with a gun, and probably every one knows how easily wood-pigeons are attracted either by feathered or wooden lures. The simplest method is, when one is shot, to prop it up in as natural a position as possible, and for the shooter to hide within a reasonable distance. An improvement on this is figured and described by Lord Walsingham (indebted to Mr. J. E. Harting),[2] which consists in cutting a piece of wire netting into a long oval, and applying it to the under surface of the body so as to clasp the bird and keep it upright when fixed on short sticks for the ground, or on branches of trees.

The next is a wooden decoy carved and painted to represent the bird ; and the best of all, perhaps, is a stuffed wood-pigeon, which, with leg-wires projecting, may be fixed upon a branch. As with pigeons, so with other birds, and ducks and many shore-birds are attracted by similar methods. Probably every shore-shooter knows that a gull or tern shot down is an almost certain lure for others, if not picked up at once ; but that they will come to bright tin or blackened paper cut to shape is surprising, and was not calculated upon by the writer, who, however, saw a man collecting birds for the feather-trade by this method. He had, with some ingenuity, built himself a hiding-place, on the bare shore, of pieces of wreck, seaweeds, broken baskets, and other flotsam and jetsam, some distance from which he had stuck up these rude imitations—in profile, be it remembered, and all head to windward, which is a rule to be

---

[1] *Instructions to Young Sportsmen in all that Relates to Guns and Shooting*, by Lieut.-Col. P. Hawker (ninth edition best) ; *The Wildfowler*, Folkard ; *The Gun and its Development*, W. W. Greener ; *Practical Wild-fowling*, by Henry Sharp, 1895.

[2] *Shooting (Field and Covert)*, Badminton Library, pp. 228 and 230.

observed in setting all decoys. The first tern which hovered near, suspiciously regarding these by no means artistic imitations, was shot before his suspicions became certainties, and from this everything was easy, for another followed at once—attracted this time by the real bird—only to share the same fate, and another, and yet another from the same small flock, and afterwards a gull came to look on. Now these dead birds were stuck up, three of them on the sand, head pointing to the wind ; the fourth, with its wings spread as well as could be, was suspended upon a stout wire stuck in the sand, and waved to and fro in the breeze as though hovering over the others. The dead gull was tied to a long line, the other end of which was made fast within the hidden shelter, and directly terns came in sight it was thrown into the air, the gunner meanwhile imitating the note of the tern with his mouth. As fast as the lined gull fell upon the sands, it was drawn quickly in and re-thrown, and quite a number of terns responded to this lure and at the sight of the natural decoys, and were forthwith shot. Gulls, curiously, were alarmed instead of attracted by the dead bird thrown up, and sheered off, but would come to the sitting terns, or to a dead bird of their own species, if the gunner kept quiet.

Many other birds are attracted by similar methods, which, allowable enough if the birds are wanted for a collection or for eating, should not be permissible for the purposes of " trade " (see pp. 201-205).

The collecting of birds leads at once to the collecting of their nests and eggs, and, unfortunately, the procuring of the latter as so many " sorts," in the same manner that postage-stamps are collected, is often the only aim of the young. Despite what may be said by those to whom a trimly-arranged egg-cabinet is the summit of their ambition, the exhibition of a vast array of egg-shells is on a par with a collection of marine shells, if the habits of the animals which evolved both of them are not known and studied. Hence the disassociation of eggs from the nests which contained them, and from the birds by which they are made, is as painful to contemplate as nautilus shells without their strange inhabitants, and there is no reason why endless rows of egg-shells upon wool, or within cunningly concealed cavities prepared for their reception, should not give place to their arrangement in glass-topped boxes of no great size, in which the lesser nests and eggs with a pair of their producers (in the skin) should be exhibited—failing, of course, their exhibition by the more complete methods sketched in Chapter X. The methods of blowing eggs are so well known now, that no schoolboy ever dreams of emptying their contents by making two holes, but neatly drills one perfectly round smooth hole on the least beautiful side, and blows out the white and the yolk by various means. The drills, which are of steel, can be readily purchased ; otherwise, one may be easily made by filing one end of a piece of " pinion-wire "—used by clock-makers—to an apex, and continuing the channels, by means of a small three-cornered file, to the point. A needle being used at first to make a small hole, is followed by the drill, which is rapidly rotated and cuts a clear hole ; the contents are then either sucked up through a fine glass tube into a bulb, or blown out by holding the point of the blow-pipe some little distance from (not within) the hole. Sometimes a syringe or a pressure-ball held in the hand, or a species of small bellows does the work of the mouth ; the egg-shell is then well washed out with water, to which a little oil of cloves is added if the egg be stale, and finally with corrosive sublimate (Formula 11). When drained and dry, a small patch of paper cut with a punch should be pasted over the hole, and the distinguishing number, referring to a catalogue containing all particulars, marked in ink upon the shell. For all the niceties of cutting out embryos, or removing them by caustic potash from "hard-set" eggs, dissolving dried-up contents by bicarbonate of soda, etc. etc., the reader is referred to works which deal specially with this subject.

The collecting of reptiles and amphibians is an easy matter in Britain, which harbours so few, that all are known and collected by the veriest schoolboy. In other countries, however, there are many better known than liked, and various books of travel and some scientific works describe their collection. Some very simple methods are described, and the present writer has "collected" many venomous species abroad by the aids of a long supple stick and a boot ; and often fair-sized lizards by the simple device of teasing them, in their holes under rocks or within walls, with a stout straw or small switch, to which they clung by their teeth and would be jerked out. Noosing lizards is a well-known device lately re-described by Mr. Stejneger,[1] who recommends fine annealed iron wire for such a purpose instead of the fine brass or copper wire usually employed. Such large reptiles as alligators and crocodiles object to be noosed, and are usually shot.

Fishes are collected in a variety of ways, which, however, may be resolved into collection by hook and by net, the latter, as in fowling, bringing the most to bag. No definite instructions can be given for getting fishes with certainty other than by the net,—the "fyshing with an angle" being an occult art known only to certain people.

The collection of animals lower even than fishes is a more difficult business until winged insects are reached. The higher invertebrates, Cephalopoda, marine crustaceans, etc., are obtained in various ways, and although some few may be collected by the amateur, yet the greater part are obtained by "those who go down to the sea in ships," and the dredge plays an important

---

[1] *Directions for Collecting Reptiles and Batrachians*, Leonhard Stejneger, Bulletin 39, U.S. National Museum, 1891.

part in procuring them. Although the ordinary trawling-dredge brings up a vast amount of material useful to the biologist—including shrimps, which, boiled in sea-water and eaten *hot*, whilst the boat runs lazily before the wind dragging the trawl, are things to be remembered,—special trawls have been invented for special purposes, and the following describes one particularly interesting :[1]—

Passing by this controversy to consider the facts obtained by the *Albatross*, we may remark that the cruise will be memorable for the use which was made of a really practical opening and closing net, "which worked to perfection at 200, 300, 400, and 1000 fathoms, and had the great advantage of bringing up anything it might find on its way up above the level at which it was towed." This apparatus was due to the ingenuity of Captain Tanner. The net is conical in form, and is suspended from a ring between two ropes, which are weighted at the bottom. About one-fourth up the net two strings encircle it, passing through loops; to the ends of these strings are attached weights which, when allowed to fall, draw them tight, and constrict off the lower portion of the net. They are, however, held up by a crank, and can be liberated when required by a sliding weight or messenger, which is allowed to run down the line. The difficulty of opening the net under water is obviated by the simple expedient of letting it down with the pointed hinder end first, the pressure of the water being sufficient to keep it pressed tightly together like a folded umbrella. Arrived at the desired depth, the vessel is put in motion, and rope enough is paid out to keep the net moving horizontally, this being judged of by the slant of the rope. After towing for, say, twenty minutes, the net is again brought to the vertical, and the messenger sent down to close it; after which it is brought up to the surface, and the contents of the upper and lower portions of the net examined separately.

This net was used on several occasions in water of considerable depth, and undoubtedly failed to produce evidence of a mid-water fauna of any variety or abundance. The number of unexceptionable trials at depths of 400 fathoms and upwards was, however, too small to justify any far-reaching conclusions.

---

[1] "The *Albatross* Expedition," *Natural Science*, August 1892, pp. 449, 450.

"Tangles," which are constructed of a cross-beam of weighted wood, to each end of which is attached a mass of old net, swabs, or frayed-out rope, are useful to drag over the sea-bottom to entangle echinoderms, corals, sponges, and other things, and are sometimes used as a trawl from the boat.

Nowadays, owing to the establishment of marine biological stations, such as those at Naples, Plymouth, and other places, it is possible to get rare forms of marine invertebrata (often alive) at a small cost, and the Directors, if appealed to, will always, most obligingly, endeavour to get any special forms not on their lists—a kindness which now calls for grateful thanks from the writer.

So many works have been written upon the collecting and preservation of insects, and the methods are so diverse, and have been explained at such lengths by various authors, that it would be impossible to touch even the fringe of the subject, or to refer the entomologist to a hundredth part of the works published. Suffice it to say that insects are collected in every situation, even in the most unpromising ones, and are taken by searching by day and night, and with insect-nets and beating, and are lured into the clutches of the collector by light, "sugar," and "assembling." Beetles are killed by benzoline, spirits, and by other means, including that chiefly used for the Lepidoptera —cyanide of potassium,—and are boxed, pinned, set, and arranged in a great variety of ways, too numerous to particularise here.

The collecting of fossil forms, treated upon in some works, especially foreign, dealing with collecting and taxidermy, is a matter so comprehensive in its details and issues that the same remarks apply to this as to the collecting of insects.

of the tail ; the greatest width in the centre of the body ; the greatest depth ; and, what is, perhaps, most necessary, the distance between the inner borders of the fore and hind limbs, *i.e.* between the humerus of the one and the femur of the other. A rough tracing of the shape may in some cases assist the pupil. Laying the animal stomach uppermost, take knives Nos. 1 and 4, and, with the latter, make an incision along the median line, commencing at some distance below the fore limbs, and continuing the cut to within an inch or so of the tail, but being sure not to make the cut too high, as it should be remembered that this can always be lengthened if necessary, and that the incision from which the body will ultimately be removed ought to be made as small as is practicable. Nearing the lower portion, care must be taken not to cut the membrane which retains the bowels. Now taking the broad knife, No. 1, it will be found easy, by working with a scraping movement, to release the body at the sides without leaving any fat or flesh upon the skin—which is, of course, an important matter, —and for this purpose, it need hardly be remarked, the knife must have a rounded, or partially rounded, point.

Continuing the scraping movement on both sides, the hind limbs will begin to show, and, probably, about here some little fat may obscure the view of the actual flesh, in which event the fingers should be dipped into dry plaster of Paris kept by the side for that purpose, and, by working with them and with the knife, all the fat may be removed, but very carefully, otherwise the thin skin may be torn. Working now with the fingers of one hand to free the skin from around the thigh (femur), push the foot up into the skin with the other hand, and continue working until the fingers meet, inside the skin, at the junction of the tibia with the femur, when the shears (No. 8), or, better still, the knife, may be slipped underneath and the femur disunited from the trunk at the pelvis. This, being repeated upon the other side, will expose the anus and the root of the tail. The skin of the former must be cut carefully away close to the flesh without cutting the outside skin, and a piece of wadding should be here used as a plug.

The root of the tail now shows much more plainly, and may be skinned a little way up, and loosened with the knife from the skin on its upper surface. The withdrawal of the tail from its sheath of skin is a necessary matter, and one which, with a little practice, is easily accomplished. For larger and longer-tailed mammals, the cutting-pliers (No. 12) are usually used, the bows being made to encircle the tail inside the skin, against which they are pressed, and at the same time held firmly down upon the table with the left hand, whilst the right hand grasps the tail at its root, and forcibly and rapidly withdraws it from the skin. Sometimes the tail refuses to be drawn in this manner, in which event there is no alternative but to sever it at the root, place this part in a vice, encircle the tail as before with the bows of the pliers, and, grasping these with both hands, pull with might and main. In a small mammal, however, such as the rabbit, the pliers are unnecessary, the withdrawal of the tail being effected by encircling the tail with the fingers of one hand dipped in plaster and drawing with the other. Properly managed, the whole of the bone of the tail will be pulled out from its sheath, without, be it understood, allowing the skin of that part to be turned inside out, but retaining its normal position.

At this stage it is a convenience to have a small hook run through the back, which hook, being attached by a string or chain to the ceiling, leaves both hands free ; or an " arm " may be used like the French " telegraph," to which the string may be attached instead of to the ceiling. It is as well to remember that the greater part of the animal should not be pulled up so high as to unduly stretch the skin, and such a matter of

CHAPTER V

THE SKINNING AND SETTING-UP OF MAMMALS BY ORDINARY
METHODS ; ALSO THEIR REPRODUCTION BY CASTING,
AND MODELLING IN PAPER, ETC.   HORNED HEADS, THE
PREPARATION OF SKELETONS, AND THE TAWING OF
SKINS.

DIVISION I

SKINNING AND SETTING-UP BY ORDINARY METHODS

FOR the purpose of this lesson, either a rat or a small rabbit
should be procured, both of which are common, although
probably the latter will be found the best, not only because
it can be at any time easily purchased for a few pence, and
is larger, but because, being the mammal usually selected for
biological investigations, a familiarity with its morphology will
be of service, and a distinct advantage to the future investigator.

The rabbit, then, having been procured in as fresh a state
as possible,—for it must be recollected that all creatures which
live on vegetable food decompose more quickly, especially
about the abdominal region, than carnivorous mammals,—
should be laid on the dissecting-table and well studied with
regard to its external morphology. The following measurements
should be taken, namely, the total length from the neck to
the tail, and—the head being thrown back upon the shoulders
—the length along the side from the throat to the insertion

adjustment can be easily managed by a pulley. The knife now
being taken in one hand will, assisted by the fingers of the
other hand, soon clear the skin all the way down the back,
when, by careful handling, the humeri of the fore limbs will
show. Take notice, however, that the skin will stick somewhat
in front, and must be gently trimmed away with the broader
knife, by this means getting the fat back upon the skin. The
shoulders, *i.e.* the scapulæ, being now free, the whole of the fore
limbs appear and may be skinned down, and, when done, each
one should be separated at the junction of the humerus with
the scapula. When these are free, nothing but the head
will remain within the skin, which, being thin at that part,
must be very gently freed around until the attachments of the
ears show as a whitish cartilage lying very far back. Pinch
them up with the fingers of the left hand, slip the knife underneath, and cut towards the *body* and close to the skull. If
properly done, the ear will be left nicely within the skin, with
only a small hole, at its lower extremity, exposed. Both ears
being freed in like manner, the delicate membrane which covers
the eye is exposed. Needless to say that at this point the
greatest care must be exercised, and the cutting must be all
towards the bone, until, by pulling gently with the fingers of the
left hand, the eyeball starts a little from the orbit, and there
is to be seen the delicate membrane which apparently attaches
the eyeball to the skin. Slip the knife in and sever this
membrane. The skin now holds very firmly at the outer angle
of the eye, and must be, with the greatest care, freed from the
bone; when this is done on both sides, the nose and under
jaw begin to show, together with the inside of the mucous
membrane of the lips; this part should be left attached to the
upper and lower jaws, but the nose must be carefully skinned
over until the nostrils appear, when the knife must be slipped
in and the cartilage cut through. Probably this will leave a

little more than is wanted on the skin, but that is far better than finding afterwards that the outer skin is cut. Continue cutting above and below the lower jaw until the skin only holds at the extreme tip of the latter ; disjoint the skull from the first vertebra, and the body is freed, and must, of course, be retained as a guide to the setting-up.

Taking one of the fore limbs next, skin down to the pad of the foot, and from this remove all the flesh nearly to the tips of the toes, which latter must be left attached. Repeat this operation upon the other fore limb, and afterwards upon the hind limbs.

Each limb, when trimmed, should be painted or rubbed in with a preservative, and in small mammals, especially those with thin skins, it is advisable to make up each limb as it is trimmed and return it into the skin, instead of waiting until the whole of the trimming is completed. This is managed by re-placing with clay the flesh previously removed from the pad of the foot, and, indeed, filling with clay the whole of the under-neath of that member, and then proceeding to wrap the next bones—the radius and ulna and the humerus in the fore limb, and the tibia and femur in the hind—with tow to the shape of the natural limb, going over the whole with a coating of clay, and taking care that the pre- and post-axial borders are kept thin.

Ordinarily the alum and saltpetre preservative (Formula 59) should be used as a " cure," but for small mammals, and especially for such a subject as a rabbit, which has a thin " papery " skin, the bird-preservative (Formula 57) will be found the best, as keeping the thin skin moist until finished, and also preserving such a skin just as well. If, however, the skin dries too rapidly, or has to be put away before being finished, a little glycerin added to the preservative will keep the skin moist and fresh.

The limbs having been modelled up with tow and clay to their natural shape, the head must now be considered. With the tool No. 7, take out the eyes from their orbits; then cut a triangular piece of bone from the palate near the base of the skull, and, with the same tool (No. 7), remove the brains through the opening thus made. With the knife and scissors, remove all the flesh from the sides of the face and all other parts of the head, getting out the wetter portions about the nose and so on by twisting in a wire with wadding, or using the tool No. 7. The cartilage of the nostrils must also be removed, and the lips split.

The lining or cartilage of the ear has now to be separated from its outer skin. Hold this lining—which is, of course, the whitish part of the ear—firmly with the fingers of one hand, and, with the others, separate it from the outer part up to the extreme edge, which is marked by a darker line; when this is done, trim away all the flesh from the base. (A more detailed description of this rather delicate operation, and also of the skinning-out of the nostrils and the splitting of the lips, is given at pp. 125 and 150, in the paragraphs relating to the skinning of those parts in a tiger's and a deer's head respectively.)

The skin of the ears, now turned completely inside out, must be painted with the preservative, and so left whilst the head is made up. This is done by packing wadding into the orbits only, and tow into all other parts of the skull whence flesh has been removed, and finally covering all with clay until the head is of the natural shape. Next paint the remainder of the skin of the body inside.

The ears of the rabbit, and, indeed, of any mammal, must be blocked, otherwise they will shrink. There are several methods of doing this, but commonly one of the ears is flattened upon cardboard, traced around, and, if cut just within the pencil-mark, the piece is not too large; for the other ear it is only necessary to lay this cardboard upon another piece, cut this to the same size, and, by reversing the latter, the shapes of the cardboard will be as right and left. Two other pieces should be cut to the same patterns, to be dealt with afterwards. Two of these should be coloured pink on the inner surface, and one of them must be introduced between the skin and cartilage of each ear, the best manner of doing this being to return the skins of the ear by opposing the point of the cardboard to the point of the ear, and gradually drawing the latter over it, compressing the card meanwhile, so that the broadest part may pass the narrower base of the ear. These cards must be fitted into the extreme tip and edge of each ear, which requires some little skill and patience. Sometimes thin tin or zinc is substituted for cardboard, either of which is a decided gain in shaping, but heavier, and apt to cut through at the edges, whilst tin is entirely objectionable for other reasons (but see p. 116). The head should now be returned to its natural position within the skin, and the wiring-up commences.

Let four wires be pointed—one for each limb—and pass one of them in at the pad of each foot and along the back edge of each limb to the inside of the skin of the body, taking care not to push the wire through the skin, nor catch the skin up in any part, but, if possible, let each wire pass within the tow and clay covering the bones, and come some little distance through. The points of the four wires being now within the body-skin, *cut them off*, and, if left an inch or so in length, they will come in useful for something else ; this precaution is taken to prevent them sticking into the hands of the operator.

Proceed next to consider the body-wire. The simplest way, perhaps, and one much affected by foreign taxidermists, is to make it longer than the body, *i.e.* of sufficient length to come through the skull at one end, and up the tail at the other ; two loops—each large enough to take two wires—are then

8

formed upon it, one for the fore limbs and the other for the hind, the distance between them being determined by the measurements previously taken. The natural body should now be in front of the operator, and the length of the neck-wire from the anterior loop must be measured by this, and sufficient wire left, after the neck is made, to come through the skull, the end of the wire being pointed for that purpose. The other end of the body-wire being thrust up the tail, the ends of the leg-wires are pushed up inside the skin of the legs, through the two loops of the body-wire now within the skin, wound round the main body-wire, and firmly secured.

The body is, with this style of wiring, literally made by " stuffing," loose tow or wadding being packed in to form the shape, and resulting usually in a bag as unlike the animal as it is possible to conceive ; and, as the removal of the limb-bones and a soft filling of the head usually accompany this soft-body system, unlimited scope is given for the development of flights of fancy, which are not compatible with accuracy of form. Another and better system is to make up the neck and body roughly on a straight body-wire, insert it into the skin, thrust the leg-wires through the tow (which should be firmly wrapped), and clench them as in the bird's body (see p. 188).

A still better system, which combines the two, is to make two loops upon the body-wire as before described, and, pointing one end, make up upon it the neck with tow to size, and on the remainder of the wire bind tow also to form a rough body, leaving, however, the loops free. The body must not be made at first of quite the full size, but merely roughly shaped. Insert this into the skin, and push the point of the wire up the skull and through the centre to the outside, keeping the loops uppermost. Through the first or forward loop push the two wires of the fore limbs, and, with the pliers, bend them around, one below and the other above the loop, and make each secure. This operation will no doubt necessitate the lower part of the artificial body being out of the skin whilst being done. This being reinserted, place the wires of the hind limbs in their corresponding loops, and make fast in the same manner. Cut off what superfluous wire may have been left at the tail end, which part, in the case of a rabbit, can easily be adjusted afterwards by a fine wire, but, in a longer-tailed mammal, this wire may, unless another wire be also used, be left long enough to go up into the tail. The rabbit is now somewhat in a spread-eagle condition, and therefore the limbs must be brought down to the sides in their proper position and roughly shaped to the attitudes desired. The body will now be too small in parts, but that is better than having made it too large by overstuffing at first, as more tow can easily be added where it cannot be so well taken away, and, when nearing completion, a little clay placed within over the tow in various positions will help the final modelling of the thinner portions, care being taken to shape each part as the work progresses. Sew up the skin, and, when the legs are fixed upon a board, through which their wires should be bolted, the head, which during all these processes has suffered considerable derangement, may be pricked out with a fine needle and the fine awl No. 26, and more clay added or taken away through the orbits as the modelling demands. The eyes may either be introduced now or left till later—when any imperfections may be made up through the orbits,—whilst, through the orifice of the ears, the modelling of the back of the head may be improved by pushing in wadding and clay, and finally, the ears should either have the two extra pieces of card bound lightly within them, shaped so as to fit the contours of the cards inside, and be bent into position, or, better still, their hollows filled with clay, and a long pin or two or fine wire driven through the base of the ear will hold each in position. *The* most effectual method, however, of dealing with the ears, in all mammals, is to entirely discard cardboard—inside and out,—and line between the skins with a thin layer of clay or of one of the modelling-compositions (see Chapter III. Division III.), and, when modelled into shape, to partially or entirely fill the outer ear with clay also, which, when thoroughly dry, can be removed, leaving the ears for ever in shape, even in such subjects as " lop-ears."

DIVISION II

THE SETTING-UP OF MAMMALS BY MEANS OF WOODEN MODELS OR MANNIKINS

From the wiring by any of the foregoing methods to the setting-up by means of a body-board or a mannikin is an easy transition, if it be considered that a small piece of board, placed within the body of a mammal,[1] or even inside that of a large bird,[2] serves as a backbone to which the head and limbs can be bolted ; from this arose the conception, not only of a board conforming somewhat to the shape of the animal to be set up, but of a " mannikin " such as was made early in the century for an elephant, and also for the large ungulates, in the Natural History Museum of Paris.

Although elephants are not " common objects of the country," yet they occasionally come under the taxidermist's and modeller's hands, and therefore a description of how such creatures are erected into a semblance of their former selves may not be unwelcome ; and first it will be best to transcribe what is, perhaps, the earliest description of the manner in which a former school of taxidermists worked at such huge brutes.

[1] See Capus et Rochebrune, *Guide du Naturaliste Préparateur*, p. 103 (on which a horse is represented *wired* as if it were a mouse !).

[2] See Gestro, *Manuale dell' Imbalsamatore*, p. 53.

The method employed by M. Dufresne, of the Jardin des Plantes, Paris, to mount an elephant which died at the menagerie in 1803, was described in his work,[1] and the following translation of the original, rendered by Bowdich,[2] has since been copied by many industrious authors.

The corpse of the elephant having been extended upon the ground, facilitated our taking and writing all its dimensions : the thickness was taken by a sort of rule, which M. Lassaigne, cabinet-maker of the museum, invented at the time. This instrument resembled the rule used by shoemakers, on a large scale. The curves of the back, the belly, etc., were taken by bars of lead, $\frac{3}{4}$ in. thick. This metal, not having any elasticity, accommodated or bent itself to the curves we wished to measure and preserved the measurements until wanted. M. Desmoulins drew the animal on one of the sides of the wall according to all these measurements, in the workshop where the model was to be constructed in its natural size. This done, we proceeded to the skinning of the elephant, which we were only able to place upon its back by means of four-corded pulleys, fastened to the platform. In this position we made an incision in the form of a double cross : the middle line went from the mouth to the anus, the two others were directed from each left foot to the opposite right foot; the tail and trunk were opened underneath longitudinally. We scooped out the soles of the feet within an inch of their edge, that the nails might remain in the skin : to effect this, we were obliged to employ the chisel and mallet. This operation was very difficult.

After four days' labour of several persons, we separated the skin from the body: it then weighed 576 lbs. ; we extended it on the ground to take away the cutaneous muscles which adhered to its interior, particularly to the head. In this state the skin was placed in a large tub ; we spread a considerable quantity of pounded alum in all its folds ; we then boiled some water with such quantities of alum that some pieces still remained at the bottom of the boiler, that is, we more than saturated the water : this water was poured upon the skin, and we continued to do so, until the skin was covered with it 6 in. deep.

---

[1] See Bibliography.   [2] Pp. 41-45, fourth ed. (See Bibliography.)

To render the dimensions of the model or shape which was to receive the skin more exact, we modelled one half of the skinned head in plaster, as well as one of the hind and one of the fore legs.

All these measures being taken, Lassaigne constructed a factitious body in linden-wood. The reader would find the detail too long and too minute if we were to describe the ingenious methods invented by Lassaigne, either to cut the wood, or to preserve the form he had given to this great mass. But to avoid all prolixity, it will be sufficient to observe, that he composed this wooden elephant in such a manner that all the parts could be separated.

He opened a panel (it is immaterial on which side of the body), and introduced himself into the interior, by means of this opening, either to diminish the thickness of the wood, or for any other purpose during its construction : the head, the trunk, all was hollow; so that the body, alarming at first from its supposed weight, might be easily transported from one place to another.

After taking the alum-water from the tub where the skin was placed, we heated it, and poured it boiling on the skin : we left it an hour and a half in this state, after which we drew the skin out to place it quite warm upon the shape. This was not an easy thing, but it was rendered still more difficult by our finding the false body a little too large : the skin would not entirely cover it. There was but one thing which could be done : we could not diminish the wood without destroying the proportions ; besides, the iron pins, the screws which fastened the work, would have lost their hold, and we should have run the risk of overturning the edifice. We then took down the skin, placed it on trestles, and diminished the thickness of it by the help of large knives, cutting it away in thick and long shreds from the whole of the inside. This work occupied five persons for four days. We weighed these shreds, and they amounted to 194 pounds. During this operation, the skin had dried, and consequently lost its suppleness. We put it back into a tub and covered it with soft cold water ; the next day we placed it afresh on the shape, and fixed it with wire-nails and large brads : those which fixed the edge of the skin were driven in deeply, the others only half way, to accommodate the skin to all the sinuosities of the model. We drew out a great many of them when the skin was sufficiently dry.

This paring of the skin answered our purpose in two essential points : first, by facilitating the means of enveloping the model entirely, the form of which had not been altered ; and, secondly, by ensuring its speedy desiccation. This last had not been the least alarming, for we feared that the humidity secreted in the skin might concentrate in such a manner (notwithstanding we had taken the precaution to give the wooden model a coat of oil-paint) as to occasion mouldiness in the parts exposed to the air. The alum with which it was saturated soon crystallised on the interior, which at first gave it a very ugly grey colour; but we entirely got rid of it by rubbing the surface of the skin, first with spirits of turpentine, and then with oil of olives.

In the *Standard* of 12th March, 1886, appeared an article entitled "The last of Jumbo," the facts presumably contributed by Prof. H. A. Ward, of Rochester, U.S.A., in which details of measurements and weights of the model and materials used in setting-up "Jumbo" are given. To this article the present writer replied, in the issue of the 15th following, that although our American cousins were generally well to the fore, if not in advance of the times, yet in this case they were quite as much behindhand in such matters as ourselves, and that the resources of the modeller, combined with those of the engineer and fitter, should have prevented the building up of so clumsy and weighty a structure as described, which was, indeed, no advance on the knowledge derived from the taxidermists (or rather " stuffers ") of the eighteenth century. There was certainly no need to build a " huge frame of wood and iron," when a much stronger and infinitely lighter structure of prepared paper and steel would have accomplished the work required in a much more effectual manner. The weight of three tons recorded was certainly great for a finished model, when it is taken into consideration that Jumbo weighed when alive no more than six tons.

The treatment of the hide was commonplace, being left too thick and heavy, as evidenced by the thicknesses given—

" half an inch, and in places one and a half inch." Its extreme weight—1538 lbs.—also proved that ; and why it should have been taken off in three pieces was difficult to understand, whilst the startling item of 74,000 nails and their aggregate weight left the untechnical reader in doubt as to whether great weight of wood, iron, and skin, in a taxidermic specimen, was the object aimed at.

After pointing out that the great weight of the model, pedestal, wagon, and special car might have been obviated by a little forethought, the writer concluded by saying that, until tradition in such matters was discarded, the science of taxidermy would never advance by its own merits.

Soon afterwards, there appeared a full description of the methods employed by Professor Ward in his taxidermic establishment near New York.[1]

The mannikins, now much affected by the best professional taxidermists, are made in a variety of ways. Mr. Rowland Ward was probably the first to publish a less complicated system of making a wooden model for a tiger.[2] A board being primarily cut roughly to the shape of the skin, seven iron rods are bolted to it, viz. two for the head, one for the tail, and four for the limbs. These latter are bent to the position required, and bolted or screwed firmly to a base. On the upstanding model are now nailed segments of board to give the idea of ribs and other parts of the body, and across these laths are nailed. The artificial limb-bones are, by some taxidermists, carved from soft wood, bored to the diameter of the leg-rods, sawn down their lengths, and afterwards tied around the rods ; but this is a roundabout way of getting effects which can be much better and more quickly managed by other processes if the actual bones cannot be used, and binding the rods with tow

---

[1] *Natural Science Bulletin*, 1st May, 1886.
[2] *The Sportsman's Handbook*, first edition, pp. 55-58 ; seventh edition, pp. 77-81.

to represent the bones, and afterwards superimposing clay for the final modelling is quite as good, the body and skull being covered with wood-fibre or tow and clay in like manner.

The skin, which, in all processes involving a "mannikin," must be split from the throat to the tail and up the insides of the limbs, and indeed treated in every respect as explained at p. 123, is now put on over the model, and sewn up, improvements being made by putting in or subtracting clay as the sewing progresses. The final modelling of the head may be executed by any of the methods described hereafter.

The setting-up of mammals by mannikins of wood, tow, or wood-fibre ("excelsior"), has been superseded in the Leicester Museum, for the last ten years, by the following process, which depends for its fulfilment upon the exact reproduction of the subject, and which, apparently unknown, is here published for the first time :—

DIVISION III

CASTING FROM THE ACTUAL SUBJECTS, AND THEIR REPRODUCTION IN PAPER

The Skinning and Setting-up of a Tiger

Some time in November, 1885, a magnificent tiger, known as "Tippoo Sahib," was killed by his companion in Messrs. Bostock and Wombwell's menagerie at Norwich. So valuable was "Tippoo"—who, by the way, was amiable enough, or so well trained, as to permit the redoubtable Captain Cardono to put his head into his mouth—that his market value was £400, as "a real, live, performing, double-striped Bengal Tiger." Unhappily, this paragon amongst tigers was, in an unguarded moment, seized by the throat by a more ferocious but less costly animal, who, jealous, no doubt, of the paragon's surpassing merits, in less time than it takes to tell it, succeeded in killing him.   A sudden spring, and four enormous canine teeth were planted through the carotid arteries and the wind-pipe, and in less than three minutes poor Tippoo lay dead.

Mr. J. W. Bostock, having refused several tempting offers, generously allowed the Leicester Museum to acquire it for a nominal sum.   By a strange fatality, Tippoo's murderer, and, in fact, the whole den of tigers, have since then come under the hands of the museum operators ; and now, in a large plate-glass case in the zoological room, " Tippoo " is represented as fighting with another over the dead body of an elephant, presented later by Mr. G. Ginnett.   The weight of the tiger (without intestines) was 280 lbs.[1]

Directly it arrived, the jaws were opened and washed ; the head was then placed upon a box, with a wedge opening the jaws to the extent required, and the muscles of the face, especially those over and under the eyes and at the corners of the mouth, having been worked up to give the necessary expression, a rapid colour-sketch of the head was made, showing the colours of the mucous membrane inside the mouth, of the great muscles leading from the inside of the lower lip nearly up to the formidable canines, of the tongue, nose, and eyes, with all other details required for ultimately reproducing the proper colours.   This, however, did not give definite form nor arrangement of parts, therefore a model was made by taking a piece of well-kneaded " pipe-" or modelling-clay, and, by the aid of the tools Nos. 27 and 29 to 36, accurately modelling by eye, assisted by measurements, the whole of the outside and inside (up to the teeth) of one half of the lower jaw.

This, being done entirely by the knowledge and aptitude of the artist, is unteachable save by experience ; a figure (Fig. 9, Plate VII.) is, however, given from a photograph,

---

[1] Not by any means excessive, as large tigers are known to attain to a weight of 350 lbs., and even, in some rare instances, to over 500 lbs.

showing the half model and also other parts of the mouth, etc.

The corresponding half of the inside of the upper jaw, though not so important perhaps, was copied in the same manner.

A cast in plaster of Paris was taken of the face, and the head was then placed, forehead downwards, upon the table, and a cast was obtained of the roof of the mouth, giving the arrangement of the palatal ridges for the final modelling. The tongue itself was taken out at the subsequent skinning, and was posed in a natural manner on clay to give it its proper curves, surrounded by a wall of clay, then cast in plaster of Paris, and, when set, was turned over, trimmed, and its under surface cast, thus making a mould in two halves, from which the paper or pulp tongue (see following pages, and Fig. 13, Plate VII.) was reproduced.

The carcase was then handed over to the skinners, who commenced by getting it upon the dissecting-bench, being assisted by a rope and pulley-block screwed into a beam or joist in the ceiling above. The animal having been placed upon its back, an incision was made in the skin, on the central line, from the throat, along the stomach, to the tail; a cross cut was then made from the chest up to the "armpit" of each of the fore limbs, extending nearly to the end of the humerus, whence it followed the course of each fore limb, running along *just* inside (so that the stitches should be hidden when the animal was finished) down to each manus and splitting the large central pad. At the hind limbs the cross cut was made to follow the inner line of the limb just inside, coming through the central pad as in the others. The removal of the skin was commenced by flaying it back from the fore limb on one side, a rope tied to each assisting the stretching out of the limbs. Both sides of the limbs were flayed back by carefully

working around, cutting meanwhile *toward the body*, in order
that the knife might not slip and cut the skin. The skin of
the side being freed, the hind limb was treated in like manner.
When sufficiently loose underneath, the foot was disjointed at
the second joint of the toes ; in the case of the fore limbs,
these were disjointed at the same point, the large or innermost
toe (= pollex or thumb), just above, being freed from its attachment, and the remainder of the toes being left in for future
operations. When skinned on one side up to the centre of
the back, the other side and paws were treated in precisely the
same manner, care being taken at the thin part of the flank
not to cut the skin.

After both sides had been sufficiently relieved, so that the
skin was loosened all along the back, the parts around the tail
were skinned out with care, and the tail itself released from its
skin. In this case the skin of the tail was split to the end,
but this will often skin and pull out, as in smaller mammals,
without cutting, so as to come out in a piece ; if, however, it
should " stick," the mode is to cut it underneath near the tip,
and flay back towards the body.

The hind quarters were then slung by the rope previously
mentioned, and the skin was pulled from underneath them by
shifting the rope to the fore part so as to lift the head off the
ground or table. The throat and neck were now skinned,
and, it being necessary that the skull should be retained to
show the teeth, etc., it was disjointed at the first or atlas
vertebra. (When, however, it is not necessary to retain the skull
within the skin, it should be freed therefrom at the junction of
the ears, care being taken not to cut to the outside. The ears
should be skinned a little way up, and, when slightly relieved,
cut off *close* to the skull, so that there may not be a large
orifice. Great care is required, as there are many attachments
here, but if the rule be observed of cutting on to *the flesh* and

not on to *the skin*, no ill results will accrue, as what little
muscular fibre or flesh is left on the skin may be easily
trimmed off afterwards.) Skinning down as far as the eyes,
the greatest possible care had to be exercised, the fingers of
the left hand being placed inside to feel for the eye, and
around the orbit or bone of the eye the skinning was close
upon the bone, in order not to cut the membraneous coats.
A thin blue skin which now appeared was cut through, and
the skinning from under the eye was quite close to the
eyeball on the bone of the opposite ridge of the orbit. This
skin, being freed from the bone, relieved the skin along the face
for some little distance underneath. The other eye having
been treated in like manner, the lips were cut away *quite close*
to the base of the teeth of the upper jaw, and the skinning
continued to the cartilage of the nose, which was cut right
through, when the skin dropped down leaving the front teeth
exposed, and these were carefully cut around. The only point
of attachment was now at the under jaw, a large mass of
muscle surrounding the large canines and coming almost inside
the mouth. This should have been trimmed completely from the
bone, when the skin would have fallen off, taking with it some
portions of the inner skin of the lips (the mucous membrane),
and of the eyes and nose; but in this instance the skull
was *not* detached. The skin was then placed upon a table,
and the operator proceeded to "split the lips," commencing
under, or at the side of, the nostrils, where the two skins
meet, or rather where the mucous membrane of the lips shows
as a shiny skin, carefully splitting or skinning one away from
the other quite up to the edges of the lips until the two skins
were held there by a thin edge, forming a complete bag. The
same process of splitting was performed upon the under jaw,
the nostrils, and the eyes, the central cartilage of the nose being
split to allow of more freedom in skinning out. Finally the ears

(on which some flesh was left at the first cutting, for safety) were trimmed, and by careful management were skinned along their edges until they were turned inside out right up to their tips.

A strong paste was made in a bucket, by mixing 8 lbs. of burnt alum and 2 lbs. of saltpetre with warm water (see Formula 59, p. 75), and this was thoroughly rubbed into the skin, especially at the thickest parts, or where any flesh had been left for further and final trimming.

After this had been done and the skin was thoroughly cured, which was accomplished by turning it and rubbing in the preservative for two or three days, the skin was damped and stretched wherever it showed signs of drying, and the skull—improperly left attached,—having been cleared of flesh, was dusted over with rough plaster of Paris (or whiting) to dry it. Preparations for the setting-up were then commenced by drilling a hole with a brace and bit through each side of the lower jaw where it is thin (close to its junction with the upper jaw), through which a stout wire was threaded, and the ends turned around the upper jaw when in position, so that the upper and lower were articulated as in nature, care being taken, however, to leave the wire loose enough to allow the jaws to open to the extent required. Tow steeped in carbolic acid or creosote was then packed into the nasal orifice, and between the sides of the face and the articulation of the lower with the upper jaw, in the orbits, and in the brain cavity. Carbolised tow having been used only in sufficient quantities to dry up any remains of flesh, etc., was followed by dry tow, and then by wadding rammed close in all parts excepting in the brain cavity, in which a small aperture was left to receive the supporting rod.

Much flesh having, of course, been previously removed from the sides of the head and face, it was replaced by tow wound around until it roughly assumed the proper shape.

Being well packed and tied around with hemp until it was sufficiently firm and unyielding, strips of common muslin about two to three inches wide were brought around from side to side, and crossed from end to end, until the tow was completely covered and bound in as a fairly hard mass giving the proper shape of the head. Half an hour being suffered to elapse, some well-kneaded pipe-clay was plastered over the nose of the model skull, along the sides of the jaws, and on the face where wrinkles or muscles were to be depicted. The "bags" of the eyelids, nostrils, and lips, and between the outer and inner skins of the ears, were well filled with clay, and then, by gentle means, the skin of the head was pulled back again until the skull assumed its normal position inside the skin. In getting it over, some of the clay became displaced in parts, but was easily pushed back into position, or more added or taken away through the apertures of the nostrils, back of the lips, orbits, ear-holes, and at the back of the head, the skin of the neck being sufficiently open to admit the hand or a "crowding" tool.

It is as well to note here that wadding pushed in behind clay gets it well into position, and should always be used where practicable in order to lessen the weight—otherwise great where much clay is used ; the aim of the modeller, therefore, should be to use no more of the latter than absolutely necessary.

The clay model of the mouth and the coloured drawing of the head now proved extremely useful in assisting the operator to obtain the necessary distances, the relation of parts, the wrinkles of muscles, and positions of the mouth and lips. Of course, the orbits of the skull (left as a shallow depression in clay) fixed the position of the eyes, and the teeth assisted the formation and position of the lips. All being satisfactorily arranged, stout "needle-points" were driven in various positions under the eyes, about the lips, and between the wrinkles, in order to keep all in position and prevent parts from starting as the work dried. The skin, having been suffered to dry for a day or two, was well hand-stretched all over, except, of course, at the head, which was carefully protected and bound down by the skin of the neck upon the modelling-table. In the meantime the skin, wherever thick and hard, was again pared and rubbed.

Prior to this the body, being entirely freed of its skin, presented itself as a complete carcase without its head ; and here it is as well to remark that the lungs should be inflated, before a cast of the body is taken, in this manner :—

After the head is removed, seize the trachea and draw it out of the neck for a few inches, dissecting around it if necessary, then insert a short length of lead piping in the case of a large animal, or glass tubing in the case of a small one, and tie the trachea tightly on to this with stout string. If the tube or cannula has a slight constriction or neck a little way from the end, any danger of its slipping out will be removed. When the tube is fixed, the lungs may be inflated, in the case of a small animal with the mouth, but in a larger one it is best to fix a length of india-rubber tubing to the pipe and inflate with bellows. When the lungs are nearly full, not quite, apply a ligature to the trachea below the tube, tie tightly, and remove the tube.

The carcase was then laid, with the neck pointing to the left hand, upon a long, stout board, and, the attitude shown in Plate VI. having been selected, the mode of procedure was as follows :—The tail was thrown up and the limbs placed somewhat in position ; this, however, had the obvious disadvantage of presenting merely a flat surface, such as would appear on a basso-relievo, the body being flat, with no curves on the upper or under surface, and the uppermost limbs (those of the animal's left side) being flat on those underneath, so that, although the limbs were parted on their plane, there was no separation between those above and below. Accordingly, each of the uppermost limbs, or those of the left side, was raised from its fellow, and propped into position by a stage of one-inch board raised to the necessary height by blocks placed underneath, but in such a manner as not to interfere with a clear view of the inside of the underneath limbs or those of the right side. The proposed attitude of the animal demanding a wide separation of the feet, the slope of the supporting board was higher at its outer edge. The body was now propped from the back into the necessary curves until it assumed the form shown in Plate VI. At the neck, which was brought forward and high to the left front, in order to get the necessary pose for the head, the staging was very much higher than anywhere else. The fore limbs were supported widely apart to show the chest and muscles. In doing this, care was taken not to hide from view, nor enclose, the underneath or right fore limb. The arrangement of the animal's carcase and consequent blocking of the supports took two men nearly a day. The carcase now showed the whole of its left upper surface, and the inner surface of the right limbs. These latter were surrounded by a wall of common fire-clay, about three inches high, and about one and a half inches from the edges of the limbs. Into the tray thus formed, plaster was poured, being made up to a thickness of about two inches over the flesh, and extending to the median line of the belly.

The plaster now covering the under limbs was used as the base for the further support, by props, of the upper limbs lying upon boards wide enough to take them. These being surrounded, as also the body, by boards and clay, were covered with plaster as before, and left for a night. The position of affairs at this stage was, that the whole of the top side of

9

the carcase was covered, viz. the insides of the right limbs and upper sides of the left, and also the left side of the body, the left limbs and body being cast in one piece, the right separately. The next morning, the top piece was carefully lifted off, being supported by two men, whilst another pulled and shook the fore and hind limbs gently to release them. This being successful, the stage which supported the whole was knocked away, leaving the under limbs free to be dealt with ; these were released in like manner. The animal's carcase was then pulled off the board, and the largest piece of casting, viz. that of the left side, placed in its stead. This casting or mould being carefully packed underneath where not quite flat, in order to make all solid for fear of breakage, the carcase was gently forced into it, the neck now, of course, pointing to the right. At one or two places the limbs were difficult to get into the *exact* former position, having been a little cast over, forming an " undercut," but by patience every line and muscle was coaxed into place, and the carcase lay with its left side downwards within the mould. The *inner* sides of the left limbs were now surrounded with clay resting on the edges of, or just outside, the mould, to a sufficient height and thickness. Into this, mixed plaster was poured as before until it rose up the chest, and at the tail, to the points where the other moulds ceased. Allowing time for the drying of the plaster (half an hour in the preceding operation), the moulds of the inside of the right limbs were blocked into position upon the others, the extent of stride and width between the limbs being found by the manner in which they could be forced, or naturally fell, into their former position. This being satisfactorily determined, and the whole of the right upper surface remaining to be cast, boards were nailed and "strutted" around the moulds in which the carcase reposed, and clay was used to plug all fissures into which the plaster might penetrate to its loss, or to the undesirable filling up of crevices in the other

CASTING FROM THE BODY OF A TIGER IN PLASTER OF PARIS.

moulds, and all being greased, as before, with a mixture of lard and oil, the plaster, mixed in a large vessel, was spread over all the flesh in sight as a thin coating, followed immediately by more and more until the required thickness was attained,—and so ended another day. The next morning the body of the tiger was removed, and the two halves and the four inside limb-moulds were set up on edge to dry. The weight of these moulds was considerable, some hundredweights of common plaster being used. Plate III. shows the moulds, etc.

Pending the drying of these moulds, all the flesh possible was cut from the carcase, which was then dismembered by the fore limbs being disconnected from the scapulæ, the hind limbs from the pelvis, and by the vertebræ being severed at the dorsal and lumbar regions, making three pieces. These, with two scapulæ, pelvis, and four limbs, made, in all, ten portions (exclusive of the skull, which was left in the skin for mounting ; this not being, however, a serious matter, as tigers' skulls are far more easily procurable than an entire or part skeleton). Each limb was, with all its parts, sewn up separately in calico, numbered, and carefully boiled in a copper until the flesh could be easily picked off the bones, but not so long as to allow it to *fall* off, nor to cause the epiphyses of the bones to do the same. Each limb, being separately treated, had its various parts drilled and wired together with copper, was boiled afterwards for an hour or so, then placed in warm water with Hudson's soap for a day to get out the grease, and was finally laid in a shallow tray out in the sun, wind, and rain for a week or so. These processes of skeletonising—except the latter, of course—took up a man's time for a week. During this time another man was preparing the paper model. One of the halves of the mould, being placed upon the work-table, was propped until it lay flat ; the inside and edges, the latter previously trimmed, were greased. A half-bucketful of flour-paste was made, and some thin but tough waste-paper, used by manufacturers in the hosiery trade, was procured. This was torn into pieces of various sizes, and taking one—pasted on *one* side only [1]—sufficient for the purpose, a commencement was made at one end by laying the *unpasted* side downwards, and working it into the inequalities of the mould by gentle but even pressure with the fingers, the edge of the paper coming over the edge of the mould being *pasted* down on the flat in order to get a secure attachment. Piece by piece the whole of the inside was covered, each piece coming to the edge being pasted down, and each piece on the whole surface being well pressed down and kneaded, as it were, into every depression and " quirk." For the next layer, paper of a different colour (a light buffy-pink) was chosen, in order to show an even distribution, and these pieces, pasted on *both* sides, were pressed still more equally into the mould. Next followed a third layer (of the same colour as the first), also pasted on both sides and pressed in with care. The next half-mould was then treated in precisely the same way, followed by the moulds of the four insides of the limbs. All had now received three layers, which had taken two men a day to manage. The next day, the process was repeated up to six thicknesses, and the next day three more, making nine in all. The moulds with the models in them now stood a week, no appliances being available for steaming so large a mass in front of a fire. During this time, a man was employed thinning down the skin and " double-skinning " the lips. At the end of a week, the models being *just* damp, were cut around where pasted down at the edges of the moulds, and carefully lifted out, coming away solid, and with every muscle and all the contours beautifully moulded. After being laid out upon racks for two days in a warm room

---

[1] It was afterwards found that the coating of the mould with a mixture of lard and linseed-oil in equal parts allowed the pasted side to be placed downwards—a great improvement resulting,—and this method is now always followed.

to dry and harden, they were put together in the following manner:—

Two pieces of $\frac{5}{8}''$ board ($\frac{3}{4}''$ before planing), 40 inches long by $6\frac{1}{2}$ inches broad, were laid lightly inside the halves as close to the back as they would come. Four $\frac{1}{2}''$ iron rods were next procured, and, having been flattened out for five inches from one end until they were $\frac{3}{4}''$ wide by $\frac{1}{4}''$ thick, and drilled for two screws, were bent in such a manner that, starting from the flattened parts which were to be screwed across the boards, they lay inside the limbs, following all the curves. Sufficient being left to come through the skin of the foot and through an inch board for about an inch, all the rods were screwed at their ends for six inches up, each to receive two nuts. Further, two short rods to support the skull were provided, and flattened and drilled for screws at those ends which were to be affixed —one to each board.

These preliminaries being arranged, the irons were laid upon the boards, which were marked at those points where the irons exercised the greatest resistance. The boards were then lifted out of the models, and the irons screwed to them where marked, once more put into the models, and two or three nails driven through the halves of the paper model from the outside into the boards to hold them in position temporarily.

The insides of the limbs were now laid on and carefully arranged at the edges, and joined by short strips of calico, or, better still, of muslin glued on at the junction. At various places where the board came into contact with the model, pieces of calico or muslin were glued to each as attachments, and wound around the rod where screwed on, to help to strengthen all together. Finally, the holes at the bottom of the legs were stopped with *glued paper pushed in*. Each half, having been treated in the same way, was left over night to allow the glued edges to set.

On resuming work in the morning, each half was set up-right and held by one person, whilst another rammed fine clean sawdust with a crooked iron rod into the bottom of, say, the near fore leg, to make all solid. Some dry paper was then rammed on top, and fixed into position by other pieces of paper glued on both sides, wound around the iron rod, and attached to the inside of the leg. As the limb filled, a wooden " crowder " was used to push in more sawdust and paper alternately, until, coming up to the shoulder, more paper than sawdust was required. Nearing the board, all was made secure by gluing paper or tow in underneath the board and to the edges of the model inside; so as to enclose all flatly up to the board. The hind limb of the same half was now treated in exactly the same way, the result being that both limbs were solid, and cased in by glued brown paper, the body being hollow at the back and front of the board. The next process, therefore, was to fill up behind with the soft paper previously mentioned, and, to assist in its retention, some long strips of calico were glued upon the board at intervals, their edges being allowed to lap over on the top of the back. The stomach was filled up in like manner, care being taken to pad out any accidental flatness which might have been caused by pressure on the model whilst damp—a matter of some importance being that, with care, no disturb-ance of the muscles and other parts previously modelled takes place. Afterwards, brown paper was glued over all until the half model was fairly flat, care, of course, being taken, whilst working, that the board kept its place *inside*. The other half was treated in the same manner, and thus concluded another day.

The halves (similar ones are shown on Plate IV.) were left for the night to dry, and work was resumed by securing the fore and hind limb of one half by its nuts, by screwing one with a washer upon the threaded portion of each rod,

IV.

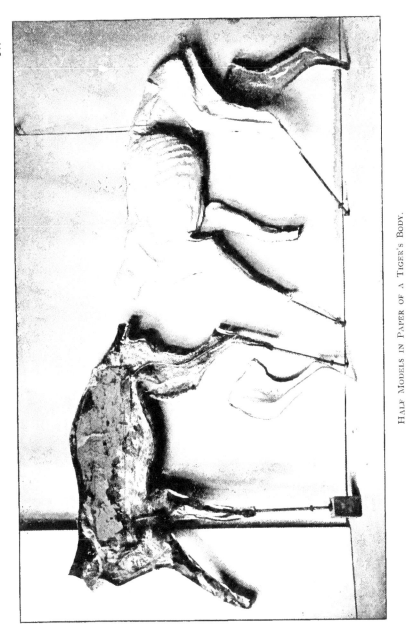

HALF MODELS IN PAPER OF A TIGER'S BODY.

then dropping the latter through holes in a piece of $\frac{3}{4}''$ board, about three to four inches wide, and finally screwing up the other nuts, with washers, to bite. Then, by means of props and stays of half-inch stuff, it was nailed into the position required on a platform of $\frac{3}{4}''$ boards large enough to take the whole. The other side, having been fixed in the same manner as the first, was brought up by supports and stays of thin board to the side of the other until the edges touched equally. By cutting slits in the sides in certain positions, screws were introduced from one body-board to the other, and the two halves were brought closely together by this means. Glue was then run along, and into, the edges, and finally muslin or thin calico was glued along the seams of the body and legs, forming all into one piece. The next morning, the whole of the model was whitewashed with a mixture of glue-water and whiting, which had the effect of making a solid, plaster-like looking model, on which any imperfections could be easily detected and remedied (see Plate V.).

In a few days, when quite dry, a coat or two of oil-paint, etc., was given, and allowed to dry, in order to prevent the wet skin, when laid on, from damping the paper model and putting it out of shape.

The next process was getting the skin on over the model. The head having been got upon the neck-rods, by pushing the latter up into the hole left in the brain-cavity for that purpose, a few stitches were made, bringing the skin together at various places to try how it fitted. To assist the coming-together of the edges, a pair of carpet-stretching pliers (a most valuable tool for stretching skins) was used, and, the "trying-on" of the tiger's jacket being satisfactory, the sewing-up was commenced in earnest, beginning at the *tail end*, the reason being that this part was sure to be right, but that, if there were any loose skin left, it might be wanted, or could be easily disposed of, at the

neck, chest, or belly.   Strong hemp, fourfold and waxed, was
used in " skin "-needles.   As the work progressed, little faults
were looked for and corrected.   At the junction, for instance,
of the hind and fore limbs with the body, it was necessary to
put in a saw-cut, to allow the skin at those parts to be properly
tucked in.

At certain places, especially on the flanks and belly, the
model appeared somewhat thin.   This was attributable to two
chief causes : one, the weight of the plaster, when casting from
the body, bearing the flesh down ; and the other, that all the
fat and a considerable thickness of the inside of the skin had
been pared away in " trimming."   The question how to replace
this evident loss was solved by tacking cotton wadding [1]
evenly over certain parts, and binding it down with hemp or
string.   (In some instances—as happened in the case of a
very thin lion,—two to three thicknesses, and in some parts
even more, of this wadding were nailed, glued, or tied on, the
weight of the superincumbent skin being quite sufficient to
press it into the hollows, or over the projections, when aided
by the hand, or by a few nails properly driven through the
skin where wanted, or even by stitching through at such places
as the hollows by the tendons of the legs.)   Throughout
the sewing, the skin was well stretched with the " carpet-
stretcher " and pulled toward the front, so as to get sufficient
skin to allow for folds and wrinkles at the neck and to deepen
the chest.

The arrangement of the head was then attended to, and
the skin of the throat partly sewn up, to get an idea of the
pose when finished.   Gradually a little tow and wadding were
rammed in where required, and, the head being satisfactory, a
rod was driven in through one of the ears to fix all securely.

---

[1] Superseded in later models by tow or wood-fibre, both of which are improvements.

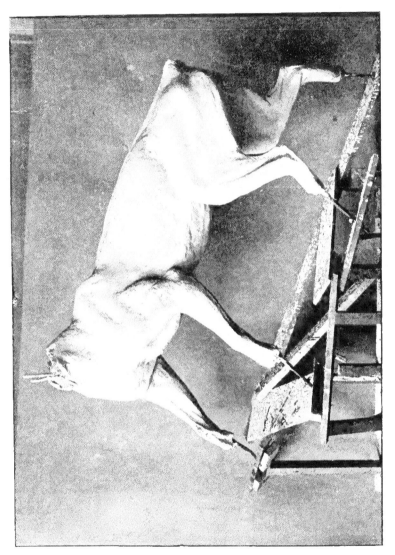

Model in Paper of the Headless Body of a Tiger.

At open stitches, purposely left along the whole of the body and throat, a few corrections were made by the addition or subtraction of the tow, etc., until the whole was sufficiently life-like ; the open stitches were then drawn together, or re-sewn, and the tiger was completed in all save the details of the head, the tail, and the feet. These latter were next attended to. The tiger, being intended to be represented as repelling the charge of another, was made to exhibit his claws by forcing clay or modelling-composition, followed by wadding, into the pads. Note that not much clay, etc., is needed,—no more, in fact, than sufficient to keep the pads from shrinking near the claws, the wadding doing the rest. The sole of one of the feet, not being quite in the right line with the supporting rod, was cut under-neath to bring it properly into position ; all was then filled out to a natural appearance, and the pads sewn up, excepting a small hole left at the back of each, just behind the supporting rod, by which errors might be corrected. The head was touched up in the modelling, but the ears, eyes, lips, mouth, and tongue were left untouched until the whole should be dry. Fine wire nails were driven in along the line of the back, on each side of the vertebræ, and in every other situation where needed.

The tail was the next thing to be executed. A stout wire or an iron rod was wrapped with tow to length and shape—thicker at the base, of course, and tapering off at the tip. It was then well smeared with clay, and inserted within the skin of the tail. The part left unwrapped (some feet) had been previously pointed, and was now thrust into the body. All being care-fully made up and the necessary action given to the tail, a second pointed wire or rod was driven in from the outside, through the thickest part of the well-bound tow of the model tail, into the body.[1]

[1] This has also been improved upon by using *one* rod, affixed to the board of one half model by screws passing through holes in a flattened portion as in the limb-wires.

When the animal's skin was thoroughly dry, it was well brushed to remove dust and clay-stains, and was afterwards wiped down with turpentine and benzoline to brighten the fur. Where any imperfection or slight gaping was observed in the stitching, that part was first cleaned out, and then filled and made up either with coloured wax or with paper pulp.   Finally the head was finished off, and the open mouth was modelled with wax in the following manner :—Good beeswax was taken and coloured to the various tints required, and, whilst hot, was painted thinly with a brush over the oiled mould of the palate (see Figs. 10 and 11, Plate VII.); this, when nearly cold, was removed (see wax model, Fig. 12, Plate VII.), and fixed upon the roof of the mouth by brushing the latter over with hot wax and uniting the two by gentle pressure, and by brushing on a little more wax at the edges.

The muscles around the teeth of the upper jaw were next made up with hot tinted wax, by means of brushes and warmed tools ; this was followed by the modelling, in the same material, of the great muscles around the teeth—canines especially—of the lower jaw ; the lips generally were also improved, and for all of this the clay model and casts (see Figs. 9 and 10, Plate VII.) were used as guides.   Next, the upper and lower moulds of the tongue were brushed over with properly-tinted hot wax, which, taken off when nearly cold, and the parts joined together at their edges, formed the complete tongue, which was inserted and fixed in the mouth, giving all a life-like effect consequent on being modelled from the natural objects.

It is quite possible in summer time, or by artificial heat in winter, to make pressure-models, and so dispense with melted wax for all the foregoing processes, as such waxes as Nos. 65 and 66 will, if made into convenient sticks, be easily broken up by the fingers, and may be well kneaded by pressure —strong thumbs being required for this—into all interstices and depressions of plaster moulds of palates, tongues, and so on. If a mould be large, pieces of wax may be added as required, and if the pressure applied be sufficiently powerful and long sustained the joins will not show (see Fig. 12, Plate VII.). The edges of the various portions of a model, such as the upper and under parts of a tongue, can be united by pressure and tooling, and the muscles, etc., around the teeth may also be made up by pressure ; hence a supply of sticks of the modelling-waxes, Formulæ 64, 65, 66, and 73, in various colours are extremely useful, are easily manipulated, and of equal value with the hot waxes.

Not only may tongues, palates, and such-like objects be modelled in various waxes from moulds, as previously described and figured, but they may be excellently reproduced from moulds by any of the pulps, especially Formula 93 (see Fig. 13, Plate VII.); and when coloured pulp is used, allowed to dry, and after-wards brushed over with a very thin layer of very hot coloured wax, the result is quite as good, and both wax and pulp processes are greatly in advance of the clay tongues recommended by Mr. Rowland Ward,[1] and of the skinned-out natural tongue filled with sheet-lead and clay recommended by Mr. Hornaday.[2]

The skin around the base of the protracted claws was also waxed to represent the natural appearance.

The artificial eyes should be—as was the case in all the examples mentioned in this division—made of half-ovals of thin glass painted to nature from the inside (see p. 193), and inserted in the orbits after the eyelids have been filled, and the cornea, etc., then made up in wax.

The second tiger-model shown on Plate VI. was managed in the same way, the only difference being that one leg (the off hind), not being sufficiently advanced, was dissected, just at

[1] *Sportsman's Handbook*, seventh edition, p. 82.
[2] *Taxidermy*, pp. 174, 175.

the place where the "knob" or head of the femur showed in the model, by a knife and a saw, precisely as if it had been an operation in the flesh. The whole of the leg, just attached at the inner surface, was moved bodily forward to the position shown. The same thing was done to the off fore limb, to allow a closer grasp of the paw on the neck of the tiger already finished.

In casting this tiger, seven bucketfuls of plaster were used on one side, five on the other, and two for the inside of the four legs—*i.e.* $2\frac{1}{2}$ cwts. of common plaster altogether.

About 8 lbs. of burnt alum and 2 lbs. of nitre (see Formula 59, p. 75) were made into a paste with warm water in a bucket and used for the skin, the paws and head being dipped into water next morning preparatory to further skinning.

To harden the tongue, a saturated solution of salt was used to remove the blood, followed by bichromate of potassa, to which a little methylated spirit was afterwards added.

In some of the specimens—notably in that of the elephant (see p. 142 and Plate VI.) lying under the fighting tigers, and in a zebra and some others,—the head, not being required to show the teeth, has been removed and modelled from by the direct paper process, and therefore no bone whatever has been retained ; and in all deer it is only necessary to retain a small triangular plate of bone to carry the horns (see "Horned Head," p. 151).

It having been found that the nine layers of pasted paper not only took a long time to dry, but were too weak for such large animals as tigers and lions, a supposed further improvement was effected by making the model of twelve, viz. three thicknesses of *pasted* paper thoroughly moulded into every "quirk" and muscle, followed by alternate layers of thin and thick brown paper, nine in number, *glued* upon each other. The strength of this was surprising even by the next day, but in a few days it was as firm and solid as possible. Since that

GROUP OF FIGHTING TIGERS WITH ELEPHANT, SET UP BY MEANS OF PAPER MODELS.

time, however, it has been found that, although increasing the number of layers to twelve or more is correct, yet that the substitution of glue for paste is a mistake, and that there is nothing like *strong thick* paste and thick paper to follow the first few coats of thin paper.

An old lion, of the weight of 252 lbs., which was also sent to the Museum by Mr. J. W. Bostock, was skinned and cast with these differences :—The body was arranged in such a manner as to allow of both sides of the body and the legs, with the exception of *two insides*, being cast in two pieces.

The Skinning and Setting-up of an Elephant

The method adopted in the Leicester Museum for the mounting of a young male elephant called "Ajax," which died of peritonitis, and was presented to the museum in March, 1886, by Mr. G. Ginnett, was somewhat similar. Its weight was one ton one hundredweight. After being skinned, which process took two men two days, the skin was placed for ten hours in a bath of salt, water, and crude carbolic acid in the following proportions to remove the blood and toughen the tissue :—

85.—Preservative Bath for Elephants' and other thick Skins (M.B.)

No. 1.

Salt	40 lbs.
Carbolic acid, glacial . . .	2 oz.
(or if crude be used, 4 oz.)	
Water (warm if possible) . .	20 gals.

The skin was then drained, and steeped in a tub containing the following :—

86.—Preservative Bath for the same (M.B.)

No. 2.

Burnt alum	32 lbs.
Nitre	8 ,,
Bichromate of potassa . .	4 oz.
Water (warm if possible) . .	16 gals.

It remained in this bath (the skin being turned and the liquor stirred twice a week) for fourteen days, and came out perfectly cured, without a blemish, and remains intact to the present day.

The skin was pared down quite thin, especially inside the feet, with the result that 63 lbs. weight of "chips" or parings were taken off, leaving the skin 1 cwt. (130 lbs. when wet). During the pickling of the skin, however, three men were employed casting from the body and making the skeleton.

The elephant was laid on its right side, placed in the required position, the legs propped apart as in the tiger (see p. 129 and Plate III.), and surrounded with a wall of clay. The upper legs were slung to the ceiling to support them at the width required ; the plaster was then poured on the insides of the lower limbs (now their upper surface), and brought up to the insides of, and half-way up, the topmost limbs in one piece. The head was next cast in three pieces—one piece at the back, one at the lower jaw, and the other on the side of the face now uppermost, which included the trunk. The next piece embraced the neck, shoulder, and the upper surface of the fore limb. The body was cast in one piece from this point up to the hind leg ; next the rump and top part of the hind leg was cast. All of these took as their boundary the ridge of the back. The carcase was now turned over by levers and pulleys, and the casting was finished by repeating the process, beginning at the side of the face left undone, and following on as before.

When the moulds were dry, they were brushed inside with grease and oil, and subsequently a direct paper model—made in the same manner as detailed for the tiger at p. 132, but much thicker—was built up, and strengthened inside by props of wood, and by packing with dry waste-paper and shavings, the skin being stretched over and sewn with thick cord entered in sail-makers' needles, and fastened here and there with a "clout" nail. When the paper model was quite finished,—the animal, which was intended for the tiger group, being shown lying prone, as if dead,—its weight was 95 lbs., or say 100 lbs. with patching and putting together, bringing the weight of the finished elephant to 212 lbs. only, or less than 2 cwt.

The writer has been often asked what should be done to cure and preserve thick skins, elephants' feet, etc., in India, and the advice given has been that, directly the animal was killed and skinned, the foot or other parts should be steeped in a bath made according to Formula 85 (p. 141). Let the skin, or foot, lie in this from two to ten hours, to discharge the blood, and also to harden the tissues, and follow with the second bath (Formula 86, p. 141) in the proportions given ; or, if the skin is at all disposed to be " high," make a thick paste, with hot water if possible, of the burnt alum, saltpetre, and powdered bichromate, and let it be rubbed in, outside and in, and it will be more than surprising should they not be perfectly preserved. Arsenic is always useless, and especially in wet weather.

If the specimens can be dried anyhow before being packed away, it is just as well ; otherwise, should the weather be continuously wet, it is necessary to look them over soon after dressing, and to rub more paste into the folds of the skin, etc., and, should mildew appear, to brush the skin over with Formula 11 (p. 36).

Modelling a Wild Sheep

A sheep, which was next done, was varied by the paper model being allowed to dry in the mould for some two weeks, when, by careful cutting around and gentle handling, the whole of the two halves came out hard and firm. This wild sheep, or more correctly mouflon, was fixed thus :—A $\frac{5''}{8}$ board, as before, was fitted to each half in such a manner as not to rise above the edges. Where the shoulders interfered,

V-shaped pieces were cut away, and $\frac{1}{4}''$ iron rods, simply flattened out at one end and drilled with two holes for screws, were provided, and, being thin and easily bent around, were *not* screwed at the bottom, but were fixed into their pieces of $\frac{5}{8}''$ bottom boards by simply bending the ends underneath and clenching them. Before this could be done, however, one body-board, with the rods attached, was placed in each half, the rods accurately fitting inside, and following the hollows of, the limbs. Three nails were driven through the model from the outside into the board to keep it in position, and glued tow or fibre was lightly packed under and over the boards, each parcel of tow being glued separately here and there until a solid mass was attained ; the boards being brought just level, or a *little below* the edges, the neck, and chest, and all parts where the boards did not touch were padded with glued material. The legs, being small, were carefully fixed to the iron rods, all being kept in place by strips of glued brown paper folded and twisted around. Each half was then finished by gluing large pieces of brown paper over the body-board and its packing from side to side of the body, keeping all flat and secure.

The next morning, the two halves were fixed upon their foot-boards, stayed up into position on the bottom board, and, a little glued tow having been used to attach the two sides, were *sewn* together at the edges of the paper model, this process having the effect of bringing the edges together in a more even manner, and giving all a better shape than any other method. The inner halves of the limbs were attached to the half-models by being filled with paper, glued, placed in position, and sewn where required. Next the head, previously cast in paper, was fixed upon the neck-rod. Muslin was glued over all the edges, and the final coat of whitewash given.

The improvements in this case were—1. Superior lightness

and facility of handling, by using tow instead of sawdust. 2. Gluing paper over all. 3. Sewing the edges.

It not being desired to show the teeth as in the carnivora, the mouth was closed, which enabled a cast to be taken of the head, and its subsequent reproduction in paper. The skeleton of this animal, by that means, was kept in its entirety, even to the ultimate phalanges or "coffin-bones" of the hoofs; thus *two* museum specimens were obtained.

Note that the bases of the horn-cores were included in the cast from the natural head, and formed supports for the horns.

The Skinning and Setting-up of a Horned Head

Whenever practicable, a head of any kind, especially a horned head, which is most frequently hung upon a wall as a trophy, should be cut off with a considerable portion of the skin of the *front of the neck* attached—say quite six inches measured in a line from the back of the eye. To take a deer's head as an example, it will often be found that game-keepers, and people who should know better, either leave a great length at the back of the neck, where it is not wanted, and leave none whatever in front, or otherwise slit up the front of the neck, which is, of course, a useless proceeding, and is directly opposed to all satisfactory modelling of one of the most important parts, viz. the throat.

At almost any time of the year, if the head has to be sent from a distance or be kept for any length of time, it should be plunged for half an hour into a saturated solution of salt and water, and, when taken out, should be covered with salt *inside and out* before being sent away, or until it can be skinned.

When ready to commence operations, remove the mass of salt, and wash the head thoroughly in cold water, removing the remainder of the salt, blood, etc., from the matted hair by means of a scrubbing-brush. At the same time, scrub the horns to cleanse them also from dirt and blood. This having been done, a bucket or two of fresh water thrown over the whole will remove all that has been left.

The head being now ready for skinning, lay it, throat downwards, upon the operating-table ; with the pointed knife No. 4 (Plate II.) pierce the skin of the head exactly in the centre and in a line with the back of the burr of the horns, and extend the cut along the back of the neck until the skin is split throughout its entire length. When this is accomplished, turn the head back to front and relieve the cut edges a little where they are retained at the back of the head, and then, inserting the point of the knife close to the burr of one horn, and rather more to the back than the centre, make a diagonal cut therefrom extending to the anterior end of the median cut. Do the same upon the other side, and the appearance presented by the cuts will be in the form of a Y, the lowest or posterior limb being, of course, the longest. Holding the head in the most convenient position for work, which is ordinarily resting on the brow-antlers, take the right or left diagonal cut, and, holding that part of the skin firmly in the left hand, first dipping the fingers in sand or coarse salt to ensure a firm grip, commence to release the skin around the burr by digging with the point of the knife close to the under side of the burr and cutting upwards. When this has been done almost to the front of the burr, the base of the ear and its attachments, showing as a cartilaginous bag, will be found to hold the skin some distance below, and the whole of these must be detached from the skull by carefully skinning around, and by cutting the last attachment at the little orifice of the ear (*meatus auditorius externus*), entering the skull.

Do not trouble at this point if there should be a little too much flesh adhering to the base of the ear, as this is a matter

for subsequent operation. Leave this part now, and, returning
to the top of the head, release the skin around the burr from
the back to meet that part already freed, still cutting upwards,
and also releasing the skin as much as possible on the crown
of the head, until the whole of the skin around one horn has
been detached.

Now lay the head upon its side, and, inserting the left forefinger into the orbit under the eyelid, skin carefully down *upon
the finger*—the explanation being that the finger will give due
notice in the event of the knife going too far. Detach the
skin a little more on the top, keeping the point of the knife
well down upon the bone, and gradually release the inner skin
of the eyelids, which will appear as a whitish membrane both
at top and bottom. After about an inch of this skin has
appeared, cut it right through, holding the blade of the knife
pressed close to the bone of the orbit. This process leaves the
actual eyeball within its orbit, whilst it has the effect of leaving
a bag of whitish skin inside, which is, of course, the inner skin
of the eyelids. At the anterior angle of the orbit, the skin
sticks more than at the posterior ; this is due to the skin near
this point entering the lachrymal sinus or tear-gland—the little
pit in front of the eye.

Very great care is required now, as the skin appears to
stick, not only just within the orbit, but outside, and the point
of the knife must be shortened in the hand and kept close down
upon the bone, rather excavating that part than actually cutting ; at any rate, the cuts must have no upward tendency.
Directly this part is free, release the skin still more at the side
of, and above, the orbit.

Probably, before the skin entering the proximal end of the
sinus can be released, it will be necessary to free the skin around
the burr of the other side, and above and below the other eye, in
exactly the same manner, until the bag of each sinus becomes

visible. Now it will be found practicable to release one of these by judicious undercutting and excavating as before, aided by a pull with the fingers of the left hand ; and, when one is thus released, the other will follow as a matter of course.

The remaining operation, down to the tip of the nose, is simple, consisting in merely skinning away the flesh from the bones of the nose and underneath the jaw, until stopped by a bag of blue skin which shows just underneath the proximal angle of the sinus. This is the angle of the mouth, and must be cut away very delicately around the bone, still preserving its bag-like character. This skin returns on the teeth, and extends a little farther backward on the lower jaw, coming, indeed, as far back as the commencement of the orbit, and should be skinned off literally from the teeth ; this forms a large bag of skin, to be left for subsequent operations. Now continue skinning on both sides of the lower jaw, keeping close to the bone meanwhile.

At this stage, the insertion of a small block of wood, between the upper and lower jaws, assists the operator to see all round the lower jaw, and by skinning carefully the front teeth are reached, and by skinning on these the whole skin is released leaving, as before, the mucous membrane as a bag. The block may now be removed, but let the head be kept in the same position—lower jaw uppermost,—and release the skin of the upper jaw, by cutting all the way around close to the bone. This, when done, admits the knife into the cavity of the nostril ; cut well within this, in the same manner as directed for the eye, and the whole of the nostril, including its inner mucous membrane, will be released. The other side being managed in precisely the same way, the entire skin will be removed from the skull.

The mask of the deer—now turned inside out—exhibits, around the lips, a thick double skin extending backwards as a

papillated mucous membrane ; a large mass of the cartilage of
the nostrils ; large bags formed by the eyelids, and a large mass
of cartilage at the roots of the ears.

Commencing with the latter, the first operation will be to cut
away any superfluous flesh which may have been left upon the
skin or the cartilage at the base, and, after freeing the cartilage
for some little distance all round, grip the freed base of the
ear with the left hand—the remainder of the ear lying, meanwhile, within the reversed skin of the head, the back of the ear
upwards,—and, discarding the knife temporarily, proceed, with
the thumb and finger of the right hand, to work up between the
outer and inner skins of the ear, until the ear turns partially
inside out like the reversed finger of a glove. Probably this
process will not have separated the skins to their extreme
edges ; resume the knife, therefore, which must not be too sharp,
and with rather more of a scraping than a cutting motion,
assisting also with the thumb-nail of the *left* hand—the middle
finger being meanwhile opposed to the thumb on the other side
of the skin,—gradually expose the cartilage to the extreme
edge on each side, and to the extreme tip. Recollect that, in
this operation, a great deal more is done with the fingers than
with the knife. Within the skin of the head, the reversed
ear is now presented as a large mass of skin and cartilage
like a huge finger of a glove, this finger exhibiting an apparent
seam down the centre, the cartilage being white, the actual
skin appearing blue. Repeat the process with the other
ear.

Taking next the bag of the eye, this, after all superfluous
flesh has been trimmed therefrom, must be entirely freed from
the actual skin until the black rim or outer edge of the
eyelid is reached. When pulled through the orifice of the eye,
the bag—which is, however, without a bottom—should project
quite half an inch, but must, of course, be returned within

the skin to await final operations. Repeat this with the other eye.

The next to be taken are the nostrils, which show within the skin as a large mass of cartilage with, probably, some flesh attached. Grasping the cartilage with the left hand and using the knife with the right, cut away the whole of the septum, or that part which divides one nostril from the other; then, using the knife and fingers as before, proceed to skin from the inside to the outside of the nostrils in the same manner as directed for the bags of the eyes, so that, coming to the extreme outer edges, the inner linings of the nostrils are practically detached, except at their outside edges, and form bags; whereas the cutting-away of these, in improperly managed heads, results in objectionable holes.

When both nostrils are done, there remain but the lips to be grappled with, and these show, as before mentioned, a thick mass of papillated inner lining, *i.e.* mucous membrane. Where the edges of this, both of the upper and lower jaws, remain attached to the inner surface of skin, they must be carefully split until the junction of their edges with the outer hair is reached, but not divided. This, being thoroughly done all round, leaves some very large bags which, like those of the ears, eyes, and nostrils, are to be left for subsequent modelling.

The last operation is to carefully examine and thin the skin over all its remaining parts. Then plunge it into the nitrate solution (Formula 59), made as a thin paste with warm water, thoroughly saturating and rubbing in both the inside and outside, taking care not to neglect the least portion, or at that place the hair will " slip." Properly, the skin should lie in this for a night, after which the superfluous preservative should be scraped off and retained, and the skin thoroughly washed in clean cold water several times and then partly dried, so that it may be but just damp when placed on the model.

Treatment of the Skull

Lay the head, horns uppermost, upon the table, and, with a tenon saw, make a cut half an inch from the back of the orbits, which is usually about one inch from the base of the burrs. Let the cut go straight across and under the horns, guiding it in such a manner that it is about in a line with the base of the burrs at the back. Another cut, as close to the back of the horns as the saw will go, should be led down into the front cut, and the horns will then fall off with a piece of bone, chevron-shaped in front and round at the back, attached. The whole extent of the piece of bone need not be more than four inches in length by three in breadth for an ordinary buck ; larger, of course, in larger deer.

Directly the bone is cut off, and whilst it is still soft, two holes should be made with brace and bit, one on either side of the frontal ridge, equi-distant, and not far, from the pedicles of the burrs ; if necessary, a third hole can be bored at the apex of the chevron. These holes should then be countersunk. Now clean and scrape the bone with a knife, then wash it and scrub it with a brush. When dry, paint it with the preservative, Formula 57.

The head itself is the next thing to be considered, and this now shows the large cavity of the nostrils, and a much larger and rounder cavity whence the horns and brains have been removed (see Fig. 4, Plate VII.) ; these, as also the orbits, must be nearly filled with paper or wool, and this covered with clay. Take note, however, that the brain-cavity must not be filled up to the top, but the filling must follow the line of the cut edges of the bone, so that the horns will fit upon it ; neither must the orbits nor the nostrils be quite filled up, but must be a little concave, and all places from which flesh has been cut must be made up with clay.

The head should now be laid, throat downwards, on a board sufficiently large to extend beyond the limits of the head at every point, and the next thing to do is to take a mould or " cast" of the head.   This is effected by first building a thin wall of putty along the skull, just off, or on one side of, the median line, coming down over the nose and the back of the head to the board.   Buttresses of putty (and putty is used because it does not stick to the clay as fresh clay would do) are built on the farther side of the putty wall to strengthen it, and when the head is enclosed within its walls by the retaining boards in the usual manner (see p. 231), plaster is poured in on one side until one half of the head is entirely covered to a thickness of about an inch and a half, and is allowed to set, and, the putty wall being removed, the edges of the half mould are keyed and oiled, and plaster is poured over the remaining half of the head in like manner.

When the plaster is set, a little care will remove the natural skull from the mould, and this is best done by tapping the mould over all its surface with a mallet, until a chattering is heard, and the joint opens ; then, by more careful tapping and by pulling with the hands, the halves come apart and one half of the mould is free; the head is now easily removed by tapping and pulling, and there results a complete cast or mould of the head in two halves.

Sometimes, if at all undercut, or if a neck is to be shown, it may be necessary to make the mould of more than two pieces, and in this case it will be better to make it in four pieces—the first by pouring plaster in on one side to extend up the side of the face as high as the orbits ; the next piece from there to the median line on the top of the head, and repeating the same on the other side, thus making four pieces which will easily relieve.

To make a model either from the two or four moulds, it is

merely necessary to oil and to key them together tightly, and, laying them on the table with the orifice of the neck upwards, to pour in plaster mixed as usual ; then, when set, by tapping gently with the mallet as before directed, the mould can be taken off, and the counterpart or model of the skull in plaster is obtained. This is, however, solid and heavy, and, therefore, when it is desired to fix the head upon a shield or to model a neck, two pieces of board should be provided—one about one foot long by three inches wide by one inch or so thick, the other just the size of the anterior cut for the horns. The smaller piece should be nailed on the top of the larger at right angles and placed that end downwards within the mould, resting upon that part which represents the anterior saw-cut in the bone. After oiling, plaster should be poured in and on top, firmly fixing the boards in position. As the plaster sets, it should be taken out with a spoon or modelling-tool to within three-quarters of an inch of the edge, and for some distance down, to hollow it and thus reduce the weight. Finally, the moulds must be removed with still greater care on account of the thinness of the model, which, of course, comes out much lighter, and with a wooden neck-block and horn-block immovably fixed. (Fig. 1, Plate VII., represents a hollow plaster cast of the head.)

The weight of the solid plaster model, with wood included, will be about eight and a half pounds whilst wet, but, when dry, six pounds. That of the plaster model partially hollowed out will be, however, about six and a quarter pounds when wet, and, when dry, about four pounds.

Hitherto the neck has not been taken into consideration in the casting, as a plaster neck, in addition to the plaster head, would be far too weighty. In this process, therefore, it is best treated as described in the following pages, but, on the other hand, if a paper instead of a plaster model is to be made of the head (see p. 157), the original moulds should embrace the neck. Solid models of a red deer's head (Fig. 5) and of a calf's head (Fig. 8) are shown on Plate VII. These were, however, cast from clay models copied from the dead heads by eye and measurements.

To put the Skin upon the Model

The plaster model having been well dried, and thereby rendered so much lighter as explained before, take the skin, just damp (*not* wet), and try it over the model, the horns having been temporarily screwed upon the small block, which shows through the plaster in the model. It is necessary to do this before the skin can be fitted, and also to determine the length of the neck and its pitch. This can be done by placing a wide board or a square at the back, so that it touches the hindermost points of the horns, and marking the piece of wood which forms the neck at the point where the board or square touches. If the neck-board be cut about an inch shorter, or nearer to the head, than the point of intersection, it will be sufficient, and will allow for the subsequent three-quarter-inch oval block and three-quarter-inch shield on which it should be finally arranged. If, however, no shield is to be used, but only the neck-oval, this, of course, must be taken into consideration. The horns, temporarily screwed to the block, may now be taken off, and the neck-board sawn off to the length and angle required. This being done, cut a long oval, or somewhat egg-shaped, block, about six inches long, by four and a half at its greatest breadth, by three-quarters of an inch thick for an ordinary head. This being screwed to the neck-board, the neck can be made up in the following manner:—Ram the hollowed-out part of the head full and tightly with rough or waste paper, and, when this is packed closely, wrap more round the neck-board down to the oval block, making up at the same time to about the natural shape of the neck, which shape is partially determined by that of the neck-block. Next take some tow, make a long loose rope of it, and wind it around the paper, and tie over all some wrapping-cotton to bind the whole together, and to make it nearly of the shape required. Take some thick paste, and paste over the tow ; cover all with a thin skin of clay, which may be pressed in and shaped, first with the hands and afterwards with the modelling-tools Nos. 33, 34. When this is done, screw the oval block upon a board sufficiently large and weighty to prevent it from toppling over when subsequently worked upon. Now take a broad brush well charged with paste, and paste the clay well over, bringing it into the form which it is to assume.

The whole being firmly screwed to the board from the back, take carving-tools Nos. 37-39, and carve out the orbits, nostrils, and lips quite as deeply as in the skinned head. After the carving-tools, finish off smoothly with the coarsest sand-paper. This sand-papering is not so much to give beauty to the cast as to reduce small imperfections, and to remove the dirt acquired by handling, which somewhat obscures the finer points. Now screw the horns permanently to the head-block, as they will not have to be taken off again.

Nothing remains to be considered but the skin, which, if at all dry, must be plunged into water for a few hours, wrung out, and put on as nearly dry as possible. Remember that every part must be thoroughly damp, though not wet, as, if at all dry, it will neither stretch nor model.

Before the skin is finally placed upon the model, fill between the skins of the ears with clay, or with modelling-composition (Formula 61 or 72), which, as before directed, must be used warm. Press the composition well towards the edges and tips of the ears and gradually bring them into shape, dipping the composition into hot water as used, to render it of about the consistence of putty. When this is satisfactorily accomplished, paint the whole of the skin inside with Formula 57 (p. 73). The eyes may now be embedded in the orbits of the model by means of *clay ;* the composition, hardening quickly, would not, perhaps, allow of subsequent alteration, therefore clay is in this case better. Pull the skin over the model, stretching it in every direction if it shows a tendency not to come together, and, if it is very obstinate, using the carpet-stretchers ; if, however, the skin has been tried on before, this should not be necessary. Sew up the cut at the back of the neck, using a skin-needle charged with double hemp well waxed, and driving the needle with a sailmaker's "palm." Then take out the screw which holds the board to the oval neck-block: this frees the latter, and now the skin should be brought over the edge of this, tacked down on the under side, and all superfluous skin cut off. Rescrew the head upon the board, and *now* fill in the bags of the eyes, nose, and lips—both upper and under— with the composition, just sufficiently to replace the flesh cut out and to thicken the edges of the lips, etc., as in life ; turn them back into their natural positions, and fix them and the ears by means of stout pins or pieces of pointed *galvanised* wire—to prevent rusting—hammered through the skin into the various corresponding cavities and depressions on the model, correcting here and there by the addition or subtraction of the modelling-composition, and taking particular pains with the arrangement of the eyes and nostrils.

Hang the whole up by the board to dry, which will happen ordinarily in about a week or ten days. Then let the whole of the hair be well brushed with a wire scratch-card, and finally wiped down with benzoline. Screw upon the shield (see pp. 416, 417), and tint to nature the inside of the ears, eyelids, nose, and lips.

Making a Paper Model of the Deer's Head

The plaster mould of the head being, as before, in halves, either with or without the neck, the paper head is made up in those half moulds separately, and the half models are afterwards joined together. To do this, first oil the moulds, and press into one half a layer of tissue-paper pasted on the lower side as before directed ; follow this with two layers of " cap "-paper, and from four to five of brown—eight in all—the extra thickness of one layer being pasted on the crown of the head where the horns will ultimately be fixed, and where the strain of their weight will be greatest. Do the same with the other half mould, and, when the paper model is quite dry, relieve each half from its mould, trim the edges until the halves join nicely, and fix them together by pasted hinges, or strips of strong calico, which, if the neck is to be added afterwards, may be managed by fixing from the inside through the aperture of the neck. If, however, the neck is part of the mould, which it may well be, the fixing from the inside will be rather more difficult, but this is so purely a matter of " gumption " that no detailed instructions need be given.

When nicely together let it dry, and then paste a strip of calico along the whole of the seam, both at top and at bottom outside, covering it afterwards with a layer of brown paper, which makes all secure.

This being allowed to thoroughly dry, cut out of the crown of the modelled head, where the V-shaped depression is, a piece of the consolidated paper 4 inches wide from side to side, and 3 inches from front to back of skull. Next procure a block of wood, $4\frac{1}{2}''$ by $3\frac{1}{2}''$ by $1\frac{1}{4}''$, and let it be cut in such a manner as to conform to the shape of the depression in the model, caused by the prior removal from the skull of the V-shaped piece of bone with the horns attached, as previously

described. The shape of this block, viewed as a section, now
being as shown in the accompanying figure, two screwholes

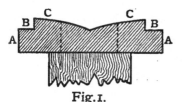

Fig. I.

should be drilled in the block
(see dotted lines), by which to
affix the neck-support mentioned
hereafter.

This block being inserted
in the space cut out from the
model, the shoulders A — A
should fit *under* the edges of the paper, whilst the sides B—B
are included within the thickness of the model, so that all fits
as snugly within it as possible, the V-shaped depression C—C
following the original lines of the model. (See also Fig. 3,
Plate VII., for an elevation of this, and for the following neck-
support.)

The neck-support, to which the head-block is to be screwed,
is made of a piece of wood 2″ by 1½″, and of such a length as
may be required—usually about 9 inches,—and, whilst the
upper extremity is left square, the lower or neck extremity
must be sawn off at such an angle that, when the completed
head is fixed upon the wall, the distal extremities of the horns
shall not touch. The head-block is screwed to one end of
this, and the T-shaped block (as it now is) is well bedded into
its proper position in the paper head by means of wadding
saturated with glue—the wadding being also packed around
the junction of the neck- and head-pieces as a further aid and
support to the screws. This must be well pressed in, and
although some regard to the ultimate weight must be observed,
yet this glued wadding must not be used too sparingly, taking
into consideration the weight of the horns which the blocks
have to carry. Outside, the joining of the wood and paper
may be filled in by the same method, and, over this, calico
should be pasted. The open space where the neck should

VII.

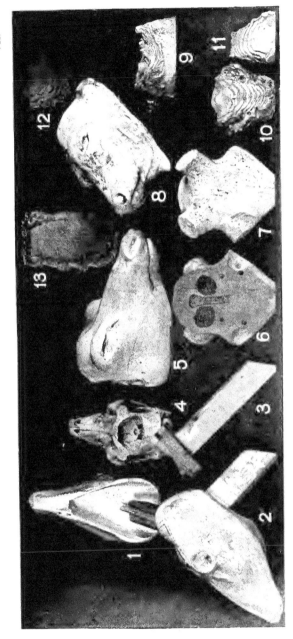

Models in Clay, Plaster, Paper, and Wax, of Heads, and of Parts of Mouths, of Ungulates and Carnivores.

come is made up by pasting strips of calico around the block, followed by pasted paper, completely closing the orifice, but leaving the required length of the neck-block outside it. When, however, the neck is cast with the head—which should, if possible, always be the case—some modification of this procedure will be necessary, which may be left to the sense of the pupil ; but in any event all must be made perfectly firm and rigid.

The model should now be painted with whiting, into which a little glue-water or paste has been stirred, and, when dry, one coat of common oil-paint of any colour to hand will be sufficient, or, failing this, boiled oil alone brushed over will render it sufficiently waterproof for the reception of the damped skin ; the subsequent proceedings being exactly the same as directed for the plaster model (see preceding pages).

The advantages of the paper over the plaster model are twofold : great lightness combined with strength, for, whereas the lightest plaster model weighs over 4 lbs., the paper one made for this lesson, when blocked complete, weighed but 1 lb. 10 ozs., and whereas a plaster model dropped upon the floor would inevitably be broken, the paper model may be (and indeed was) dropped and banged about with impunity. (See Fig. 2, Plate VII., for a view of the completed paper head.)

The manifest advantages of paper models of heads, limbs, and carcases of mammals cast from the natural objects are so enormous from every point of view, that now this system, so easily managed, is published, it is hoped that incorrect and rule-of-thumb methods of setting up mammals will for ever be discarded, in favour of what must be at least scientifically accurate.

When models of the internal organs of any mammal are required, it is better, before making a mould, to inject thin plaster as described in many works on biology,[1] and such methods may be modified to suit various classes of the animal kingdom.

DIVISION IV

THE PREPARATION OF SKELETONS AND THE TAWING OF SKINS

Skeletons

Skeletons, which are necessities in all that relates to anatomical investigation, and are therefore objects to be desired in all museums, may be justified as being certainly scientific, and, when well made, artistic. The making of skeletons, however, involves so many disagreeables, that their preparation should be handed over to those whose business it is.

Most works on taxidermy treat bones in a light-hearted manner, which makes one wonder if the writers know anything at all about their preparation. The time-honoured method is to cut as little flesh from the subject as possible, and to place the mass in a tub and cover it with water; the flesh in the course of a few months or a year, according to size and situation, decomposes, and the bones are then fished out, one by one, from the horrible slime, washed, drilled, washed again, sun-dried, bleached by lime, and wired together, the taxidermist or professional bone-maker losing, meanwhile, a few of the minor bones (which mean anything less than the skull or long-bones) and considerately replacing their loss (if he ever misses them) by other bones taken, if possible, from another of the same species of animal, but not allowing himself to be fettered by any considerations as to sex or age, nor as to the normal position of such trifling objects as the phalanges, which are, as he thinks, pretty much alike in most mammals.

----

[1] See *Practical Zoology*, Marshall and Hurst (last edition), Introduction, pp. xxi.-xxiii.

The system adopted in the Leicester Museum is to skin and eviscerate any animal, to take out the brains, to trim as much flesh as possible from the bones, and to let the carcase soak in strong salt and water, constantly changed, for a time ranging from a few hours to two or three days, or even longer, according to the size of the subject, to remove the blood. When it is taken out, the long-bones are drilled from end to end with tool No. 21, and the marrow, etc., removed by water forced through by a syringe. Then the bones are all properly scraped with the backs of knives or with blunt tools, such as No. 32 and others, and finally rubbed with salt, which clears them nicely of the periosteum, care being taken not to disarticulate the smaller bones, and all are then wired in their proper positions.

Probably this wiring, in the larger mammals, may be provisional only, being roughly done, and with galvanised wire to be afterwards replaced; but in quite small things the wiring is artistically done, and the silver or copper wiring is definitive. The bones are next put into water, which is often changed— say twice a week in warm weather; they are then taken out, dried by exposure to the sun and air, put into water again, and so on until nicely whitened, and no bleaching by chloride of lime, nor by chlorine in any form, nor by lime in any form is ever necessary, and therefore bones managed in this way are strong, sharp, and clear, and there is no fear of losing the smallest bone, whilst the cleanly and inodorous character of the process is a sufficient recommendation.

Of course with large subjects, and indeed with nearly all, the carcase may be conveniently divided into six parts—the skull, the body or " cage," and the four limbs—whilst being cleaned and wired.

Boiling the bones, after steeping in salt and wiring, is the quickest and most cleanly process of all, but is apt, unless all of the bones are well drilled and syringed at first, to cause grease to set within the porosities or cancellated tissue, and to remove this the cold water process is necessary, although re-boiling in plenty of water charged with Hudson's soap is often efficacious.   Strange to say, skulls seldom or never grease in boiling if proper precautions are taken, and fishes' skeletons never, if the flesh is just scalded off the bones.   Sometimes, however, in spite of the utmost care in boiling, there is one bone or another, either in a mammal or bird, which will persist in remaining greasy, and this bone must then be treated by itself.

In hunting expeditions, it is impossible to do more than roughly trim the bones, to disarticulate the skull and limb-bones, and to pack them within the "cage" of the body to take up as little space as possible.   Nearly every arsenic-advocate advises the thick painting of such a rough specimen with his favourite poison ; such men should be allowed to do nothing else than to try to trim, macerate, and bleach arsenically- prepared skeletons, which, if it did not make them wiser, would certainly make them sadder men.

The actual methods of wiring the bones together, and the preparation of ligamentary skeletons, are so much matters of individual expertness that they need not be described, coming easily with a little experience.   A correspondent has, however, described his method of dispensing with wires in making a ligamentary skeleton of some size, and, as this appears to have borne the test of practicability, it is worth mentioning :—

I find that after clipping and macerating has gone on till the flesh ceases to "fur" in the water, the ligaments remain tenacious.   At this period I wash the entire skeleton with chloride of lime and water, using, of course, great care, and, after brushing the object with a soft brush and rinsing it, I set it up with props in the required attitude (of course the skull has *always* to be detached).   The skeletons dry in the required position with the ligaments, which shrink to nothing, and hold for ever. I have not only used this method with moles, bats, a jerboa, etc., but with cats, monkeys, large fish, and even human limbs—all with great success. This I term the "natural" method, but although I discovered the process for myself, yet it is probably well known.[1] It has the merit of saving an infinity of trouble, and shows no wires. Should a joint come apart I fasten it again with gum tragacanth, and usually the skull in this manner. Tragacanth, as you are doubtless aware, dries with hardly any bulk. LIONEL E. ADAMS.

A cartilaginous sternum is best treated, after careful steeping in water, by the process given at p. 34 (Formulæ 7 and 8).

Ordinarily, animals are represented with the bones arranged in one of the positions the animal assumes in life, and this has been carried even farther, for a dog's skeleton has been represented as holding that of a rat, and so on until the culminating point was reached by the arrangement of the skeleton of the man and horse as in motion at the South Kensington Museum, all duly enhanced by a background, in black velvet, showing the contours of the bodies.

For biological students, other methods of setting up have been devised, and probably the plan now followed in the Leicester Museum is, although somewhat diagrammatic, a little improvement on some of them, whilst the charting of the bones—both of existing and extinct vertebrate animals—by distinguishing colours is believed to be confined at present to this institution.

Leather

The making of leather hardly comes within the scope of such a work as this, but, as there may be some persons hardy enough to do the dirtiest possible work, involving a maximum of trouble with a minimum of gain, they are referred to an article upon leather by Mr. James Paton, Curator of the Corporation Galleries of Art, Glasgow, *Encyclopædia Britannica*, ninth

[1] This is so ; see Boitard, Granger, Gestro, and others.

edition, vol. xiv., pp. 381-390; but, as it may be useful to know how such skins as those of deer, rabbits, moles, etc., are dressed, the article upon the making of "calf-kid" (or White Leather) *i.e.* "Tawing"—is given here (see *op. cit.*, p. 389) :—

The tawing itself is accomplished in a drum or cylinder the same as the currier's stuffing wheel, into which is introduced for one hundred average skins a mixture consisting of 20 lbs. of alum, 9 lbs. salt, 40 lbs. flour, 250 eggs (or about 1⅓ gallons of egg yolk), ⅞ pint of olive oil, and 12 to 16 gallons of water. In this mixture, at a temperature of not more than 100° Fahr., the skins are worked for about forty minutes, by which action the tawing is completed. After the withdrawal from the drum the skins are allowed to drain, dried rapidly by artificial heat, damped, staked out by drawing them over a blunt steel tool, and then wetted and shaved down on the beam to the required thickness. Next they receive, if necessary, a second treatment with the tawing mixture.

It would appear by this that the proportions for a small skin would be :—

87.—Tawing Solution

Flour	.	.	.	.	6½ oz.
Alum	.	.	.	.	3¼ ,,
Salt	.	.	.	.	1½ ,,
Olive oil	.	.	.	.	1½ drachms (fluid)
Eggs	.	.	.	.	2 to 3

Water (warm), a sufficient quantity to mix with the above and to cover the skin. Treat as above directed.

A variant of the preceding is a recipe given to the writer by a correspondent. He writes :—

The following is a recipe for "white" dressing of skins, which was given to me by a tanner. In my opinion, it reduces the work to a minimum : Wash the hide clean ; shave or scrape the flesh down thin. (In small skins I find that a good washing does almost as well.)

88.—Tawing Solution

Rock salt	.	.	.	.	2 lbs.
Alum .	.	.	.	.	1 lb.
Sal ammoniac	.	.	.	.	1 oz.
Water (warm) .	.	.	.	.	2 gals.

Spread the hide, stretched flesh side up, in a shady place, and cover it with a coating of solution. When dry, continue as before until the flesh is white; then it is "tanned" through. Cover the hide with bran to remove salt. Soften by rubbing over a shovel-blade or by beating with a club. Large skins should be softened during the drying. Of course it would be best to thoroughly clean before applying the solution, but for experiments I have dressed rabbits' skins without even washing them, and they have come out all right. This is the only preparation that I have successfully dressed cavies' skins with. J. E. KNIGHT.

NEWPORT, MONMOUTHSHIRE.

CHAPTER VI

THE SKINNING AND SETTING-UP OF BIRDS BY VARIOUS METHODS

DIVISION I

THE CLEANING OF FEATHERS, THE SKINNING OF BIRDS, AND THE MAKING OF A "SKIN"

UNDENIABLY the most popular section of taxidermy is that vulgarly known as "bird-stuffing," and, like some other vulgar terms, it is literally true in the sense that the origin of the art was founded upon the actual stuffing-out of the creature's skin, performed by what is called the loose method, and by means of wool, wadding, moss, tow, shavings, straw, hay, and so on. Although, as just stated, of great popularity and of respectable antiquity, the methods have not altered very much since Captain Brown—whom the Americans and others take as a guide—wrote his treatise more than sixty years ago, and the "stuffers" of the present day deviate as little as possible from the ancient and incorrect systems, and almost unanimously agree to do their worst in a manner as devoid of artistic feeling, and as unlike nature, as may be compassed by clumsy fingers guided by an unlearned or a clouded brain. Further, there are some amongst them who never improve ; to them a bird is a "skin," and they invest it with their own sombre personality instead of with the bird's own *riante* elegance and perfection of form.

The difficulties and pitfalls which surround "bird-stuffing" are most amusingly told by the Rev. Henry Housman.[1]

Directly a bird is shot, the mouth and *nostrils* should be plugged with cotton wool to prevent the flow of blood and other matter, this being very important as tending to keep the bird clean and preventing future trouble : so important is it, indeed, that, whenever possible, it should be done in the field, and, if no wool be at hand and the bird bleed much, moss should be used, or even sand.

Each bird should be wrapped in a separate piece of paper, and, when practicable, another receptacle in addition to the game-bag should be carried, in which birds intended to be set up should be placed by themselves : an ordinary fish-basket —a "bass" as it is termed—will do very nicely, and can be easily carried by the attendant who carries the cartridge-bag. If shooting without an attendant, however, it would be as well to have a game-bag made with an outside pocket, in which the specimens could be placed, and thus kept distinct from the ordinary game. Otherwise, it is possible to procure at a small cost, at any gunmaker's, a handy, leather-lined, tanned-canvas game-bag, inside the mouth of which are attached loops of cord on which discs of leather play freely, and in these loops regulated by the discs, from three to six brace of partridges can be suspended by the neck, whilst birds of other kinds, intended for preservation, lie in the bottom of the bag, well protected by paper and wadding from any drip from the game-birds above.

Cleaning Feathers from Blood and Stains

The cleaning of a dead bird's feathers, whether from blood or dirt-stains, is an all-important process, without which the

---

[1] *The Story of our Museum : showing how we formed it and what it taught us,* pp. 30-37.

bird will never look well when set up.   In instances where the flow of blood emanates from the mouth or nostrils, the method should be to mix a little salt with warm water, and, by means of wadding dipped in it, sponge the feathers before the bird is skinned, changing the wadding as it becomes soiled.   If, however, the blood emanates from a shot-hole in connection with some artery, the blood will again flow directly the warm water and salt touches it, and this in spite of previous plugging ; in this case, therefore, the bird should be skinned first, and well cleaned before setting-up.   Although the addition of salt, as pointed out some years since in *Science* (U.S.A.), has a certain action on the hæmoglobin, yet the removal of the blood-stains by no means completes the process of restoring the feathers to a satisfactory state, for, as soon as the cleansing is accomplished, the feathers must be wiped " the way of the grain " with wadding dipped in benzoline, and, when a stain no longer appears, common plaster of Paris should be lightly dusted on, shaken off, fresh put on, and the specimen laid by until the feathers are clean and dry, when they should be gently beaten with a bunch of feathers, or with the softest part of the wing of a large bird, and afterwards with a soft brush, such as No. 19.   If properly done, the feathers become glossy and stainless, especially if finally brushed over lightly with benzoline or spirit.

Mud-stains are best treated with water and salt, followed, as usual, by the benzoline-and-plaster treatment, but grease-stains are not amenable to water-treatment, and therefore benzoline and plaster only must be used.   In very old and greasy skins, it will sometimes be found necessary to use turpentine to remove the stains, but, as this is in itself of a greasy or oily nature, it must be followed by the benzoline-and-plaster treatment.

Birds with black or very dark plumage require that the

plaster should be well beaten out of their feathers, and, if they should still look dull and dead, a very little benzoline lightly applied with wadding or a brush will restore the gloss, or, if not, a light application of methyl-alcohol will be sure to do so. In point of fact, all birds, before casing up, will be benefited by a brush-over either with benzoline or spirit, and, in instances where moths are suspected, the specimens may be absolutely plunged into turpentine followed by benzoline and plaster, or, if not in a very bad state, in benzoline alone followed by plaster.

It should be noted that the common benzoline (" benzol," " benzine " C_6H_6), at, perhaps, a shilling a gallon, is quite as efficacious as the very much more expensive " benzine collas."

The Skinning of a Bird

This, the alpha of the bird-taxidermist's art, bears the same relation to the setting-up as forming letters correctly does to finished writing, and, until a skin can be accurately shaped and neatly arranged, the beginner must not be allowed to "set up."

The first process, whether for making a skin or for setting up, is, of course, the removal of the body, leaving the skin and feathers intact ; and in all books, dating from the earliest times, the advice invariably given is to lay the bird upon its back, and to make the incision, through which the body is to be afterwards removed, *in the centre of the breast.*

Nothing is more wrong in theory and in practice ; it has not one single advantage to recommend it, whilst it bristles with numberless disadvantages. These are, that in the beginning the learner often cuts too low, or through the thin membrane which covers the intestines, and in either case a nasty mess is the result, and the bird is half spoiled ; again, the skin is usually torn at the edges and flattened out. In making up, great difficulty is experienced in getting the shape of the breast anything like the original, and in nearly every instance it must be sewn up. To say nothing of the difficulty of getting the feathers to lie in position and not show a draggled and untidy line, there is the *certainty*, especially in white or light-breasted birds, of a greasy or dark line showing sooner or later, and, in fact, *the* very part of a bird which should be least disturbed is clumsily cut into and as clumsily rearranged.

It is supposed that this method of flaying, probably derived from the practice of some primæval butcher, is easier for the beginner to learn than any other system.   Nothing of the kind ! and so convinced is the writer, from observation of the proceedings of numberless pupils, that a sound method of skinning can be learned as easily as an unsound one, that no description of the " flaying" method will be perpetuated here ; the proper method—that of *skinning out from under the wing*, which has everything to recommend it and absolutely nothing against it— being given, in the hope that it will entirely supersede the crudities of the older method.

At the outset, it may be stated that a bird of sufficient size should be procured.   A starling, although one of the best of birds for such a purpose owing to the extraordinary toughness of its skin in proportion to its size, is, however, rather too small for the beginner to practise upon.   Really a rook is the best bird, but, as this cannot always be procured, a domestic pigeon, which can be, is perhaps the next best,—that is to say as regards size. It must, however, be observed that the skin of a pigeon is by no means tough, and difficulties may occur, which are to be guarded against when skinning over the back ; and, if the pupil is too clumsy, or too well endowed with extra-sized fingers, he would do well to try upon a starling, which only a budding taxidermist with more than ordinary strength can very well damage. However, for the purposes of this chapter, and especially for the sake of the figures, a pigeon has been chosen throughout, this being a bird, moreover, which most text-books of biology choose for demonstrations, and thus familiarity with some of its parts may make it a stepping-stone to further research.

Let the pigeon, therefore, however killed, have a plug of wool placed in the throat, pushed down and pulled out again by means of the crooked awl, to cleanse the mouth from any blood or other impurities ; let one also be run through the nostrils in like manner, and finally insert another plug of clean wool through the nostrils and in the throat, not, however, so large a piece as to unduly distend the latter. Now lay the bird upon its back on a clean sheet of paper, and make a note of the colour of the eyes, bill, legs and toes ; note also the positions assumed by the legs and wings in relation to the body, and the general shape and length of the bird as a guide to future operations.

Let the bird's head point towards the right hand, and, taking the pliers, No. 10, in that hand, seize the quill feathers with the left ; stretch the wing to its full extent, place the nose of the pliers close to the junction of the wing with the body and snap the bone with them. Do the same with the other wing. Now observe which side of the bird is the better, that is to say, the less shot or the cleaner, and choose the worse side upon which to make the first incision. In determining which is the better side of a bird, the condition of the head should be the first consideration, and, if this be much shot, that damaged side will be chosen as the worse, not only on account of the difficulty which the tyro will experience in dealing with such a specimen, but also because the better side will ultimately be the " show " side, and the head is, perhaps, the most important part in giving character to a bird.

Having, therefore, selected the worse side, turn the bird's head diagonally to the front and to the left, and, taking the scalpel No. 4 or 6 in the right hand, part, with the left, the feathers just under the wing at the side of the breast, and there make an incision with the point of the knife for not more than half an inch, the fingers of the left hand meanwhile holding the wing away from the body, whilst either the thumb or the finger rests upon it as the case may be. Through the small opening thus made, the flesh of the body appears; and now, exactly reversing the position of the bird so that the tail will point away, hold down the wing with the fingers of the left hand, slip the point of the knife in between the skin and the flesh, and, cutting upwards so that only the skin and not the flesh is cut, continue over the first joint of the leg, *i.e.* the femur (see Plates VIII. and X.), where it should end. This, in a pigeon, makes an incision exactly three inches in length, and is shown on Plate IX., Fig. 1, the cut having been opened out rather more than would otherwise be the case, for the purpose of demonstration.

Now, with the cutting-edge of the knife directed towards the flesh, loosen the edges of the skin for some little distance over the back—say half an inch or so,—holding it away meanwhile with the fingers of the left hand. Do the same along the other edge over the wing, breast, and thigh (femur). This, being done with a scraping movement, although the cutting-edge be directed toward the flesh, will loosen the skin without any fear of cuts. Having freed all around rather more than directed for the back, insert a thin layer of wadding between the flesh and skin to prevent the soiling of the feathers.

Holding now the wing closed, the fingers and thumb of the left hand opposing, free very carefully around the wing towards the broken bone, and then, slipping the knife underneath, make an upward cut and entirely sever the wing from the body, at the fracture. If the bone is not properly broken, or if they come handier, the shears (No. 8) may be used instead of the knife. Probably, with all care, a little flesh will still remain attached to the skin and to that part of the bone of the wing

VIII.

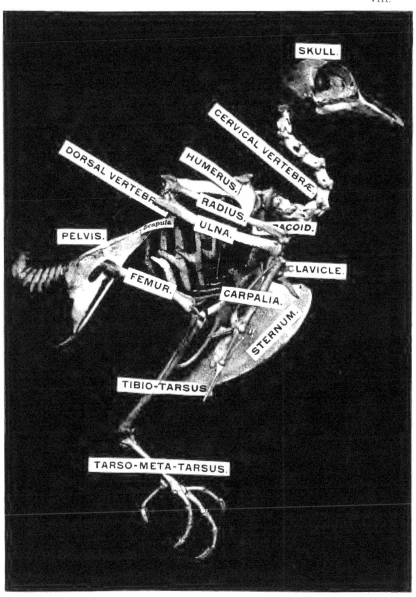

SKELETON OF A PIGEON.

left upon the body ; if so, this must be delicately freed from
its attachment, and the greatest care is to be taken now, as
this is the place, if any, where holes will be made. The skin
having been released all round, the wing falls away from
the body, and the broken bone shows plainly. Leaving this
part, push the leg up a little from the outside, and, holding the
foot in the palm of the hand, place the thumb and fingers in
such a manner that the front and back edges of the junction
of the femur with the tibio-tarsus appear, so that the shears
(No. 8) may be introduced underneath to cut the bone through.
Probably the whole of the flesh will not be quite freed from
that which holds it below ; in that case, take the knife and
entirely free it, when, the foot being pulled from the outside, the tibio-tarsus will fall within the skin leaving the femur
attached to the body. Now, returning to the neck, observe
a little membrane—that of the crop—and push it away from
the skin and on to the body with the fingers, then, seizing it
with the right hand, take the head of the bird in the palm of
the left hand, gently push the neck within the skin, pulling the
crop-membrane *gently* away meanwhile with the right hand
until just under the fingers and thumb of the other hand. Now
holding the skin and feathers away from the flesh, the neck and
windpipe will appear, and, pushing the point of the scissors
underneath these in such a manner as not to cut the underlying
skin, snip them through. Again, as in the leg, perhaps a little
flesh or membrane may attach one to the other or to the underlying skin, and, if so, this must be snipped away. Letting the
head fall out of the fingers of the left hand, insert a little more
wadding under the cut edges of the skin, and wrap a piece of
wadding around the neck, or push a piece of wire through it, as
a further support by which to grasp it firmly. Fig. 2 on the
same plate shows the bird at this stage.

The skin, it will be observed, is still held at three points, viz.

the wing on the "best" side, the leg on the same side, and the tail. Again gripping the body with the left hand and keeping the feathers from touching the flesh, with the right forefinger and thumb release the skin a little more on the back and over the shoulder of the uncut wing. Release it also upon the breast on that side by working gently with the fingers, aided now and then by the knife when any little sticking occurs. Ease it on the body with the fingers, working towards the tail, and skin away a little more on the back with the knife, being careful to note that on the back the skin is extremely thin, and must therefore be laboriously scraped, as it will not bear the slightest pull with the fingers. If this be properly accomplished, the skin may be so loosened on the body as to come away from under the wing, giving an opportunity for the knife to be slipped in as before, and the upward cut made, to entirely detach the wing at its broken portion. Great care is as usual required at this point, as the skin comes well underneath the bone, and will be cut right through if not carefully watched. Still skinning by scraping upon the flesh, the other thigh (femur) is exposed, and should be pushed up from the outside as before, and cut through in the same place with the shears, taking care not to include any skin, trimming away with the knife any small pieces which prevent it clearing. Having done this, the progress toward the tail is necessarily slow, the skin becoming thinner and thinner over the back until it has to be positively scraped from the bone, to which it clings with tenacity. The skin must also be released from the abdomen, to which it also clings, and the cutting here must be hardly appreciable; otherwise, the membrane which covers the bowels will be cut into, to the great damage of the feathers of the specimen. With such a bird as a pigeon, all this scraping and gentle cutting-away of the skin may take a quarter of an hour or more, until, the bird being still kept in the left hand, neck pointing upward, the feathers preserved from contact with the inside of the skin, and the wings and head resting on the operating-table, the lowermost points of the pelvis (*i.e.* the pubes)—points of two small bones which stick out and rather impede the way—are passed. At this juncture it will, perhaps, be as well to let the body lie on its back upon the table, merely supporting the tail part above and below with the fingers of the left hand while gentle scraping goes on, and turning it from front to back if necessary, until, in the front, the vent is reached, and, at the back, the oil-gland of the tail; the knife must be slipped underneath and around each until the final severance is made which disconnects the skin from the body. The sex should then be determined—an important matter in all cases, too often neglected by the ordinary taxidermist. Cut through the ribs, therefore, of one side with a pair of scissors and pushing aside the intestines, etc., look in the hollow of the back, and if the bird is a male there will be observed two whitish-yellow (sometimes blackish and small) oval bodies, one rather lower than the other, attached to the upper *lobes* of the kidneys and close against the vertebræ. But if it is a female, one irregularly-shaped mass, showing variously-sized (often small) egg-like bodies, will be found in the same position and partly covering the *left* kidney only (the right ovary only appearing in the embryo). Except in the breeding season, these organs both in male and female birds are small and often difficult to determine, and a further complication may arise from the *adrenals* being mistaken for the male organs. The adrenals, however, are longer, yellower, and for two-thirds of the year much smaller than the testes; moreover, they are situated a little higher, viz. at the upper *ends* of the kidneys.

The Trimming of the Skin

The body having been removed from the skin, the trimming of all flesh from the tail, legs, wings and head com-

mences, and the tail, being already in the hand at this point, will
be the first to be trimmed. With, therefore, the scissors (No. 9)
and the knife, cut and trim away all flesh and fat, not only
from around the tail itself, but from the skin which surrounds
it, should any have been left on. The legs next require the
skin freed from them down to the joint (the junction of
the tibio-tarsus with the tarso-meta-tarsus), taking care, when
cutting the ligaments away, not to cut so low as to pierce
through to the outside. The ligaments being cut all around
with the point of a knife, the whole of the flesh may be stripped
from the bone with the finger and thumb. The wings are now
to be trimmed, and are, perhaps, the most tiresome. All the
flesh in sight must be trimmed away, as also the pieces of
broken bone, but the part still attached to the wing must be
left for the present, as it is something to lay hold of. It will
be observed that there are two skins, as it were, to the wing,
i.e. that above and that below the wing, and the one on the
under side must be loosened until the flesh surrounding those
bones known as the ulna and radius (see skeleton, Plate VIII.)
becomes visible. This requires a considerable amount of
delicate management to expose a little pocket of skin in which
the flesh lies. In some cases, however, it is possible to expose
these bones by laying hold of the humerus. Now disjoint the
small piece of broken bone, or all that remains of the humerus,
and, by cutting with scissors and scraping with a knife, the
flesh remaining on the ulna and radius can be removed. It is
important that this should be done, as there is much more
flesh in that part than would appear; it must be quite
understood, however, that the skin is not to be freed from
those bones on the *top* of the wing. Both wings having been
freed from flesh, nothing remains but the head and neck;
this latter being seized in whichever hand is more convenient,
the fingers of the other hand are employed in pressing the skin

over the neck towards the beak until, the back of the head being reached, the skin is found to stick on each side of the skull, namely, at the ears, and, if the finger and thumb be dipped in plaster or sand, it is possible to " pinch " these away, or to pull them right out from their attachments ; otherwise, the knife must be used, but in all cases a pull is preferable. The eyeballs now appear, and the skin is attached as a thin membrane to the centre of each. This must be very carefully severed by cutting downwards, or, rather, towards the back of the head, and, when quite free, the brain-scoop (No. 7) must be put into the orbit on the side nearest the beak, pushed well under the eyeball, and, by the aid of the thumb pressing gently against it, this must be pulled out, care being taken not to burst it. In any case, press a plug of wool into the orbit, directly the eyeball is removed, to clean it out. The skin is still held on the top of the skull, and must be relieved with the knife or the brain-scoop until well up to the base of the beak. A little more skinning away is required under the orbits, and at the sides of the face, and also in front of the orbits, so that the skin will only hang just by the base of the beak, care being taken not to cut so far as the gape.

If the tongue is not required to be kept, slip the knife between that and the skull, pull forward, and the tongue and windpipe will come away. Disarticulate the neck where it joins the head, but do not cut away the back of the skull as is usually done, as the brains may be extracted easily from the back of the orbits. Figure 3 on Plate IX. shows the skin at this juncture turned inside out.

Take now the preservative (Formula 57), and well paint every part of the skin, the skull, the bones of the wings, legs, and tail, taking care not to paint the feathers during this operation. Return the skin to its normal position—*i.e.* with the feathers outside—and then will come—

The Making of the " Skin "

Fill the skull, through the opening at the back of the orbits, with some chopped tow (made by cutting it up with scissors); the orbits themselves may be filled with wadding, but this must never be used where there is any possibility of a wire or pin being needed, as it will not allow even the sharpest wire to pass. All of this must be thinly plastered over with soft clay (or with modelling-composition Formula 71), to allow of the shape being corrected when the head is turned, and also to prevent shrinkage of that part. Especially must the clay be well forced in about the beak and at the sides of the face. The throat is also to be partially filled, where needed, with cut tow. The skin of the neck should now be gathered up in the fingers of both hands, and the thumbs and forefingers used to return the head through the neck to its proper position, care being taken that the bill does not catch in the skin and tear it. By judicious handling the bill will appear, and, by pulling this gently and by pushing with the fingers, the head will ultimately be returned as in nature. To assist this, a thread may have been previously. tied in the nostrils and around the beak. Arrange the ruffled feathers with a fine needle, and if some part stretches or forms ridges upon the clay inside, use the needle as a pricker to bring the feathers backward or forward—usually backward. The hollow bags of the wings, lying over the bones from which the flesh was removed, now require filling with cut tow to replace this loss, and a threaded needle should be passed through the hollows between the bones (ulna and radius) and around the radius of each wing, the ends of the thread being then drawn together until the distance between the wings is as in nature.

The leg-bones are the only members left which require consideration, and these are to be bound with tow wrapped around them to the shape of the flesh removed, and, if this be done well and tightly, there will be no need to wrap it over with binding cotton. Having done this, pull the legs back to their proper positions.

Nothing now remains but to make a false body and insert it, for although the body for a skin is not made so tightly as for a bird about to be set up, yet the advantages of a made body over a loose one are manifold. First place the bird upon its back, and, bringing the whole of the skin—especially that of the neck—to a little less than the length of the bird in life, take a piece of fairly stout wire (No. 17 will do nicely), of such a length that, one end coming up into the skull (not through it) when the neck is properly shortened, the other shall fall just within the tail, the measurement of such wire being determined by the notes previously taken (see p. 171) and by the natural body (see Fig. 6, Plate IX.), which should be kept in front of the pupil as a guide.

Now, calculating the depth of the skull inside to where the neck joins, leave a corresponding length of the wire uncovered —probably about half an inch—and, taking some tow or very fine "packing," wind it upon the wire below until it assumes the length and shape of the natural neck. From this point, guided by the natural body, proceed to swell the tow, winding it firmly, but not too tight and hard, until it assumes the shape required ; at the same time, do not make it of quite the height of the body from back to breast, as a "skin" should be much flatter upon the breast than is quite natural, for convenience in packing it away in cabinets, etc. Note that the body rapidly narrows toward the tail ; at that end of the wire, therefore, the tow must be wrapped around thinly and come to an apex, and, to prevent slipping, the wire may be just turned up upon the body.

From time to time, flatten the artificial body, and where

refractory bind it with hemp; but this should be used as sparingly as possible for a skin, and, indeed, not at all when practice has made perfect. No notice need be taken of the femora when making a skin, and, therefore, the artificial body will be a pear-shaped object, and not so full as shown in Fig. 5, Plate IX. Taking the artificial body in the right hand, raise the bird's skin with the left, and, having cleared the orifice of the neck with the tool No. 17, or by blowing up it—which may be done with a blowpipe,—insert the point of the wire, followed by the artificial neck, into the palatal part of the skull, and, if possible, without the end of the wire being sharpened ; then, with a little dexterity, the whole of the body may be inserted into the skin, the breast feathers brought over the breast of the artificial body, and the tail into contact with its apex. Turn the skin over, settle the wings in proper position, get the feathers around those parts generally, and the whole of the back into good order, using the flat-nosed pliers No. 14, the awl No. 26 or 27, and the brush No. 19, to aid this process, and further, to prevent the wings dropping, secure them in position by passing long pins through them into the false body.

With care the bird may now be turned over, and rested either upon a strip of soft paper or within the trough used for shaping skins. The latter is simply a piece of board with two sides of any height according to the size of the "skin," but in this case of about two and a half inches, over which is tacked a piece of "strawboard" (a common and cheap kind of cardboard) in a concave position as described by an American writer.[1] In this trough, in which a thin layer of wadding should be placed, the bird rests breast uppermost, and that part now requires attention. The feathers must be finally settled in position, brought over the butts of the wings, and neatly arranged upon the breasts and sides, the legs just crossed and

[1] Batty, *Practical Taxidermy.*

IX.

PIGEONS, EXHIBITING METHOD OF SKINNING FROM UNDER THE WING (FIGS. 1, 2, 3); A MADE "SKIN" (FIG. 4);
A NATURAL BODY (FIG. 6); AND AN ARTIFICIAL BODY (FIG. 5).

tied, or, in some birds, brought together by a stitch passing
through the skin underneath, and at the junction of the tarso-
meta-tarsus, and the head arranged as shown in the figure, turned
on one side, which, though more difficult to subsequently set up,
is, perhaps, better for the cabinet, and is decidedly so in the case
of long-billed birds. All being settled, cotton or hemp may
be wound a few times around to keep any refractory feathers in
position, but can be dispensed with in time.

The paper strip or band is more used by professionals, as
giving less trouble and taking up less space than a series of
troughs, and is easily arranged around a bird after the feathers
are settled, and the two ends brought together and pinned.
Mr. Maynard [1] recommends a skin to be wrapped closely "in a
very thin layer of nice cotton batting (wadding), taking care
that the feathers lie perfectly smooth, although these may be
partially arranged through the cotton, which must be thin
enough for the feathers to be seen through it. The skin is then
laid aside to dry, without placing it in the form" (trough).

In the Leicester Museum, two or three cross bands of thin
tissue-paper have been used with advantage to supersede this
last method. In all methods it may be necessary to look at
the skin before it sets, and to correct any irregularities. Finally,
a card should be attached to the legs, containing all information as
to sex, stage of maturity, date and place of capture, and initials of
collector on one side, and on the other should be written notes
as to the colours of the irides, bill, legs, and soft parts. These
matters should be noted for all animals, and especially when
collecting abroad. A well-shaped skin should appear as shown
in Fig. 4, Plate IX.

[1] *Manual of Taxidermy*, p. 54.

DIVISION II

THE SETTING-UP OF BIRDS WITH SOFT BODIES AND WITH-
OUT WIRES

Waterton's system of setting up birds, as explained by the late Rev. J. G. Wood [1] who knew him well, is based upon—(1) soft-body stuffing ; (2) the disuse of wires entirely ; and (3) by arranging and propping the specimen in a box with cotton wadding until nearly dry, and then finally setting it up in position by bending the legs and toes to any required angle.

This, it will be seen, is really nothing more than a " skin " with the eyes inserted and legs bent, and although it is not gainsaid that such a method will give good results in the hands of a man who has the requisite time, patience, and space at command, yet at best it is but an amateurish "fad," serves no useful purpose, and, whilst likely to get the amateur into bad methods of work, is an impossible system for the professional.

Why it serves no useful purpose, and why it should get the learner into bad methods, is because, in the first instance, the practice of skinning a bird upon the knee instead of a bench or table is inconvenient upon the face of it ; the soft system of stuffing also, which looks so very easy, is of that delusive nature which, with or without wires, is only well done by the very advanced, and the total removal of the skull leaves too much also to the immature judgment of the beginner ; indeed, the cutting away of the superciliary ridge, in the very bird (a hawk) selected by Waterton for the lesson, destroys all that peculiar character which gives expression to the Accipitres, and which no learner would know in the least how to restore. The recommendation to make the body larger than in life to

---

[1] *Taxidermy.* See Waterton's *Wanderings*, 1893.

allow for shrinkage is false in practice, for that is the very thing which is always done at first by the learner, with the result that the bare tracts—for, be it well remembered, the whole of a bird's skin is not covered with feathers—are unduly puffed out, and no subsequent treatment can restore them to the hollows in which they lay, and the feathers about the neck, wings, and breast start, and cannot be brought together in a natural manner. Let the learner take such a bird as a gull or a grebe (worst of all) and make the body too large, and then try to get the breast feathers into position without causing an unsightly line, and the feathers to part in opposite directions, and he will speedily find that there is no help for his troubles but taking some of the packing out, or, in the case of a hard body, replacing it by a smaller one.

Waterton's method, though very pretty in theory—and, in his hands, in practice,—is not one which commends itself as having any scientific value.

DIVISION III

THE SETTING-UP OF BIRDS WITH SOFT BODIES AND WIRES

This, the most ancient system of setting up birds, presupposes the incapacity of the worker, or his ignorance of the art of skinning out a bird's body from under the wing, as it is based upon the principle (or want of principle !) of "flaying."

There are many variations of wiring, but, of the foreign methods in vogue with the Italians, French, and Germans, the prettiest, neatest, and best figured is that by Granger.[1]

This wiring and soft-body making may be modified so as to be applicable to the skin opened under the wing, in which case the wiring need not be so elaborate, and a more simple method is as follows :—

[1] *Manuel du Naturaliste*, pp. 244-246, Figs. 230, 231, 232.

Let four wires be provided ; one—the longest, pointed at both ends—is the body-wire ; two others, also pointed, are for the legs, and the fourth one, bent in this manner ⌐‾‾‾‾‾⌐ is for the wings. Let the ends of this latter be pushed into the hollow bones of the wings, after a sufficiency of wadding or tow has been laid inside the skin along the back. The length of the bar is determined by the distance between the wings in nature. The longest wire is next taken, and a loop made in it to come about the centre of the skin. One end (the longest from the loop) is then pushed up the previously stuffed neck and head until it comes out at the centre of the skull, and so far through as to let the other end fall within the skin ; when this is so, push that end through the root of the tail from the inside, taking care that the wire is well packed underneath to prevent it, and all others, from touching the skin. The leg-wires only remain now to be considered, and these, being pushed up the legs in the ordinary manner, are thrust through the loop upon the body-wire and twisted around securely so that all is perfectly rigid. Proceed by shaping the various parts, and by filling in with the packing until finished sufficiently to sew up. As stated just before, soft-body setting-up is only well done by those who have great experience, and does not in any way help the learner, as setting-up by the hard-body plan does, unless, indeed, the skeleton is used as described later, at p. 199, and shown on Plate XI.

DIVISION IV.

THE SETTING-UP OF BIRDS WITH HARD BODIES

Probably the origin of the hard body was the wine-cork, through which a wire extended from head to tail, the leg-wires, and sometimes the wing-wires, being pushed in at an angle and their ends turned down and made fast where they came through. This was the system affected by "Joe Wise," of Mr. Housman's book. Then came the body formed from a piece of peat; it was undoubtedly an advance upon the cork, inasmuch as it was shaped into some rough semblance of a body, but it was hard and unyielding, and was a dirty, awkward plan with nothing but quickness in manufacture to commend it. Bodies made of moss, hay, straw, and shavings have been used, but there is nothing comparable with the fine wood-fibre ("excelsior") now used in packing various goods, or with tow, commonly used by all except American taxidermists.

Assuming the skin of the pigeon to be ready for setting up, nine pieces of wire are first of all got ready, and filed into a point which is either three- or five-sided, these "bayonet points" being far superior in penetration to the rounded points; one piece, gauge No. 17, a little longer than the bird, say about ten inches in length; one piece, gauge No. 18, about seven inches in length, bent for the wings (see preceding figure, p. 184); two others, of the same gauge, about five inches in length, also for the wings; two, gauge No. 15, about fourteen inches in length, for the legs; two, gauge No. 18, about four and a half inches in length, for the thighs; and the ninth, gauge No. 18, about five inches in length, for the tail.

Next comes the question of the artificial body, and for this the natural body (Fig. 6, Plate IX.), having been retained, is, as before, taken as a guide. Its measurements are, still presuming the pigeon to be the model, five inches in length, and two and a half inches across the back at its widest part, where the wings have been cut away, and gradually tapering to the tail. Its greatest height from breast-bone to back is also two and a half inches, but it will be seen by the figure that it rapidly slopes from this to the tail. One point usually lost sight of, and to be well considered, is that the thighs are of the same width across the back as are the wings, viz. two and a half inches, and it must be settled now whether the artificial body is to taper regularly, or to be swelled out there to allow for the thighs (femora), or whether these shall be made up independently of the body upon the leg-wires.

Take the body-wire, and make an artificial body of tow upon it in the same manner as directed for the making of the "skin," but with these differences:—1. The neck must be longer, that is to say of the exact length of nature. 2. The body must not be quite so flat upon the breast. 3. It should be well wrapped with thread or cotton, and made firmer than for the skin. 4. As a further advantage, greatly assisting the natural shape of the bird when set up, false thighs, *i.e.* femora, should be added.

These are made, each one separately, by winding tow around a piece of thin wire to the shape and length of those left on the natural body, the free ends of the wires being pushed into the artificial body, and arranged to be brought forward or straight according as the bird is intended to stand, and bound upon the body with thread ; or they may be left free, providing the other ends of the wires are made fast by turning in, and this is an advantage when the exact position of the bird is not quite determined upon, as the thighs can then be moved forward or backward at will.

Another matter constantly lost sight of is, that in nature there is a distinct hollow between the clavicles, in which the neck fits when the bird is at rest, and the excessive filling-up of this always results in an unnatural or strained appearance at that part, caused by the fact that, although the bird's artificial neck is of the natural length, yet there is no hollow arranged for, wherein to fit it, to shorten it for certain attitudes. This trouble may be easily obviated by beating, and pressing, and binding the tow in at that place so that the neck may rest within it if necessary, and in any event the straining across the breast, which is so unnatural, is avoided. Figure 5, Plate IX., shows the artificial body rather larger than the natural one (Fig. 6), which was that of a small pigeon (Fig. 3).

With these exceptions the making of the body is practically the same as for a " skin," but before the artificial body is coaxed into the skin the wings must be wired, and this is done by pointing the piece, gauge No. 18, at both ends, bending it into the shape shown on p. 184, and pushing the ends into the hollow bones of the humeri, which should be left, or, if removed, into the hollows of the ulnæ, in which latter case the bent ends of the wire must, of course, be longer, and in either case the points must bite, or must come through the bones and be turned. Fill up, as before described, any spaces whence flesh has been removed, and place the bones, now held by a cross-bar of wire, in their natural positions ; a *very* little tow or thin paper should underlie the wire bar, and upon this the body, shortly to be inserted, should rest. It is as well to consider that the wings, though springing from very near the top of the back, are not quite so high as the artificial body, placed upon the *top* of the wire, makes it appear ; the bar, therefore, must be a *trifle* longer than the width in nature, so that, when the body comes upon it, it can be arched a little, and so cause the wing-bones to fall into their correct position in relation to the back.

After the wings are placed in position (*and note beforehand their distances, when closed, from the end of the tail*), the body must be carefully coaxed into the skin, and in this instance the neck-wire, being pointed, with a much longer end free than for the " skin," is to be thrust into the skull and through to the outside of the head. Next take one of the leg-wires, and, the tibio-tarsus having been bound as it was for the " skin," hold the leg of the unopened side in the left hand, and, with the right, insert the wire at the sole of the foot, pass it up the skin at the back of the leg, and, holding it firmly at the tarso-meta-tarsal joint—where the point of the wire will endeavour to break out, but must be repressed,—continue past that and get the wire up through the tow, or at the back of the wrapped tibio-tarsus, until it appears within the body. Now slip the artificial body out of the skin at the lower part, and observe where the distal[1] end of the artificial femur appears; thrust into and through the body the point of the wire, and, clenching it on the opened side, bring the proximal end of the tibio-tarsus against the end of the artificial femur, and bend the wire so that the leg lies naturally. Probably to do this the leg will have to be drawn up or down the wire. If the toes and legs are dry, or any difficulty occurs in getting the wire up, the leg-drill (No. 20) must be used to prepare the way.

Now re-insert the body, do the same thing with the leg on the opened side, and, after bringing it against the femur, which is easily seen through the opening, make it fast by the aid of the pliers wherever most convenient. A professional would doubtless get it through to the other side and fix it by touch, but, as a learner would be more than likely to rip the skin in attempting this, he must be content to make it fast where he can. The bird may now be roughly set up in position, and the ninth wire pushed up through the root of the tail into the artificial body without being clenched.

The bird is now ready for fixing upon a stand or perch, which, usually of turned wood, but sometimes of metal or ivory for exhibition purposes, is replaced for actual work by a roughly-constructed one. This is invariably either one piece of wood nailed end-ways upon another, or a T-shaped piece, but, the

---

[1] *Proximal* is that end of a limb or bone nearest to the body or to the point of attachment, whilst *distal* is that end most remote, a familiar example, and one to be easily remembered, being that the upper bone of the arm—*i.e.* the humerus—has its *proximal* extremity at the shoulder, and its *distal* extremity at the elbow.

former being unsuitable in allowing no freedom of action, and the latter being always insecure and ill-balanced, one of the assistants in the Leicester Museum put together the much more stable and easily-made article shown on Plate XI., an improvement upon which is one with the top piece sloping downward, so that the bird may be arranged with one foot higher than the other to give variety. The distance between the feet, and their relative positions being determined and measured, corresponding holes are bored in this top piece, through which the ends of the leg-wires are inserted and bent under to hold firmly.

The bird is now upon the stand, roughly shaped, and probably more out of shape from the fixing. It must next be arranged in the position it is to finally assume, the legs placed properly, and the neck, as that of a perching bird, bent downwards to fall within the cavity, and then bent back upon itself (see Plate XI.). This is a difficult matter to describe, but—done with both hands—comes with practice. All imperfections in modelling are now to be made good by the insertion of small pieces of tow through the opening under the wing, but, before deciding that these are really imperfections, bring the feathers into position, and bear in mind what is systematically ignored, even by fairly-skilled professionals—that the arrangement of the feathers by pricking the skin with a fine needle from *tail to head*, and from side to side, is, in many instances, of much more value, and gives better results, than the sleeking of feathers from *head to tail*. Be quite sure that the abdomen falls neatly into shape between the legs and by the tail, and, when all is fairly right, take one of the two five-inch wing-wires, insert the point through the first two or three primaries at about two and a half inches (in the pigeon) below the flexure of the wing, or, taking the skeleton as an example, below the lowest (*i.e.* the second) digit, pass it underneath, following the natural arch of the wing, and push the point into the body high up ; the effect of this is that the lower part of the wing, as the upper, rests upon an arch of wire, the top end of which is thrust into the body, and the other end through the stiff part of the wing below, this being a better method than that of sticking a wire or a pin straight in as is usually done. Having quite settled the question as to more filling on the opened side, pin up the feathers of the flank under the wing of that side, wire the wing as on the other side, and the bird is complete, all but binding or " cottoning." The head-wire must, however, be cut off, and this is done by forcing the head gently upon the neck, thus temporarily shortening the latter a little, then cutting the wire, and afterwards pulling the head up until the wire rests *within* the skull ; if done, and the feathers pricked over, before the skin dries, the hole will never be seen.

Every bird, whether set up in a flying, or perching, or any other position, must have the tail, if not spread, at least with the feathers nicely overlapping one another from the centre, and these will not remain in that position unless certain precautions are taken in addition to binding. Take, therefore, a piece of thin cardboard, and cut it of double the width of the tail when spread to the extent desired, and of a sufficient length. Fold this in the middle and give it a slight curvature, and in the centre of one half make two holes a little distance from each edge. Through these holes thread a wire, just stout enough, when one end is pointed, to penetrate the body, and of a length to reach beyond the middle of the tail when firmly inserted. Push this wire, armed with the cardboard strip unfolded, into the body under the tail until the strip rests about the centre ; spread the tail as much as required, and, keeping it so, fold down the top half of the strip and stick a pin through the free ends to keep them together, another in the centre, and so on, regulating each feather whilst proceeding, and this, with the curvature previously given to the cardboard, will hold the tail firmly in position until the feathers are set. Often it will be found practicable to use the tail-wire, instead of an independent one, for this purpose ; and two separate strips of card will do, but not so well, as one folded. In large birds, it may be necessary to keep the curvature of the cardboard from getting out of shape by threading another wire throughout its length. Another method, but hardly necessary, is the making of arches of light wood to be used under the tail, with a permanently fixed wire, and a thread which passes over the arch from side to side and is held by slits therein, for the retention of the tail-feathers on their upper surface.

The binding is done after the bird is finally "feathered," which latter consists in pulling, and pricking, and brushing feathers into place. Procure some sharp pins ; fine steel pins with glass heads are the best for large birds, and may be used many times, and long entomological pins for small birds. Insert one or more of these in or along the centre of the back, one or more in the breast, one under the tail, and sometimes two in the flanks, making, with the ends of the two wires sticking out from the wings, several points of attachment.

Tie one end of the thread to one of the pins in the back, wind it over to one of the flank-wires or pins and back again, and so on, making use of any pin or wire which may be convenient, and binding with a light hand until quite sure that the feathers falling over the butts of the wings are well bound. When the back is done bind the breast, also from side to side, assisted by the centre pins, but there is no particular rule for doing this ; the only things to be considered are, not to tighten the threads too much, and that an expert will use half as much thread or cotton as a beginner, and do more work with it.

What is stated to be an improved method of binding was given by Mr. Frederic S. Webster,[1] and consists merely in

---

[1] *Second Annual Report American Taxidermists*, 1881-82, pp. 41-46.

using pointed wires instead of pins, and crooking them at one end, the binding-cotton resting within the crooks instead of upon the feathers. By this it is claimed that the feathers of the breast and back are not unduly pressed out of shape, but it is hard to see what end this serves, inasmuch as the binding-cotton is prevented from resting upon the very parts where it should take effect, and moreover, as already stated, it is only a very clumsy or untechnical taxidermist who gets his bird out of shape by binding ; indeed, the reverse should be the case, as often parts not quite satisfactory may be corrected by close binding.

To represent a bird upon the wing, the inside wiring is the same with these differences :—(1). The wires for the legs may be very much thinner, as they have no weight to support; (2) the addition of a strong wire, pointed and passed into the body through the incision, bolted securely by turning in the end, and of length sufficient to pass beyond the extent of the spread wing on that side, and to leave enough to be bolted into an upright stand whilst being set up, and into any background when finished ; (3) the outside wires are supplemented in some instances by two others which, inserted from the outside, pass along the flexures of the wings between the skin, and are hidden by the feathers ; (4) the binding is supplemented by many pieces of thin cardboard, which are pinned across, and under, and over the wings, and these, with more pins stuck into the body at the flanks, and more cross threading, serve to keep the feathers in position.

The appearance of a " bound " bird is shown on Plate X.

Artificial Eyes

The glass artificial eyes for some mammals and most birds are of two classes—black, without iris or pupil, and coloured, with a black pupil and a variously-coloured iris. French and

HAWK (KESTREL), SHOWING METHOD OF BRACING AND BINDING THE FEATHERS.

German-made eyes are far before the English in point of artistic excellence and variety of colour, but, although some prefer the rather flatter, thinner German eyes, there is no doubt that the French are the best. There is, however, a clever maker in Birmingham, who, when he likes, can make eyes to any tint and size, and has made some marvellously good imitations of human eyes, said to be superior to those made by the French.

Albeit the French and German eyes for mammals are often carefully and beautifully made, and in addition are veined, streaked, and cornered, some of the eyes for the Carnivora and Ungulata being very good, still, for high-class work, there is nothing which approaches half spheres, or, better still, half ovals, of thin glass, which can be painted in oil-colours from the inside in such a manner as to absolutely imitate the exact hues of any given eye. Unfortunately they cannot be made small enough for ordinary-sized birds, but for the larger birds and for medium-sized mammals, reptiles, and fishes they can be made. Commonly, eyes for the latter are made "clear," *i.e.* of white glass with a black pupil, and are coloured or gilded at the back by the taxidermist.

Although eyes should not stare, to obviate this there is no need to have them so flat as some do, for nearly every animal has a full, liquid-looking eye—some extraordinarily so—and therefore the French eyes are the best to use, and, if well set in the orbit, with the top eyelid drawn down a little, and both lids rather elongated at their corners by pinning them up with very fine entomological pins, a staring wooden expression will be avoided. The fact is, that eyelids are usually stretched too much and made too round, whilst the posterior angle of the eye is not brought forward enough to make the animal look to the front ; the eyes are flattened to the sides of the head in such a ridiculous manner that often the anterior angle looks backward,

13

and the animal could not possibly see in front of its nose or bill unless it protruded its eyes like a chameleon.

Many persons insert the eyes whilst the bird is being set up or directly afterwards, but the disadvantage of this is that, should there be any shrinking of the face or any other part of the head, the faults cannot easily be corrected, whereas, if the eyes are left out, corrections may be made through the orbits, if those parts be damped ; there is no doubt, therefore, that the best plan is to let the animal dry first, and, after damping the eyelids with cotton wool (wadding) dipped in warm water, and replacing, by small pieces of clay rolled in wadding, any clay which may have been dragged out, insert the eyes last, fixing them in their proper positions, and pinning the eyelids up to proper shape when required, with the finest entomological pins.

DIVISION V

THE MODELLING AND SETTING-UP OF BIRDS BY SCIENTIFIC PRINCIPLES

Although the principles enunciated in the preceding pages for the setting-up of birds are substantially correct, and are those which usually obtain with trained professionals, yet it must be evident, to both skilled and unskilled readers, that success is largely, nay, indeed, entirely dependent upon great skill and experience, and it is not too much to say that the niceties of pose, and especially the shape of the body and proper position of the head, wings, and legs are not fully appreciated, even by those who get their living as taxidermists, under a great number of years, and even then a great deal depends upon ripe anatomical knowledge and outdoor observation. These facts are so patent to the educated mind, and so subversive of any respect for what is really a pleasing art and not a clown's pastime, that it was felt that students of taxidermy might be assisted, in form at least, if scientific principles were given for the making of a properly-shaped body, which should denote the exact positions of neck, wings, legs, and tail, all of which had hitherto been matters of chance and left to the discretion, or otherwise, of the operator. Accordingly, one of the first of the improved processes adopted in the Leicester Museum is now given.

Take a bird—say a pigeon, as before—and, having skinned it, lay the skinned carcase, divested of its neck, upon its side, embed one half in modelling-sand surrounded by a zinc strip, and proceed to take a cast as detailed in subsequent pages.

Turn it over, leaving the body still in the half mould ; cut keys, oil the edges, repeat the casting process, and, when the mould is sufficiently dry, remove the body, and there will result two halves accurately giving the intaglio or impression of the bird's body. Dry these moulds, and either boil or oil them as detailed hereafter, then press into each half mould a layer of pasted tissue-paper followed by one of cap-paper, then one of pasted brown paper—three in all. Fill each half mould with tow well packed to tighten and solidify it. In one of these halves fix a pointed wire for the reception of the head ; fix it by pasting brown paper over it, and paste brown paper over all, letting it come over the edges of each half mould. Dry in the oven as rapidly as possible, remove from the moulds, trim each half at the edges, join the two together, and the result will be a perfect copy in paper of the bird's body, showing the exact position of the neck springing from the hollow formed by the junction of the clavicles, the positions whence spring the humeri of the wings and the femora of the legs, as also the position of the tail.

The wiring, etc., is precisely the same as detailed at pp. 185-192 for the hard-body method, and gives, of course, better results, although the body is a little heavier.

Even the preceding method, differing but little from that previously described for mammals, does not fully educate the learner into the niceties of form and pose, and, indeed, one of the prime reasons why taxidermists and others fail in the correct form of a bird and the relation of parts to a whole is— as regards perception of form—want of artistic training, but there is no doubt, even given a fair knowledge of easy and natural outlines, that the greatest shortcoming is want of anatomical knowledge, and the conclusion is irresistibly borne in upon one that, without some elementary knowledge in this direction, the taxidermist is but a bungler, and will remain so until the end of his days. Let a bird be watched when standing, walking, perching, or in any position, and one thing is strikingly manifest, viz. *balance*, that is to say, the body is perfectly balanced about its centre upon the legs ; yet, take the work of nine hundred and ninety-nine amateurs out of a thousand, and this self-evident law is utterly and absurdly ignored ; the legs are always too far back, so much so that the bird could not stand one moment in the attitude in which the " stuffer " and his wires place it, but would immediately tumble upon its beak ; at other times the " stuffer," dimly conscious that something is wrong, elevates a bird's chest and beak to the skies, and then the unfortunate creature appears as if a gentle puff of wind would cause it to fall backwards upon its tail, and it really seems as if the ordinary taxidermist takes especial care to get the legs of his specimens as far back under the tail as possible, and these faults are so frequent, and so little recognised, that a method has been devised, which, supplementing the teaching of the skeleton, is, although a little tedious and requiring care, a fine lesson, and turns out a bird absolutely correct in its relation of one part to another, and in shape and size (see Plate XI.).

A bird being laid upon the table, strip the feathers from

the wing of the worse side until the bones appear, then make an incision from the gape of the bill to the anterior edge of the wing, and from here extend the cut over the wing down to the tail. Make another incision thence, passing just *inside* the leg to meet the one at the anterior angle of the wing, the effect being that an oval piece of skin can be stripped from the body, exposing the whole of that side, including the wing and leg. Now take the cut edges in the fingers of the left hand and lift the skin in the ordinary manner with a knife away from the flesh of the other side, leaving it attached only at (1) the bill ; (2) the angle of the eye ; (3) the wing at the junction of the humerus, radius, and ulna (see Plate VIII.); (4) the leg just above the tarso-meta-tarsal joint ; and (5) at the end of the tail. No members, it will be observed, are cut off, and, where the attachments of the skin are noted, the skin is merely freed around and at the leg and wing as when skinning a bird for mounting.

Place wadding between the skin and flesh, so that the former, and the feathers outside, may be kept clean, and remove the intestines and other organs, leaving, however, the windpipe attached at the chest and throat. This done, remove all flesh from the bones with the knife and scissors, getting them as clean as may be, but being careful not to cut the ligaments which hold the joints together. Remove the eyes, and, through the orbit on the opened side, extract the brains.

Before the removal of the flesh, it will, of course, have been necessary to take note of the amount of flesh upon the bones of the opposite side to the incision, for purposes of reproduction. If this cannot be done by the eye aided by the memory, it will be necessary to cut the breast part off in one portion, and strip the flesh from the leg in the same manner, and keep them for reference. When the bones are well cleared of flesh, run a pointed wire through the skin from the outside, in at the top of the skull, and let it traverse the orifices (or neural

canals) of the neck vertebræ until it comes out *inside* the body
at the *dorsal* vertebræ.   In like manner run a suitable wire
(not too thick) inside the bones of both wings ; this will be
more difficult, and will require care and the bone-piercer (No.
20) before successful accomplishment.   Finally, wire both legs
throughout their length from the outside inwards, making the
points fast inside the skeleton.

Now paint the bones and the skin liberally with the preservative, Formula 57.   Arrange the bones somewhat in the attitude
required, and wrap the leg and wing of the unopened side with
tow to the shape and size of the flesh removed, and with wadding
or tow replace also the flesh of the body.   A piece of board or
a stand of sufficient size should next be procured, and holes
made therein in which to insert the leg-bones, which done,
arrange the attitude of the bird in an easy position, add to or
withdraw the wadding or tow until the body is shaped correctly, and, with a needle and thread, catch up the skin of the
body here and there and make fast either to the leg, or to the
skin of the back of the opened side of the neck, then, with
ordinary care in placing the wing and feathers, the whole skin
can be adjusted beautifully *and correctly*, as in nature, on one
side, leaving the skeleton partly exposed on the other, and,
when dry, the stitches and the neck-feathers on that side, and
any others interfering with a full view of the internal skeleton,
can be cut away, leaving the bird as shown on Plate XI.

Observe now in the figure how the bones of the wing fold,
and where they come into place ; also, most important of all,
observe how far forward the knee (*i.e.* the junction of the tibio-
tarsal with the femur) comes, and how the length and bend of
the latter allow it to do so.   Note further, on the other side, how
the feathers fall over the anterior border of the wing, and how
neatly and wedge-shaped they lie between the legs to the tail.

Let a bird treated in this way—which is scientifically

XI

PIGEON SET UP TO SHOW RELATION OF BONES TO SKIN.

correct, and can be used as a museum object—be ever a guide
to the relation of one part to another, and never again let the
legs fall under the tail as if they sprang thence.   A good guide
to the overlapping of the secondary upon the primary feathers
of the wing is to leave them attached to their respective bones,
and to pluck off all the others, above and below, as shown in
the figure.   This will settle any doubts as to the proper place
and overlapping of these greater feathers of the wing.

Really the proper way to mount animals scientifically and
correctly—and this will, or should, be a *sine quâ non* in the
museums of the future—is to utilise the entire skeleton on which
to mount the skin, and the objections as to the time it would
take, and the danger of the roughly-trimmed skeleton attracting
insects, can be easily disposed of thus—

Take any bird—a rook, a starling, or a pigeon as before—
and open it under the wing as previously directed.   This being
accomplished, there remain two methods of dealing with the
body : one is, after the body has been freed from the skin
around it, and the skin drawn over the head, to disjoint it at
the atlas vertebra ; at the junction of the radius and ulna with
the humerus ; at the junction of the femur with the tibio-tarsus ;
and at the last vertebra of the tail.   This, it will be seen,
entirely frees the body, which is taken out, cleaned, rolled in
plaster to dry it, and painted either with the preservative
(Formula 57), carbolic acid wash (Formula 34), or bichromate of
mercury solution (Formula 11).   The other and better method
is, failing the entire removal of the body, to leave it attached at
certain points, and to clean off the flesh, which is more easily
done than would be imagined.   In either case the head must
be filled to the correct shape as before described.   The
wiring is managed by pushing the wires within the bones
where possible, or, where the bones are too small, by running
the wires along by the side of each bone, making them

fast within the skeleton, and attaching them firmly along each bone by winding small pieces of copper or other soft wire around. The wiring of the head is done as directed in the preceding lesson. The skeleton with skin is then fixed upon the stand or perch in the position it is intended to assume, and filled in with wadding and tow as a soft body, which, with a little judgment, will nevertheless give the natural shape of the bird, whilst by this system its length, etc., must be positively exact.

The leg-wires, if not properly attached to the pelvis, and so supporting the body as they should do, may be assisted in this by a pointed wire penetrating the breast and abutting on the sternum, and fixed at its other end to the stand or perch on which the bird rests. The ligaments, in drying, stiffen the skeleton, when this wire may be withdrawn. Many specimens have been set up by this method, which is so easy of accomplishment, and gives such fine results, that in the Leicester Museum, in future, all mammals and birds, when not modelled, will be executed by this process.

Several birds were set up in this manner before it was discovered, as usual, that there is nothing new under the sun, " Bowdich "[1] (*i.e.* Dufresne) recounting that " Becœur of Metz " was the first one to mount both mammals and birds by practically the same method.

Special difficulties arise now and then in skinning certain subjects, such as ducks, woodpeckers, flamingoes, and other birds whose heads are larger than their necks, and so will not come through to the inside as in the generality of instances. There are three ways of getting over such a difficulty : one is to cut the neck off close to the head, and with strong scissors or shears (No. 8) cut out a triangular piece from the base of the skull, and, after extracting the brain and eyes with the scoop

---

[1] Footnote, pp. 11, 12.

(No. 7), compress forcibly the sides of the head from the outside, endeavouring at the same time to press and coax the head—now much more elastic—through the neck. Some birds there are whose heads are so thick and unyielding as to resist all coaxing, even after the removal of part of the bone, and with these the second plan may be adopted—namely, that of cutting away the roof of the mouth from the outside, and removing the brain, eyes, and flesh through the orifice. It is a tedious operation, however, and likely to be dirty, and as both methods cause difficulties to arise in the modelling and returning of the head when pulled out, the very best plan is to make an incision on the *top of the head*, and to get the skull out that way. It may then be easily trimmed, modelled, returned, and sewn up, and if the bird be crested or have any length of feathers, the stitches will never show if carefully done, *i.e.* the stitches drawn tight, and no feathers pulled in with them.

Although the heads of the greater and lesser spotted woodpeckers refuse to be skinned out by the neck, yet the head of the green woodpecker, which appears so very much larger, will come through with care. The head of the little grebe is also rather large, but will pass with care, whilst that of the coot is very much better cut upon the top, for although it passes the neck it stretches it badly, and gives trouble to make it look natural.

Be extremely careful, in instances where birds, such as the eider duck, have fleshy swellings at the sides of the face or by the base of the bill, or protuberances thereupon as in the swan, to clean them well from flesh or fat, and to well preserve and remodel them.

The use of birds' skins or feathers for purely decorative purposes, whether for personal adornment or for domestic embellishment, cannot be too strongly deprecated, and the abominable cruelties perpetrated by callous wretches, instigated by presumably tender-hearted and gentle ladies worshipping the Juggernaut of Fashion, bring a blush of shame and resentment to the most hardened masculine cheek ; yet the women appear not to know nor care that mother-birds—lovely white egrets and other fairy-like things—are caught upon their nests, their breast and back feathers, often with the skin, *torn out whilst the birds are still alive*, and the poor, bleeding, quivering, dumb things cast upon the ground to die a cruel, lingering death, whilst their unhappy young die of starvation before their eyes, and the butchers hasten on, too busy in snatching fresh spoil, and too callous to kill their poor maimed victims.

"Wings" are obtained with but little less cruelty, and although the birds from which they are cut are mostly shot and trapped, yet the destruction of bird-life for the sake of a few feathers is appalling, and never was this more forcibly brought home to the writer's mind than when, geologising on the Yorkshire coast, he met a man engaged in slaughtering as many terns or sea-swallows as he could, for the sake only of their wings and tails. With some skill, he had arranged for himself a decoy (see p. 101), and the sum and substance of his remarks upon the "trade" was this. He was a first-class shot, quick yet cool, and, fortunately, in nearly every case killed his bird dead, whilst he had such business-like precision in loading and firing quickly that, with an ordinary and common under-lever breechloader, with hammers and without ejector, he was seen to kill seven terns out of one passing flock, and said that he had killed nearly thirty on one occasion as fast as he could load and fire. He had slaughtered about four hundred, and considered that less than a thousand did not pay him. Gulls were of no use, being "out of fashion," and "women were such fools" that they would not wear the natural heads and wings of the "sea-swallows," but the heads, tails, and wings must be pulled to pieces and re-made in any nonsensical way dictated by Fashion. Asked whether the " Society for the Protection of Birds " had not done something to stop bird-slaughter, he replied that was so, but they " managed to dodge all that sickly sentimentality by tearing up the wings and remaking them in the fashion. Some of the members (ladies) of that Society he would like to broil, but he gave it straight to one of them. She saw him once dangling a bunch of birds, and remonstrated with him upon his cruelty, whereupon he replied, 'You eat lamb, don't you?' 'Yes,' said the lady. 'Then have you no compassion for the little lambs slaughtered for you? What is the difference between my trade, by which I have to live, and your *pleasure ?* ' "

Venturing to remark that the cases were hardly parallel, as he slaughtered thousands to make an ignominious living, whilst his natural talents fitted him for something higher and nobler, and that the lady had lamb killed only now and then for the perfectly legitimate purpose of eating to live, he rather begged the question, and stated, what is indeed comforting news, that where there were formerly many like himself, he is now the only one in England who makes a living at it, and this but a precarious one, whilst in the "old days" he had followed the birds in every part of Britain, and slaughtered *many thousands* of terns alone in one year. Even then he "had an order from one firm for *ten thousand wings*, but did not know how he should get them, birds were so scarce."

He was an interesting though misguided personality, and perhaps the luxury of killing will pall some day, and he will become a "collector" for the love of the bird, and not for the love of the few pence their poor wings make.

Ladies, it is to be feared, will never see these, to them, dry-as-dust pages, but their husbands and brothers are asked to point out to them the cruelty which lurks within each fibre of their " ospreys " and " wings."

So with humming-birds, which are killed in incredible numbers—hundreds of thousands—for the adornment of ladies, and which must, in a very short time if the fashion be persisted in, result in the extermination of several of the " fashionable " species.　As to the trimming of dresses with robins' or swallows' breasts and heads, and such like survivals of a savage state of life, nothing can be said, because probably both designers and wearers are too thoughtless or too callous to heed our words.

Is it of the slightest avail trying to strengthen what has been written before, and to give pause to the abominable cruelties practised in the name of Fashion and threatening the near extinction of many species of animals, by quoting the following from an American paper and repeated by Professor Ward in his *Natural Science Bulletins ?*

THE HALO

W. C. Gannett, in Unity

One London dealer in birds received, when the fashion was at its height, a single consignment of 32,000 dead humming-birds ; and another received at another time 30,000 aquatic birds, and 300,000 pairs of wings.

> Think what a price to pay,
> Faces so bright and gay,
> 　　Just for a hat !
> Flowers unvisited, mornings unsung,
> Sea-ranges bare of the wings that o'erswung,—
> 　　Bared just for that !

> Think of the others, too,
> Others and mothers, too,
> 　　Bright eyes in hat !
> Hear you no mother-groan floating in air,
> Hear you no little moan,—birdlings' despair,—
> 　　Somewhere, for that ?

Caught 'mid some mother work,
Torn by a hunter Turk,
Just for your hat !
Plenty of mother hearts yet in the world :
All the more wings to tear, carefully twirled,—
Women want that !

Oh, but the shame of it,
Oh, but the blame of it,
Price of a hat !
Just for a jauntiness brightening the street !
This is your halo, O faces so sweet,—
Death : and for that !

So late as November, 1895, one of the secretaries of the " S.P.B." published an appeal, and stated that during that first season, " in one warehouse alone of the many engaged in the traffic, there were no less than 60,000 dozen mixed sprays disposed of."

In fine, the adaptation of the feathers of anything, save those of domestic birds—and ostriches are classed with them, —for decorative purposes is an outrage on every feeling of humanity, when it is known in what a brutal manner they are procured, and therefore no directions for " making up " will be found in these pages ; nor, indeed, will any instructions be given for another form of setting-up likely to lead to a mischievous form of collecting—that of making up gulls, owls, hawks, and other birds as hand-screens,—although there may be some excuse when birds such as jays and magpies, inimical to game, are shot by keepers and used for such purposes, but it must be remembered that, after all, such *objets de luxe* are admittedly unnaturally set up.

The making-up of a rare and valuable bird piece by piece is sometimes necessary, and for this purpose an artificial body of tow is constructed, in the same manner as described at p. 186, to which the legs of the bird are bolted, and the whole is fixed

upon a perch or stand ; this, it will be seen, is simply a headless artificial body supported by natural legs.   Assuming that
the pieces of skin and feathers, whether resulting from accident
or extreme age, are nicely relaxed and free from grease, the
commencement should be made at the head, and the pieces
arranged on the model in proper order, and observe where the
model is faulty and remove or add until correct.   Having fitted
every part in proper order and marked the places they should
finally assume, remove them from the model, and give the
latter a good coat of thick flour paste (Formula 90).   Upon this
rearrange the feathers, or pieces of skin with feathers attached,
and probably it will be found more expedient to work from tail
to head than from head to tail, to allow for the overlap of the
feathers.   Where any paste comes through on to the feathers,
sponge it off.   No exact instructions can be given, but the
learner must be guided by circumstances as to whether the
breast-pieces should be fixed first, as they usually are, or not,
and, when it is necessary to swell out the feathers in certain
positions, let a piece of pasted wadding be inserted under them,
lifting up the surrounding feathers with some tool handy for
the purpose.   When the wings and head are finally fixed,
sponge the bird down with wadding dipped in warm water if
any more paste has appeared, and afterwards with benzoline followed by plaster, which, being dusted off subsequently, will help
to dry as well as to clean it.   Put the specimen in a warm or airy
situation to dry, and, lastly, rectify any imperfections through
the orbits, and put in the eyes.

The original idea in making a "skin" is that it may be
used as a cabinet - specimen for reference, but, as it often
happens that the collector makes a skin to save time and
space, well knowing that it must be subsequently set up and
mounted when more favourable conditions exist, the art of
what is called "relaxing" was invented many years ago, before

which time skins were roughly wired, and, with the exception
of being upon their legs, were no more like a properly set-up
bird than may be supposed.

"Relaxing," therefore, is an important and delicate operation, and is one which fails if the worker does not take pains,
or is not skilful. In the infancy of the art, the skin was
unpacked and water poured through with great care so that it
should not touch the feathers; and later, perhaps, came the
" plaster-box," which has been described by nearly every writer
upon Taxidermy, and consists simply of a strong box thickly
plastered inside with plaster of Paris, which is allowed to set
and dry. When required for use the box is filled with water,
which saturates the plaster lining, and, the surplus water having
been thrown out, the skins are placed within and the lid tightly
closed, and the skins, being allowed to remain for a certain
time, become more or less relaxed. To Waterton is due the
credit of inventing the apparently impracticable operation of
plunging skins entirely into water to relax them, but it cannot
be said to be a success executed as he describes it, and the
improvement of the method lies in the after-treatment, not then
known to Waterton. The skin is, in the first place, entirely
covered with water, and, although professionals should have lead-
or zinc-lined wooden tanks in which to submerge their specimens, yet an oval galvanised-iron vessel or foot-bath, to be
obtained for a shilling or so from the tinman's, is a respectable
substitute when skins are not large. A round bucket is, though
deep, of such small diameter as to cramp wings or tail, which
must on no account be allowed; nor must a *tin* vessel be used,
and there is really little expense in having a small zinc-lined
wooden trough made, which is *the* safest.

If of any size, the bird's skin will probably require weight-
ing to keep it submerged, and this can be done by resting
a piece of thin wood on the specimen, and keeping it down

with a brick or stone ; no metal must on any account be used to do this, or, as with the vessel, rust or stain will make its appearance and spoil the specimen.   In very cold weather use a little warm water, but it must be kept where it will not freeze ; and, at any time, warm water is more efficacious in relaxing than cold.   If the skin is suspected to be tender or old, put a little vinegar or stronger acid in the water.   When the skin has been in the water for a length of time varying from hours to days, according to size, take it out and, if the opening be sewn up, search for the stitches, cut them and remove the "stuffing," but not before the skin is thoroughly relaxed, or the stuffing will adhere to it and tear it.

The skin must *now* be drained thoroughly on a sloping board, and, whilst yet damp, be well wiped down with benzoline, and treated with plaster to be subsequently beaten out as described at p. 168, but on no account must the plaster be put on the wet feathers until they have been well dressed in every part with benzoline.   The skin having been permitted to lie for some considerable time in plaster, this should be removed and fresh substituted, until, when beaten out, the feathers come into proper order and appearance, whilst the skin itself is just damp enough to allow of its being set up as though it were a fresh specimen.

The subsequent setting-up depends upon whether the skin has been made as directed for the hard-body system or for the soft-body method, as is the case with most.   In the former instance, the made body is entirely removed, but the head, if properly modelled, is left intact, a fresh body is made, and the bird set up, cottoned, and finished as previously directed, whilst, in the latter event, the wool or other packing is removed, the skin turned inside out, even to the head, and scraped, if at all fat, as all ducks' skins and some others are, the head is modelled, and the bird set up. .

Take notice in all cases, whether in a " skin " or in a newly-skinned bird, that the removal of the fat and grease is much accelerated if plaster be thrown on and removed from time to time.

The colouring of the bills and legs of birds is seldom well done, the colour used being often some crude paint which fills up all detail and shows what it is at once ; or, if there is any approach to the original hues, there is a distinctly shiny or varnished appearance which is most objectionable. As there is not a large surface to be covered, artists' tube oil-colours will be found the most suitable, and they may be thinned upon the palette with turpentine, which often gives a sufficient gloss, but the turpentine and varnish formula (No. 84) will do still better, and gives just enough " quality " to be natural. It must not be supposed that any given bill or leg is of one uniform hue ; close inspection will reveal many gradations, and it is only necessary to observe the colours of these parts in a bird of any size to prove the truth of this assertion.

The really troublesome matter to be grappled with is the fact, that not only do the bills and legs lose their characteristic hues after death, but that they *shrink* very considerably, and that is the only thing which prevents a properly-mounted bird from looking natural. Bills, especially of such birds as snipes, shrink in some degree, but not nearly so much as do the legs of all birds. There is no way of arresting it, save for a short time by glycerin, and therefore such parts must be made up. Young birds which have a full and fleshy base to their gape, of various tints of yellow, lose this soon after they are set up, when it shrivels to a thin leathery-brown or whitish-yellow hue. This must be made up, and the appearance and colour restored.

Notes should have been previously taken of the colours in the living or recently-dead specimen, and sometimes it may be

14

possible to work from the members of a later brood, but, if not, it is always possible to make a little wax model of one half of the upper and lower gape, and to copy the colours at the time from the nestlings themselves.

After the birds are set up and the bills are dry, take wax (Formula 98, or beeswax), and, having stirred in a little tube oil-colour, say cadmium, aurora yellow, or aureolin—whichever is most like the colour of the natural gape,—brush a very little turpentine over the parts to be modelled upon, and then, with a small, common, camel-hair pencil, paint on the hot wax, shaping it with the brush, and with any of the small tools, Nos. 26, 27, 34, 35, and 36, just warmed. The inside of the mouths, if shown open, must be *previously* painted with wax of another colour, and, if several small pans of coloured waxes are made, they will always be useful, and can be blended one with another like pigments if quickness and skill are exhibited. Indeed, the young herons in the Leicester Museum (see pp. 402-405 and Plate XX.) have the insides of their mouths coloured in two or three hues of wax, and their bills in several others, and there are many other groups in which the mouths and gapes have been modelled. This, when it can be done properly, is far superior to superimposing colour upon wax, as the colour being within, locked up as it were, gives a certain brilliancy and mimics nature remarkably well. When, however, this cannot be done, colouring upon the wax, if skilfully managed, leaves little to be desired.

The combs and wattles of fowls and other of the Gallinæ, which are fleshy and afterwards shrink, should be skinned out with care, then filled with clay or composition, and afterwards coated with wax and coloured; or, better still, should be cast from whilst the specimen is fresh, and modelled in wax (Formula 64), and should either entirely replace the dried and shrivelled originals, or be superimposed upon them when *thoroughly dry*.

The legs of birds are more tiresome and difficult to deal with, for they are, as will be seen, covered with scutellæ or plates, each shrunken one of which will have to be subsequently covered with wax and carved into shape. This is done, either from the legs of a fresh bird of the same species or by estimating the amount of shrinkage, by putting on the wax to the required thickness on one leg, and copying the scutes, etc., from the other, being careful, however, to note that the direction of the lines of one limb is reversed in the other. At present there is being tried in the Leicester Museum a new method, from which great results may spring.

The keeping hot of the variously-coloured waxes during the operation of brushing them on, is best managed by the water-bath, which, in this instance, may be a vessel of boiling water, in which rest little gallipots containing the various waxes, or, for larger quantities of wax, Clarke's pyramid food-warmers with the stand complete, used with a spirit-lamp first, and afterwards with the night-lights supplied, are the very things, and are, indeed, indispensable when plants are modelled (see Chap. IX.). Hot plates and iron plates—kept hot by a gas-jet,—on which rested "patty-pans" of coloured waxes, have been used, but there is always a danger, by any other method than a water-bath, of burning the wax and the colour with it, and entirely spoiling a tint which has been troublesome to make.

In all cases where practicable, these methods of wax-colouring should be resorted to, as the hard and "painty" appearance presented by the shrivelled and coloured integument may thus be entirely obviated. In quite small birds the waxing is a tedious process, but when it is stated that the gapes of birds such as young thrushes, whin-chats, robins, and tits have been successfully restored in the Leicester Museum, the difficulty, it will be seen, is merely one of degree.

CHAPTER VII

THE TREATMENT OF REPTILES, AMPHIBIANS, AND FISHES[1] BY TAXIDERMIC AND OTHER METHODS

DIVISION I

BY TAXIDERMIC METHODS

Fishes

AT the outset, when considering the wisdom or otherwise of writing this chapter, it seemed useless to attempt to give directions for skinning and setting up such objects as those denoted by the heading, for the reasons given in the following pages ; but as there may be some taxidermist foolish enough to go to some trouble in order to painfully and successfully elaborate a shapeless mummy, the ensuing pages are written in the hope that the taxidermic processes detailed therein will, if he follows them, make him a sadder and a wiser man. As an addendum and further severe discouragement may be quoted the following pertinent remarks from one of the Badminton Library series : [2]—

The exhibition of casts of fish by Mr. Jardine and others, few as they were numerically, sounded, I believe, the death-knell of taxidermy.

---

[1] The arrangement of these chapters—which is necessarily from highest to lowest form, owing to the difficulty of interesting the amateur in his work if the invertebrata be taken first (as they should be)—is here broken for a similar reason, *i.e.* that fishes are better known (and liked) than reptiles ; the heading, however, shows the sequence obtaining in this work. [2] *Fishing*, pp. 149, 150.

In all that constitutes the perfection of simulation or the art of making the unreal appear as the real, casting is immeasurably ahead of fish-stuffing. You have, in fact, the exact representation of the fish, scale for scale, as he appeared fresh out of the water, in full length and unshrunken proportions. With a stuffed fish, on the contrary, neither his length nor his girth is ever really accurate. Fish vertebræ are separated by a sort of gelatinous substance, forming a separation between the several joints, which, after a short time, becomes desiccated or dried up, thus contracting the several bones and shortening, not inconsiderably, the total length. A similar shrinking process, though from somewhat different causes, takes place in the girth. The colouring also in the cast is that of the fish just after his decease—

> Before decay's effacing fingers
> Have swept the lines where beauty lingers.

And last, not least, the fish-casting is practically indestructible by time, and does not cause the disagreeable smell produced by the old mummified specimens of the art of the taxidermist, no matter how scientifically tittivated in the ordinary manner. Besides Mr. Jardine's pike,[1] aforesaid,—alone worth going to the Exhibition to see—there was in the same gallery a very beautiful cast of a grayling of about 2 lbs. weight, which was a model of fish-loveliness, and seemed to do everything but swim. I am very sorry that I have forgotten the names of the artists by whom these casts were made, so that I am not able to associate their names with their exhibits.

The fish-taxidermist, being by this time, probably, reduced to a proper condition of mind, is recommended to begin with a perch, which, by reason of its thickness of skin, is best suited to the occasion.

The perch, after capture, is at once mercifully killed by the insertion of a penknife through the gills, severing the spinal cord, or passing into the brain (when it can be found); the fish is then wrapped in damp rag or paper—*not grass*, which marks it in stripes not calculated upon in the scheme of evolution,—and carried carefully.

[1] Executed by the late Frank Buckland, and coloured by Rolfe.

Laid upon the dissecting-table, the first process is to take all necessary measurements or trace an outline on stiff paper, and, selecting the better side of the fish—that less bruised or ripped, or from which the fewer scales are missing,—cover that side with tissue-paper or muslin, which will easily adhere to the slime[1] with which all fishes are coated. This serves to hold the scales in their places, and, moreover, gives a certain stiffness or "set" to the skin whilst the flesh is being removed.

Turn the specimen worse or uncovered side uppermost, and keep all the fins (in which is included the tail or caudal fin) moistened by wet rags, or by dipping them in water, or by brushing them with glycerin, for on no account must they be permitted to dry during the operation of skinning, etc.

Lift the operculum or covering of the gills, and observe that its edge just covers a somewhat silvery or golden arch of bone between it and the body; sever this, which is the pectoral arch and rather thick, with the shears (No. 8), and now, taking either a smaller pair of scissors or the knife No. 3 or 4, make a clear and not deep incision thence through the skin of the body exactly in the centre, and continue it up to the insertion of the tail-fin. Afterwards, with the same or with a broader knife (No. 1 or 2), separate the edge of the skin on either side of the incision, by holding one part, whilst the other hand guides the knife with a scraping motion to free the skin from the flesh. The knife should be held in a somewhat slanting position toward the operator, and great care must be exercised, when nearing the fins, not to cut outward, or a hole may ensue, which will leave the fins attached to the *flesh*, and not to the *skin* as required. The first fin to be freed is, of course, that one lying close to, and just underneath, the commencement of the incision; this is called the pectoral fin,

---

[1] Mr. Rowland Ward mentions in *Sportsman's Handbook*, p. 92, seventh ed., that this may be removed by sponging with diluted vitriol.

and the one below that—also a paired fin, and called the ventral fin—cannot be freed from the flesh until more room is given by further releasing the skin of the ventral half of the body for some considerable distance. This having been done, the ventral fin is cut away, and the last fin, that near the tail—the anal,—is freed by slipping the point of the scissors underneath, and cutting it away from its attachment. Working from this toward the tail, release the skin all round, and the whole of the ventral half of the skin of the body will be detached from the flesh.

The skin along the dorsal half of the body is now to be dealt with, and is a rather easier matter, because it is usually thicker there. Commencing at the head as before, skin back the upper portion of the pectoral arch and free the skin of the dorsal fin ; now slip the points of the scissors or shears underneath, and sever the bones inside to detach that fin from the back. Continue to free the skin until, coming to the next, or sub-dorsal fin, the bones of this may be severed inside in like manner, and, cutting on to the tail, relieve the skin at that point.

In cutting away the fins from the inside, there is no need to trim them carefully at that stage ; a little flesh, more or less, left on is much easier to deal with than to remedy holes cut through the skin in the anxiety to trim too closely at first.

The skin of the fish being entirely freed on one side of the body, and also along the back, the skinning-out of the other side is done by first working along the back from the sub-dorsal fin toward the tail, keeping the cutting-edge of the knife pressed down on the flesh, and scraping away the skin with the back of the knife. Do the same on the lower half of the fish from the anal fin to the tail, and in large fishes this process may be materially assisted by using the fingers, or the handle of a scalpel or some similar instrument, to separate the skin, until this is only held some little distance up the body and at the base of the tail.   Now slip the point of the shears or scissors between the skin and the flesh, and sever the bone near the base of the tail ; this part is now free, and the skinning progresses toward the head until stopped by the bone of the ventral fin on the under side ; cut this through.   The next thing, on nearing the head, is the bone of the pectoral fin of the under side ; this must be cut through in like manner, and the trunk of the fish will only remain attached to the head by the vertebræ ; with the scissors or shears, cut through the vertebræ as near to the head as possible, and the whole body will thus be removed, leaving merely the head to deal with.

During these various operations, and especially when cutting away the ventral and pectoral pairs of fins, as much care as possible should be exercised not to cut into the internal organs of the fish, or an effusion of blood and other troubles may ensue ; and therefore it is always wise to be prepared to plug all such accidental openings with wadding, and also to slope the fish and pour water inside to cleanse it if the flow of blood, etc., is serious.

All the large pieces of flesh having been removed from the skin of the body, nothing remains but the head and the trimming of the fins to be grappled with.   It is immaterial which is done first, but, assuming that the bases of the fins are cleared of flesh, the head is managed thus :—

The first process is to remove the gills with the knife or shears, cutting away their attachments at top and bottom ; this will expose what is left of the vertebræ and flesh ; cut all away with the shears or broad knife until the brain is exposed, which, of course, remove.   Remove the eye, and by the side of the face, just behind the orbit, resting upon the pre-opercular bone, is a mass of flesh, in some fishes of considerable volume, which, either through the orbit or from the back of the head, can be removed by judicious use of the knife and scissors, or by the tools Nos. 27, 34, 35, and 38, and all the flesh from between the skin and the bones of the face, and all flesh adhering to their inner sides, must be laboriously pulled, cut, torn, and coaxed out from the various cavities, etc., in which it rests. Some of the edges of these bones being very sharp, care must be exercised not to cut the fingers, nor to lacerate them with the teeth, which, in the case of such a fish as a pike, are formidable, and are situated in unexpected positions.

From the pectoral fins, a fleshy process with a silvery outer skin extends until it touches the inner angle of the lower jaw ; being partly overlapped on each side by the folding membrane which covers the branchiostegal rays, this rapidly narrowing wedge of flesh is by no means easily extracted from the fine silvery skin which envelops it, so that some patience must be exercised to do this without tearing the membrane. At its junction with the distal ends of the large bones of the hyoid, *i.e.* the cerato-hyals, it is also attached to a thin bone (the basi-branchiostegal, = uro-hyal of Owen and Günther), which must not be detached, but must be cleared around, and left within the cleared skin.

What flesh there is underlying the teeth, especially along the lower jaw, must be cut away, and this is managed by making an incision from the back of the head below the eye, and removing the flesh piecemeal through this by the aid of the tools previously mentioned, or a special curved tool may be made. Consider how extremely thin this membrane is, and that the slightest carelessness will rip it away from the bone or cut holes in it, and be patient accordingly. Some operators cut this entirely away and replace it with various modelling-materials, but, if the fish's mouth is to be left open, this plan will not do ; otherwise it does not matter.

If the mouth is to be left open—which gives a by no

means satisfactory appearance to the specimen, and causes far more trouble,—the tongue must be cut underneath, the flesh removed, replaced by clay or some other medium, and the skin sewn up.

It may be mentioned that some fine sand or plaster in which to rub the fingers from time to time facilitates the operations of skinning-out and trimming.

The Setting-up of the Fish

This is accomplished by two or three methods, all equally objectionable and unscientific, but, as they are the only methods known to the users of arsenic and ignorers of lines of beauty and natural shapes, they must be given here, in the hope that the "stuffer" will in time become a modeller, and so progress by degrees from the infinitely bad to the really good.

The skin, having been painted inside with the preservative Formula 57, is measured for length and corrected by previous measurements, and a piece of wire is selected of proportionate thickness to the size of the fish, and of considerably greater length. One end of this wire is bent around to form a large pear-shaped oval, and is twisted firmly around the main stem. Some distance from this, determined by the length of the fish, the main stem is twisted upon itself to form a small loop ; nearer the tail, the stem is twisted again in like manner, and, at the remaining extremity, either a smaller pear-shaped loop is formed or the end is pointed ; perhaps the latter is the easiest to manage, although the loop is the most secure, and the wire forms in reality an artificial backbone, the large loop being subsequently thrust into the head, and the small one into the tail of the specimen, the small loops between being for the reception of short wires, which are made fast by being twisted around the main stem, these subsidiary wires being used to attach the fish to the backboard upon which it is afterwards mounted. The length and bearing of this " backbone " are rendered more exact by its being formed upon the fish before it is skinned, as some lengthening of the skin is sure to take place afterwards in the hands of the tyro.

Around the artificial backbone wrap paper, or wood-shavings, or that packing-material called by the Americans " excelsior," and tie on with hemp or string, shaping it roughly to the size of the fish ; tow also may be used to supplement this, or both paper and tow, or one alone may be glued, or glued or pasted paper may be worked over the mass to give it shape and smoothness. When this is satisfactorily accomplished, pad the face of the fish between the skin and bones with putty, or with the modelling-composition Formula 61, and also all other parts of the head and throat from which flesh has been removed, especially between the silvery skin running, as aforesaid (p. 217), from the pectoral fins ; between the skin of the gums, under and within the tongue, and, indeed, wherever any shrinkage would be observable. Pad also the bases of the fins, including the tail, with the putty or composition, and, if a thin covering is laid over all the inside of the skin, it may improve it. Clay, which is ordinarily so useful for everything else, will not do for filling or modelling the skin of fishes, as, although apparently satisfactory at first, it draws and wrinkles the skin after a few days, and entirely spoils what little success may have been achieved by this method. Whatever space may be left between the skin and false body when inserted, should be filled with sawdust, well rammed and shaken in.

The large loop of the artificial backbone or false body resting now within the head, and the smaller loop within the tail, or, if a sharpened point, through the root of the tail, the skin may be got together by sewing. First, however, drill the bone of the pectoral arch with an awl, No. 26, and bring that part together with a piece of soft wire or thick thread ; next drill the gill-cover, through which pass the skin-needle (No. 23, but finer than shown) threaded with strong hemp, and so, working towards the tail, lace the skin together, bringing the edges into apposition, but not allowing them to overlap. This must be executed with care and patience and some little " gumption," and, if the fish is well shaped and fairly tight on that side, it is presumably so on the underneath or " show " side. From time to time, where defects occur, insert a little more sawdust, pushed into place by tow, which should follow it for this purpose, working it well to the underneath. Some-times it may be expedient, or even necessary, to recommence sewing from the tail end, and so meet the stitches from the other.

As the work progresses, and as soon as the stitches are made fast around the two protruding wires, the fish may be lifted cautiously by them to examine the under side, and where any irregularities occur these should be made good. Judicious tapping on the sewn side, with a rather heavy and flat piece of wood shaped like a small bat, will often improve the shape, which must conform, of course, to the original measurements, and the skin must be shortened when it shows signs of lengthening.

The fish, having attained, on the upper surface, a fairly respectable shape, is ready to be turned over, which is done by measuring the distances between the wires of the artificial body and marking corresponding distances upon a board some-what larger than the fish, and, holes being made through the board, it is brought down upon the wires, which are pulled through, their ends turned over, and the fish and board reversed by placing the hand underneath to support the weight of the head and upper part of the trunk. The fish is now right side uppermost, and as, no doubt, the putty may have been flattened and pushed a little out of place in certain parts, notably the head, this must be rectified by lifting the opercular region and inserting more "stuffing." The head, "neck," and tail must be properly adjusted afterwards, and, by pressing and patting the skin deftly with the hands and with the wooden bat previously mentioned, all the lumpiness may be reduced and the underlying putty or composition rendered even.

In arranging the head, some pointed wires, hammered into the board on each side of that part, will be found useful for keeping it in position, and, if the mouth is to be shown widely opened—a most reprehensible practice unless there is a distinct reason for it,—one wire may go through the "nostril," another under the tongue, and a third or more, parallel to it, under the jaws. If any of the teeth are loose in their sockets, they must be arranged in proper positions, and the rays and membrane of the gill-covering must be brought into place, and kept so, either by fine stitches or by "needle points" driven in, and finally wrapped with hemp or cotton (in the same manner as a bird's feathers), to keep them from springing up in drying.

The fins are now to be displayed by placing underneath them pieces of sheet cork (entomological cork), kept to the height required by elevating each piece upon a wire driven into the board, laying the fins, still kept wet, upon the cork, and pinning pieces of cardboard over them, or binding them with cotton.

As a means of still better preserving the skin and keeping down any smell resulting from its drying, a wash of the carbolic formula (No. 34) may be passed over the whole of the outside, and, as this dries in an hour or so, the skin may afterwards be varnished with a thin coat of clear "paper-varnish," which has the advantage of setting the scales firmly in their seats and of preventing the skin from rising. As carbolic has, however, the effect of bleaching and removing the colour from the skin, it is, in the case of those who are not artists, and do not know how to reproduce the natural colour, advisable to omit this, and to varnish the skin as quickly as possible after the fish is finally arranged ; some part of the colour will often be retained for a time, and, indeed, the fish-mummifiers rather pride themselves on the fact that they *do* varnish their fishes and *do not* colour them—which is, perhaps, just as well in their state of knowledge, as a leathery effigy is, possibly, preferable to one overloaded with green and red paint and gold and silver leaf!

The fish will be properly dried in a month if kept in a warm situation (it may be hung up on its board near the ceiling of the work-room), and the corks, braces, threads, and wires may be removed, the eyes inserted, the skin, if not previously varnished, may be slightly oiled outside and coloured, and the fish will then be ready for removal to its proper back-board, which is either a coloured or papered tablet, or to the case in which it is to rest, the wires being necessary, in either alternative, to affix it.

All the preceding instructions, though ostensibly dealing with a species of fish which never grows to any size—4 lbs. being phenomenal,—are yet applicable in their entirety to much larger fishes, and, indeed, a pike has been in the writer's mind whilst describing the use of some of the tools and some of the processes.

Improved Methods of Setting up

The following is an improved method of filling the skin, by which, probably, better results may accrue as regards the shape, with, perhaps, greater facility of execution :—

Let the fish be measured as before, and, having provided a piece of stiff paper, mark it quite an inch smaller, all around, than the size of the fish, allowing also for some reduction of the length ; that is to say, if the paper rests at one end just by the base of the tail, the other end should come just past the gill openings. Let a board be cut to the shape of this paper pattern, and, at distances determined by the length of the fish, drive two stout wires through it, and clench them securely at the back. This is the artificial " backbone " to be used afterwards.

The fish, after it has been skinned by the method detailed in this division, and the head and bases of the fins been well crowded with paper, tow, and putty or composition, is laid, incision uppermost, upon a separate board larger than the specimen, and *dry* plaster of Paris—which is far superior to sawdust, bran, or sand as a filling-material—is ladled in, beginning at the tail, and is well pressed and rammed with a short stick, shortening up the skin meanwhile, which, at the tail especially, has a remarkable tendency to lengthen out.

In sewing up, when about a third has been completed, let the stitches be fastened off, and fill in at the other end, being careful to firmly press and ram the plaster everywhere to remove all wrinkles and depressions, lifting head and tail gently from time to time to look underneath and see how matters are progressing. When nearing the middle of the body be sure to deepen that part, and when full sew up the remainder of the skin. Take another board and place it on the top of the fish ; lightly tie both together, turn the fish over, and, what is now the upper board being removed, the fish is revealed right side uppermost. No doubt it will be found rather flat where it has rested upon the board, and this must be improved by passing a wet cloth over the skin, and, when damp enough, patting it into shape by means of the bat-shaped piece of wood ; but, should the modelling not be true, note the positions where faults occur, and, reversing the specimen again, crowd in more plaster between the stitches, or cut a few, if necessary, to do this. When the skin is re-sewn where any stitches have been cut, and is again brought better side uppermost, it will be seen that the head is perhaps too flat and has dropped down too much upon the board, causing the gill-covering to open widely ; this must be remedied by propping the nose from the board with wedges of wood, kept in place by nails. The mouth may now be set and the fins spread as before directed, and the specimen may be treated and dried as usual. When it is thoroughly dry, the stitches are cut and the plaster shaken out, care being taken meanwhile not to crack nor injure the skin in any way.

The specimen is now completely hollow, and might remain so, but, to prevent possible accidents, it will be as well to pack it inside with paper, or tow, or shavings, just sufficiently to keep it out, and, when nearly full, the shaped board previously mentioned at p. 223 is brought into use, and is inserted in the skin, and the edges nailed down upon it with tacks, the protruding wires fixed in the board being used to fasten it upon anything else. The wires *may* be dispensed with and long screws used instead, or screws may supplement the wires, as circumstances determine.

The advantages of this method are, that the plaster appears to more perfectly adapt itself to the filling out of the skin, and, when removed, leaves the specimen light and firm. It is possible, but not very practicable unless great dexterity has been attained, to fill the skin of small fishes with *wet* plaster, bringing the cut edges together, and putting all rapidly into shape before the plaster has time to set, but only thick-skinned and small fishes can be managed thus.

Heads only of large fishes are sometimes set up, and then plaster may be run in between the skin and bone, and all the parts of the mouth made up with any of the modelling-compositions mentioned in Chapter III.

If it be absolutely necessary to retain the skin of a fish,

and not to delineate it by any of the following methods, it will be found a good plan for ensuring greater accuracy to take a cast of the best side, and, having skinned the specimen, to replace its skin within the plaster mould and fill it with dry plaster until it entirely conforms to the shape of the original fish ; there is, however, some difficulty in doing this which the beginner may not be able to overcome, and the best method of reproducing such objects is by casting.

Professor Kingsley [1] gives a description of the Davidson method of setting up a fish, thus :—

The necessary materials are thin pieces of soft wood about one-eighth of an inch in thickness ; square sticks measuring from three-fourths of an inch upwards ; plaster of Paris, glycerine, tissue paper, pins, and double-pointed carpet tacks.

The outline of the fish without fins is marked on two pieces of board, which are held together by pieces of the square sticks tacked across the ends, and then the portion corresponding to the body is cut away, so that we have strips of wood, one following the dorsal and the other the ventral contour of the fish. The fish is then placed in this opening, and the various fins are extended and fixed in position with pins, the board in the meantime being supported so that one side of the fish can freely extend through the opening in the joined boards. Strips of tissue paper wet with glycerine are then laid smoothly over the fish, and next a coating of plaster is poured over the same side. When the plaster is hardened, the boards, etc., are reversed, and the rest of the work is carried on from the opposite side of the body. All that portion of the fish which projects through the opening is first cut away, and then all of the muscles, bones, and viscera are carefully removed, until nothing remains but the skin supporting the fins and its plaster backing. In this condition one side of the skin is entire, and on the other side a narrow strip of skin extends around the median line of the body from a quarter to half of an inch in width. The interior of the skin is now dusted with arsenic. The eye is then placed in position and the skin is filled with plaster, mixed to about the consistency of cream.　The double-pointed carpet tacks are then taken, and their points, having been bent as shown in the adjacent figure, are hooked into the strip of skin, and the loop embedded in the plaster. A small strip of wood (previously coated with shellac, to prevent undue expansion from the moisture) is also embedded in the plaster, its upper surface being even with that of the plaster.　The two halves of the board are separated when the plaster becomes dry, the skin, with its plaster interior, is removed from its mould and washed, and the fins placed in clips, so that they may dry flat.　When thoroughly dry, the specimen is mounted on a wooden tablet by screws passing into the embedded block, and the whole is ready for exhibition.

No means have yet been found of preserving the natural colours of the fish ; and the only way of representing them on the specimens thus mounted is by means of paints.

This process, which has been thus briefly described, is the property of Dr. H. E. Davidson of Boston, and to him all inquiries as to the rights to use it should be addressed.

Upon the foregoing it may be remarked, that it is hard to see what useful purpose is served by a process which is, at best, but a compromise between stuffing and casting, and also how Dr. Davidson can reserve any rights to published methods of work.

Amphibians

Some writers have advised the skinning-out of frogs, toads, and amphibians through an incision made on the median line of the stomach, filling with wadding or tow, and finishing and wiring them in the manner in which birds are wired by the old systems (see *ante*).　This has been modi-fied by skinning them out through the mouth, which requires a delicate touch, and, when done, is just as useless, for no batrachian can be successfully " stuffed," not even by the inter-vention of a " mannikin " ; the only way in which such things can be made as in nature is by casting, as explained in the following pages.

Reptiles

Snakes, lizards, and so on, have been stuffed by the methods adopted for batrachians, but the same remark applies here, and those who advise the reproduction of any such, even the largest, by taxidermic processes, are not artists, nor have they much regard for anatomy.

Tortoises and turtles are easily mounted by removing the plastron and skinning the head and limbs, and, after 'the flesh has been removed, leaving them attached to the carapace by the skin of their upper surfaces, subsequently filling them out by any of the methods mentioned in these pages, and replacing the plastron by wiring and making up with shellac, or cement (Formula 60 or 61). Mr. Frederic A. Lucas, in a very interesting article " On the Mounting of Turtles," [1] gives full directions for the skinning and setting-up of the creatures ; but really the only way to satisfactorily reproduce even these easily " stuffed " reptiles is to cast them, as has been most successfully and beautifully managed by the American modellers,[2] albeit they have been executed in an objectionable material.

If the actual shell, and not a model, be required, the head and limbs may be cast, reproduced in any of the materials mentioned hereafter, and arranged naturally within the carapace and plastron.

DIVISION II

REPRODUCTIONS IN PLASTER BY VARIOUS METHODS

Fishes

There are many objects in nature so difficult or impossible to satisfactorily preserve by any processes of taxidermy, or

---

[1] *Third Annual Report of the Society of American Taxidermists* (1882-83), pp. 84-90.

[2] See Shufeldt, *op. cit.* Plates XXXII., XXXIII., XXXIV.

by liquids or such media, that the recognition of this fact is beginning, though slowly, to be borne in upon the mind of the naturalist preparator—to give an English rendering of a French term, so much more comprehensive than our "taxidermist," and so much more elegant than its common variant, "stuffer,"—and hence some of the more advanced in a beautiful art, which has had but few educated or able exponents, are realising that certain things must have a mould cast from them, from which a model can ultimately be made.

At present, a plaster cast represents the limit which has been attained in the delineation of the lower vertebrata, and even this is, as yet, rarely met with. At this stage of these remarks, it may be as well to state emphatically what was before insisted upon in *Practical Taxidermy*, viz. that no taxidermist ever has mounted, or ever will mount, a fish, amphibian, reptile, or cetacean even decently, or with more than a remote approximation to nature, by any of the resources of their art known to them, and in this sweeping condemnation are included all who are in any way famous in fish-taxidermy ; they and their patrons are self-deceived and misguided, and the sooner this patent fact is recognised the better for art.

Take a pike as a familiar example, and take a thousand taxidermists ; how many of this number are there who can make such a fish other than a ghastly elongated mummy, all ridges and bumps, and utterly unlike nature in many points ? Probably one, and that one the great fish-taxidermist *par excellence* (whoever he may be) ; and even he, although by his mistaken art making it plump and fairly respectable in shape, never does, and *never can* do anything with the head and the fleshy bases of the fins. Those parts are simply *mummified ;* all the cartilage has shrunk, and there is a grinning death's-head upon a plumped-out body.

The replacement of shrunken cartilage, by wax or other

modelling-media, inside or outside the skin, is a fallacy, and only in the hands of a most expert and artistic modeller does it attain a measure of success.

Be quite sure, therefore, that if any taxidermist, or his patron, tells you that he can "stuff a fish like life," he deserves the retort discourteous.

If fishermen—unless their notorious shyness of the truth blinds them to their own interests—would recognise these facts, and would not be so anxious to save the mere skin of their "finny prey," and would be clever enough to appreciate an absolutely exact copy of it, unchangeable and indestructible, it would do more to put a stop to the making of ugly mummies than anything else, and make the "stuffers" turn their attention to art. Perhaps, however, there is something to be said even for the worst of them when their patrons, with the usual rectitude which distinguishes all fishermen, hint that, as the pike they have just brought in "doesn't look his weight, doncherknow— sixteen pounds two and a quarter ounces, weighed after he had been out of the water three hours and three-quarters " (quarters are very important in all weights and measurements, as is well known !), "he had better be filled up a bit, as there is no doubt he weighed quite two pounds more when first caught, the dryness of the air "—and so on, and so on.

The home-coming of that gorgeously-bloated beast is a triumph for the 'cute taxidermist, and, as a friend present remarks, "He looks quite as big as what's-his-name's twenty pounder—no, twenty pound three and a half ouncer." Struck with the remark, the fortunate captor revels in the fact that no doubt, as he weighed eighteen and a quarter pounds (by fishermen's calculation), he would, if left another day or so to feed, have been quite twenty pounds in weight ; therefore that pike of, probably, fifteen pounds original weight, goes down to posterity as "just over twenty, old chappie, but he was so beastly old and half starved, that he should have weighed quite five-and-twenty."

Is it possible that considerations of such a nature can militate against the possession of a faithful reproduction of such a finny trophy? Quite impossible! but an instance has occurred in which a pike of some considerable weight was cast, and showed the perfectly natural depression of the stomach. An angler, who saw it then, remarked that "he didn't seem very well fed"; so the operator rammed some artificial "food" into the stomach of the fish and made another cast. When the two moulds were modelled from, the "improved" fish looked most unnatural, but that one was the fisherman's fancy!

Be this as it may, most persons of sound judgment prefer a thing as nearly correct as may be, and the casting of a fish taken as soon as possible after capture is *the only* method which gives anything like satisfactory results. The late Frank Buckland, whose geniality was only equalled by his enthusiasm for fish-casting,[1] made many fine models, as his fish-museum testifies; these are, however, all cast in plaster of Paris, and some few—but very few—museums have followed his lead, and those chiefly in America, where, judging from the excellent photographs published by Dr. Shufeldt for the Smithsonian Museum,[2] they appear lately to have attained to some proficiency in this art; but plaster models, from their weight, brittleness, and other bad qualities fully considered later on, have been discarded for many years in the Leicester Museum, and have been replaced by paper, paper pulp, and other compositions, all described in the following pages.

[1] *Life of Frank Buckland*, by George C. Bompas; and *Curiosities of Natural History*, by Francis T. Buckland.
[2] See Plates XX.-XXVI., *Scientific Taxidermy for Museums*.

For all methods of making moulds or models of any object, whether by means of plaster of Paris or of any other medium, the first thing to be provided is—

The Casting-box

Leuckart's embedding-boxes[1] have given the writer an idea for an improvement, not, perhaps, on the embedding-boxes for their especial purpose, but on the ordinary casting-box, and this is made in a more simple manner, whilst doing, more efficiently, the work for which it is intended.   Take, therefore, four pieces of one-inch wood of any suitable length and width — say two feet, or two feet six inches, in length— two of them an inch or so wider than the others.   At about an inch from one end of each of the wider pieces cut a slot just large enough to allow one of the narrower pieces to easily pass through it, and, inserting one of the latter into each slot, place the opposite ends of the narrower pieces at right angles to the inner faces of the wider pieces, so as to form a rectangular box, every side of which is movable, and whose length and width may be varied at will—limited only by the extreme length of the sides—by sliding the narrower pieces through the slots, and their other ends along the faces of the wider pieces.

It is necessary, be it observed, to oil the insides of the walls, and also to place, along the bottom edges and corners, some putty or clay to prevent the liquid plaster from running out.

Direct plaster casting is the easiest to manage, and is the system most in vogue.   It consists in laying down some natural object—say a snake or a fish, as being the easiest—and pouring plaster over it until a mould or cast is made therefrom in the manner now described.

[1] *Journ. Roy. Mic. Soc.* [N.S.], ii. p. 880 (see *Microtomist's Vade-mecum*, Lee, p. 172).

The Casting of Fishes and Simple Objects

As a preliminary, it may be stated that fishes are not injured in the slightest degree, if moderate care be exercised, by a mould being taken from them, but, if required for eating afterwards, they must only be washed and hardened for a short time in salt and cold water. Otherwise, they may be hardened much more rapidly by placing them in formol (Formula 31), alcohol of 90 per cent., a strong solution of potassium bichromate, or of alum and saltpetre (Formula 44), which are enumerated in their order of merit.

When a fish is merely to be represented with the fins closed or partially spread, as if lying upon a bank, etc., after capture, a quick method of casting is to simply lay it upon a smoothly-planed or paper-covered board, or upon glass, and to build up with sand, clay, or putty the under surface of the fish, so that only the upper half is seen without any under-cutting left underneath. This having been surrounded by the adjustable walls (see *ante*), plaster is poured over it in the ordinary manner and allowed to set for a short time; the object is then removed, and the inside of the resultant mould is either oiled or soaped, or the whole plunged into water. Into this pour plaster, after surrounding it (the mould) with the walls as before, and, having allowed it to set for a quarter of an hour or more, according to the size of the object—and consequent mass of plaster,—trim the edges, and tap all along them, and at top and bottom of the mould and model, and, as soon as a line appears and the halves "chatter," the model is loose from the mould, which may be carefully drawn off, working it usually from head to tail, the mould being previously marked to show which is which. Such a mould is shown by Fig. 1, Plate XII.

If properly managed, the plaster model of the object

XII.

Moulds and Models in Plaster of various Marine Fishes.

should be presented lying upon a tablet, also of plaster, without a blemish, and by this means easy subjects, such as perch, roach, or even much larger fresh- and salt-water fishes, can be cast, and the mould may make several copies if the same care be exercised.   See Fig. 2, Plate XII., which is a model made from Fig. 1.

With some of the tools Nos. 29 to 36 and a long "firmer" chisel, the fins, where spread, may be undercut and the tablet planed with advantage, and, therefore, in an hour a fish may be moulded, cast, and finished all but colouring—for which, of course, the plaster must be dry.

A much more scientific method, however, and one which gives far better results, is the following :—

Improved Method of casting Fishes

The specimen, having been kept for a few hours in any of the media mentioned on the preceding page, and well washed therein, is laid, better side uppermost, on a slab of slate or thick glass if a flat fish, but if, say, a perch, it will be best to lay it on a piece of board a little larger than itself.   Other small pieces of half-inch board, say 4″ × 3″ and 6″ × 3″, and some putty being provided, the pieces of board are arranged to lie underneath and support the dorsal, the *lower* ventral, the anal, and caudal fins, but *not* the uppermost ventral and pectoral fins, care being taken that the edges of the small pieces of wood do not meet *under any of the fins*, especially the tail, or an unnatural and unsightly ridge will occur in the subsequent casting.

Where the sides of the pieces of wood come against the sides of the fish but do not quite touch, pack in putty with a modelling-tool, and also where gaps occur between the end of one piece of wood and another.   Where the pieces of board are not thick enough to support the fins at the height required, wedge up with putty, or add other pieces of board, thinner or thicker as the case demands, and, in fishes with a long dorsal fin, a piece of wood sufficiently long and broad to save a join must be used. All boards must be wetted or oiled, and the reason for using boards instead of glass, slate, or cardboard is that, as the fins, especially the tail, often float up as the thin plaster goes over them—thus locking or spoiling them,—their being arranged on boards allows one or two fine entomological pins, *with their heads cut off*, to be used to keep them down. When the pins are driven in—one at each outer edge of the fins will often be quite sufficient—they must be cut quite close down on the fins, so that they will draw easily through the fins when the fish is turned over and the boards are removed. Keep the fish and its fins damp by applying water, or glycerin and water, with a *soft* brush, and remove all specks of dirt or putty from its surface.

At this stage, it must be decided whether the pectoral, and sometimes the ventral, fin is to be raised or allowed to lie flat upon the fish ; if the latter, nothing need be done further than to see that it *does* lie flat. If the former, however, the fin must be raised and held up with the fingers until the first cast or so sets it in the position required, and, if the fish be not very thick, the greater part of it will be above and outside the mould when the fish is cast, and will pull out, leaving a hole in the mould when finished.

All being ready, build the wooden walls, as detailed at p. 231, or the zinc walls (see pp. 341, 342) if the fish be small, and stop crevices with putty ; damp the fish as before, and pour in the plaster carefully, a thin skin at first, and so on as for other delicate objects. When dry, remove the walls, turn the half mould, with the fish in it, upside down, and remove the boards and putty.

If all has been done as it should be, the under half of the

fish now appears, all the rest being in the mould. Nothing should be disturbed, but that side should be gently brushed and wetted, and the surface of the mould now visible should have keys cut in as usual, and must be oiled—*this must not be forgotten*. Replace the walls, which, if propped, need not go close down upon the modelling-table ; make up the crevices with putty, and pour on plaster as usual, and when dry, which will be in about a quarter of an hour, the halves will come apart by gentle tapping and pulling, and the fish can be easily removed from the mould, care being taken not to rip the fins where they may be slightly held by the pins. Let it be noted that, if the fins have been upheld and protrude from the under-neath or first half mould, some provision must be made, such as supporting the mould on pieces of "quartering" (wood $3''$ by $2\frac{1}{4}''$), to prevent it from lying upon and crushing the fin.

When the fish is out of the mould and washed, the next process is to take a separate cast of the pectoral and ventral fins, and this is done by laying the fish again upon the board and placing a piece of board or glass under each fin, building a little wall of putty around, and pouring plaster on in the usual manner. Usually, both sides of the fins, and both sides of each right and left paired fin, must be cast ; but in some cases it will be sufficient to take moulds of both sides of the fins on that side of the fish determined upon to be the show side.

This system of lifting the fins upright when casting the trunk, and subsequently casting the fins, is only necessary when the fish is lent, may-be, for casting, or when the perfect skeleton is afterwards required ; but if neither of these causes is in operation, the best plan—after having taken a cast with the pectoral and ventral fins flat and the others spread, or else as a dead fish with nearly all the fins closed—is, undoubtedly, to remove the pectoral and ventral fins at their bases with a sharp pair of scissors, and place them beside the fish when arranging it for casting ; thus, the plaster being poured over all, the upper and under surfaces of both fins appear on the same block with the fish—an obviously valuable precaution against loss or mistakes.   Such a mould is shown by Fig. 3, Plate XII.

Dry the mould near the fire, but do not bake it to make it chalky and brittle, and, when dry, give it one or two coats of colza-oil, but not sufficient to fill up the pattern or to cause a skin of oil to form upon the plaster.

Although many authorities recommend treatment of the mould with water previously to making a model, yet this has certain disadvantages not found in oil, and the difficulty of distinguishing which is mould and which model is accentuated, in the case of the water process, in the trimming of the edges, unless the mould be coloured to distinguish it from the model.

Only simple objects such as those previously described will come out or relieve when plaster is cast into a plaster mould, and although many fishes can be made from such, yet there are others which are too " undercut " to relieve without breaking. In such cases, either the character or composition of the mould itself must be materially modified, or the substance of which the model is made must be changed.

The first alternative—that of modifying or changing the character of the *mould* so that a *plaster* cast or model may be made—leads to a consideration of—

How to make Plaster Casts of Undercut Objects

There are several methods of arriving at a satisfactory solution of this difficulty, which may be summarised under the following headings :—

1. By waste moulds in plaster.
2. By piece moulds in plaster.

3. By glue moulds.
4. By gutta-percha moulds.
5. By ordinary wax moulds.
6. By paraffin wax moulds.

Waste Moulds in Plaster.

These, so called because they are ultimately broken away piecemeal and only admit of one copy being taken, are commonly managed thus : [1]—

If the work is a medallion—and perhaps it will be as well to make your first mould as a trial one on a piece of clay, roughly formed like one—the work is easy.

First brush over the groundwork all round with the moulding composition. Mix a *little* of the red powder with some water into a paste in a basin, then add more water until the basin is three parts full, put your plaster in until it appears as a sort of hill in the basin with some water all round, beat it up with the spatula, and pour or spread it over the model, say to the thickness of an inch, or nearly so, all round and over it.

Let this set ; it will be better that it is not touched for an hour or so.

Then lift it up, and it will relieve from the groundwork ; you can now pick out the clay.

Soak it for about ten minutes in the pan of water ; then, while in the water, brush it carefully, so as, while leaving it clean, none of the fine parts are worn away.

Now place it on the table, and, to take the cast, mix your plaster ; then see that there is no water left in the mould, which should only seem just shining with the damp.

Pour some of the plaster in, shake it gently, lay the mould down and fill up with the plaster.

Let it rest for, say, an hour or longer, then turn it over, take your mallet and chisels and gently cut and break away the mould, which is no longer of any use, and is for that reason called a waste mould.

---

[1] *A Guide to Modelling in Clay and Wax, etc.*, by Morton Edwards, pp. 46, 47.

The white cast will soon show itself in places, and, with care, relieve from the coloured mould.

The work is then complete, and you have the plaster cast.

A modification and improvement on this is to stir into the plaster intended for the first coat a sufficient quantity of any common powder-colour (say Venetian red or red lead) to tint it. Let this be poured on as a *very* thin coating over all parts of the specimen—assume it to be a fish,—let it set, then oil or soft soap it all over, and follow with another thin coat of plaster of Paris *uncoloured;* oil again, and follow with another thin coat of uncoloured plaster, and so on, until a just sufficient thickness is attained to prevent breakage when the fish is taken out. Make a note of the number of layers, or the colours might even be varied after the first coat with any other cheap powder-colour. Instead of oiling or soaping each successive layer, brown paper may be introduced between, but is not certain in its effect.

The fish or other object, having been removed, reveals the mould with a tinted inner surface. It will not be necessary to dry this, for the sooner it is cast into the more easily will it break away. Soap or oil the mould (some authorities recommend merely soaking it in water, but this does not always answer), and pour plaster into it. Let it set for an hour or so, and then proceed with the modelling-tools Nos. 29 to 39, or with small chisels and a hammer, to break and prise away layer after layer, until, coming to the last pink one, greater care is necessary, and the model, being white, gives due notice of its presence below, so that, by delicate handling, the last coat is removed and the complete fish is revealed. It is a very pretty process, but one which taxes the patience and ingenuity of the operator.

In the case of a fish, snake, or lizard, a tablet should be allowed for in the plaster itself, and this is, of course, determined by the edges of the mould being protracted beyond the object cast, and also by the original surface being made flat and smooth. When this is not the case, the various tools, Nos. 29 to 33, and a long "firmer" chisel may be used to relieve and pare flat the plaster tablet of the model. A fish executed by this process is shown by Fig. 4, Plate XII.

Piece Moulds in Plaster

Piece-mould casting is a method by which the artist skilfully builds up a mould, piece by piece, in plaster of Paris in such a manner that although, in casting from an object, he takes in undercuts and under surfaces, each piece, though joining its fellow exactly, "relieves," and when the pieces have been put together and the whole filled with any medium, each piece takes off easily in a certain sequence, leaving the resultant model complete in itself. Such piece moulds of a sepia are shown by Figs. 1, 2, 3, and 4, on Plate XVI., and of a gigantic salamander, *Cryptobranchus japonicus*—in which one half of the tail is made as a "piece"—by Fig. 1 on Plate XV. This method is explained perhaps sufficiently under the heading of "The Cuttle-Fish" (see p. 284), and from such a mould several models can be made.

The method by which extremely large fossil reptiles have been modelled and built up is described by Mr. B. Waterhouse Hawkins,[1] and although not bearing upon the methods just described, is interesting reading, especially to visitors to the Crystal Palace, where these huge restorations still remain.

Glue Moulds

The glue mould is one which, with care, is capable of producing more than one copy. It will not do very well, if at all,

[1] "On Visual Education as applied to Geology, illustrated by Diagrams and Models of the Geological Restorations at the Crystal Palace." Read before the Society of Arts, 27th May, 1854, and published in the Society's Journal, No. 78.

for anything wet or damp, such as fishes or fungi, but if these are dry it will copy them ; such things as snakes and most reptiles can be cast admirably, and many copies delivered, by this process, which is used by plasterers, and modellers in plaster, clay, and wax, to get copies for centres of ceilings, trusses, brackets, busts, and statuary. It comes away so perfectly from undercuts and complicated corners by reason of its elasticity and toughness, that, to make an exact copy—say of a small bust or an apple—it is, in some cases, merely necessary to cover the object with the glue, and, when cold, to split the mould all the way down one side, pull it open, take out the object, and fill its place with liquid plaster.

There is no need in similar objects to adopt the complicated and useless process described at p. 213 of *Practical Taxidermy* and perpetuated by Mr. Hornaday ;[1] a description of how the glue mould of a large vertebra of a fossil reptile was managed will show the greater simplicity of method and consequent saving of time.

The vertebra, having been oiled, was supported, on one of the faces of its centrum, by a small pedestal of clay, about an inch or less in diameter, raising it about the same distance from a piece of glass upon which it rested on the casting-table. The vertebra was then surrounded by a square casting-box well oiled inside—as was also the glass on which it rested, —and a sufficient quantity of modelling-glue (Formula 95) was poured in to completely envelop the specimen. When cold, the mould was split and the vertebra extracted, and where it had rested upon the clay a hole was formed, through which (after the inside of the mould had been painted with oil-paint —red and white lead mixed with plenty of " driers ") the plaster was subsequently poured, and thus reproduced the original, as shown by Fig. 8, Plate XVI. In some cases it will be found

[1] *Taxidermy and Zoological Collecting, etc.,* pp. 265-267.

practicable, and indeed advantageous, to rest the object upon the heads of three nails driven into a piece of board.

This method dispenses with two tiresome and lengthy processes, namely, coating the specimen with clay and making a "jacket" of plaster.

There is certainly nothing half so safe as the modelling-glue of which to make a mould from a delicate or undercut fossil, where a plaster mould would be of no avail, and might break the specimen, even if not undercut, and where wax and gutta-percha would do the same, or stick and refuse to come away. The good modelling-glue (Formula 96), which must always be used for delicate specimens, will perfectly relieve, and come away sweetly, without the slightest danger, from a slightly oiled fossil.

In all cases the glue mould must be thinly painted, or, better still, varnished—care being taken not to fill up any sculpture—before the plaster is poured into it.

To cast a Fish in Plaster from a Glue Mould

The fish, being laid upon the board and prepared for casting as before described, is dried by gently patting it with a soft cloth. It is then oiled all over, but with only just sufficient oil to damp it and not to flow over it. When all is ready, pour over it a thin coating of the glue composition, Formula 95, followed by another, and so on, until a fairly thick glue mould is obtained, the crucial part of the operation being not to have the composition too hot, nor, indeed, so hot as is required for making a model in the ordinary way, and letting each coat, subsequent to the first, grow colder by trickling on the half-warm glue. Set the board with its contents out in the air, if possible, to cool, which takes about an hour. When it is cool enough, give the glue mould—without moving anything in the least or turning it over—a coating of thick white paint with

16

plenty of driers in it, and in a few hours it will be ready for use. If this cannot be waited for, cover the mould with a thick skin of putty, upon which arrange two strings crosswise. Surround with the casting-walls of wood or zinc, pour over all a sufficiency of plaster, and, as this is setting, pull up the strings, which will cut the mould into four parts. When set, turn all over, and the appearance will be presented of the fish resting in a mould of glue backed up by a jacket of putty and plaster, the oil-putty to prevent the wet plaster from liquefying the glue mould, and the plaster jacket to keep the glue mould stiff and in shape for the casting of the model.

Take the fish out, and into the glue mould (after the walls have been arranged around it again) pour plaster in the ordinary manner. When set, turn all over again, and the plaster jacket of four pieces will easily come off; next remove the putty, and lastly the glue mould, when a plaster fish will appear, with fins and "undercuttings" more perfect—owing to the elasticity of the mould—than can be obtained by any other method, excepting the paraffin wax mould. This is, of course, but a half cast, but if the edges of the first glue mould are sufficiently protected, it is possible to get the remaining half.

A later improvement, which simplifies matters, is to take—

89.—Glue composition (M.B.)

Formula 95 glue composition, hot	.	.	3 parts
White or red lead in boiled oil } as a stiff paint	.	.	1 part

Mix intimately.

With this as a mould, anything, from small boulders or fossils to fishes and fruits, may be reproduced, not only in plaster, but actually by any of the paper processes, so waterproof is it, and a jacket of plaster may be used over it as a stiffening support if necessary.

Gutta-Percha Moulds

The gutta-percha and wax composition (Formula 76, p. 85), melted in a water-bath, does very nicely to pour over objects such as small fishes, as it sets so rapidly as not to burn them, and gives wonderfully sharp detail ; it is, however, subject to the same drawback as the moulds made entirely of wax (see following), that, unless poured over in one unbroken layer, it shows lines of junction. Both this and the following, if thin, should be backed with a " jacket " of plaster.

Ordinary Wax Moulds

Beeswax or Japan wax moulds have certain advantages over the glue moulds, in being impervious to wet or damp, and so may be used for fishes and such objects. They are, however, subject to "blows," and, unless for small things, or unless done very quickly, show wavy lines where the wax flows but does not unite with another rapidly-cooling edge. All waxes for casting must give place to the following, which is, at present, probably used for such purposes only in the Leicester Museum.

Paraffin Wax Moulds

Paraffin wax, which is quite as cheap as the unmixed Japan wax, unlike it, does not answer as a modelling-composition, having no tenacity. It will occasionally serve for making a model of a small specimen, but its chief and most valuable use—in this far excelling any other wax, or, indeed, any other material —is that to which it is now applied in the Leicester Museum, namely, the casting of such objects as fishes, etc., or groups of fishes, for reproduction in plaster. For this it is unrivalled, as, although setting directly upon a cool surface, it liquefies immediately, and unites without the slightest blemish upon more paraffin being added, and it is so clear and liquid that the underlying specimen can be seen, and any floating-up of parts— which seldom happens, owing to its weight—can be instantly rectified. The subject should be slightly damp (*not wet*), and is not burned by the hot paraffin, but comes out easily, leaving the sharpest of impressions, quite hard, without a sign of a " blow " or joining. Into this mould, without any previous oiling, plaster is poured, and results in an extremely sharp model. In some cases, where the subject is not much undercut, more than one copy can be taken, but as its greatest service is for such objects and for complicated groups, it must be considered as a waste mould, and melted off the plaster model resting within it, and the wax may be used over and over again ; this, combined with its exceedingly low original cost, is a further recommendation, in which particular it is only paralleled by one or two other materials. Small meat-tins with sloping sides are the best to melt it in, and, as it liquefies at a low temperature, a water bath is not absolutely necessary, although it is always safer and better ; failing this, however, it may be placed upon the stove or in an oven to melt, care being taken that it does not burn. Its disadvantage—of not uniting with any other substance—is here a very great advantage, for any dirt, dust, chips of plaster, or what not, sink at once to the bottom of the melted wax, which may be strained off into another tin, and will come out, when cold, as a solid block, easily packed away until wanted.

The exact methods of building up the walls for the moulds and for the resultant models have not been given in all these processes, as they are practically the same as those described before ; the boards or glass on which the specimen rests must, however, be *wetted* for paraffin.

By this process such undercut objects as seven plaice, one over another, and nine or ten small codfishes, also in a heap, have been beautifully reproduced for the Leicester Museum (see Figs. 5 and 6, Plate XII., for models of a smaller number).

Another valuable property which paraffin possesses, is that of giving not only an ivory surface, but an ivory interior, to plaster casts ; and to do this it is only necessary to warm the plaster well and to dip it rapidly, or, in some cases, let it lie in very hot paraffin wax, which penetrates the plaster so efficiently that, by cutting with a knife, the brittleness of the plaster will be found to have vanished, and there appears an ivory surface which possesses the inestimable advantage of taking colour and drying softly, and so solving the difficulty at once of giving a proper surface to the ordinarily intractable plaster. The waxing of the plaster is applicable not only to models, but also to moulds, and has partially superseded borax (see p. 310) for leaf-moulds.

In *The Stonemason*, No. 58, 1887, pp. 73, 74, it is stated that

If the plaster has been mixed with milk and water, or if it be brushed over with a mixture of oil and wax, the surface will, when dry, take a good polish, and will after a while acquire the appearance of old ivory. Another method is to keep the cast in an oven of about 300 degrees F., for forty-eight hours, and then to steep it in olive oil. Afterwards immerse it in warm water, and polish with whiting. The plaster for casts may be tinted any desired colour by colouring the water with which it is mixed with soluble dyes. Gum arabic and alum mixed with the water will make the plaster as hard as the hardest wood, so that it may be used in ornamenting furniture.

DIVISION III

REPRODUCTIONS IN PAPER BY VARIOUS METHODS

Objects constructed in paper have always possessed a certain fascination for all art workers. The cheapness of the material, its lightness, freedom, when properly treated, from cracking or

warping—to which wood is peculiarly liable,—and its extraordinary toughness and applicability to many purposes, have
ever rendered it a favourite ; and now that it can be worked up
into large masses for purposes for which wood, or even iron, was
previously used, and can be waterproofed and made to withstand much more than wood possibly can, it is rapidly coming
into prominence, not as an aid to the fine arts merely, but as a
material to be dealt with in the building and other trades.

In No. 3 of a most useful periodical which came out in
1889,[1] is to be found the commencement of an interesting and
valuable article on " Papier-mâché : How to Mould It and
Ornament It," by Sylvanus Ward,[2] which gives the origin of
the process or processes now known under the comprehensive
term of Papier-mâché, or sometimes " Carton pierre," as thus:—

Papier-mâché, which, literally translated, means "chewed paper," is
a term which we have been accustomed to hear applied to a great
variety of products made by a pulping process, and some of which
contain no paper whatever.   If we look for the origin of the name we
shall find that it was first applied to a coarse, unglazed paper reduced
to a pulp, and then mixed with gum or glue paste, thus forming a
substance plastic whilst wet, and, when dry, as hard or harder than most
woods, and, unlike them, not liable to crack.   As the name would seem
to indicate, the inventor, or reputed inventor, was a Frenchman—one
Lefevre.   About 1740 this person is said to have imparted his discovery
to a German snuff-box maker named Martin, by whom it was found to
be of commercial value in his trade.   In or near the year 1745, John
Baskerville of Birmingham, the famous printer, took the matter up, and
before long the manufacture of papier-mâché became an important
industry in Birmingham and its district.   Later on, various fibres or
fibrous materials, pulped and mixed with adhesive substances, have
been known as papier-mâché ; scrap leather, wood fibre imported from
Sweden, potato peelings, and even sawdust having, it is said, been

---

[1] *Work: An Illustrated Magazine of Practice and Theory for all Workmen, Professional and Amateur.*

[2] Pages 33, 34.

made to take the place of paper; whilst in some preparations china clay, a substance apparently little suited for the purpose, has formed a large, if not an important part of the admixture.

In another periodical, published in 1895,[1] is another interesting article,[2] too lengthy to reproduce here, but which points out that—

Paper is now made from almost everything which can be reduced to pulp. The good old linen rags are now very little used, and only for the very finest kinds of hand-made writing-papers, and for paper to be used in printing the most costly and luxurious special editions of books. For ordinary purposes new products, unheard of in the paper trades until comparatively recently, are utilised on an immense scale. Esparto grass, wood fibre, stems and leaves of all sorts of plants, grasses, and even sea and fresh-water weeds, are pulped, and made either into paper, or by different processes transformed into innumerable forms capable of taking the place for many purposes of wood, stone, and even of iron. When strong fibre is used the resulting substance may be made so hard that it can hardly be scratched.

The article goes on to mention that rafters, roof, walls and their plastering, ceilings, floors, and all the interior and exterior parts of a house, all the furniture, including even the piano, can be, and have been, constructed in specially compressed and water-proofed paper; that a church, a factory chimney, gas-pipes, tobacco-pipes, horse-shoes, false teeth, carriages, telegraph-poles, boats, flower-pots, " glass," bed-quilts, stockings (!), cigars, carpets, and so on—a sufficiently comprehensive list,—have been, and are, made of paper or vegetable pulp of one kind or another, and it will, therefore, not surprise the reader to learn, that the desire to substitute some strong and light material for the objectionably heavy plaster, led the writer first to study the principles of " mask-making " at a theatre, and later to investi-

---

[1] *Old and Young*, vol. xlvi. No. 1264, pp. 4, 5.
[2] " Paper and its Uses," signed " Ben Olio."

gate the principles of stereotyping, and this suggested what may be termed—

The Direct Paper Process

This can be applied to the making of copies of such objects as fishes, although the heavy beating required by the prepared paper in stereotyping—which is all very well upon a metal base—is far too rough when applied upon a plaster mould. A judicious blending, however, of both theatrical and typographical paper moulding resulted in the successful accomplishment of the model of a huge skate which, previously done in plaster, taxed the united strength of several men to lift, and was then far too heavy to be trusted upon the walls of any museum. But when finished in paper it was light enough to be held out easily in one hand, and, although not so well done as subsequent specimens have been, yet, as it has remained unchanged for ten years, it may be as well to note the method pursued, and the improvements upon it since that time. The mould having been oiled, thin white paper, such as is called "lining paper," and is sold in rolls of twelve yards by the paper-hangers, was laid down in moderate-sized pieces, dry upon the side next the mould, and pasted upon the upper surface, followed by four more layers of the same paper, pasted, and afterwards by five layers of brown paper glued—ten layers in all, all carefully laid, and beaten with a stiff brush.

When dried and lifted out of the mould, it was seen that the first paper had not properly united, but hung in ribbons, and therefore required pasting down, which took out a great deal of the sharpness.

Further experiments showed that the paper used first should be tissue-paper, *pasted on the side next to the mould*—to which it does not adhere when dry, if the mould be suitably greased or oiled,—and that each piece should be laid as free from wrinkles as possible, and gently patted down with a brush (the shape shown on Plate II., Fig. E, being the best), that several layers of tissue-paper should be followed by slightly thicker paper, known as " cap-paper," and this finished by layers of thin brown paper, all well pasted and *not glued*.   By these means a very fine model of a large " angel fish " was made, and still exists.

A more detailed description of some fishes, large and small, made during the past few years by this direct method may be useful.

The Casting and Modelling of an unusually large Fish

A ground, or six-gilled, shark, *Notidanus griseus*, was caught in the North Sea, and sent from Grimsby, in 1893, as a present from Mrs. Dobson of that port.   It was 8 feet in length, of proportionate girth, and of such a weight that four men could barely lift it.   Directly it arrived, it, being a trifle " high," was thoroughly washed and brushed, and a mixture of salt and weak solution of permanganate of potash was thrown over it.   It was then laid on its stomach, fins extended, upon the paved floor of the casting-room, and a box built around it ; a thin and narrow line of clay was then built along its back, not quite in the centre, but in such a manner as to give rather more to the better half.   (Here it may be noted that there is a " better half " to most things, and that should be the show side whenever possible.)   All being ready, plaster was mixed in a large pan or tub, and, when rather thicker than cream, was ladled out by buckets and gently poured over the better side, covering it as quickly as possible, fins and all, with a thin coating.   This required several bucketfuls before the whole was united, and required the constant attention of three assistants, so that no part of the first coat set before the whole was covered.   This, when about a quarter of an inch thick, or rather more, was allowed to partially set, so that no excessive weight coming after should distort the shape of the specimen, and the process was repeated several times, the thickness of the coats, however, being gradually increased until a sufficient thickness was attained, rising high above the line of clay.   Naturally it may be asked how this was possible, and why the clay was not built up to the full height. Because, had the clay been built along the back to the full thickness required, the weight would have been too great for the fish to bear on that side without distortion.   Therefore, after the first coats were on, the plaster was made a little thicker, and, not being so liquid, was piled up, as it were, along the edge above the clay by holding pieces of board just outside this, and " dodging " any overflow.

When the first side was completed the clay was removed, and the edge of the plaster half mould examined for any thin papery edges or overflows next the skin, and these being trimmed off carefully, and the skin of the half of the fish still exposed having been washed and freed from small chips of plaster—not too easy a task with a rough-skinned fish such as a shark,—the edges of the half mould were well oiled (a most important matter, by the way, as those who forget it will find to their cost), and the casting of the remaining half—with the exception of the tail, which, lying flat, was included in the first cast—was proceeded with in like manner, the plaster now coming up to and against the edges of the first half mould. The stomach was not cast, as in this case it was not necessary to show that part.

When of the same thickness as the other half, it was trimmed until the edges of the join showed as an oily line, and the whole was allowed to set for some time, and then came the task of getting the fish out, or rather, in this case, the mould from off the fish.   This, it may be imagined, was no easy matter, the dead weight being enormous, considering that, to the original weight of the fish, was added that of the mould, consisting of some hundredweights of plaster together with a vast amount of water. However, by pressing more men into the service, and by leverage and gently rocking the mass to and fro, also tapping with a wooden mallet along the seam, one half loosened, came away, and was removed. The other half, being the weightier, was more difficult, but was at length levered on edge against the wall, and the fish dropped out when the planks were removed. It was washed and dragged to the tank, where it now remains in bichromate solution (Formula 43) awaiting skeletonising, and is as fresh as when it came in.

The two halves of the mould, taking a long time to dry, were not fit for use for some months, being too heavy to move about into the sun or near the fire. At length, being dry, they were thoroughly dressed inside with grease and oil, and this was repeated every other day for a week.

It stood for some little time, and then came the making of the model by the direct paper process. One half of the mould having been well oiled—this time with colza-oil,— tissue-paper of good quality was pasted on one side with the paste (Formula 90), and laid carefully down in fairly small pieces, *pasted side downwards*, inside the mould ; this first coat should be, and was, extremely well laid, all tendency to wrink-ling being patted or "stippled" with one of the brushes (Fig. E), and where it tore, as it did occasionally, a fresh piece was pasted over at once ; so it progressed until the inner surface was completely covered, the paper being moulded and coaxed and patted and stippled into every depression. This skin was followed by another treated in precisely the same manner ; the third was, however, *pasted on both sides*. These three thicknesses of tissue-paper were followed by three thicknesses of "cap" paper, and these by one of thin brown paper, one of "cap," one of thin brown, and finally by three of thick brown paper, mak-ing twelve layers in all. Strengthening ribs of six thicknesses of thick brown paper, about 4 inches in width — nine in number—crossed the inside of the body at intervals from the nose to the tail, and, lengthwise over all, one 4-inch strip of six thicknesses of brown paper extended from head to tail, making the whole extremely strong without unnecessary weight.

The other half of the mould was treated in precisely the same manner, and both halves were left to dry until they showed a disposition to lift along the edges, which did not happen for some weeks. This is, of course, dependent upon the dryness of the weather, and also upon whether moderate fire-heat or warm air can be brought to bear. Note, however, that placing large masses, whilst wet, in front of a fire, or even in hot sunshine, has the effect of drying them indeed, but in such a manner that they are often drawn completely out of shape and ruined.

As some of the edges gradually dried and lifted, the remaining edges were slightly relieved, either by the hand or by cutting with a knife ; this, taking care of the fins the while, had the effect of letting the air under the body of the animal between the paper skin and the mould, and in a few days parts could be lifted to let in more air, the head, toward the jaws, being the last to "stick." At length the whole could be lifted, despite the undercut nature of the mould ; here and there, indeed in one place near the gills, it was found advisable to slit it along a prominent edge with a knife, to cause it to relieve properly.

When out, it was looked over for blemishes caused by the paper sticking a little to the mould in places, as it sometimes does ; these, if hanging loosely, were pasted down at once or made up.

The joining of the two halves and the repairing of the slit near the gills were now effected. The two edges, being slightly damped, were brought together and propped up from the underneath, and united by four strips of calico, $2\frac{1}{2}$ inches in width, put on diagonally, and then left to dry. Where the edges were obstinately disinclined to come together they were left until next day, or until dry, and the strips of calico applied at those points. Strips of brown paper next covered all in four thicknesses, crossing the work again, and when dry, the outside, where open or not quite level, and the cut near the gills were made up with tissue-paper, pasted and rolled up, and wedged in as pulp. Finally, a little pasted tissue-paper over the seams made all good.

Although so strong when dried that two men, equal to a weight of 22 stone, sat upon it without the least fear, and without making any impression upon the model, and although the fish, as before stated, weighed some hundredweights, yet the finished model was—incredible though it seems—but 9 lbs. 12 oz. in weight! Hence it may be claimed that, having absolute truth of detail, strength, a certain elasticity, and inappreciable weight, and that more copies than one can be made, the paper processes, both direct and pulped, must supersede all other methods for the delineation of large objects for museum purposes.

As it was inexpedient to exhibit it as if lying extended upon its stomach on the ground, as at first intended, it was decided to show it suspended upon a wall without any back-board, and therefore some half-inch pieces of deal were procured, and one, intended as the supporting centre-board, was cut 4 feet 6 inches in length, by 3 inches in breadth, and a $\frac{1}{2}$ inch in thickness.

One end (that by the tail) was cut diagonally, and was arranged to rest within and against the post-axial border of the anal fin, this being a distance of exactly 3 feet from the extreme tip of the tail ; and the other end lay inside, within a foot of the snout. Two "key-holes," 1 inch in length by a $\frac{1}{2}$ inch in width, were cut crosswise in the board, one at

18 inches from the snout or 6 inches from the end of
the board, and the other at a distance of 3 feet 2 inches,
or about 8 inches from the end of the board near the tail.
On the inside of the board the key-holes were covered with
pieces of zinc, each cut 3 inches in length by 3 inches in
breadth and bent in this manner :— ⌐⌐. When nailed
down, two pieces were fitted at the open ends and nailed on to
the edge of the board, thus forming a box, which was further
secured and closed in with pasted brown paper to prevent anything getting inside the model (see A, Fig. 2, Plate XIII.).

Across the pectoral fins a piece of half-inch wood, 3 inches
wide and nearly 2 feet in length, was fitted, and the line
of the fish and the projected centre-piece being arranged on
the same plane, this wood was nailed *underneath* the centre-piece,
forming a cross (B, B, Fig. 2); underneath this a small post,
about 7 inches in length, was nailed as a strut to support the
wood now as a cross-piece at that end. At about 18 inches
from the tail end another strut was fixed in like manner.
Along the inner surface of the tail a long lath was pasted as
a strengthening bar (C, Fig. 2), and from about the centre of
this another lath (D, Fig. 2) extended to the underneath of the
tail-end of the centre-piece to make all fast. On or under the
cross-piece were nailed two short laths extending inside the
pectoral fins as supports (E, E, Fig. 2). A similar lath, but of
less length, proceeded from just inside the snout to the fore end
of the centre-piece, and was made fast (F, Fig. 2). These and
the bottoms of the small struts or props were firmly attached
by strips of linen and paper to the inside of the model; the
struts, of course, abutting against what should be the backbone
of the fish. All this, being satisfactorily fitted and pasted in,
was suffered to dry, and then several 2½-inch strips of common
calico were brought over the centre-piece, cross-pieces, and struts,
and well pasted down inside the model, brown paper being

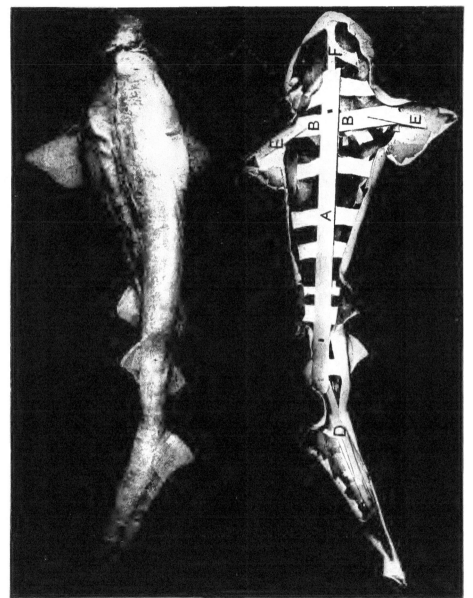

XIII

MODEL, BY THE DIRECT PAPER PROCESS, OF A GROUND SHARK, SHOWING UPPER AND UNDER SURFACES.

ultimately fastened over those for greater security.   When dry, the whole, although so light, was beautifully rigid, and could be lifted by any part of the framework.   Finally, it was filled with shavings, and very thick brown paper was folded and laid along on the top of the shavings to come in between the edges of the model and the centre-piece, and the whole was covered with well-pasted brown paper, which united all in one plane. The finished model, right side uppermost, is shown as Fig. 1 on Plate XIII.

The Wolf-Fish or Cat-Fish [1]

A fine specimen of the spotted variety of this "Gigantic Blenny" or "Shanny" reached the Museum through the kind offices of the same lady, and, in this case, was laid upon the casting-table *on its side*, the large pectoral fin spread out fully, but closely appressed to its side, and a cast in one piece was made of it.   This was permissible, owing to its configuration, and also by reason of its being intended as a side view, not taking in both sides, but only, say, three-quarters.   To do this, the under surface, or rather that part next the slab, was filled up with clay (damped sand would, perhaps, have been better) around the whole of the fish until only rather more than half was exposed ; this was to prevent the thin plaster running underneath and locking up the fish.   Plaster was poured over it in successive coats as over the shark, and when set, which would be in a quarter of an hour after the last thickness had been laid on, the fish tumbled easily out of the mould, which then represented, as an intaglio, rather more than half of it.

The fish, having been washed and freed from any small pieces of plaster, etc., was laid down again, and, as it had been decided to represent it as if swimming, a rather ingenious device was resorted to to get the muscles of the large pectoral fin into

[1] Not the American "Cat-Fish," *Amia calva*.

proper position, whilst yet not locking the fin in the mould.
This was managed by holding or fixing the fin in a swimming
position, away from the body, whilst the plaster was poured on.
As the mould was thickened, the part immediately around the
fin was, after being sufficiently strengthened, left uncovered by
any more plaster, and consequently the edges rose around it, leaving the end of the fin exposed.   When, therefore, the mould was
finished, the fin, not being covered in to its full extent, withdrew
easily with the fish, and left a cavity, of which the use will be
described.   The fin was now cleanly cut from the fish along a
certain line which would give the best results in future joining,
and a separate cast made of its upper surface.   (Both upper
and under surfaces must be cast if the fin is to be subsequently
shown straight out instead of a little relieved from the side.)
There were then two moulds made—one with the fin close to
the side, the other with the fin extended ; and the reason why
the fin was not cut off in the latter instance before the fish was
cast, as is done in some instances, is that it has been found
that fishes such as this, with very fleshy or muscular pectoral
attachments, do not subsequently make up at that part so
naturally when the fin is cut off as when the muscles are extended by the fin in position.

The moulds, having been dried and oiled as before (after
the hollow of the pectoral fin in one case had been partially
filled in with clay or putty), were modelled into by the same
process as used for the shark, the number of layers of tissue-
paper and other papers being the same, the " ribs " and longitudinal strip being, however, dispensed with, this not being
required for any but very large fishes.

The completed model being trimmed of superfluous paper
around the head, fins, and tail, and rounded off by knife or file,
so as to follow the undulations correctly, the fins and tail
should be thinned at their under edges by file or sandpaper, and

the loose fin attached to such part of the base shown upon the body of the fish as was determined upon before. This attachment is simply made with paste and tissue-paper, and by pulping a little of the tissue-paper or using wax (Formula 71) to fill in crevices, and to make up clearly and naturally.

When the fin has been cast on both upper and under surfaces, two moulds will, of course, result, and each mould must be modelled into with tissue or other paper to half the natural thickness of the fin ; then, when pasted together in the manner detailed for the edges of fungi (see p. 375) and the base filled in with composition or wax, it will be of the right thickness.

Sometimes, owing to various causes—nine times out of ten the fault of the operator,—the model will have small blemishes, or will have taken away some specks from the interior of the mould. If this happen, make up with tissue-paper and paste, and brush gently when dry. Oil the model well with colza-oil, and, when absorbed, repeat the dose—perhaps twice—and put away out of the dust.

The Mounting of the Model

The finished model was arranged, like that of the shark, with a back-board of wood with keyholes, the wood being 3 feet 6 inches in length, by 3 inches, by a $\frac{1}{2}$ inch, feather-edged for a foot from the tail end. At 14 inches from this end a keyhole was made, and another at an interval of 18 inches, both being boxed in as described at p. 254.

The weights of the model were as follow :—

Model complete, but unmounted . . 1 lb. 6 oz.
,, with wood, zinc, packing and backing, under 4 lbs.

whilst the weight of the actual fish was nearly 30 lbs.

This system of mounting, although, perhaps, not quite so attractive in appearance as when the hollow model is cemented

17

to a board, has two advantages. One is, that the weight of the mount (a canvas-covered and coloured board) would be about $4\frac{1}{2}$ lbs., which, added to the original weight of 1 lb. 6 oz., is about 2 lbs. in excess of the completed model when simply backed and arranged in the keyhole method; the other being that those models not on mounts take up less space. Still, it must be conceded that not only is a model, when mounted, of handsomer appearance, but there is space on the mount, under the model, to affix a label with the necessary information.

To Colour the Model

For this purpose, a fresh fish of the same species should always be procured; notes and sketches may help, but they are at best but extraneous aids, and, missing the greys and nuances of colouring, must always result in disappointment when compared with a fresh fish. In this case the fresh fish, well washed, was placed on a sloping board in front of the artist, and the model, also laid upon a board just underneath it, was then brushed over with a full body of linseed-oil, afterwards wiped dry, and the following tube oil-colours, etc., were used and laid on by artists' large, flat, hog-hair brushes:—

Ivory Black	Caledonian Brown
Vandyke Brown	Aureolin
Permanent Blue	Terre Verte
Purple Madder	Flake White
Vermilion	Roberson's Medium

The two latter, well blended by the palette knife, formed the base with which the colours were mixed by the brushes used. The colours thus mixed to the tints desired, were laid on rapidly and with a "full brush," and, when the general hue and tone were achieved, the characteristic markings of the body, head, and fins were blotched and stippled on, whilst the remainder was wet, the eye, as a special organ, being truthfully copied, so that, by studying the greys and lights, the appearance of liquidity and depth was arrived at.

Needless to say, it is impossible to describe exactly *how* it was done; only the colours can be given as a guide, and no two artists would agree in this. They are merely indicated, therefore, as a record of what was actually and satisfactorily accomplished with them.

Not only is the direct paper method useful for modelling such objects as have been described, but it is of the highest service to delineate correctly rocks of various formations which it is desirable to introduce into cases as accessories. Ordinarily, the "rockwork" is a fancy conception (see pp. 381, 382), but, if a plaster mould in two or more pieces be made of any stone, those pieces may be tied together, and paper pasted within them to a sufficient thickness, as for other objects, and the mould may be removed when the model is dry, leaving a perfect reproduction of all the characteristics of the original. In this way certain rocks in the Leicester Museum have been modelled, and, to give an idea of the saving of weight, there is a small flint boulder of the original weight of over 7 lbs., the model of which weighs but a trifle.

That the English are as far behind in such matters as the Americans, a visit to the British Museum will demonstrate. There the resources of paper are almost unheard of. Skeletons of large extinct animals and others, for which it is admirably adapted by reason of its lightness and toughness, are cast in the old-fashioned heavy and brittle plaster, and although, for such objects as the cetaceans, the paper process is invaluable, the resources of taxidermy not being sufficient to even decently portray these mammals, yet the British and American Government Museums do not appear to have recognised this fact, or in but a half-hearted manner.

The Pulped-paper Process

Although the direct paper process is so valuable for large objects and for those in which minute definition is not required, yet there are other objects, such as the smaller fishes, the scales of each of which possess a certain distinctive pattern, and for such as these a species of papier-mâché was introduced into the laboratory of the Leicester Museum some six years ago. In working out this system, numberless experiments were made, and a short *résumé* of the successes and failures may help others in like experiments, and may give them a choice of methods.

As flour pastes enter largely into all paper - work, methods of making good pastes are now given.

90.—Flour Paste (Water) (M.B.)

Flour	.	.	10 oz. by *measure* (or 7 oz. by weight)
Water	.	.	10 oz. and 5 oz. by *measure*
Oil of Cloves	.	$\frac{1}{2}$ oz.	,, ,,

There is a particular method to be adhered to in making the above paste ; for this purpose, therefore, take 10 oz. by *measure*, of good flour, and to this add gradually 10 oz. —also by measure—of cold water, stirring them well together for some minutes to break up all lumps. Put the mixture into a saucepan, rinse the vessel in which it was mixed with 5 oz. more of cold water, and add this to what is in ·the saucepan. Stir constantly over the fire until unable to stir it any more by reason of its thickness, when it will be done, and should be *very* stiff. Lastly, empty the paste into a large jar or a small pan (brown stoneware, glazed inside, is the best, being the strongest for laboratory purposes), and add the oil of cloves.

91.—Flour Paste (Oil) (M.B.)

Flour	.	. 10 oz. by measure (or 7 oz. by weight)
Linseed-oil	.	. 5 oz. by measure (or nearly 5 oz. by weight)

Stir well together, and boil slowly in a water bath (glue-kettle) for two or three hours, and afterwards unite this with the water paste in the following proportions and manner :—

92.—Combination Pulp (M.B.)

Water flour paste (Formula 90)	.	. 5 oz. by measure		
Oil　„　„　(Formula 91)	.	. 5 oz.　„　„		
Tissue-paper	.	.	.	. 6 sheets

The two pastes are mixed together, and spread thinly with a spatula upon the sheets of paper, and these are laid one upon another as done. The whole of them are then rolled together and kept in a cool place, in an air-tight jar or other receptacle, until wanted, but not for less than three days, when they are well and intimately pounded in a metal mortar with the addition of a *very little* Venetian Red. The composition, which is *to be used fresh*, is well and firmly kneaded like putty in the fingers, and pressed into the mould with the fingers and with a rough cloth, and finally with wadding to remove super-fluous oil.

Should the pulp, however, after lying by for some time, be found to become dry and unworkable, 2, and sometimes 3 oz. of flour paste Formula 90 must be added.

The mould should not be oiled immediately before using, but some days should intervene. The pulp model is finally backed with six layers of brown paper for subjects of ordinary size, the number of layers being increased for large fishes, etc.

The detailed method of applying the combination pulp is, when a sufficient quantity is got together, to press it into the mould (oiled some time previously) with the fingers to the thickness of from an eighth to a quarter of an inch, and "stipple" it in with a stiff brush, and press it with a rough cloth in such a manner as to knead it well into every interstice, and cause it to take the print of every line.

Although there should be a sufficient thickness of pulp to well cover the inner surface of the mould, yet if a sixteenth of an inch will do this, there is no need to pile more on. When the pulp has been well beaten in—care, of course, being taken not to damage the mould with too hard usage,—paste on several thicknesses of tissue-paper, followed by thicker "cap" paper, and again by thin brown paper for larger fishes; but no glue must be used, as it often "pulls," especially if there should be any reason for putting the model near the fire for quicker drying, and also because it will not allow the oil subsequently put on to penetrate the substance of the pulp and paper.

When laying down the composition, it should be very thinly spread upon the fins, and finished off, indeed, to a thin outer edge with only one or two thicknesses of tissue-paper backed by a piece of pasted muslin. The fins, which may have been removed from the subject and cast upon the same block with it, are better managed by the direct process, *i.e.* with tissue-paper, *pasted side downwards*, well worked in with a brush and followed by other thicknesses, say six, of tissue-paper backed with muslin, the hollow part at the base (if only one side is cast) being filled up with tissue-paper crumpled and pasted in, or, better still, with composition (Formula 61). If, however, both sides of a fin are cast, the thicknesses of paper should be reduced, or the edges will be too thick when the two sides are joined together—which they may be with paste, and tied together temporarily with thread or hemp, after being trimmed around to the exact shape printed by the mould.

The model will require a few days to dry, according to the warmth of the atmosphere indoors and out, and, if very large, the edges of the paper covering the pulp and overlapping the edges of the mould may be raised all around to let the air in to dry the remainder,—the head and lips, where the pulp has to be pressed in to some thickness, being the last to dry ; from four days to a week in a warm room is generally sufficient, but this is a matter of experience, and the greatest care must be taken to let it be sufficiently dry, although there is a stage only known by practice when, after a certain amount of drying, the mould may be put near, *not before*, a fire, and the model " sweated " out. Usually, the tail and fins being freed, a gentle pulling from the *tail end*, with a rocking and upward tendency of pull to free the lips, will relieve the model without injury to it or to the mould.

Directly it is out of the mould, and before it has time to get " bone dry," it should be tacked down upon a board by the waste edges of paper, and allowed to dry. Subsequently, the waste paper around the margin must be trimmed off with a sharp knife, the fins, if necessary, trimmed thinner, and, assuming the model to be a half cast, this must be laid upon a calico-covered board or mount, and fixed by a little pasted wadding under the head and tail, or under any part where it touches the board, and all crevices made up afterwards with pulp (Formula 93).

Probably, however, the latest method adopted—which is applicable to all direct paper or pulp models of a certain size— is better. Directly the model is removed from the board on which it was tacked to dry, a piece of half-inch pine (thinner for small fishes), exactly conforming to the shape of the model, is fitted within it so that it falls a *little below* the edges all round, and these are made fast to the board by pasted muslin or thin calico. When nearly dry, the model is turned right side uppermost and re-tacked by its waste edges upon the drying-board, and, when *quite* dry, these edges are cut away.

The model is then affixed by screws passing from the back of the tablet into the fixed body-board, and, where the edges of the model do not quite touch, they are made up with one of the pulps, wax-, or other compositions. It may be, but seldom is, necessary to fill in large fishes made with very thin pulp. In this event, a square hole is cut in the body-board, through which, after it is fixed and dry, sawdust or wadding is introduced, and the hole is then closed again.

The latest addition to the pulps used in the Leicester Museum is one which has given the very best results in quickness of making, toughness, and extreme definition; by it very fine models of fairly large fishes, fossils, and other objects have been made with gratifying success, and its lightness is so extreme that it may be calculated, in almost every instance, as being *half an ounce* in the model to every *pound* weight in the original. For instance, a 12 lb. 9 oz. carp weighed but *six ounces*; a 5 lb. 5 oz. bream *three ounces*, and a 6½ lb. block of stone, on which were ammonites, *four ounces*, after the thickness of the model had been made up on its sides and under surface to resemble the original stone.

93.—Carton Pierre (M.B.)

Tissue-paper, 4½ sheets	.	. or 1 oz.
Flour paste (Formula 90)	. ' .	. 5 oz.
Powdered pipe-clay .	. .	. 1 oz.

The above should be well beaten in a metal mortar until reduced to a fine pulp, and afterwards worked, a small portion at a time, by a muller upon a stone slab, or by a strong spatula upon a piece of thick glass, until it becomes as a thoroughly homogeneous paste without showing knobs or traces of unworked paper. When squeezed between the fingers it should not be " short," nor break up easily, but should be tough and closely adherent.

When a sufficient quantity has been made, oil the mould thinly and press the pulp firmly into it, kneading the pulp well into every depression, but *as thinly as possible*, for, wherever this precaution is neglected and it lies as a thick mass, so surely will a loss of definition be subsequently observed, the increased thickness not allowing sufficient pressure of the fingers and thumbs being brought to bear to force the pulp into all the patterns and interstices of the mould.

When the mould is thinly covered with the pulp, lay upon it some pieces, not too large, of muslin, well pasted on both sides, to form one layer at first, this being superior to paper, which has sometimes been the chief cause of the troublesome thickening of the folds in the deeper cavities, and a consequent loss of definition ; this also has been due to the tissue or other paper with which the pulp was formerly backed getting out of place, or working up as a thick mass. About three layers of muslin will give sufficient strength as a backing, but in fins and small specimens one is sufficient. It is necessary, some hours after finishing, to examine for " blisters " in the muslin, and these parts must be re-pasted and rubbed down with the fingers. On an irregular surface the muslin must be put down in small pieces, cut to shapes best adapted for being laid down without wrinkling ; otherwise they will lift or contract over the depressions when drying. The muslin must overlap the pulp at least half an inch all round to prevent curling. When relieving the model from the mould, pass a thin knife under this edge of muslin, and gradually relieve everywhere. As before stated, these models should be dried slowly, at least a week being allowed. Should the weather be damp and it be found necessary to expose them to a fire, they should be placed at a considerable distance from it, or they will be twisted out of shape.

By means of the backing of muslin, the model, when dry,

comes out perfectly sharp, strong, and exceedingly light, and may be steeped in linseed-oil to toughen and further preserve it, as well as to render it fit for the reception of colour; this adds but very little to the weight, the model of a $4\frac{1}{4}$ lb. bream weighing but *two and a half ounces* after steeping.

Sometimes, for certain objects, more paste and clay may be added than given in Formula 93, but, although probably harder, it is less tough.

The addition of 1 oz. of glycerin to the above renders the model slightly elastic and very tough, and can be used in such things as reproductions of seaweeds, but it is difficult to manage, and is better left out for most things.

A pulp quickly made, not, of course, of such fine quality as Formula 93, but which is valuable for taking the place of clay (see p. 77), for inserting within the skin of mammals, birds, and other animals, is thus prepared:—Take pieces of tissue-paper, not too large; paste them on both sides with the thick paste, Formula 90, and work up with a spatula or knife upon a slab or glass; as it becomes broken up and pulpy add a little finely-powdered pipe-clay, just sufficient to assist the binding together of the mass. This is much lighter than clay alone, and can be used in all situations where that can be used, and, indeed, surpasses in some cases the cements given for ears, etc., as it does not set so quickly, but, on the other hand, must be more quickly dried artificially, or it is liable to mildew the skin.

Let it be noted as a valuable trait in the character of all water-paste pulps, that they may be coloured to any tint by the addition of dry powder-colours; hence very little is needed to finish the colouring of the models of tongues of mammals, those of various anatomical dissections, and of the pileus of fungi.

The best pulps are also highly valuable in reproducing

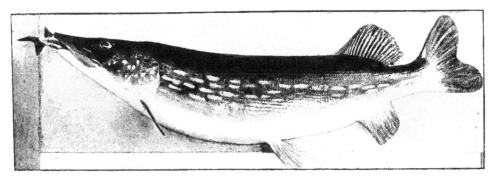

XIV

FIG. 1.—MODEL IN PAPER PULP OF A 20-LB. PIKE STRIKING A ROACH.

FIG. 2.—MODEL IN PAPER PULP OF A DOGFISH SWIMMING.

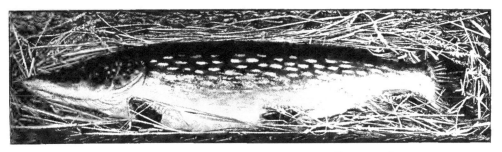

FIG. 3.—MODEL IN PAPER PULP OF A 20-LB. PIKE IN A BASKET OF STRAW.

many fossil fishes, whose great weight and bulk, when done in plaster, are a serious consideration in any museum. An instance amongst many may be given. Some years ago, the Messrs. Ellis, who have been great benefactors to the Leicester Museum, presented a rare fossil fish in fine condition—the *Hetero-lepidotus serrulatus*—but retained the counterpart themselves. Permission was obtained to make a mould from this, and a copy was made in pulp, in which every scale, and the pattern of every scale, was exact, and, when finished and coloured, the model could not be distinguished from the original; and whereas the latter was as much as a man could lift, the model weighed but a few ounces.

At the present time, the compositions may be said to have successfully resisted all alternations of heat and cold, exposure, and some knocking about, and are therefore justly prized.

Their strength and toughness are so great that they bear considerable weight and ill-usage without bending or breaking, and some idea of their extraordinary lightness has been given before. The combination-pulp models (Formula 92), especially if subsequently soaked in oil or brushed over with hot beeswax, are somewhat heavier; nevertheless, even their weight is hardly worth mentioning, and it will be sufficient to note that the model of a pike of the original weight of 20 lbs. weighs but 1 lb. 13 ozs. (see Figs. 1 and 3, Plate XIV.).

It has been stated previously that even large reptiles should not be executed by any process known in taxidermy, and when the direct paper process weighs so little, and the newest pulped-paper process so much less—viz. half an ounce in the model to each pound the natural specimen may weigh,— it will be seen that even crocodiles and large snakes may be perfectly reproduced, without the horrifying results attending the stuffing of such objects.

DIVISION IV

MODELS FORMED OF AN ELASTIC COMPOSITION

It will have been seen by the preceding pages that a glue composition is sometimes used as a means of making moulds, into which plaster may be poured to make the resultant model. The disadvantages of plaster, when used to represent a natural object, are manifest, and have been commented upon at length. If, however, the process is reversed, the plaster of Paris being used as a *mould* and the glue composition as a finished *model*, then the advantages are all on the side of the softer material, owing to its elasticity and the readiness with which it relieves from the most intricate undercuttings in the plaster mould.

Hitherto, the use of any glue composition has been limited by the important consideration of its durability, and repeated experiments with the ordinary glue—plasterers' modelling-glue—composition have proved its uselessness. There are, however, modifications of this which, in elasticity, definition, beauty of appearance, applicability to almost any purpose, adaptability to colour, durability, and freedom from shrinking, are of the highest importance. Quite impossible, indeed, is it to overrate any medium which will successfully interpret the texture and matters of detail in such diverse objects as a caterpillar, a slug, a cuttle-fish, any species of fish, an amphibian, a reptile, the body of a bird and of a mammal, and the internal organs of all. Such valuable properties are possessed by some of the compositions which follow, the best being probably Formula 96 or 97, which has been used in the Leicester Museum, with the best results, for subjects ranging from a slug up to a 12 lb. fish.

Apparently the first, however, to recognise the valuable

properties of glycerin as an aid to elastic or glue compositions was Dr. Cathcart, in 1885, whose method is described by Hamilton.[1]

The next published was—

94.—Shufeldt's American Modelling-glue (see *P.Z.S.*, 1894, p. 136)

Glue (best Irish) .	. . . .	4 oz.
Gelatin (photographers') .	. . .	2 ,,
Glycerin .	. . . .	4 ,,
Boiled oil .	. . . .	$\frac{1}{4}$,,

This has been well tried in the Leicester Museum, but has not been found to dissolve nor unite, owing, probably, to the omission of any directions for its preparation, and also to the want of water, which is not mentioned. Moreover, the utility of gelatine is by no means apparent, its cost is great, and " boiled oil," as will be seen from subsequent remarks, is, neither in colour nor quality, of the same value as linseed-oil.

The following are those used with the best results in the Leicester Museum :—

95.—Modelling-glue (M.B.)

Glue (best Scotch)	. . .	6 parts
Water .	. . .	1 ,,
Glycerin	. . . .	6 ,
Linseed-oil	. . . .	3 ,,

This, it will be seen, makes 1 lb. of composition, which, in a water bath over a spirit-lamp, takes three hours, with constant stirring, to prepare.

96.—Modelling-glue (M.B.)

Glue (best Scotch)	. . .	6 parts
Water .	. . . .	1 ,,
Glycerin	. . .	7 ,,
Linseed-oil	. . . .	2 ,,

---

[1] *Pathology*, pp. 716-718.

The following is the outcome of recent experiments, and, although last in order, is, without doubt, the very first of all glue modelling-compositions from every point of view.

97.—Modelling-glue (M.B.)

Glue (best Scotch)	6 oz.
Water	1 ,,
Glycerin	7 ,,
Canada balsam	2 ,,

Remarks upon the Making and Use of the Modelling-glues

The method to be adopted in making all the glue modelling-compositions is the same, viz. the glue is broken up small, and to do this it should be wrapped in a strong cloth and beaten with a *wooden mallet*, and afterwards pounded in a mortar. It is then put, with its allowance of water, into a water bath, and by this is always meant, in these pages, a vessel set or supported in another in which water is boiling ; an ordinary glue-kettle is, therefore, a water bath, but " Clarke's food-warmers," set over a spirit-lamp, serve admirably for half the quantity given.

Whilst the glue is being got ready, the glycerin and oil are heated separately, each in a water bath also, the glycerin taking about an hour, and the oil about two hours, to get hot, but sometimes they will warm sufficiently in an oven, and indeed, in the case of Formula 97, the glycerin and Canada balsam may be mixed, and warmed with ease in an oven in a short time. If a sufficiency of glue-kettles cannot be procured, strong " gallipots," or, when quantities are required, large stoneware jars such as are used for salt, set in a saucepan of boiling water, will do for the glue, etc., provided the surrounding water is not allowed to boil over into the inner vessel.

In the cases of Formulæ 95 and 96, when the glue is

melted, add the glycerin gradually, as the glue will take it up ; and, when united, add the oil, also in small quantities, and boil all together, keeping thoroughly stirred. Some time will elapse before the whole is satisfactorily united, sometimes, as for Formula 95, a whole day's boiling being insufficient ; especially is this the case if oil floats on the top, or if it can be seen as bubbles or shining patches in the mass, and it then requires more boiling and stirring, even to the extent sometimes of two days over an ordinary fire, but over a gas-jet the mass will be done in a day. For Formulæ 96 and 97, however, three hours should be sufficient when half the quantities are taken.

The properties of each are dissimilar, inasmuch as, although the modelling-glue Formula 95 is a fairly good medium, and flows and delivers well, it has rather too much oil in its composition ; Formula 96 is much the better of the two ; it flows and delivers much more easily, is very elastic, and of a better and lighter colour, approaching that of candied sugar, and takes tube oil-colour finely when a small quantity is stirred into the hot mixture. Formula 97 is, however, the very best, and is of a fine, light, whitish-yellow, flows and delivers beautifully, is very elastic, and comes out of a properly oiled mould (colza-oil) finely. It takes tube oil-colour admirably when it is hot, and, being many tones lighter than the compositions made with oil, is so much more valuable for colouring upon its surface afterwards. In some cases it is advisable to colour the composition to the groundwork of the object—say of such as a star-fish—and to touch up with other pigments those parts not partaking of the general colour. Further, this composition does not seem so liable to " blows " as any of the other glue-compositions, and probably this is due to the chemical affinity between the balsam and the glycerin, both uniting perfectly with each other and with the glue, which is more than can be said for oil and glycerin, which only appear to unite by the intervention of the molecules of glue ; hence, probably, arises the tiresome behaviour of any modelling-glues which contain a greater proportion of oil than Formula 96, some of the models made from them breaking and being unduly affected by changes of temperature. Even this objectionable cracking and break- ing, however, may be obviated in great part by stirring in either dry red lead or flake white or tube oil-colours, but there is no need to make inefficient glue-compositions in face of the admirable behaviour of Formulæ 96 and 97. Others which were made contained either too much water, too small a quantity of glycerin, common glue instead of best, or boiled oil instead of linseed, and were unsatisfactory. In none is the weight or expense serious, as 1 lb. of any of the compositions will model a $2\frac{1}{2}$ lb. perch, if the model be hollowed out when made, and, when cast and trimmed, the weight will be $\frac{3}{4}$ lb.

To make really good casts with this, free from " blows " and other defects, is by no means an easy matter unless certain rules are observed ; these are—

1. Brush the plaster mould *thinly* with warmed colza-oil, and on no account let it be varnished ; then let it be well warmed all through—if small, in an oven, but *not* in front of an open fire, or the mould will be liable to crack.

2. Let the modelling-glue be hot, but not boiling ; otherwise bubbles will burst on the surface of the mould and leave holes in the model.

3. Small objects such as caterpillars, slugs, and snails, minnows, gudgeons, etc., amongst fishes, and small newts and snakes may be cast solid, but larger objects, even fishes so small as $\frac{1}{2}$ lb. in weight, as well as larger fishes and reptiles, should be cast hollow ; and there are two very good and sufficient reasons for this, the first being on the score of weight and expense, and the other because, when made thick and solid, the tendency to " blow " is accentuated, and, when

cold, the difficulty of getting such an object as a large coiled snake out of its mould is almost insuperable, owing to the resistance and want of elasticity of such a large mass when lying in undercut folds, each fold in that case blocking the other; whereas, when made hollow, the folds are compressible when being skinned out, as it were, from the mould. Not only that, but there is danger of future deterioration or cracking in thick masses of composition, unless, probably, protected by pigment within or without.

It may be safely affirmed, therefore, that, even if the coating of composition is so thin that every detail of the mould can be clearly seen through it, it will be thick enough, provided it delivers without tearing; *breaking* is a sign of bad materials, and is quite different from *tearing*.

When models are accidentally made too thick, as they often will be in certain places, they may be further hollowed with a knife or scissors; fins also may be cut thinner and pared.

The method of applying the compositions, when small objects are cast solid, is simply to introduce them by means of a spoon or brush into the hollow mould, and turn this about until the composition runs into every crevice, and, when the mould is full, set it in some cool place to allow its contents to solidify. Very small objects will be fit to remove from the mould in a couple of hours, but such a thing as a common ringed snake is better left all night before being taken out. Figures 4 and 5 on Plate XV. represent such an object coiled and extended.

When, however, objects are cast hollow—which should always be done, and can be done even when they are small, but is absolutely necessary when they are of any size,—the method of procedure is, first to warm and oil the mould slightly, then pour into it a sufficient quantity of the composition to form a thin skin over all. This quantity, which experience alone

18

teaches, should be rapidly yet firmly brushed over the whole surface, care being taken to work it well into every crevice and undercut with a medium-sized brush, and, if there are lengths or small channels—such as would occur in the mould of the tentacular arms of a sepia,—with an artist's small hog-hair brush. Carefully yet quickly done, this, with rules Nos. 1 and 2 attended to, will prevent any vexatious "blows," or vacancies which the composition has not filled.

When the coating is sufficiently thick, varying from a sixteenth to a quarter of an inch according to the size of the specimen, it should be left to cool, and will be ready to lift in about two hours in the case of a small fish, and in double that time in the case of a fish of the original weight of 10 or 12 lbs.

Sometimes it will be found advisable to fill separate parts of a piece-mould, and afterwards to put them together and brush in hot modelling-glue to join and finish, and sometimes parts of a piece-mould can be brushed in and put together afterwards, or bodies may be made hollow by brushing instead of pouring in, or a mass may be poured into each part and the mould closed and turned about until cold, and difficulties may be overcome in various ways which experience will suggest.

The joining-together of separate parts of a glue model is managed by means of glue-composition, ordinary glue, glued paper, or small splinters of wood, pointed at both ends, glued, and inserted into the two ends or surfaces to be united.

An easy method of getting a cast without "blows," and also of making it deliver easily from a mould, is to wet the mould with hot water; but it certainly makes the model watery and apt to crack or break off short in more places than one, and is, therefore, not recommended.

When sufficiently cool, the glue model will be, if properly made, tough and elastic enough to lift away from curves and undercuts. Use the fingers to prise and pull, and follow up every advantage without undue violence. Sometimes, when getting out such an undercut object as a coiled snake, in which the head—though properly above—is at the bottom of the mould, and therefore the last to be got out, it will be best to relieve the tip of the tail first and follow the coils around. These, when the model is cast solid, are so held at certain points as to absolutely hurt the fingers, pressing them upon the sharp edges of the mould as each fold is delivered; therefore, thrust in a piece of rag as a wedge, until, coming to the head, a gentle pull with a rocking motion will relieve the whole.

Imperfections in these glue models of fishes are dealt with in a variety of ways. Supposing there are " blows " or holes in the body, these, if small, may be plugged with a small piece of the trimming taken from the model, *i.e.* a piece of cold composition, and this just warmed in by the application of a slightly heated tool (say No. 34); but this is, needless to say, a very delicate operation, as the heat of the tool may melt more than is necessary. A better method, in the case of small holes, is to fill them with thick white lead (flake white) and leave this to dry, but when the imperfections are large, the very best plan is to boldly cut out the piece irregularly, no matter where it occurs, to replace the model in its mould, and to pour into the gap a sufficiency of *very hot* composition; if well and quickly done, no join will be observable. Imperfect fins may also be cut away and replaced by the same method without the least fear.

When fins are cast separately from the remainder of the model, and are to be modelled and affixed in a certain way as if swimming, they should be made very thin at their distal extremities and of the full thickness at their bases; this is accomplished by brushing the composition very rapidly and thinly over the mould of the fins, and afterwards filling up the hollow bases with more composition. These, when trimmed—

either with a sharp knife or pair of scissors,—are affixed to the model either by a piece of stiff brown paper *pasted* upon and backing the fins, or by a sliver of wood pushed into the base, the junction of the fins to the trunk being made by using a piece of the "trimmings" and melting it in with a warm or moderately hot iron tool.

Fins, if too thick, may be pared, but this process is by no means so satisfactory as making them thin originally. Both sides of the fins may be joined together with pasted tissue-paper between, but not so satisfactorily as if made entirely of paper, and, therefore, if both sides of the fins of a glue model must be shown, it is best to make them entirely of paper (see p. 262), and affix them at their bases by a sliver of wood and modelling-glue.

The hollow casts or half models of such objects as fishes, especially when large, are too slight and thin to keep their shape without backing or packing, and this is managed by crowding them quite tightly either with wadding, tow, shavings, wood-fibre ("excelsior," such as boxes of sweets and various groceries and china are packed in), sawdust, or paper, but experience in the Leicester Museum has proved that sawdust is the best, especially if the model should have been left unbacked, and have collapsed some time after casting.

After the fish-model has been relieved from the mould, therefore, and examined for imperfections, it is trimmed and replaced in the mould, to which it again easily adapts itself; whilst therein, it is painted inside with common white or red lead containing plenty of "driers," and, when this is quite dry, the model is partly filled with coarse, clean pine sawdust, or sometimes with wadding, and this is followed by soft paper, some folded and some torn, until it is *firmly* packed nearly up to the top edge. At this stage, a piece of stiff cardboard (common straw-board is good enough and cheap) in the case of small fishes, and of actual board a quarter of an inch or half an inch thick in the case of larger ones, is cut to the shape of the fish, and is so laid upon the paper that it just sinks below the fins, or in a line with the edge of the half model, to which it is firmly attached by brushing the edges and filling them in with some of the same modelling-glue used for the model ; this, if done properly, makes board and fish all in one, and in the case of cardboard it may be glued, or, when backed with wooden board, screwed, to any tablet or background.   Care must be taken not to over-run the body-board upon the fins, especially upon the tail, as those parts are to be kept thin.

When fixed upon a backboard, although screws judiciously applied will usually bring the edge of the model close at any point, yet places may be occasionally found where the trimming has not been done with perfect accuracy, and where spaces occur, in consequence, between the edge of the model and the board.   Such defects may be remedied by filling in the spaces with pieces of "trimmings," and applying a warm iron tool (preferably of a rounded form) in the manner already described (see p. 275).   Where the melted composition runs upon the linen-covered board, it will, if coloured over, present a shining appearance, which is a disadvantage, as the background should be dull.   The repaired portions should be trimmed, therefore, by cutting down upon the board with a sharp knife, carefully following the natural lines of the model, and avoiding the cutting of the covering of the board ; this done, the superfluous composition must be removed from the board by *scraping* (not cutting) with the knife.

The glue models, when finished, take oil-colour admirably, and the texture and appearance of such things as reptiles, fishes, and invertebrates are lifelike when properly managed, added to which, positions may be slightly varied by bending and wedging upon tablets, and, when painted *inside* and out, they appear to be sufficiently waterproof to resist ordinary moisture.

This has been discovered to be a *sine quâ non*, some fishes, etc., made of Formula 95 composition a year ago, and left uncoloured but filled in with *paper*, having been placed in a damp situation, collapsed in greater part ; on the removal of the paper filling, however, and the substitution of *sawdust*, they were restored to their proper shapes in all but one or two bad examples, and, having been painted, inside thickly, and outside *very thinly*, with quickly-drying flake white, they are now efficiently protected thereby. Those executed at the same time, and coloured, underwent no change.

The weights of various objects modelled in the glue compositions, Formulæ 95 and 96, are given below :—

A roach of the original weight of 8 oz. was cast solid, and weighed just double, *i.e.* 1 lb. By paring and hollowing out, 11 oz. was removed, thus leaving the model 5 oz. only in weight —a gain of 3 oz. on the original.

The same fish cast hollow weighed 4 oz., and, when filled with wadding and backed with cardboard, but 6 oz.

A perch of the original weight of 2 lbs. 5 oz. was but 7 oz., and, when backed and finished, 11 oz.

A bream of 5 lbs. 5 oz. weighed, when modelled, $1\frac{1}{2}$ lbs., and, when backed and finished, 2 lbs.

A ceratodus of 15 lbs. original weight weighed, when cast, 2 lbs. 10 oz., and, when backed and finished, $3\frac{1}{2}$ lbs.

A carp of 12 lbs. 10 oz. was modelled to a weight of 1 lb. 10 oz., and, when backed and finished, was 2 lbs. 13 oz.

A ringed snake cast solid weighed, when completed, $8\frac{1}{2}$ oz.

A large rock snake of some considerable weight, when cast hollow, weighed but 2 lbs.

Some of these, the ceratodus for instance, were not cast quite so thinly as others.

More difficult, however, than either fishes or snakes, are lizards, frogs, and such subjects, which have legs and toes to be considered, and therefore a description of the method of procedure to be adopted in casting these creatures is here given.

Casting and Modelling a Frog

Some common frogs were procured, killed, and hardened for a few hours in the solution Formula 31. They were then placed in various positions on a block of stone, or, rather, upon the paper model of a block of stone, to which they were affixed in characteristic attitudes by means of fine entomological pins, one of these being used to support the head, the throat of the subject resting upon the head of the pin. Plaster was poured over the frogs and over the surface of the block on which they rested, and from this resulted a mould which, naturally, was deeply undercut in places ; the glue-composition (Formula 96), however, made light of such difficulties, and the models of frogs delivered nicely with care. From one of these groups, the specimen shown as Fig. 2 on Plate XV. was cut, and was laid upon a tablet for the purpose of illustration. The model was then coloured from a living specimen, and, although apparently easy, taxed—as did the snakes (Figs. 4 and 5)—the resources of the palette to the utmost. A more detailed description of a similar process, applied to a lizard, follows.

Casting and Modelling a Lizard

A large lizard, which happened to be the well-known and but little-liked *Heloderma suspectum* or Mexican poisonous lizard, was cast in the autumn of 1894, and is taken for the purposes of this explanation.

In this case the lizard was laid upon its stomach as if walking, its head a little erect and turned to the left, a natural sweep given to the body and tail, and the limbs and toes in easy positions ; as, however, neither the fore nor hind limbs would have delivered if left unprepared, the inferior space, resembling an open Λ, formed by the flexure of each limb, was filled in with a thin wall of putty ; the head was also supported in its erect position by a wall of putty placed under the lower jaw, just off the median line. As it was considered that, even then, the limbs would be difficult to relieve, or, rather, to model into, if the creature were cast entire, a thin wall of putty, rather more than a quarter of an inch high, was built along the back, just off the median line, and was "stayed" by buttresses of the same material, springing from the slab on the opposite side, and curving over the body on that side until united with the wall ; this was, of course, to prevent the breaking away of the thin wall by the pressure of the oncoming plaster.

As usual, the specimen was washed, and, the casting-box (see p. 231) having been placed around, was ready for the casting. This was performed, as is usual for small objects, by mixing plaster and water in a basin to the consistence of cream, and putting it on gently, a thin skin at a time, by means of a large spoon. When the summit of the putty wall was reached, the mould was thickened at that edge by the same method adopted for the shark, namely, by lumping it on thickly and dodging overflows with a strip of zinc. When thick enough, it was allowed to set ; then the putty walls were removed, the edge of the mould was nicely trimmed, keys were made, the mould was oiled (an important matter), and the other half was cast in like manner. When properly set, the fresh edge was pared down until the oiled line of division became visible; the mould was then reversed, the halves taken apart, and the lizard came out easily enough, every knob, pustule, and line being exquisitely delineated (see Fig. 3, Plate XV., in which, however, the creature is represented in the modelling-composition before

XV.

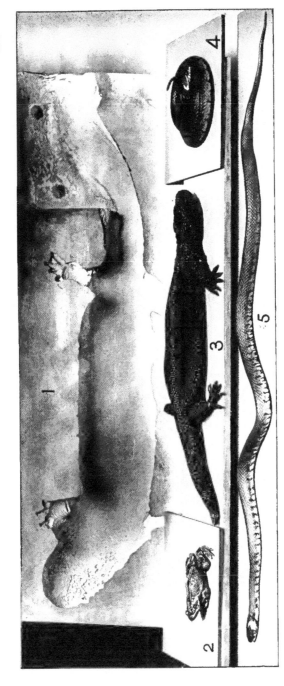

Mould in Plaster of a Gigantic Salamander, and Models in Glue Composition of a Frog, a Lizard, and Snakes.

colouring). Two toes only stuck, they having been floated up
by plaster getting underneath ; " floated up " meaning, of course,
buried when the creature was stomach upwards, careful digging
with a modelling-tool soon freed these toes, and the mould was
placed upon the stove to dry. It was afterwards found, when
casting another of the same species, that it was quite unnecessary, and indeed objectionable, to cast the animal in halves, and
that, when cast in one piece, the best compositions relieved easily
from the mould.

Very fine models were made in the Leicester Museum with
white gutta-percha, which was soaked in hot water and pressed
firmly into moulds, and although, by certain technical manipulation which need not be entered into here, they came out exceedingly sharp and with a good surface for the reception of
colour, yet that very colouring was the cause of their becoming
brittle in a short time and breaking into pieces,—manufactured
gutta-percha, like indiarubber—which was also tried,—having
a certain impatience of oil or grease of any kind, although it
must be stated that some gutta-perchas and indiarubbers were
found to withstand this better than others, and there is one
modelled fish—a chub of 5 lbs.—which still remains intact after
some years, due, probably, to its enclosure under glass.

DIVISION V

MOULDS AND MODELS OF METAL, ETC.

Should the zoological artist feel impelled to perpetuate
some fine piece of modelling in imperishable metal, he will not
find directions for executing such work under this heading,
which only deals with one method connected with the taking of
clichés in fusible metal or foil, which does not require the aid of
the foundryman or electro-plater to bring to a successful issue.

This extremely easy process—given by Mr. Goodchild[1]—consists in beating tinfoil with a brush, etc., on to fossils, and thus getting a *cliché*. As a copy, the result is satisfactory, yet it must be pointed out that, even when backed as directed, it dents with the slightest pressure, and although it has been well tried in the Leicester Museum, and certain improvements made upon it, yet it cannot, of course, compare with any of the paper processes described in this chapter.

LITERATURE UPON MODELLING, ETC.

Born, *Arch. f. mik. Anat.*, xxii., 1883, p. 845. Boulby, "New Material for Casts," *Brit. Med. Jour.*, 1882, ii., p. 783. Cathcart, "Material for making Casts," *Trans. Med.-Chir. Soc. Edinb.*, iv., 1884, p. 273. MM. Lebrun, Magnier, Robert et De Valicourt, *Mouleur* (Illustrated). Selenka, "Metal Models of Microscop. Preparations," *Sitzungsb. d. phys.-med. Soc. zu Erlang.*, xviii., 1885, p. 26. Strasser, *Zeitschr. f. wissensch. Mikroskopie u. f. mik. Technik.*, iii., 1886, p. 186; *Ibid.*, iv., 1887, p. 168. Urquhart, J. W., *Electro-plating*, 1888 (second edition), gives some methods of casting and modelling.

---

[1] J. G. Goodchild, F.G.S., *Geological Magazine*, 1892, pp. 206, 207.

CHAPTER VIII

METHODS OF REPRODUCING VARIOUS SUBJECTS AMONGST THE INVERTEBRATES

ALTHOUGH models of these creatures are sometimes executed in plaster, there is a difficulty in properly reproducing them in a material which ever gives a certain hardness of texture incompatible with their soft-bodied character. Paper is very much better, but the glass models made by the famous Blaschka, numbers of which are found in most museums, have a vitreous and unreal appearance which, although the colouring is undoubtedly prettily rendered, stamps them at once as *models*.

Two processes, however, stand out in bold prominence for the natural rendering of these soft-bodied animals : one the wax, and the other the glue method. There is little but praise to be said for either ; both are eminently pliable, both have a certain softness of texture, and both receive colour admirably.

Probably, on the score of durability, wax would come by far the first, as it is, if of pure and good quality, practically indestructible ; but, on the score of working, it is far more difficult to manage, and taxes the capabilities of the artist far more in overcoming difficulties of various kinds than does the glue process. This latter, although easier to manipulate, and of equal value as far as appearance goes, is as yet upon its trial, and although the formulæ Nos. 96, 97 appear to be all that is desirable, still there is no knowing how they will behave under certain circumstances, nor how they will stand the test of time.

Descriptions follow of how animals should be executed by either method.

The Cuttle-Fish (Sepia)

This creature is not a "fish" at all, but one of the higher Invertebrata, and, being generally preserved in spirits, is, in consequence, usually a most unsatisfactory object—as most spirit preparations are, however well displayed ; in America, however, according to Shufeldt, they appear, in the State Museum, to have hit upon the idea of representing it, out of spirits, modelled in the gelatine process (Formula 94), but, so far as can be gathered from the pages of the book [1] which describes their methods, and which is illustrated with very fine process-blocks of specimens, they nevertheless seem not to get their models from a direct cast of any invertebrate, but rely upon figures of such objects, from which they evolve a model in the manner now described :—

Take, for example, such an elegant reproduction of an Octopus as is shown in Plate XV. (*O. vulgaris*). This triumph in the matter of an exact model, perfectly preserved, of a large soft invertebrate animal is accomplished through the use of the plaster mould and gelatine cast now so successfully brought to such perfection. Under the careful supervision of Mr. F. A. Lucas, whom I must thank here for the selection of the six specimens illustrating this department, the proper specimens are first picked out from the collection or are chosen from plates, and pass next in order to the most skilled modellers, casters, and colourers. Of the series I here present, Mr. A. H. Baldwin has made the models after the drawings of various artists which will be hereinafter mentioned. After a model has been made, a mould is next taken, and from it a gelatine cast is secured, which, later, is finally trimmed to life and faithfully coloured to nature. Mr. J. W. Scollick is responsible for the delicate manipulation required in securing

---

[1] *Scientific Taxidermy for Museums*, pp. 389, 390, Plates XV.-XVII.

accurate moulds and castings from the models, and then they once more pass to Mr. Baldwin's hands to be coloured. After this operation, and when perfectly dry, they may either be tastefully mounted upon properly tinted pieces of small boards of a suitable kind of wood, dressed down to a right thickness, or they may play their part in a group, wherein all the natural surroundings of such creatures are reproduced, save the element in which they exist. This specimen of *Octopus vulgaris* was based on the figure given by Verany, as was also the model of *Sepia officinalis*, shown in Plate XVI., and in one of *Histioteuthis bonelliana*, shown in Plate XVII., and so may be relied upon as being more or less true to nature.

Unless one has seen one of these unfinished gelatine casts of such an animal as an Octopus, it is hard to realise what a perfect representation it gives us of the living animal; and, the cast being perfectly pliable, much as is the best of good rubber, it still further enhances the resemblance to the original. But to produce this requires skill and art of a very high order at nearly every step of the process. In the first place, if we are to model from a drawing, that drawing must be known to be accurate; if we model from a specimen, we must be sure about placing it in a posture that the animal is known to habitually assume. Great skill is next required in making a perfect model or copy of the design or specimen, and then it goes without saying that it is only through long experience and care that the necessary moulds and casts are obtained. Much depends at last upon the ability of the artist to faithfully colour the result of all the previous efforts; that is, the trimmed cast.

By this it appears that, strange to say, their Invertebrata, certainly the Cephalopoda, are not cast direct from the natural objects, but are made up as wax or clay ("plastic") models from figures in some book! From these, moulds in plaster are made, from which the gelatine models are cast—a method which will not, of course, commend itself to a scientific person, however pretty and striking the results may be, for they are purely artistic conceptions, and not scientific delineations of natural objects; and the plates, being fortunately derived from photographs, show this to be the case, for even in the sepia—too common an object, one would suppose, to be modelled from a book-illustration,—the want of scientific accuracy is evident, especially in the tentacles and other parts. The triumph of the modeller —no doubt great—is discounted by the fact that no two artists, especially if of different nationalities, will interpret anything to be modelled by eye and measurements in the same manner. Probably, while an American would make it as large as possible, the Englishman would give it a respectable and eminently solid appearance, the Frenchman an elegant and poetic shape, whilst, to carry the idea still further, the German might interpret it as a weird and grotesque monster. Hence it is desirable not to trust to chance, but to nature alone for its rendering ; and how such a simple thing to cast from as an octopus should have been executed in the far-fetched manner described is hard to say.

Perhaps a description of how a more difficult object, viz. a "cuttle-fish" or sepia, was cast from in the natural state will prove of service.

The cuttle-fish, having been brought from the sea in the bichromate pickle, was further hardened for a short time, then well washed in cold water, and laid, dorsal surface upwards, upon a smooth board covered with brown paper and well wetted. The tentacular arms and first pair associated with them (*i.e.* the largest or ventral pair underneath) were arranged as shown in the figure, the other six arms—those dorsad to the mouth and beak—being supported and held from touching the underneath parts by two pieces of soft woolly string, one end of each being loosely tied around three of the dorsal arms, whilst the other ends of the string were each attached to a long "French" nail, one on either side and behind the sepia, hammered a little way into the casting-board. Three sides enclosing these parts up to the string having been formed—two of zinc and the top (third) one of wood,—a barrier of clay or putty was built across, just below the string, extending from the zinc sides *up to* each side of the specimen at the springing of the arms, but not extending *across* the specimen. Thus a square box was formed, of wood at the top, zinc at each side, and clay at the bottom, which enclosed the two tentacular arms and the two dorsal ones, and extended up to the mouth. Plaster, mixed in the usual manner, was carefully poured on, a little at a time, until it covered the four under arms, and came over the mouth, and up to the underneath of the six dorsal arms still upheld by the string. As soon as this happened, the string was cut and the six arms rested upon the surface of the plaster, into which, being fairly liquid, they were rapidly arranged and pressed, and any plaster which overran their upper surfaces was immediately scraped off with the modelling-tool, and the arms finally washed clean with water and a soft brush.

When the plaster had set, the walls were removed, disclosing the first square as a sufficiently thick block, whose upper surface, having had "keys" cut in it a little beyond and outside the arms (or rather *feet*), was oiled, as was also the square edge whence the clay had been removed.

No. 2 was arranged to take in the exposed upper surfaces of the six dorsal arms, and the head, and eyes, and "neck," up to the body. First, therefore, zinc walls followed within the line of those of No. 1, and one crossed its upper surface beyond the keys, and, to complete the square, clay walls extended to some height from the lower ends of the side walls to touch the junction of the body and the "neck," rising at that part, coming on to the body or "mantle," and following its sigmoid curve, leaving the edge exactly true with the surmounting clay wall. A floor of clay was laid within the square to prevent the liquid plaster from running underneath the head, etc., to the ventral surface ; hence it will be seen that, when the plaster was poured on and filled up the square of No. 2, it overlapped No. 1 to some little distance beyond the arms, and, falling over the lower oiled edge of No. 1, made all the part lying behind that and the lower clay walls of No. 2 considerably thicker than the remainder, the plaster being, it may be remarked, allowed to fill in the "neck" or space between that and the body. The clay walls being removed, the curved edge of the plaster was oiled, and No. 3 piece was arranged for by packing the body with clay up to the underneath of the surrounding "fin," which was well stretched and pressed flat upon the clay (or putty), fine pins, with the heads cut off, being pressed down through the edges here and there to assist its retention. Two sides and a bottom piece of zinc being arranged around the body, plaster was poured on and within, completing the upper portion of the mould, which now covered the entire sepia.

When dry, and the walls removed, a board was placed upon the mould and the whole turned over, exposing the under side of the creature. No. 4 piece-mould was made by removing the clay which covered up the underneath of the "fin," placing two sides and a bottom of zinc around the body, the upper or top end being formed of clay, which now came upon the "neck," following and leaving the sigmoid curve of the body free ; this, when the plaster was poured within, completed the whole of the under side of the body up to the "neck." The walls being removed and all edges oiled, the remaining portion was surrounded with walls in the usual manner, and plaster was poured in, forming piece-mould No. 5, and last, taking in the "neck," the syphon, and the under side of the tentacles and dorsal arms.

All the edges having been previously oiled as described, the pieces readily came apart and released the sepia within. Looking at the "pieces," No. 1 showed the impression, on the side first cast, of the pair of long tentacular arms and of the two ventral ; on the other side, the impression of the *under* surface of the six dorsal arms ; and at the junction, that is, on the edge of the mould, the impression of the mouth and beak (see Fig. 1, Plate XVI.). Piece No. 2 showed the *intaglio*, on the one side, of the *upper* surface of the six dorsal arms and of the head and " neck," whilst the other side showed the print of the " collar," which lies below the " neck " under the mantle (see Fig. 2). No. 3 showed the *intaglio* of the upper surface of the body (see Fig. 3), No. 4 showed the impression of the entire under surface of the body, and No. 5 showed the remainder, *i.e.* the under surface of the tentacular and of the two ventral arms, the syphon and its orifice, and also the " collar " coming within the mantle on the under surface of the body. Another and larger sepia was managed in four pieces only, Nos. 4 and 5 of the preceding being united (see Fig. 4, Plate XVI.).

The moulds, having been slowly dried for some days, were well warmed in an oven (*not* close before a fire, which invariably cracks a dry mould), and just brushed over with colza oil, particular care being taken not to load the surface with much oil, nor to do as was once done in the Leicester Museum, where a fine mould of this very object was utterly ruined by being steeped in boiled oil for a week, with the result that the oil clogged the surface to such an extent as not only to spoil the sharpness of detail, but to form a kind of varnish, which clung to the glue composition, and refused to leave it or let it go, so that the mould had to be broken away with a mallet, piece by piece.

Sometimes the plaster clings to the glue, or the glue to the plaster, and, in preparing very special moulds, every precaution must be taken to have them quite dry and well oiled for some time previously ; or plunging them for a few moments into very hot paraffin wax, as before directed, will often prevent anything from sticking to them.

19

In either case the moulds should be warmed ; and, this having been done, and the modelling-glue (Formula 96) heated, it was led with a brush into every part of the No. 1 piece of the mould, and was made up with the brush to the required thickness above and below.   The next piece was then brushed over in the same manner, and so on until nearly filled.   Finally, the body halves were completely filled with the composition, and all were rapidly put together upon a board, the whole being then so tilted that the glue ran into parts not yet full.   Having been left for a night in a cool but dry place, the moulds were removed in the inverse order to their being put together, when a sharp and perfect copy appeared (see Fig. 5, Plate XVI.), in which the " arms "—really feet—surrounding the mouth were brought out beautifully, showing their upper surfaces with membranous attachments and their under surfaces with all the cusps, hollowed as they should be, exactly reproduced.

About a pound of the mixture is required for casting such an object, which will weigh, when trimmed, considerably less than the original.

The colouring, which was done from a very fresh specimen sent from Plymouth for that especial purpose, is almost impossible to describe, the creature being of a whitish, pink-yellow, semi-transparent nature ; the under surface, however, is much whiter.   Suffice it to say, that no conception of the beautiful hues and subtle gradations of tints possessed by this animal can be formed, unless a living or fresh specimen be obtained.   The long tentacular arms are of a dazzling china-like or vitreous whiteness, which no white pigment can, however, in any way interpret ; analysed, it appears to owe its extreme and dazzling whiteness to the incidence of light upon a bluish, semi-transparent, jelly-like substance, encased in a silvery sheath, and the resources of the palette are taxed to the utmost to gain a semblance of reality, for black, blue, pink, and

XVI.

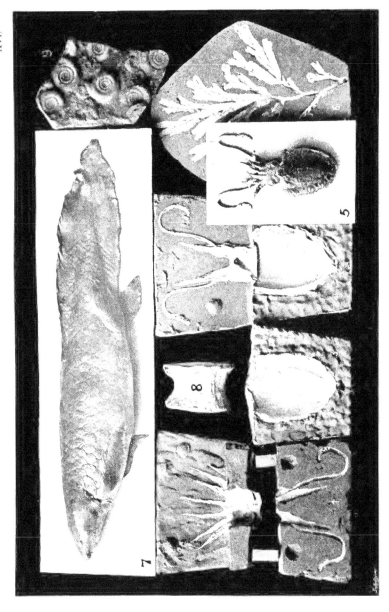

PIECE MOULDS IN PLASTER OF A LARGE, AND MODEL IN GLUE COMPOSITION OF A SMALL, SEPIA; MODEL IN GLUE COMPOSITION OF THE AUSTRALIAN CERATODUS; MODEL IN PAPER PULP OF AMMONITES; MOULD, IN PLASTER, OF SEAWEED; AND MODEL, IN PLASTER, OF A VERTEBRA.

yellow with white, in infinite *nuances*, are there. The other "arms" are light pinkish-yellow above, with the cusps of the under surface of the same puzzling white as the tentacular arms; the dorsal pair are, however, finely striped with fawn and yellowish-white. The head is fawn, yellow, bluish and pinkish-white, with a suspicion of greenish; the dorsal surface of the body the same, but finely striped with zebra-like markings of whitish, pinkish, and yellowish-fawn upon a darker ground of brownish-yellow; the "fin" paler, dusky, whitish vitreous; the under surface of the body, head, and dorsal "arms" white.

From this meagre description it will be seen that, where hues are subdivided into such myriads of tints, it is impossible to give exact instructions for colouring; indeed, all such instructions are merely relative, and it must be quite understood that, as all colour owes its existence to long or short waves of light and their incidence upon various substances with consequent selective absorption, it is as well to choose as suitable a material as possible with which to make a model, and so let the resources of the artist's pigments and his knowledge be aided by some material which gives an approximate texture; hence it will be found that, for such things as sepias, slugs, larvæ, and so on, nothing gives better results than the glue compositions, especially Formula 97.

The Casting and Modelling of a Caterpillar

Larvæ ("caterpillars" or "grubs"), especially those of the Lepidoptera, are so abominably done, even by the "blowing-up" process and its recent improvements, and look so like what they are—empty skins, with the segments of the carcase as bulbous distensions following an attenuated head, the whole devoid of life-like attitudes, stiff, uncompromisingly "stuffed," and, even when managed at first with some little traces of colour, so rapidly fading—that it is with a feeling of relief we turn our backs upon this ancient method, and try something newer.

A large and hairless larva being necessary for the following processes, a very large and fine "goat moth" caterpillar was procured.

This larva, having been killed painlessly, was left for a night in spirit to harden, and the next morning was laid, feet downwards, upon a small piece of glass, the better to turn it about; a little lateral twist was given to the body, and, by means of a bit of putty placed underneath, an undulating curve, as if the creature were rapidly crawling, was indicated. Fine damp sand was now tooled underneath the segments of the body, just coming up to, and following, the lines of the little inverted arches, and the sand smoothed out to the same thickness for some half an inch beyond, and all around, the body; thus only the "legs" were hidden up. The zinc strip being bent around and puttied up outside to prevent the plaster from escaping, this latter was poured on thinly in successive coats, to prevent crushing, and, when set, the mould was turned upside down, revealing only the under surface of the larva. Keys were made, the edges were oiled, and, the zinc strip having been readjusted, the casting was repeated. When dry, the two half moulds came readily apart, and the larva, though sticking a little by its few stiff hairs, came out as readily, revealing a perfect and beautiful impression.

The moulds (two complete ones were taken from the same larva) were dried and boiled as usual, and, when ready, were dipped in hot water, and one half (the top) filled with melted wax; the under part was then placed upon it, fitting by its keys, and the whole rotated and turned about in the manner usual when making wax fruit. No result accrued, the wax sticking and refusing to come away at all, which necessitated melting out on the stove after all else had been tried and failed. Next, therefore, the moulds were warmed in hot water as for leaves, and sheet wax pressed in and backed by fabric. Again no result, the wax again sticking and having to be melted out, which was singular, seeing that leaves come away from the mould when done by the same process.

Something was evidently wrong, and, being convinced that the wax itself was not in fault, it was considered that oiling the moulds might give better results. This was done, and the same wax was used in successive layers, each thin sheet being pressed down with the fingers until the combined thickness was too great to be cut by the sharp edges of the segments ; on this a strip of white art fabric (see p. 302) was welded by pressure, and then the whole was systematically pressed into each small depression by placing within the mould a small piece of rag, folded to the thickness required, and kneading it in with a *rounded* stick or piece of bone until the white fabric took on a ruddy tint from the underlying red wax. This was a perfect success, the bottom half—that showing the legs —coming out easily, with even the feet perfect ; the upper half, however, being deeper, required more coaxing, but came out finely, and of nearly the exact colour of the back of a living specimen.

The next to be tried was an orange-coloured wax, made by adding, to melted white wax (Formula 98, p. 303), chrome yellow and alizarin crimson (both tube oil-colours), and this was used for the bottom half, and a deep crimson (alizarin again) wax for the upper half or back.

The upper and under portions having, of course, to be united, they were trimmed around with a small pair of sharp scissors, supplemented by a very small knife, the outlines impressed upon the wax being carefully followed, and the whole thickness of each half model being cut at such an angle as to permit the *outer* edges to come together. When this was satisfactorily accomplished, the edges were warmed just sufficiently to allow of their being united by gentle pressure, after which the junction was finished off by means of the stem of a modelling-pin used lightly and with care.

As chrome yellow is not truly permanent, although wax "locks it up" better than anything else, it would be necessary to replace this for very delicate and pure tints of wax by aureolin, aurora, cadmium, or orient yellows. Alizarin crimson also, being a heavy, somewhat opaque crimson, should be replaced, for delicate tints, by rose madder.

Making a Model of a Block of Stone showing Fossils

Ordinarily, such an object as a block of stone exhibiting fossils would have moulds made from it in the manner previously described for other things, but a different method was adopted in one particular case ; this, which was a piece of limestone showing moulds or *intaglio* impressions of ammonites, was interesting, not only as exhibiting the capabilities of the modelling-material, but as enabling a correct diagnosis of the species to be arrived at, the distinguishing characters not being observable in the natural impressions, but coming out beautifully in the model.

The impression was obtained directly from the block, as if it were a mould—which indeed it was,—and was executed in the pulp (Formula 93), and in the manner described on pp. 264-266, the only modification being, that the pieces of muslin used as backing were cut small and triangular to fit within the whorls of the ammonites.

To obtain the block or model of the natural thickness of the stone, about six layers of "cap" paper were pasted around the edges (oiled) of the stone itself, and overlapping top and bottom about an inch. This, when dry, was relieved by cutting at the corners, which were afterwards repaired with pasted paper. The pulp model, being reversed, had now to be joined to the *under part* of the paper block, and, that the edges might agree, they were fixed with a stitch here and there. In some places spaces had to be made up, whilst other portions of the block required trimming away. When the latter had been done, the spaces were filled with cotton wool (pasted), a foundation for the same sometimes having to be made up with crumpled paper, slightly pasted and pressed in. The bottom of the block was covered with "cap" paper, and, where the join showed on the top, a thin layer of pulp was worked on in the usual manner, and afterwards beaten in with a stiff brush to obtain the rough appearance of the surrounding matrix. It was then left to dry, any little fault being afterwards trimmed up with a sharp knife and file, and filled in again with pulp or other composition, pasted over, and plaster of Paris dusted on. Finally, when dry, it was coloured with powder-colours mixed with turpentine, and touched up with tube oil-colours, to get the natural effects and texture. The weight of the actual stone was $6\frac{1}{2}$ lbs., but the model weighed only 4 oz.

At the beginning of the instructions upon casting, it should have been stated that, contrary to the generally received opinion as to the "cleanliness" of plaster—an impression derived prob‹ably from its delusive whiteness,—there is hardly any substance so dirty, and so persistent in its endeavours to thrust itself into situations where its presence is undesirable, and that, therefore, not only should all casting be carried on as far from the dwelling as possible, but the modeller should have a special blouse or covering, of strong hurden (or harden), made high at the neck, close at the wrists, reaching to the heels, opening only at the back, and tied or buttoned around the waist by a band. Large pockets in front to hold tools when modelling are an advantage; and with this dress a cap should be worn, and every precaution should be taken to free them from plaster after use.

CHAPTER IX

CASTING AND MODELLING FROM NATURAL FOLIAGE, FLOWERS,
FRUITS, ALGÆ, FUNGI, ETC., AND THEIR REPRODUCTION
IN PRACTICALLY INDESTRUCTIBLE MATERIALS.

WHEN first the art of modelling in wax was evolved, it no
doubt occurred to the earliest exponent that nothing was so suitable for reproduction in that medium as flowers and fruit, and
there are few old people now living who do not recollect how
fashionable an amusement it was, in years gone by, for ladies ;
and few there are who cannot remember the graceful alabaster
vases, copied from the antique, filled with drooping sprays of
laburnum, passion flowers, fuchsias, and roses, which usually
made up the sum of their contents, all duly enshrined beneath
a glass shade. Although, in some cases, the flowers were
exquisitely modelled and coloured, yet the foliage was invariably ill done and stiff, and both possessed the great disadvantage
of being composed entirely of wax, so that in course of time
—usually a very short time—the wax hardened, became
brittle, and the least shake or sudden jar caused the petals to
break or drop off in a most unnatural fashion ; or the sun
gained access in some unlucky moment, and then the petals
drooped, more naturally, but with equally disastrous results.
Then came the last scene of all : the colours were not " fast,"
and a few years at most sealed the fate of the once elegant

group, upon which so much time and misplaced trouble had been expended.

Now all these heart-breaking difficulties and disadvantages have been removed, and primarily by the skill and inventive genius of a family—the talented Mintorns—whose friendship and guiding assistance the writer has enjoyed and valued, and hastens gratefully to acknowledge.   The representatives of this family, sprung from the union of a pictorial artist and an equally artistic lady, were two boys and two girls, two of whom, at the ages of eleven and seven respectively, gained a gold medal for their flower-modelling, and were appointed Queen's modellers on the occasion of Her Majesty having, at a banquet given by the City of London, raised an artificial flower from before her in order to inhale its perfume!   Let not the reader imagine this a concocted or far-fetched incident, for it is but within the last few months that the writer, although knowing full well the resources of the surviving brother and sisters, was yet deceived by some modelled sprays of Golden Rod (*Soli-dago sp.*) carelessly resting in a glass vessel, and for some time believed them to be stems of the natural plant.

When, or by whom, the notion was first devised of employing modelled foliage and flowers as artistic accessories to taxidermic studies is not known, although the writer remembers commissioning a lady to model the bilberry plant for that purpose quite twenty years ago, and there are "boxes of birds," as they are locally called in the "Black Country," quite fifty years old, embellished with stamped leaves of the primitive millinery order.   In any case, all early attempts were in the direction of wax and stamped leaves, and it was reserved for the Mintorns to invent the beautiful and imperishable material known as the "Mintorn Art Fabric," and afterwards to be the introducers of this, accurately and beautifully transformed into the semblance of living foliage, for museum purposes.

To a Leicester man—Mr. Theodore Walker—is the credit due of having been the first to recognise the importance and the capabilities of the new fabric, and he it was who, in 1877, had the first group—that of pheasants—mounted with primroses, bluebells, and ferns modelled in the new material ; this, after being exhibited for a short time in the Leicester Museum, was presented by him to the Natural History Museum, South Kensington, thus introducing this art, as a pleasing innovation, into museum arrangement.   The Leicester Museum was, therefore, the first to show the world that blending of artistic taxidermy and artistic modelling of plants, which has done so much to enhance its popularity and efficiency as a teaching factor, and has removed the dry-as-dust character which formerly clung to it, and to all provincial museums not abreast of the times.

It is most unfortunate that no examples of the early work in modelled groups—far inferior, however, to the present-day performances—exist in the Leicester Museum, Mr. Walker having, for good and sufficient reasons, given some other cases to South Kensington before the present Director came into office.   Although not of the highest merit, either in design or execution,—some, indeed, being spoiled by the introduction of stamped leaves—these were the foundation of the beautiful collection of groups now located in the galleries of the great hall, and in the centre of the bird-galleries, of the British Museum, South Kensington ; Dr. Günther or Dr. Sharpe having applied in 1879 to Mr. J. H. Mintorn, who, not being able to devote himself to such work, engaged his sister, Mrs. E. S. Mogridge, who executed the foliage for a series of groups.

In the *Daily News* of 26th February, 1892, in an article headed " Curiosities of Bird Life," it is stated that " Mr. Bowdler Sharpe's splendid services in the Natural History Museum may be seen in that most popular gallery, where the birds are made to appear as in life, with the minutest surroundings of foliage and ground faithfully reproduced," which is perfectly true so far as the foliage is concerned, but leaves one in doubt as to whether to Dr. Günther or Dr. Sharpe are due the initiation and credit of the groups, the later ones of which are uniformly good in the design and execution of the foliage, and usually very poor in the groundwork and in the modelling and arrangement of the birds.

As no recognition of the best and most artistic part of the work—namely, the modelled foliage, much of which it is impossible to overrate—appears to have been officially given, it is perhaps but bare justice to record that the greater part of it was executed by the brothers J. H. and H. Mintorn and Mrs. Mogridge, whilst, during the latter's absence in America, some foliage was executed by her niece under the direction of Dr. Günther.

In 1880, Lord Walsingham was imbued with a grand idea, and employed Mrs. Mogridge and Mr. H. Mintorn to model a number of plants, upon which the larvæ of various Lepidoptera were represented as feeding. Soon afterwards, Mr. Carruthers, of the British Museum, sent for them to make some enlarged models of botanical specimens for the use of students. After twenty specimens had been done, the work was stopped, owing to the lateness of the season ; then Mrs. Mogridge—after hoping to model the foliage for the Gould collection of humming-birds—left with her brother, Mr. H. Mintorn, for America, where they were engaged by Mrs. R. L. Stuart to model foliage for groups of birds of New York State to be presented to the Natural History Museum of New York, the execution of a number of groups occupying three years. (This work is now being continued for the Museum by Mr. John Rowley, a pupil of Mrs. Mogridge and Mr. Mintorn.) They were afterwards engaged on the Morris K. Jessup wood-collection, illustrating the destruction of timber-trees by insects ; this lasted until 1892, when they went to Washington, engaged by the United States Government to model plants for their exhibit at Chicago in 1893, under the direction of Professor Riley, who sent Mr. Mintorn into Louisiana—a distance of 1400 miles—in order to study thoroughly the growth and destruction of the cotton-plant by the "Boll worm," which shows the enterprise of the American Government even in their museum organisations. In America the Mintorns appear to have earned literally golden opinions, and their work has been recognised by press and Government alike, the former breaking out into headlines such as—

TWO ARTISTS WHO MAKE BOGUS FLOWERS AND
PLANTS WHICH DECEIVE THE EYE,

and the latter, in praiseworthy contradistinction to our own Government, scrupulously printing on all their descriptive labels : "Foliage (or 'Plants and Flowers') modelled by Mrs. Mogridge and Mr. Mintorn." At the end of 1894 and for a few months in 1895, in addition to their world-wide engagements, they assisted the Curator of the Leicester Museum in modelling foliage, chiefly for the exposition of the food-plants of lepidopterous larvæ, and of plants attractive to various orders of insects.

As showing the amount of work done by these artists, and the thorough way in which the American Government encourages such, it may be mentioned that, in one small group of little mammals called "Woodchucks" (*Arctomys monax*), there were—

540 leaves of white clover
30 blossoms   ,,   ,,
50 leaves of red   ,,
6 blossoms ,,   ,,
A large quantity of { Sorrel
                              Daisies

This necessary preamble now leads to a consideration of "how it's done," and first, of course, comes the question of tools and materials. The tools are few, and simple in construction, and are figured on Plate II. :—

Awls (Figs. 26, 27)
Blanket-pins (O)
Brushes (stub), various sizes (F)
Corolla modelling-tools in pear- or lime-wood (K and M)
Cutting-pliers (Figs. 10, 11, and C)
Flat ivories
Knives (Figs. 4, 6)
Modelling-pins, steel with china heads, several sizes (N and P)
    „   „   boxwood, with a knob at each end (J)
Modelling-tools, steel (Figs. 29-39)
Punches (L)
Scissors, small and sharp, one pair straight and one curved (A and B)
Scratcher (needles set in a handle) (Q)
Stands
Tweezers (G and H)
Wire-gauge (D)

Materials

Alcohol	Net, white cotton, finest mesh
Arrowroot	Oil, olive
Borax	Paper-varnish
Bristles (white)	Plaster of Paris, best; "S.F."
Canada balsam	(superfine)
Colours	"Steel tails"
"Down"	Wax, lump
Honey	„ sheets, of various colours
Mintorn art fabric, of various	„ paraffin
colours and thicknesses	Wire

Wire, silk- and cotton-covered

The preparation and tempering of the wax, the cutting of it into sheets of varying thicknesses and sizes, the colouring of it, the material and covering of the Mintorn art fabric, although known to the writer, are professional secrets, the property of the Mintorn family, which he is asked not to divulge ; hence these materials are to be purchased, which is just as well, did the reader know the complicated processes and machines necessary for their preparation.

In a work, however, published by Messrs. J. Barnard and Son,[1] there is a description with figures of a simple machine for cutting wax blocks, which may be of service :—

The most important thing is to cut it into sheets. To accomplish this, you must be provided with a carpenter's plane, called a "trying plane." Place it on an angle, with the iron towards you, as shown in the diagram A. Then a contrivance to fix the block of wax in, as shown in diagram B,—simple in itself, as the longitudinal section will show, being a piece of wood, about an inch wider all round than the block of wax, with a stop at each end, leaving a space of about half an inch between that and the wax, so as to admit of a wedge to keep it steady in its place. The two *hand-holes*, as shown on each side of Fig. 3, will convey all the necessary ideas, so as to require no further explanation ; and the following diagram will show at once the full working of this method of cutting wax, though the sheets of wax purchased at the shops are cut by machines constructed expressly for the purpose, which can be set to a gauge of any thickness required.

The various white waxes of commerce rarely possess the toughness and tenacity indispensable in sheet-wax for plant-modelling, nor, indeed, are they suitable even for the preparation of the fabric, unless treated with Canada balsam ; each sample, therefore, must have balsam added in the following proportion, and, when cold, must be tested by cutting :—

98.—Modelling-wax (M.B.)

Best white Madras wax	.	.	.	1	lb.
Best Canada balsam .	.	.	.	1	oz.

Melt the wax and stir in the balsam.

---

[1] Charles Pepper and Madame Elise, *The Art of Modelling and Making Wax Flowers and Fruit*, pp. 10-12.

Any admixture of spermaceti ruins the wax, and white Japan wax is of no avail.

In the work just referred to, the following formula is given :—

99.—Modelling-wax

Pure white wax	.		.	.	1 lb.
Tallow	.	.	.	.	2 oz.
Canada balsam	.	.	.	.	3 oz.

Melt and thoroughly mix.

This appears, however, to have far too great a quantity of Canada balsam, and the tallow should probably be omitted.

Colour with tube oil-colours to whatever hue is desired, and pour into the small baking-tins mentioned at p. 244 ; let it remain until cold, when it can be taken out as a block and cut into sheets with the machine.

If in a great hurry to get a small sheet, pour some thinly, or brush it, over a piece of damped glass, from which it will peel off.

Pigments for Modelled Flowers, etc.

These should be of the very best quality, as, although dear at first, they are cheapest in the long-run, for what can be more vexing than to see the once brilliant model, vying actually with nature, now a miserable failure, the crimsons a dirty brown, the pinks a faded drab, the yellows greenish or blackened, the lilacs a bluish-grey, the blues whitish-grey, the greens black, and some other tints vanishing altogether, which inevitably happens with ordinary colours? Hence it is of the utmost importance that the palette be of *permanent* colours, and by permanent colours are meant those which are absolutely un-affected by ordinary light, by foul air and gases, or by admixture one with the other.

The present writer has derived so much knowledge of the

chemical composition of pigments and of the properties of colour from a long study of Field's *Chromatography*, as to lead him to strongly recommend a perusal of that valuable work to all those engaged in art matters.

Three sets of pigments are necessary for first-class professional work, viz. a set of powder-colours, of water-colours, and of oil-colours in tubes. The pigments in each set are identical in name, and the amateur may be content with one set, and that dry, at the commencement of his labours.

Mrs. Mogridge recommends that, in all cases, Roberson's special dry colours for wax flowers be used, considering these to be the best make of colours for this particular purpose, and contends that even such heavy and fugitive colours as indigo, Prussian blue, scarlet lake, and magenta, of their make, are far richer and more permanent than those of any other maker. Be this as it may, the learner must be guided by facts and experience, and will find a full list of colours given at pp. 88-93, with remarks upon their characteristics.

The uses of the tools are explained under the various processes which follow, but the uses of such things as "down," honey, etc., are better explained here.

"Down" is either pulverised dry blotting-paper, or woollen cloth torn or scraped into dust, and is used to give a woolly or downy appearance to certain leaves, stems, and flowers.

Honey is found preferable to gum for retaining the "down" on artificial leaves, stems, and flowers.

Arrowroot powder, which should be of the finest and whitest quality, is used to rub or brush into wax to give a delicate bloom, and also to deaden any tendency to gloss in the wax or art fabric when modelling flowers or leaves of certain characters. Like most small though important "kinks," it was discovered by accident—some arrowroot required for culinary purposes in the Mintorn household having accidentally come into contact with some sheets of white wax, which it was at first deemed to have spoiled.　Arrowroot must be rubbed or brushed firmly in, and sometimes on both sides of the wax or fabric, and nothing will remove it except washing.　Dry colouring is, therefore, the only available method when treating, say, an apple-blossom, as wet colours, unless very carefully managed, run and look streaky.　Add a little dry flake white, rubbed up with the arrowroot, should the latter not be sufficiently white.

To make Ribs for Modelled Leaves

The large veins or "ribs" vary so much in different plants as to necessitate separate instructions being given for making them.　In some leaves a large central vein extends from the leaf-stem or *petiole* to the apex, and is called the mid-rib or *costa ;* other leaves have three or more large veins, called ribs, proceeding from the base to the apex ; whilst others again, consisting of five or more lobes, and called respectively *palmate* or *palmatifid*, have a rib in each lobe—all branching from one point, either at the base, or a little above the base of the leaf.　Although there are, it is needless to say, many other forms of leaves, these are all which need be considered with special reference to the making of ribs, and, in all the forms under notice, the ribs have one characteristic in common ; that is to say, they are all extremely fine at the apex, and gradually increase in thickness towards the base.　In most leaves, the rib or ribs have a somewhat transparent appearance, and in all cases it is better to use uncoloured wax, and fine wire encased in white silk, or, better still, *bristles*, wherever they are available.

Commence, therefore, by cutting a strip of wax, rather longer than the rib to be imitated if for a small leaf, beginning almost as a point, and gradually increasing the width to the other extremity. This strip must be cut *lengthwise* from the sheet (*i.e. with the grain*), or it will be liable to break up when folded. Next take a bristle, and, if for a small leaf with a slender rib, another bristle or short piece of very fine wire, holding them together lengthwise between the left thumb and forefinger, with the point of the first projecting beyond the tip of the finger, and the point of the second bristle or wire where it will extend far enough into the leaf to form a sufficient support, but no farther than is called for by the increasing thickness of the natural rib. Usually more than two bristles or wires are required, the number and size being, of course, determined by the thickness of the rib and the weight of the leaf to be supported, and the point of each succeeding one being placed a little lower than that of the preceding.

For short leaves, the requisite number of bristles or wires must be taken at once, and the strip of wax folded and pressed around them, and rolled between the thumb and finger, until a smooth and nicely graduated rib results. For the ribs of long leaves, however, two or three of the bristles or wires may be taken first, and, when these are partially covered from the tip downwards, the remainder can be added as required, and a rather wider strip of wax used for the covering ; care being taken, however, to join the wax neatly and evenly, so that no lump or sudden thickening shall appear.

It is a good plan to make a number of these simple ribs, of various sizes, and store them in boxes ready for use, so that, when it is desired to copy leaves or sprays whilst fresh, no time need be lost in doing that which could have been done equally well beforehand, and especially during the winter months.

For *palmate, palmatifid*, or any other form of leaf in which a number of ribs branch from one centre, the ribs are made in the manner described, and, each one having been measured,

from the apex of the lobe for which it is intended to the point
of junction, and the wire cleared from that point by cutting
and drawing off the superfluous wax with the finger-nails,
they are then joined together by pressure, or by the merest
shred of art fabric wound once or twice around at the junction.

If, when joining these ribs, it should be found that the
combined wires or bristles would make the leaf-stem too thick,
one or more of them may be cut away.

For the ribs of very small leaves, the silk-covered wire
needs only to be rubbed with wax to give it a sufficient
coating.

Making Moulds from Natural Leaves, and their Reproduction

Let the student provide himself with some best (S.F.)
plaster of Paris, a basin, and some water, and, having put on
the modelling-dress (see p. 295), retire to the casting-shop or
bench and proceed thus :—Let the leaves to be copied be of
the easiest character, say hawthorn or willow for the first
lesson, and commence by placing them in a basin of water for
a few minutes to clean and toughen them ; then brush with a
soft camel-hair brush to take off dust and superfluous water.
Begin at the top of the spray to be reproduced, and pick off
three or four leaves, marking them 1, 2, and so on. Then
mix plaster and water with a spoon to the consistence of thick
cream, hold the leaf with the left hand over the basin, and
pour on just sufficient to cover the leaf thinly, taking care not
to weight the leaf with so much plaster as to take out the
natural curves, or, worse still, to flatten the leaf ; lay the leaf
upon a piece of cardboard or stout paper previously moistened,
and treat another in like manner, and, by the time three or four
leaves (not more) are first coated, the first one will be ready to
receive a second coat, and with deeply-cut, cleft, or twisted
leaves, the one half—that lying down—will be the one to re-

ceive the second coat, the under surface of the leaf being supported in its natural curl by a piece of wool or crumpled-up tissue-paper ; give the remaining two or three their second coat in like manner, and then, over all, a third coat, which completes a fairly thick convex covering. Directly this has set, which happens sufficiently by the time the third or fourth leaf is covered, remove the mould from the table or board, turn the leaf uppermost, and trim away quickly as much super-fluous plaster around it as may be without cutting into the edges of the leaf, trimming into the deeper notches or clefts of the leaf so as to present a rather more concave surface at those places. Do this rapidly, if roughly, leaving the finer trimming until the leaf itself is removed, which must be done at once, before the plaster sets hard. Take hold, therefore, of the stem, and, lifting gently, remove the leaf. At some places it may be accidentally covered with a little plaster and will tear ; if this happen, take the knife and carefully trim down upon the leaf, when, no doubt, the covering scale of plaster will chip off, care being taken, nevertheless, not to scratch the mould in removing the small pieces of leaf. Finally, scratch on the backs of the moulds 1, 2, 3, etc.

Then take the next highest set of three or four leaves and treat them in precisely the same manner, and so on until the branch is stripped ; this should then be placed in water in a bottle or vase for future study. The foregoing, although very well for small or simple leaves, is by no means satisfactory for large, twisted, or thin and " floppy " leaves such as " dock," etc., which must be hardened and cleaned in water for some time, and then laid face uppermost upon the casting-board and packed underneath with casting-sand, ordinary fine sand, clay, or putty, following the natural curvatures of the leaves, and thus rigidly supporting them. The plaster is then put on in thin layers carefully, and the result is a truthful copy, and not a flattened-out impression.   Some leaves there are, such as those succulent thickened ones found on certain common sea-coast plants, and some small lanceolate leaves, such as those at the top of the stem of the sea-aster, which do not require moulds for their reproduction : the first class because they are simple, fleshy leaves, ovoid in shape, and with no appreciable rib ; the other class because they are but long, narrow strips, with a simple rib, which the wire, when inserted in the material, imitates very well (see Plate XVII. for leaf-moulds).

All the moulds, being marked from No. 1 to 20, or whatever the bottom number may be, are then dried in a slow oven or before the fire, and left until the next day, when, if dry, they should be boiled for a quarter of an hour in the following :—

100.—Borax Solution (M.B.)

Borax (common)	.	.	8 oz.
Water (boiling)	.	.	1 gallon

When cool, they should present a smooth, glossy appearance, and be nearly as hard as marble ; if not satisfactory—and only experience tells the exact stage,—they should be boiled again.   Put them in, to prevent cracking, just before the water boils.

It having been found, however, that a certain efflorescence ensues which is detrimental to the subsequent processes, and taking also into consideration the liability of the moulds to crack in boiling, the plan has been adopted in the Leicester Museum of using the solution, when *cold*, with which to mix the plaster.   This gives the required hardness and satiny surface, but for this method the leaves must be supported underneath (see *ante*) and left for *twelve* hours, so slow is the plaster now in setting.   It is better, therefore, to arrange to cast by this process in the evening, and by the next morning the borax will have precipitated, leaving a fine, hard surface next to the leaf, without the least suspicion of "blows," and without the risk attendant on boiling. Alum in the same proportion makes the plaster hard, and sometimes the moulds, after drying, are plunged into very hot paraffin wax (*instead* of borax), which gives, as explained before, an ivory surface (and interior), to which the white wax, in some processes hereafter described, does not adhere.

The moulds, having been protected either by the borax or by the paraffin wax, are used as follows :—A sheet of green wax rather *lighter* than the natural leaf is selected, and the mould, face downward, is laid upon its *dull* and grained surface, lengthwise with the grain of the wax—this is important,—and near its edge, so that waste may be prevented ; it is then marked around with a modelling-pin or by any other method ; the mould is removed, and the wax is cut with the scissors where marked around. The scissors, be it remembered, will not cut the wax clearly, or perhaps at all, unless the blades are damped, which may be done by passing them over a damp rag (putting them in the mouth is a professional dodge not to be imitated). The rough wax pattern is laid lightly upon a piece of art fabric of the colour of the under side of the natural leaf, traced around, and cut out.

The mould is now plunged into hot water, taken out, dabbed dry, and the wax pattern, laid upon it face downwards as before, is well pressed down (kneaded really) with the thumbs and fingers into every depression. When the weather is cold or the wax brittle, this must be done by the fire. The rib of the leaf (see p. 306) is now laid upon the wax in the position it naturally occupies, and over this the art fabric is placed. More and heavier kneading with the thumbs is now required to weld the fabric and the wax together ; too much pressure, however, must not be brought to bear directly *upon* the rib, although the fabric should be made to fit closely

around it ; care must also be taken that the artificial leaf does
not slip upon the model, otherwise a double impression and a
spoiled leaf will be the result. When sufficiently pressed—
which experience alone can teach—the leaf is easily removed
and a perfect impression is revealed, this being, of course, in
reverse to the model, but exactly of the form and venation of
the natural leaf.

Holding it by the stem, very carefully trim around the
edges, following exactly the serrations marked upon the model.
The edges will be somewhat too thick unless the wax and
fabric are chosen of a less combined thickness than that of the
natural leaf, but in any case they will require to be carefully
rolled with the head of a modelling-pin upon the edge of
the left forefinger, care being taken not to obliterate the inner
venations, nor to destroy the natural curves and symmetry of
the leaf.

The late Mr. J. H. Mintorn thus described [1] his method of
how to model such a large leaf as that of the water-lily :—

The mould should be immersed in warm water for some ten or
fifteen minutes ; then take it out of the water and gently wipe it. Some
green wax must be melted as described for the mould-making, and
coloured to the proper shade by using (ground in oil) chrome No. 2,
P. blue, and burnt sienna. This colour must be mixed in a spoon with
a little of the melted wax, and this well mixed into the body of the
wax; and having it quite melted or liquid, I proceed thus :—Holding
in the left hand the mould, and having removed the vessel containing
the wax from the hot water, place the mould so that one end of it rests
over the centre of the vessel containing the wax ; and then, taking a
large tablespoon filled with this, pour it over the whole surface of
the mould. This will require repeating several times to insure its being
completely covered. Should the wax crack it will indicate that the wax
is too hot or the mould too cold. To decrease the warmth of the wax
allow it to stand a few moments ; by this time the wax will be cooler

---

[1] *Lessons in Flower and Fruit Modelling in Wax*, pp. 99-101.

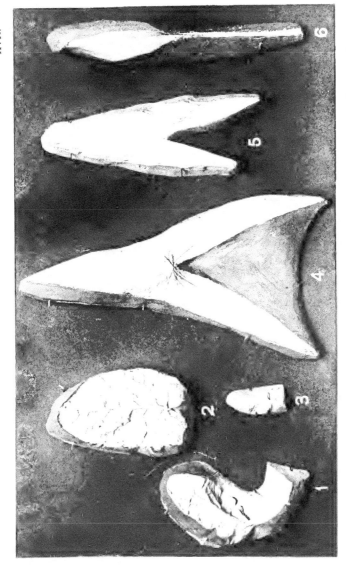

XVII

MOULDS, IN PLASTER, OF LEAVES OF MARSH RAGWORT (FIGS. 1, 2, 3); OF ARROW-HEADS (FIGS. 4, 5);
AND OF SEA-ASTER (FIG. 6).

and the operation more successful. The mould must be quite *warm*, or the seams, showing where all the streams of the liquid wax meet on it, will be visible.

It is a rare thing to get a good impression the first time. Small moulds may be dipped into the wax, but with larger leaves it would require a large vessel and so much wax as to make it scarcely worth while.

Nothing remains but the colouring, and, as this varies in each species, and often in each leaf, no general details can be given, but, under the heading of some of the species described hereafter, special directions will be found.

A clean and light hand is, it need hardly be stated, of the utmost importance even in leaf-modelling, but in the making of flowers it is a *sine quâ non*. It may also be as well to mention that no one, unless a past master of the art of taxidermy, should attempt to embellish his work with modelled foliage, or it may be that one bad piece of work will be supplemented by another.

Perhaps, however, a worse condition of matters than even that is to be seen in the Government Museums of Britain and America, where, in many instances, the birds are unscientifically and awkwardly mounted, and surrounded by exquisitely modelled foliage, which is far worse than if birds and foliage both exhibited the same degree of positive badness or mediocrity.

General Instructions

In all cases, where practicable, the plant to be modelled from should be dug up, placed in a pot of soil, and kept moist, or in a vessel of water, whilst being copied. This, with the one destroyed in making the moulds of the leaves and pasting down the flowers for patterns, necessitates the procuring of two specimens of the same plant. For temporary preservation of plants—most useful in many instances—see Formula 50 (p. 58).

Plants may be dried and kept as patterns, and, when wanted for use, will revive and swell out to their original size if immersed for a short time in warm water, but petals, calyces, leaves, and other parts of plants, whose outline is required for reference, may be preserved in several ways.

The easiest method is to paste (*not gum*) a stiff sheet of notepaper or thin card, and lay the parts, right way upwards, on the pasted side, pressing a sheet of blotting-paper over them, the only drawback being that there is a slight shrinkage of the petals, etc., when dry ; but a whole flower may be preserved by snipping off the stalk close to the calyx or sepals, and with care the stamens and carpels may be removed, leaving the petals, in many cup- or star-shaped flowers, attached to one another.

Another method, where the actual plant is not preserved, is to trace the parts around with a fine hard pencil ; but a better plan is to make a stencil of the parts by laying them down upon paper, holding them firmly, and dabbing all around them with any rather gummy water-colour almost dry—say one of the brownish or purplish madders,—which leaves a white impression when the flower or leaf is removed.

The very best method, however, is to make a flower or leaf print its own venations, and this reverses the preceding, for now the colour is dabbed upon the part of the plant to be printed, and this is then laid upon white paper, with blotting-paper over it, and rubbed gently for some little time, when a print of the form, of the venations, and of accidental holes will appear, and, by careful arrangement, many leaves may be printed side by side, giving a record of their sequence, which leaves little to be desired. Oil-colours may be used instead of water-colours, and are, indeed, better for this latter process, and this is practically the manner in which nature-printed ferns, etc., are managed. For this no brush should be used, but a " dabber " of cotton wool enclosed in fine linen (" nainsook " is the best) is used instead ; the tube oil-colour, of whatever hue desired, is put out, a very little at a time, upon the palette, and the dabber is filled with it by constantly working it upon the colour until it is in such a state as, when dabbed upon the leaf or flower, to mark every raised part without clogging the depressions. The printing is managed upon paper by laying blotting-paper over the leaf in the same manner as with water-colours, and beautiful impressions result, as, if desired, the tints can be varied on the same leaf by using several dabbers, each charged with a different colour.

Calyces and involucres are almost invariably made of fabric lined with wax, and are sometimes cut from a strip, as for the violet, coltsfoot, sea-aster, etc., but more frequently, perhaps, in a stellular form, as for the ranunculus, apple-blossom, hawthorn, etc. In the latter case it is easier to cut a disc first, and from this to cut the calyx of three, five, or any number of sepals. Such discs are easily struck with compasses, or, when a number of the same size are wanted, are more easily and quickly cut out by a punch (Fig. L, Plate II.). Probably the best plan of all, however, is to learn to cut by eye, practising upon paper first, until not only discs but calyces with any number of points can be cut accurately without mechanical aid.

To cut a folded edge of wax or of art fabric for stamens or similar purposes, lay the strip along the left forefinger, with the folded edge uppermost and nearest to the body, and, taking the small sharp scissors (which must work quite easily) in the right hand, rest the fingers of this hand lightly and easily within those of the left, and snip the wax or fabric—commencing at the end nearest to the right hand—in such a manner that the points of the scissors do not quite meet. The scissors and the hands should be held in the same position throughout, the strip itself being gradually pushed along as required by the thumb of the left hand. Resting the left hand upon the edge of a table is usually found to assist the regularity of the cutting.

Wires for flowers must *always* have a knot made at the end by turning a small piece over once or twice, otherwise the flower is certain to slip off before completion.

Some silk-covered wire is liable to strip, or does not hold the fabric well, and in such instances it must be rubbed with wax; beeswax will do.

Thick, fleshy leaves, such as those of the hyacinth, tulip, and lily-of-the-valley, are (so say the Mintorns) better cast; that is to say, plaster moulds are made, but *not* boiled with borax, and the leaves are made by pouring hot wax upon the moulds, which are previously saturated in warm water.

Very small leaves which are, as in such plants as the ox-eye daisy, ragwort, and others, closely appressed to the flower-stalks, need not have a wire inserted, but will adhere and remain erect if tooled on to the main stem.

Thick stems, such as those of the dandelion, are made upon more than one wire. Cut wax into long wedge-shaped strips, and, taking two wires, and placing the end of one some distance below that of the other, cover with a strip of white wax to a little beyond the top of the second wire. Add another wire some distance lower, cover with another strip, and continue to add wires and wax until a sufficient thickness and strength have been obtained. If necessary, the wires may be turned up at the bottom and made up in the stem for strength. When rolled smooth, cover with white fabric and draw lightly between the fingers, so that it will look transparent.

Woody stems may be made with brown fabric alone upon steel "tails," or as described for apple-blossom, p. 331.

The modelling-pin plays so important a part in this beautiful and fascinating work, and so much depends upon its skilful handling, that the method of holding and rolling it must be described. The stem of the pin, therefore, must be held lightly and easily with the right hand, the thumb and forefinger being an inch and a half or two inches from the head, and the other fingers curving slightly towards the underneath of the pin on the side farthest from the operator; it is used by applying the head of the pin to the surface of the petal, sepal, or whatever is to be modelled—which must always rest either upon the palm or the forefinger of the left hand,—and rolling it toward the body, then raising it and repeating the process until the desired thinness, concavity, or curvature has been obtained. The stem of the pin is used in a variety of ways, such as rolling up and down a stem to give smoothness, squareness, or any other effect. Indeed, it would be impossible to describe in a short space the number of purposes to which this simple tool can be applied in modelling, and they must be left for the ingenuity of the student to discover, except when they are described in subsequent pages.

Figwort Ranunculus (Lesser Celandine)

Ranunculus ficaria, *Linn.*

This beautiful little yellow flower, closely allied to the common "buttercups," is, like the latter, a well-known denizen of the meadows and plashy pastures, but, unlike it, is amongst the earliest flowers of the year, and is therefore interesting, not only to the general observer, who hails it as the floral harbinger of spring, but to the artist in modelled foliage, as being one of the very first to break the enforced idleness of winter.

Properly and carefully managed, this makes a fine object, and one or two clumps, with short grasses interspersed, are very suitable to introduce into groups of various early birds of passage. It is, though apparently a simple flower, by no means easy to make, but is an excellent lesson, as it calls into play many technicalities which will be found useful, if thoroughly mastered, in the delineation of other plants.

The first thing is, of course, to get a fine, well-grown plant, and to snip the leaves off just where the stalk joins the under surface, and then to cast them and finish the moulds as explained in leaf-casting (pp. 308-311).

The Making of the Flower

The flower is, for botanical purposes, divided into—

1. The Carpels—which, combined, form a globular head or the centre of the flower.
2. The Stamens—a fringe of little yellow threads, broadened at their tips into *anthers*, surrounding the centre.
3. The Petals (eight or nine)—which are oblong, glossy, and yellow.
4. The Calyx—consisting of three small, light green processes or *sepals*, arranged triangularly underneath the petals.
5. The Flower-stalk underneath.

The Carpels.—Patterns having been taken as already described, and another flower being placed in front of the modeller as a further guide, first prepare, in the usual manner (see p. 316), a piece of white silk-covered wire, a little longer than the natural stem, and then proceed to make the carpel or green centre by taking a piece of green wax, about an inch in length and two-thirds in breadth, doubling it lengthwise, and snipping the finest possible fringe along the folded edge (see p. 315) to the depth of about one-sixteenth inch. It will now be seen that this fringed strip is wider than necessary for the carpel, although the width *was* necessary for the convenience of holding whilst cutting; cut off a portion of the base, therefore, and wind the "fringe" loosely around the knotted end of the wire, in a some-

what convex or conical form, taking care not to press the cut
edge together.

The Stamens are made by inserting a strip of yellow or
white wax, about one-sixteenth of an inch in width, between a
folded piece of *thin* yellow fabric, and snipping the folded edge
—within which rests the strip of wax,—not quite so finely as
for the carpel, to the depth of about three-sixteenths of an inch.
When necessary, colour the stamens with that yellow powder-
colour which most nearly resembles nature, the especial reason
for colouring them at this stage being to prevent them from
sticking together during subsequent manipulation ; for an inverse
reason, the extreme bases must *not* be coloured, or they will
not adhere to the carpel when required.   Now let the tips rest
upon the forefinger of the left hand, and roll them with the
steel stem of a modelling-pin (Fig. N, Plate II.), flattening them
out to form the anthers, afterwards working a channel in the
centre of each of these with the head of a blanket-pin (Fig. O,
Plate II.), which not only gives it character, but separates each
from its fellows ; on the other side work each with the pin
to give it a slight curvature.   Taking the strip with the stamens
thus prepared, roll it around, pressing its base upon the base of
the carpel, until the strip meets, and then cut off the remaining
portion.   Take the pin, and, with the point, separate the stamens,
turning each alternate one in toward the centre regularly, and,
with the finger and thumb of the disengaged hand, slightly
round the extreme tips.   Resuming the strip of fringed fabric
representing the stamens, wind it around with the tips just
below those of the first row until it again meets ; cut off, and
in this instance separate the stamens and draw each alternate
one *outwards ;* repeat the process of tooling and pressing until
the double row of stamens looks easy and natural.

The Petals, which are made of white wax lined with yellow
fabric, must be cut separately from a combined strip, of a

width corresponding to the length of the petals, and the edge of each must be thinned by rolling with the head of the modelling-pin on the waxed side, and then channelled or veined with the head of a blanket-pin.   The petal is now turned over, and veined, and modelled into a somewhat concave form on the fabric side, which is the upper surface of the petal.   Each, if not quite correct in colour, must be made so by rubbing on powder-colour with one of the hard brushes (Fig. F, Plate II.), and, in this connection, it is as well to remark that a number of brushes of this kind are required, as each colour should have one brush devoted to it.   Now fix three of the petals by their base to the base of the fringe of stamens, preserving fairly regular intervals between them, and, as the others will come slightly over them, it is as well to colour their under surfaces, before proceeding further, with a faint greyish-green, but this is to be of moist water-colours, applied with a camel-hair or sable pencil. If the colour will not readily take upon the waxed surface, rub in a very little arrowroot (professionals usually moisten with the tongue, but this cannot be recommended either for flavour or elegance).   Fix the remainder of the petals either in threes or as the natural flower dictates, and probably in the older blooms the edges of the outermost petals will be found to turn back towards the base.   Finally, touch up with moist water-colours where needed, and give the insides of the petals their shining appearance by touching them with a little of Roberson's medium.

The Calyx.—The sepals are not cut separately, but the calyx is cut in one piece from pale green wax backed with light green fabric, first cut as a disc, of the exact size of a three-penny piece for the smaller flowers, as previously described, and a hole is pierced in the centre, by which it is slipped upon the stem-wire.

The Flower-stem is made of doubled green wax, worked

smoothly at first over the covered wire, but, as the natural stem becomes gradually thicker and squarer towards the base, another strip of doubled wax, cut to an apex, is superimposed upon the other, and this, when tooled at the back, gives the requisite squareness.

The Flower-bud is made by preparing a wire as for the stem, and building upon it a foundation made thus : Take a strip of yellow wax, three-eighths of an inch or less in width, and fold it lengthwise in such a manner that the upper portion shall be single and the lower double, and the whole width from three-sixteenths to a quarter of an inch, according to the size of the natural bud. Roll this strip, with the fold *inside*, around the prepared end of the wire to a somewhat conical form, afterwards modelling it with the stem of the pin into a triangular shape.

Next cut a disc of pale green wax backed with fabric, and from this cut three combined petals, as was done for the calyx of the flower, but larger. Thin their edges with the head of the modelling-pin, mould the lines and shape on the fabric side, then make each concave on the other side, and, having pierced a hole in the centre, slip upon the wire and affix to the base of the foundation, taking care that each petal rests upon a side of the triangle. The sepals are better cut separately for the bud ; thin their edges and tool them as before, and arrange them over and between the petals, still preserving the triangular shape, and, if the bud is to appear as though just opening, the enclosed triangular cone should show the yellow apex, which, if not of quite the correct hue, must be made so with moist water-colour.

The Leaf and Stalk.—The plaster moulds, having been made and prepared as directed previously, should now be in front of the modeller, together with a sufficient number of ribs (see p. 306). One of the leaf-moulds being selected, wet it, as

21

usual, in warm water, and press upon it a very thin sheet of rather olive-green wax, on which, when the first shows sufficient definition, press another thin sheet ; the reason for this being that one sheet of thick wax will never show such delicate veinings in the same manner as one thin one followed by another will do. Upon this double wax lay, in the proper position, a thin but nicely-covered rib, long enough to form the stalk as well. Next take a piece of green fabric, as nearly of the colour of the underside of the leaf as may be, and cut a slit in its lower part where the rib leaves the leaf and goes to form the stem, which, in this particular leaf and in those of the marsh marigold, violet, ivy, and many other heart-shaped or ovate leaves, is at about two-thirds òf its length, or in the cleft of the heart. Press the fabric well upon the wax, taking care, whilst pressing close to the rib on both sides, not to press *upon* it, as this would be likely not only to flatten the rib, but to force it from its position, and also to split the wax underneath. When properly pressed and united, remove the leaf from the mould and trim it with the small scissors to the irregular edge shown by the pressure upon the mould ; this edge will, however, be rather too thick, and must be thinned by rolling it gently upon the finger with the head of a modelling-pin, curling it afterwards with the fingers if at all straightened by this process. Next double a piece of green wax, cut a long wedge-shaped strip as directed for the flower-stalk, and roll it loosely upon the covered wire, gradually broadening it as it nears the base ; at this part, however, the stalk becomes whiter, especially at the back, and the best way to imitate this is to roll around it a small wedge of very thin white wax and tool it well into the green, which shows through the white, and gives the transparent effect of nature. The stem, being rounded at the back and flattened or hollowed in front, is nicely tooled with the stem of the modelling-pin. Finally, colour to nature by rubbing in powder-colours, and polish the upper surface of the leaf with a very soft tooth-brush or small plate-brush.

The putting-together of the whole plant is easily managed by placing the flower-stalks, buds, and leaves together as in nature, winding a strip of white fabric around their bases, and uniting the whole by tooling with a modelling-pin.

Sweet Violet (The *Violet*), Viola odorata, *Linn.*

This universal favourite, sweet and modest herald of spring, vying with the primrose in tender presagings of that happy time, is not so difficult to imitate as might be imagined. Mrs. Mogridge and Miss Squires are responsible for the following description of its method of reproduction, which method may, of course, be adapted to the scentless forms—all valuable as woodland accessories.

Cut *on the cross*, out of white art fabric, four petals in the form of diagram No. 1, one of No. 2, and, out of light green

fabric and wax combined, a calyx in the form of No. 3, the *sizes*, however, being determined by the flowers to be copied.

Colour both sides of the petals by brushing on, with a stiff brush, permanent violet and ultramarine powder-colours, mixed together with as little water as possible. The base of each petal should be left uncoloured, No. 2 being only coloured from the dotted line ; the darker markings can be added by means of a fine soft brush, with permanent violet and a little red (pan colours). Now roll the petals upon the palm of the hand with the head of a modelling-pin, laying the two upper ones face downwards and modelling the back, and the three lower ones upon their back and modelling their front surface, the lower centre petal, it will be seen, requiring to be of a deeply concave form.

Next take about four inches of fine wire ; turn over the end as usual, and wind around the tip a narrow strip of the palest green wax, folded under at the bottom edge, to form a small finely-pointed knob (Fig. 4)—*i.e.* the stigma—of which the extreme point must be tipped with cadmium orange (dry). Take a small strip of cream-coloured fabric about a quarter of an inch in width ; thicken one edge by folding over ; cut very finely five stamens, the thickened edge representing the anthers, and arrange these half-way around the stigma. Outside the stamens fix the two upper petals ; in exact opposition to these place petal No. 2, and, on each side of this, one of the remaining two. The stem must next be made by covering the wire, as far down as where the bracts appear in the natural stem, thinly and evenly with a narrow strip of light green wax or fabric, then cut and fix the pair of bracts, and complete the stem, which must be curved into the natural form.

It will now be seen that another part of the flower has still to be made, namely, the spur of the lower petal. Cut, therefore, a short half-inch strip of white fabric, fold over about one-third of the width, and roll sufficient at one end to form an object somewhat resembling an apple-pip in shape. Colour this spur, the stem, and the *fabric* side of the calyx with permanent violet, alizarin, and blue, and affix the spur with its point extending underneath the lower centre petal. Hollow each sepal of the calyx by rolling the *wax* surface with a small modelling-pin ; compress the "neck" slightly by pressing it upon the finger with the pin itself, laying the pin across the calyx on the *outside ;* attach the calyx around the upper portion of the flower, and the violet is complete.

The Clover

The well-known plants coming under the generalised term of " clover " are of many species, and are of the greatest service, as accessories, in nearly every field-group set up by the artist ; indeed, there are few groups, whether dealing with such subjects as larks and pipits, which nest upon the ground, or mice and voles, or a group of bees, which are not beautified, and their value enhanced, by these charming and truly pastoral plants.

Although there are numerous species, those which will most readily commend themselves to the artist and modeller are the—

Crimson clover,	*Trifolium incarnatum,*	Linn.
Purple clover,	,, *pratense*	,,
White (or Dutch) clover,	,, *repens*	,,
Alsike (or hybrid) clover,	,, *hybridum*	,,

but it may be as well to say, that it is only in rare instances advisable to show more than one species in the same case ; and there should be a good quantity shown, nothing looking more paltry and unnatural, as may be seen in some would-be "groups," than a flower-head or two with, perhaps, three to six leaves.

In extenuation of this, it may be urged that it is a most difficult and tiresome flower to model and put together, and consequently expensive. The obvious reply is, that if our Government is too parsimonious to do it properly, it will be better to leave it out of the groups altogether. The American Government has done it thoroughly, and cheerfully paid a bill of some hundreds of dollars for a representative mass of clover for one group alone.

The following description, for which the writer is indebted to his friend, Miss F. M. Squires (after Mrs. Mogridge), will give all but the necessary patience requisite to model this flower, so extremely valuable, in every sense of the word, when well done, and will also pave the way to the making of many others of the pea-flower tribe to which the clovers belong.

The Flower

First take a piece of thin white art fabric and cut a number of corollas in this form—

the size and number being determined by the. flowers it is desired to copy. Place these one by one upon the left forefinger, holding the lower point or stem with the thumb, and, by rolling with the head of a blanket-pin, slightly indent as shown by the dotted lines. Then, with the right thumb and forefinger, lightly press the edges together, at the same time gently stretching the curved points, without flattening them together too much, and bear them down within the partially folded centre point, giving to the whole a backward curve over the finger, or rather between the appressed finger and thumb. When sufficient of these corollas are made, they must be coloured before being put together.

Now wax a piece of rather fine wire ; turn over the end as usual, and cover the knot with pale green wax. Snip a short fine fringe of delicate green fabric, and fix, fringe upwards, around the tip thus prepared, and, around this again, fix four, or five, or six of the flowerets by pressing their thin stems upon the wire, and letting their points curve inwards above the green tip. Snip a fine fringe of dull brownish or of pale green fabric, as the case may be, and wind once around the little stems, which the straight uncut edge will bind together, whilst the fringed portion will spread, and represent the sepals of the tiny calyces amongst the blossoms. Now fix another row of the flowerets with their tips curving in between the first row. Bind with the "fringe" as before, and repeat until the blossom is sufficiently large.

Apple-Blossom, Apple Pyrus, Pyrus malus, *Linn.*

This lovely flower, which, in the spring, fills the orchards with blushes of virginal freshness, is most useful as an accessory to the nests of many of our orchard- and hedge-building birds, giving just that delicate pink which is so valuable in almost any picture-group. The method of reproduction as here described is founded upon that of Mrs. Mogridge, but corrected and improved upon by Miss Squires, who also planned the diagrams.

The centre of the blossom, *i.e.* the pistil, is made from a strip of pale green art fabric, turned over narrowly at the top edge, and snipped very finely with the scissors to form the carpels—usually five. Attach to the wire, and around the base of this pistil wind a strip of folded green wax for the ovary, which, though rarely (if ever) visible, is necessary to the proper formation of the base of the flower. For the stamens, take a strip of pale lemon (almost white) art fabric, fold the top edge over once, or perhaps twice, according to the thickness of the fabric and the condition and size of the natural anthers ; snip it very finely for some little distance, being careful not to cut the fabric through at the other edge, and being careful also to keep the folded part *uppermost.* Damp the scissors frequently ; most professionals do this with the mouth, which, although a speedy method, is not recommended. Now take a needle and draw forward every alternate, or every second and third little strip, and cut them neatly away at the base. Figures 1 and 1a show the preliminary and the finished stamens before winding on. Wind once around the ovary so that the stamens will be of the length of the *inner* ones of the natural flower, which are considerably shorter than the outer

ones. Colour the anthers with a full body of pale yellowish
powder-colour, dragged on, as it were, so as to give the rough
appearance of pollen. Wind the strip around a second time,
bringing the stamens of this row within the gaps left in the
former, and taking care that the uncut base of the strip shall be
rather below the top edge of the ovary. Press the stamens

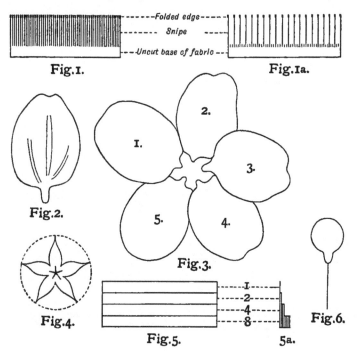

Fig.1.   Fig.1a.

Fig.2.

Fig.4.   Fig.3.

Fig.5.   5a.   Fig.6.

around, just above the ovary, with the stem of a modelling-pin
to form a "neck," and, having tinted the anthers as before,
arrange the upper portions of the stamens as in nature.

Next come the petals—five—cut with a stem, as shown by
Fig. 2, out of very thin white art fabric. Rub arrowroot upon
the upper surface, avoiding the extreme base, however, and then
thin the petals by rolling well on both sides with a modelling-

pin, and make the sharp channels and markings which occur in each petal, and which are slightly indicated in the diagram, by rolling on the palm of the hand with the head of a blanket-pin. Next, tint the *under* surface of each petal, and the colour will show through sufficiently to impart a delicate tinge of pink to the upper surface ; be sure, however, to take a natural flower as a guide, the colouring being very irregular upon the petals, according to their exposure to, or protection from, the sun's rays.

To support and strengthen each petal, take a fine white bristle, and cover it thinly but thoroughly with a small strip of white wax ; hold a petal between the left thumb and fore-fingers, place a covered bristle underneath the *stem*, allowing the point to reach nearly to the *centre* of the petal, and then, with the thin end of a modelling-pin, make a minute fold or pleat down the stem and lower portion of the petal, enveloping the bristle and assisting the natural contour of the petal itself. This is an extremely valuable "wrinkle," and is applicable to a great variety of flowers of like character. As the flowers expand, it will be observed that the petals become less con-cave, a distinct keel appearing up the centre of each, and causing the petal to partially fold backwards. In attaching the petals, let it be noted that there is a certain order of arrangement to be adhered to, of which the diagram, Fig. 3, taken from an actual flower, will give a fair idea. From this it will be seen that petals 1 and 3 are entirely *inside* the whorl, 2 and 5 entirely *outside*, whilst No. 4 is half in and half out, one edge overlapping No. 5 and the other overlapped by No. 3. In this connection, it must also be noted that petals 2 and 5, being outside, will be the most highly coloured. Re-roll and re-curl the petals, and attach securely by the "stem" to the ovary.

Cut a calyx of five points or sepals (see Fig. 4 and p. 315) out of pale green fabric lined with wax, leaving an uncut centre of about a quarter of an inch in diameter ; thin the edges slightly, and roll the broad part of each sepal on the wax side with the head of a small modelling-pin, until sufficiently concave ; pinch the extreme points between the thumb and finger, and, piercing the centre with a point of the scissors, cut small slits in the form of a star ; slip upon the wire, and, arranging so that the sepals show *between* the petals, press closely around the ovary by rolling with the stem of the pin, and give to the sepals, which are mostly recurved, the curves exhibited in the natural flower.

To make the stem or peduncle, take a broad strip of light green wax and roll *loosely* around the wire to the thickness required, to give it transparency, being careful to unite the stem thoroughly with the calyx, and to work the edge of the wax (which is better torn than cut) invisibly into the stem by means of the steel part of the pin. Now cover the calyx and stem with honey, applied with a small camel-hair brush, and dust on fine white "down" (see p. 302).

In making a bud, the first thing to be done is to form a foundation resembling, as nearly as possible, the shape of the natural bud. The best and easiest way to do this is to cut off about one-third of a sheet of white wax and fold it lengthwise *not quite* in the centre, thus allowing one edge to extend a little beyond the other. Fold again, bringing the doubled edge not quite up to the second cut edge, and finally fold again so that the strip shall be as shown by Figs. 5 and 5a, the figures showing the numbers of thicknesses. Roll sufficient of this around a wire (turned over as usual), with the thickest part *upwards* and the folds *inside*, to make the foundation of the requisite size, and model with the thumb and finger, assisted by the stem of a modelling-pin, into the form shown by Fig. 6. Cut three or four petals only out of white fabric, rather smaller than for the flower, the size being, of course, in accordance with that of the bud to be copied ; tool them as for the flower, but making the concavity still more decided. Attach one petal, wrapping it closely around the foundation, and tint with powder-colour ; but this, being the innermost petal and least exposed to the light, will be paler than the others. Now affix the other petals, letting them overlap each other as in nature, but do not press them so closely as the first ; tint according to the natural bud, using pan colour for the brighter touches, and then make and add the calyx as described for the flower.

The putting-together of the completed blossoms and buds is so simple as to need no instructions, but the little stipules and bracts, which are made of fabric and wax combined, must not be forgotten. The leaf is made in the usual manner by means of a plaster mould (see pp. 311, 312), and all that now requires notice is the woody stem, which is made by folding wax around a strong wire to the desired thickness, covering with fabric of a brown or any suitable colour, and working it with the steel part of a modelling-pin to give the natural knotty or rough appearance. Any special knots or rugosities can be added by cutting a strip of fabric " on the cross," stretching it, and twisting or winding it unevenly around the branch or twig, and finally working it into the natural semblance by means of the pin as before.

Common Hawthorn, Cratægus oxyacantha, *Linn.*

The modelling of this blossom, as executed by Mrs. Mogridge, is, with slight alteration, described by Miss Squires as follows :—

For the pistil, take a small piece of pale green art fabric, turn down the edge very narrowly, and cut one thread-like strip. Press this upon the end of a fine wire prepared in the usual manner, and wind around at their junction a narrow strip of pale green wax, modelling it with the fingers, assisted by a modelling-pin, into the shape of the ovary.

Take a strip of creamy-white art fabric, roll the edge over very neatly, and snip as finely as possible for the stamens, two rows of which will be required. To prevent these being too crowded, it is necessary to thin them as for the apple-blossom (see p. 327). Arrange around the ovary, placing the inner row low down and cutting off the remainder of the strip where it meets, and placing the outer row a little higher, to give the stamens greater length. Press firmly around the base, and trim away with the scissors any superfluous fabric.

Out of the creamy-white art fabric cut five petals, taking a natural petal as a pattern. Roll each one with a modelling-pin upon the left forefinger until sufficiently thin and concave, and then attach, by the stalk-like process, to the ovary, or rather to the base of the stamens.

The calyx, of five sepals, is cut (see p. 315 and Fig. 4, p. 328) out of pale green art fabric lined with wax ; tool each sepal on the wax side with the head of a small modelling-pin, pinching the extreme tips to make them more pointed. Piercing the centre of the calyx with the small scissors, cut little slits in the form of a star, slip it upon the wire, and model neatly and closely around the ovary with the stem of a modelling-pin. Colour the anthers to nature with powder-colours as dry as possible, cover the wire very thinly with delicate green wax, apply a thin coating of honey to the calyx, and dust on fine white " down."

To make a bud, first form a foundation by winding a narrow folded strip of cream-coloured or white wax, folded edge uppermost, around a prepared wire, and moulding it into shape with the fingers. Over this fix three small petals, cut and tooled as for the open flower, and around these place the calyx, modelling the whole carefully with the stem of a pin until of the natural form.

The putting-together of the flowers and buds is perfectly easy if a natural cluster be taken as a guide, and no instructions are deemed necessary.

The leaves are made by means of plaster moulds as usual ; the stipules, which do not require moulds, are made —like the leaves—from wax combined with art fabric, and the thorns may be made of brownish art fabric cut into wedge-shaped strips, and rolled up and modelled into shape with the fingers.

Common Honeysuckle or Woodbine, Lonicera periclymenum, *Linn.*

This climber, very valuable and handsome when surrounding or enclosing a nest of some hedge- or arbour-building bird, is, though rather difficult, yet so interesting as to repay the time spent upon its reproduction.

Miss Squires, under Mrs. Mogridge's instruction, describes the method thus :—

The corolla, which consists of an elongated tube and two lips—the upper one four-lobed and the lower one entire,—can be cut in one piece, somewhat in the form shown here, out of white or cream-coloured art fabric faced with white or cream-coloured sheet wax. Lay upon the palm of the hand, wax surface downwards, and roll with the head of a modelling-pin in the directions shown by the dotted lines, until each lobe, viewed from the front (*i.e.* the *under* side), presents a rounded or fluted appearance, this result being further assisted by pressing the pin lengthwise *between* the lobes on the wax surface. The lower lip (marked A in the diagram) is rolled and hollowed, in the same manner, but on the reverse side, and omitting the tip.

Now take some fine white sewing-silk, and stiffen it by drawing many times (in front of the fire if necessary) through a small piece of creamy or yellowish wax; cut five bits of fabric and roll them, with the thumb and finger, into the form of anthers; to each of these attach an end of the silk by rolling, in one direction, between the thumb and finger, thus winding the silk tightly once or twice around the centre, and then cut off each piece of silk a little longer than the actual stamens. The pistil also is made of the silk, tipped with a small knob of pale green wax. Now prepare a fine wire in the usual manner (see p. 316), cover the tip with wax, press the pistils and stamens upon the wax tip, bind all together and thicken the stem a little by folding wax around, and then fix the corolla over all. Colour the *outside* irregularly according to the natural flower, tint the anthers, and finally make the calyx by winding around the base of the blossom a very narrow strip of folded wax or fabric, in the upper edge of which five minute teeth have been cut.

To make an unopened bud, fold down an edge of wax to the depth of about half an inch, and cut the folded strip of a *width* corresponding to the *length* of the bud to be copied. Prepare a wire, and wind the wax lightly around it with the fold *inside* at the top, subsequently moulding it into shape with the fingers. This may be turned into an *opening* bud by covering it with a corolla, cut as for the open flower, but smaller, and modelled so that the lips will close over each other instead of curving outwards. Finish off the base, and colour as before.

Sufficient blossoms and buds having been prepared, fix as many together as there are in the natural specimen, taking care to preserve the shape of each ovary. Cover a small portion of the stem with wax, and fix another whorl of blossoms, repeating this until the cluster is complete.

The stems require no special instructions, and the leaves are made by first taking plaster moulds, as previously described, and afterwards modelling upon these with wax and fabric in the usual manner.

Coltsfoot, Tussilago farfara, *Linn.*

This herb, whose golden blooms—borne upon a practically leafless stalk, save for the small scales appressed thereto—come long before the large radical leaves appear, is found commonly upon stony clays or waste dry lands, and, like the lesser celandine (see p. 317), is one of the earliest, if not *the* earliest, flowers to welcome the wheatear or the chiffchaff, shuddering in the wintry breeze which "lingers in the lap of spring."

It is, for all its commonness, a lovely thing, and may take some credit for being extremely difficult and tiresome to model correctly. Commence by taking two wires or doubling one, turning over the ends, and arranging upon them a small piece of folded yellow wax to form a centre. Take a strip of yellow fabric and cut very finely to form the florets; wind around until the ends meet, cut off the remainder, and press the base of the florets on to the base of the centre. Resuming the strip of fabric, wind it again around, but at a little higher elevation than the first, and cut off as before; repeat this operation yet a third time, and, when tinted to nature, lay it upon the fingers of the left hand, and scratch and separate the florets with the set needles (Fig. Q, Plate II.).

The involucre is made from double fabric, and in this instance is not cut from a disc but from a straight strip, and is modelled to shape with a blanket-pin; the tips should be tinted to a brownish hue, and then the combined involucre is wound around the base of the flower. The whitish fleshy stem is made by rolling doubled white wax around the wires to the desired thickness.

The stalk-leaves or scales are cut to shape from white wax and backed by a smaller piece of green fabric, in such a manner as to allow an irregular edge of white to show beyond the green. Tool them up and attach to the stalk by pressure. Vary these by superimposing brown fabric upon the white wax, and sometimes the wax may be placed outside for the sake of variety, but the natural flower will dictate this. Colour their tips, etc., but observe, before finally arranging the scales, whether the stalk requires more tooling, the addition of more wax, or colouring.

The leaves (radical) do not come with the flowers, and, if required, must be cast (see p. 312).

The Sea-Aster, Aster tripolium, *Linn.*

This very striking and beautiful plant, flowering in September, is found lining the edges of brackish-water dykes, and on the salt marshes, of Lincolnshire, Norfolk, and other counties. When growing in the ditches, pools, and dykes, where the salt water occasionally or but rarely gains access, so that the water is brackish or but slightly impregnated with salt, it grows from 3 to 4 feet in height, much branched, each branch and the top of the main stem carrying a profusion of yellow-centred lilac flowers, which brighten up the water-courses with a broad belt of pleasing colour for hundreds of yards in length; the main stems, which are of some thickness, are of a fine red, and the leaves, except at the bottom of the plant, are somewhat thin and lanceolate. On the salt marshes—where it grows close to the sand, or at normal high-water mark, and forms broad belts or meadows of colour and verdure for miles,— it assumes a more stunted and less branched form, the main stems being from 12 to 20 inches in height, whilst the leaves are less lanceolate, extremely thick and fleshy, and there is a large proportion of flowers of which only the yellow and reddish-yellow florets of the disc show, the florets of the ray being pale, sparse, and in some cases hardly discernible, save as a short, thin, and half-developed fringe. Owing to this cause, the sea meadows, at some little distance, present a yellowish-green appearance rather than the lilac to be expected. However, it is amongst these dwarf plants, in which the yellow predominates, that the marsh-waders derive their sustenance in the many little pools of sea-water full of cockles, mussels, crabs, and other crustaceans crawling over the—to them—inviting ooze, and from amongst them birds, such as teal, whimbrels, curlews, and redshanks—especially the latter,—rise, and fall to the gun. This striking flower, so garden-like and seemingly out of place on salt-marshes, is therefore chosen as a fitting and beautiful accessory to a study of, say " redshanks at home," and as it has, probably, never been used for such a purpose until attempted by the writer for the Leicester Museum, it will have the charm of novelty to recommend it.

The Flowers

If a number of flowers are examined, it will, of course, be seen that they have attained to various stages of development, some of their centres or *discs* presenting a compact and even appearance somewhat resembling a bouquet of microscopic crocus-buds, whilst others—more advanced—appear more open and uneven, owing to the outer ring or rings of "buds" (*i.e* florets of the disc) having opened, each revealing a long pistil, tipped with brilliant pollen, and surrounded by five minute recurved petals. Others again, still more mature, have all the florets of the disc expanded, some or all of the pollen having disappeared, leaving the tips of the pistils (*i.e.* the stigmas)

22

whiter, and the tiny petals having become of a rich russet hue ; at this stage also, the florets of the ray (popularly known as " petals "), instead of standing out stiffly as in the newer flowers, become curled and twisted, and the entire flower presents an irregular and ragged appearance. Yet a little later stage, and the florets have all disappeared, and have been replaced by a tuft of silky hairs called *pappus.* It is obvious, therefore, that these various aspects must be reproduced by various methods, and that, unless they *are*, each and all, reproduced, the modelled plant, when finished, will lack that variety which is so great a charm.

Commencing with a newly-opened flower, the disc may be imitated, like that of the daisy (p. 344), by turning over one edge of a narrow strip of yellow wax, winding the strip, folded edge uppermost, around the prepared end of a suitable wire, and pressing it, in front of a fire or stove, through a piece of the finest white net. In this case, the base of the flower within the *involucre* (*i.e.* that part answering in some other flowers to the calyx) must be made up afterwards by folding a strip of wax around the wire, and moulding it with the fingers to the natural shape.

To represent the next stage—a centre surrounded by open florets—take fine white sewing-cotton, cut off an inch or more, double it, and twist loosely to form a small loop ; dip the loop into hot wax tinted with aurora yellow tube oil-colour, and, when set, take a very little dry lemon yellow (deep) upon the finger and roll the tip lightly, and the result will (or should) be an exact imitation of the florets or " buds " in the centre of the disc. Make a sufficient number of these, fix them around the prepared end of a suitable wire, and then proceed to make the outer florets thus : Take a strip of the thinnest art fabric, as nearly of the natural colour as may be, and cut it along one edge as shown by Fig. 1, afterwards cutting from this strip as many pieces as may be required of the shape of Fig. 1a. Should the fabric not be of the correct tint, brush powder-colour upon the points only, and, laying one of these small pieces upon the finger, curve the points by rolling the stem of a pin across them ; turn it over and mould the basal portion into a tubular form around the pin. Now wax some fine yellow sewing-silk or cotton, cut off about an inch, slip it through the little tube, and press the end of this to retain it in position. Having treated all in like manner, tip each *stigma* (*i.e.* the ends of the pistils represented by yellow silk) with pollen, by brushing on a little pan-colour and then dipping

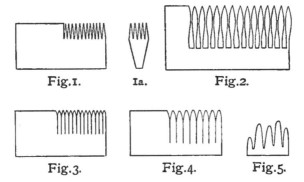

Fig.1.   Ia.   Fig.2.

Fig.3.   Fig.4.   Fig.5.

them into fine dry primrose aureolin powder-colour, and arrange the florets around the central " buds " of the disc. Next make up the basal portion of the flower to nearly the natural size, as before directed.

The florets of the ray ("petals") are now required, and as these—in this plant—show no quilled bases as do those of the garden varieties and of most daisies, they may be cut in strips (see Fig. 2), instead of singly, from thin white art fabric, and each strip of florets, before being used, must be coloured by brushing in a combination of permanent mauve, cobalt, and white powder-colours, the uncut base of the strip, however, being carefully avoided. The colouring being satisfactorily accomplished, lay the florets upon the left forefinger and impart the requisite curves, etc., by means of a blanket-pin, and then fold a strip around the disc, taking a natural flower as a guide to the number and arrangement of the " petals."

For buds of which the discs are hidden, the entire foundation may be made by folding wax around the wire and modelling it to the desired shape, and strips of " petals " may be cut as for the flowers, but much more simply (see Fig. 3), the length of the points, and the width of the uncut base, being determined by the size of the bud to be copied.

The earlier stages of the flower having been successfully reproduced, the representation of later developments may be left to the skill and intelligence of the modeller, excepting, perhaps, the latest of all those mentioned, and in this the pappus has been fairly represented by frayed-out worsted, cut thistledown, etc., but, as these require colouring, the *best* medium is the natural pappus. Remove the involucre therefore, insert a prepared wire, and bind the tuft as low as possible above the seeds with waxed silk, cotton, or very fine wire.

The involucre is all that is now required to complete the flower in any stage, and this may be cut in two parts, from a strip of light green fabric lined with thin wax, in the forms of Figs. 4 and 5. Tool each point on the wax side with the head of a blanket-pin, and then fold the first piece (Fig. 4), fabric outside, around the basal portion of the flower (which must, of course, be of the correct shape, but a trifle smaller to allow for the addition of the involucre) until it meets ; cut off the remainder, unite the ends, and colour to nature. Around this fold the other piece (Fig. 5), and impart the natural depressions and form by tooling with any of the pins most convenient. Colour this also to nature, using Vandyke brown, Rubens madder, burnt sienna, and white, as required.

A small modelled corymb of flower-heads is shown on the left of Plate XVIII.

The Leaves

The stem-leaves, as before stated, are either long, thin, and lanceolate, or short, thick, and lanceolate, while the *radical* leaves (*i.e.* those at the base of the plant) are large, broadly spatulate, twisted, and—including their long, stout stem—some 6 to 9 inches in length. The former are so simple as to require no special instructions for their casting and reproduction, but the latter, which are not quite so easy as would at first sight appear, owing to their unusually thick and transparent rib and stem, are managed as now described. The leaves, having been steeped in water for an hour or so, and gently brushed to remove the mud and sand which often thickly encrust them, should be treated with plaster as previously directed ; but, after they have been covered sufficiently by the spoon - pouring process to give them the necessary rigidity to support a greater weight of plaster, when laid upon the cardboard or thick brown paper—which is better than wood, especially if the paper is laid upon a sheet of glass (plate glass is the best, from every point of view, and need not be very large or of superior quality)—they should be surrounded with walls of zinc, and the plaster thickened to, say, an inch, by pouring on a little at a time, with intervals of rest between to allow the one layer of plaster to *just* set before the next is superimposed. Otherwise—and this is the most satisfactory plan with the larger, or twisted, leaves—they should be laid upon the casting-board and packed underneath with sand or putty.

The zinc walls are simply strips of about 18 inches in length by 1 inch in width, bent around the leaves, and held in position and blocked at the free end by a piece of wood,

$1\frac{1}{2}$ inches in height by some few inches in length, in which saw-cuts, an inch in depth, have been made at one-inch intervals for the reception and retention of the ends of the strip at the width needed.

In some instances, when casting not only leaves but other small objects, it is convenient to use two strips of zinc and two pieces of cleft wood, which, when the zinc strips are inserted within the clefts, will make either a square or a long narrow box, thus supplementing the casting-box described at p. 231, which is, perhaps, more suitable for larger objects.

The moulds having been completed and prepared as usual, commence the modelling by making a rib as previously directed (see pp. 306-308, and 316), but increasing the thickness rapidly in the lower third of the rib proper, as the stem—which must be made at the same time—is of about equal thickness throughout. In making the actual stem, double or four-fold strips of wax should be used and rolled rather loosely, for the sake, not only of transparency, but of subsequent modelling.

Next take a large sheet of wax, a little lighter than the leaf to be copied, and press upon one of the moulds sufficiently to mark the outline of the leaf. Remove the wax and cut all around a little *outside* the outline, and mark and cut a piece of fabric in like manner. Replace the wax, and press it thoroughly upon the mould to get a good impression of the veins, and then, with a small sharp knife, cut out a very narrow wedge-shaped strip from the lower portion to allow the transparent rib to show through. Place the rib in position, first warming it slightly if necessary, and press just sufficiently to make it adhere to the wax, but being extremely careful that the wax, where slit, is not torn and pushed out of place. Press the stem well into the mould, holding it at the *sides* and not pressing it *upon the top*, or the result will be anything but satisfactory. Lay the fabric upon the wax, mark where it

XVIII

MODELS, IN FABRIC, OF SEA-ASTER AND FLOWERING RUSH.

comes upon the stem, and slit about half-way up.   Replace it, and press and knead thoroughly all over, but avoid direct pressure upon the rib, and do not strain the fabric over this, but press down closely on each side of it as far as the slit, along which the edges must be welded, by means of any convenient tool, to the sides of the rib.

Great care and some little skill are required to execute these leaves satisfactorily, but the joining of the fabric and of the wax to the rib can be so managed that each of the former appears to blend imperceptibly into the latter.

The Making-up of a Plant

When making-up, it need hardly be stated, a natural plant is indispensable for reference ; this having been provided, there-fore, commence at the top of the main stem, or *peduncle*, and, having made *pedicels* of the proper length for the first two flowers, unite their extremities by pressure, and make the peduncle to where the next flower branches therefrom by folding a strip of wax around both the wires to the required length and thickness.   Add another flower, and continue the peduncle until the first little " branch " is reached ; make this up separately and affix it afterwards in its natural position, and so proceed, adding wire " tails " from time to time to strengthen the main stem sufficiently to support the increasing weight.

The bracts and leaves must by no means be omitted, and these, when quite small, can be easily copied without casting, and may be affixed by pressure upon the wax stem, whilst the larger ones should be cast and have a fine " rib " inserted for their support.

The Daisy, Bellis perennis, *Linn.*

This " wee, modest, crimson-tipped flow'r " is one of the nicest things as an accessory if skilfully made, and, as it is not

one of the hardest to make when the method is grasped, it will
not be amiss to give full directions for its successful accomplishment.

The first thing to be done is to make the yellow centre
or *disc* of the flower, which looks a hopeless task, and has
been roughly and unsatisfactorily imitated by pressing wax
with a thimble, but which is very easy to make, like many
other things, when one knows how. Take, therefore, some
yellow sheet-wax and cut off a strip from a quarter to three-
eighths of an inch in width, turn down the edge about a sixteenth of an inch, so that it is doubled on the top edge along
its whole length, and wind it around a suitable piece of wire (end
turned over as usual), gradually lowering it so that the centre
is the highest part, looking to the natural flower as a guide
to the degree of convexity, and being careful not to squeeze
the turned-down edge of the wax, which should be just loosely
folded over. When sufficient is wrapped around the wire, and
the *base* of the wax is pressed firmly to the wire, cut a small
piece of the finest white net of the smallest mesh, and—
after the wax has been well warmed (but not melted) in front
of a fire, or by a lamp—pull the net firmly down upon the top
of the wax until it buries itself and sinks out of sight, whilst
the softened wax starts through the holes of the net as little
rounded points, and in less time than can be imagined the
centre is beautifully imitated. Now cut a small strip of art
fabric, snip one edge very finely with the scissors, and wind
once around the centre; tease it out slightly with a needle,
and the outer ring of the florets of the disc, which is looser,
and, as it were, blooming, appears.

The petals, or rather *florets of the ray*, are, as is well
known, white, and often tipped with pink. They must be
imitated in thin white Mintorn art fabric, and—task though it
seems—each must be cut out separately, the natural floret being

taken as a guide, from a strip of fabric of a width corresponding to the length of the florets. To give to the florets the peculiar whiteness which distinguishes the natural flower, arrowroot and flake white are mixed together in equal proportions, and rubbed into both surfaces of the upper portions with the thumb and finger, the bases being carefully avoided, or they will not adhere when arranged in position. Each is then tooled, first on one side and then on the other, with the head of a blanket-pin, and the narrow base is quilled by rolling around the point of a pin or needle.

To put together, press the quilled bases upon the base of the centre, and arrange them irregularly, one here and there, putting now and then one floret under another, and fill in afterwards, which gives an easy and natural appearance.

The involucre, consisting of a number of equal bracts, is made of fabric lined with wax. First cut a disc, and from this, with the small scissors, cut the complete involucre to shape. If the pupil is not sufficiently skilled to do this by eye, the natural involucre may be laid upon the disc and dabbed down with moist colour to mark it. Mould on both sides with a blanket-pin, pierce in the centre, slip upon the wire, and fix in position, pressing it well between the bases of the florets with the pin, as this will greatly assist the modelling.

The stem is so simple as to need no special directions.

To make a bud, take a strip of white fabric of a size to suit the natural bud, but say an inch and a half by half an inch. Cut the strip into petals or florets, without detaching them, and tool each of these with the blanket-pin. For the foundation, prepare a wire as usual, and around the end wind evenly a strip of white wax, folded to about four thicknesses. Next wind the strip of florets *twice* around, snip away the angular edge at the base, and, having cut and modelled it to the natural size and form, make the involucre as for the flower and arrange as in nature.

The top of the stem and base of the involucre, being slightly downy, are painted over with honey and sprinkled with fine white "down."

Common Prunella or "Self-heal," Prunella vulgaris, *Linn.*

This very interesting plant—one of the labiate family, like the red, white, and yellow "dead nettles"—is a great acquisition to almost any group it may be associated with, and, being commonly found in meadows and along the sides of streams, it may be introduced into almost any situation. It is, however, although a strikingly beautiful object with its spikes of purplish flowers and well-veined ovate leaves, so much more difficult and tedious to make than even the "dead nettles," that Mrs. Mogridge must be left to tell the tale of "how it's done."

Taking the natural plant as a guide, the corolla first claims attention, and this, although of a fine purple with blue in nature, must yet be reproduced primarily in white art fabric.

Cut the corolla in two parts, of white art fabric on the cross, in the forms shown in diagrams 1 and 2 ; the calyx, also

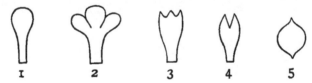

in two parts, of pale green fabric doubled, in the forms of 3 and 4, and the bract-like floral leaves, which occur under each whorl, of fabric faced with wax, in the form of No. 5.

Colour both sides of the "petals" (omitting the bases) with purple powder-colour, magenta, and ultramarine. Model into shape with a small-headed modelling-pin, rolling the upper lip (No. 1) upon the finger with the pin until it becomes deeply concave, and for the lower lip take the natural flower as a guide.

For the stamens, of which there are four arranged in pairs, turn over, as narrowly as possible, the edge of a small strip of white fabric, and, holding this upon the left forefinger, folded edge *upwards* and nearest to the scissors, cut four thread-like strips, each of which will have a minute knob at the tip to represent the anther. Prepare a *very* fine wire by turning down the end and covering it with wax ; fix the stamens on one side of this wax tip, and, having retouched the petals with colour, which will have become partially removed during the process of modelling, arrange the upper lip to curve over the stamens, and the under lip in its natural position. Roll each part of the calyx with a modelling-pin upon the edge of the left forefinger ; vein with the head of a blanket-pin ; tip and streak both sides with crimson lake and purple, and attach the three-pointed portion above the upper lip, and the other below the lower one.

For the buds, cut two petals in the form of No. 1 ; colour one side only, and model the *uncoloured* side of each into a concave form. Make the foundation of the bud with a small knob of white wax, and around this arrange first the lower lip of the corolla, and next the upper lip, partially enfolding it. A calyx from which the corolla has fallen may be made as for the complete flower, and arranged also around a small knob of wax.

To make up a spike of flowers, turn over the end of a fine wire, tip with light green wax, and around this, nearly hiding it, fix a minutely-scalloped strip of green fabric tinted slightly with crimson lake. Around this, and rising well above it, arrange six blossoms or empty calyces, with the *two*-pointed portion of the calyx on that side farthest from the wire. Then roll two of the bract-like floral leaves with a modelling-pin until nicely thinned and somewhat concave on the waxed side; vein well on *both* sides with the head of a blanket-pin; edge one half irregularly with crimson lake, and fix one of these around each half of the whorl of flowers, allowing the first to overlap the second on each side. Follow these with another whorl and two more " bracts," and so on until the spike is complete.

Should there be sufficient space between the whorls to show a portion of the stem, this must be made in the usual way, by folding around the wire a small strip of green wax and working it into the characteristic quadrangular form by means of a modelling-pin—*not* the head, but that part of the pin near the head.

The leaves, which are perfectly simple, are cast from and modelled in the ordinary manner.

It will be observed that none of the preceding colours can be called permanent, nor are they those which any one acquainted with the properties of pigments would use; nevertheless they *were* used—in spite of the faint remonstrance of the writer—by Mrs. Mogridge, in the complete assurance that such colours were, when of good quality and procured from her favourite maker, quite permanent. However, the result has amply justified the contention that, in this instance, both theory and practice were wrong, for the flowers modelled and coloured with such care have faded, in *less than a year*, from their rich purple to a dirty bluish-lavender, and this, be it understood, not in direct sunlight nor even in what might be called a strong light. Violets also, coloured with the same disregard for the chemical composition of pigments, have suffered in like manner. The writer, not having yet made the self-heal, cannot indicate the exact hues to be employed, but refers the pupil to the list of permanent colours at pp. 90-92.

The "Dead Nettles"

Henbit lamium,			*Lamium amplexicaule,* Linn.		
Red	,,		,,	*purpureum,*	,,
White	,,	(the " Dead Nettle ")	,,	*album*	,,
Yellow	,,	(the "Archangel")	,,	*galeobdolon,* Crantz.

The whole of the "dead nettles" are most elegant and valuable objects as accessories, but are extremely difficult to render faithfully, and therefore only those who have gone through the curriculum of flower-modelling embodied in these pages should attempt such objects, which require the most skilful manipulation and ripe knowledge. However, a description of how a white lamium was modelled by Mrs. Mogridge and imparted to Miss Squires, who improved upon the patterns, will perhaps help the student.

Although in the natural flower the corolla is in one piece, as shown in diagrams 1 and 2 (after Bentley), it is necessary, for the purposes of modelling, to cut two portions, which are afterwards united. For the open blossom, therefore, cut *on the cross*, out of white art fabric, two pieces in the forms of Nos. 3 and 4. Mix a little arrowroot and flake white powder and rub into each side of these pieces, avoiding, however, the narrow basal portions which are required for uniting. Now with a modelling-pin roll and model these "petals" upon the palm of the hand until the upper lip assumes a deeply concave and arched appearance, and a sort of median keel is formed throughout the entire length of the "petal," the curve being assisted by folding and gently stretching the "keel" with the fingers, the dry powder preventing the fabric from sticking. Tool the lower lip until it takes the natural form; thicken the basal portion by lining it with wax, and slightly tint the keel of each with the same powders as before, to which a little dry aurora yellow has been added.

For the stamens, double a piece of fabric, turn over one edge, and cut—commencing at the thickened edge—six thread-like strips about half an inch in length. Do not detach these, but cut off in one piece about an inch in length, the lower half being undivided. The anthers, whose colours vary with the development of the natural flower, may be represented by colouring the tips of the stamens with any suitable pigments. Fix the stamens around a *very* fine white wire prepared in the

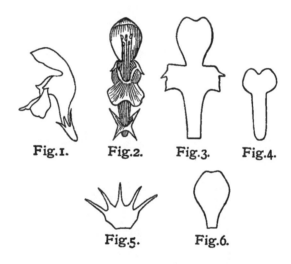

Fig.1.   Fig.2.   Fig.3.   Fig.4.

Fig.5.   Fig.6.

usual manner; then place the larger portion of the corolla with the upper lip curving gracefully over, and nearly hiding, the stamens. Next attach the lower portion of the corolla, and neatly join the sides of the tube by rolling lightly with the median portion of a modelling-pin.

The calyx is the next part to be considered, and this, having five long fine spreading teeth—the posterior one the longest,—is cut, out of delicate green fabric lined with wax, in the form of diagram No. 5 ; thin the edges by rolling on the finger with the head of a modelling-pin ; fold around the base of the corolla, which, if not quite thick enough, can be thickened by the addition of a small piece of wax. Tint the base of the calyx with purple madder let down with a little Vandyke or Caledonian brown, and touch the points with brighter green.

For the bud, first make a foundation by cutting a strip of wax or fabric three-quarters of an inch or less in *width*, according to the *length* of the bud to be copied ; fold over one-third of the width and wind it loosely around a fine wire, folded edge uppermost and the fold inside. Model this foundation with the fingers, making the base thin and the extremity rounded ; then cut out of fabric thickened with wax two " petals " similar to diagram No. 6, the size of these also being larger or smaller according to the size of the natural bud. Rub the powder upon the fabric side only ; model the wax surface of each portion until it becomes nicely concave, and fix in position, allowing the upper lip to partially envelop the lower one. Now put on the calyx, and tint as for the flower.

To make up the Whorls and Leaves

In examining the natural plant, it will be observed that the stem is quadrangular and the leaves are always *opposite*, one leaf immediately under each cyme of flowers, which are so closely clustered that two opposite cymes appear like one whorl. Each cyme contains either seven or nine flowers, arranged in a Vandyked pattern like the letter W, and it will be observed that, although the smallest leaves and buds are at the *top* of the raceme, yet in each individual cyme the smallest buds or least advanced flowers are at the *bottom* points of the W.

The leaves having been cast from and modelled as directed at pp. 308-312, take a prepared stem and affix the smallest pair of leaves, and, taking a natural plant as a guide, follow these at the proper distance by the next pair on the other, or unoccupied, sides of the quadrangular stem. Model this latter to the correct size and form to where the next leaves or cymes should come, and affix these in the natural position on the same sides of the stem as the first pair, and so continue, thickening the stem, where necessary, by adding more wires and wax (see p. 316), tooling each portion into shape before attaching more flowers or leaves, and taking care not to place two successive pairs on the same sides of the stem—following nature, in fact, as nearly as possible,—until the raceme is complete.

The downy appearance can be given to the flowers and buds by first applying honey with a soft brush, and then dusting on fine white " down."

The Flowering Rush, Butomus umbellatus, *Linn.*

This lovely plant, often to be found in canals and sluggish backwaters with its umbel of rosy flowers reared above the water, is one of the most striking objects which can engage the artistic modeller's attention, and, when properly finished, fully repays all the care and skill bestowed upon it. So far as can be discovered, it has not been attempted by the Mintorns or any other modellers ; the processes which follow, therefore, are probably original, and for them the writer and his friend, Miss Squires, are responsible.

When freshly plucked—that is, the whole of the flower-stem with as many attached leaves as possible, plucked up by the roots,—the flower-stem should be cut off about six inches below the head, and placed in a tall vessel of water, a narrow preparation-jar, for instance ; the remainder of the stem, perhaps a yard in length, being reserved and kept fresh in water, a much larger and taller preparation-jar holding this and the leaves.

The Flower.—A leafless stem arises from the water, carrying at its summit three bracts or leaf-like processes surrounding an umbel of pinkish flowers and buds, each on a long stem, or rather pedicel. Each flower has six rosy petals, which are, however, called collectively the *perianth*, arranged in two whorls or sets of three each, those of the outer whorl being smaller, darker, and more pointed ; these surround nine flattened white or pinkish stamens—pink as the flower opens, whitish afterwards,—each surmounted with a fine red anther, which changes to golden when fully expanded. The centre is of six fleshy segments or *carpels—i.e.* seed-vessels,—much more rosy than any other part of the flower, and, as the flower develops, the *styles* (*i.e.* the upper portion of the carpels) become whitish at their tips.

To model this flower, be provided with thin " Mintorn art fabric," white and of fine quality, white sheet-wax (pale pink is useful also, but not indispensable), green cotton-covered wire of suitable size and strength, and the usual tools and colours. If more than one good flower is available, dissect one by means of a small sharp knife, trace each whorl on white paper, cut out carefully, and, laying these patterns upon the fabric, so that each " petal " will be slightly *on the cross*, cut out a number of whorls in readiness for subsequent treatment. Should there, however, not be a flower available for this purpose, the following diagrams (Figs. 1-1a, 2-2a), taken from actual flowers, will prove of service.

It will be observed that the *carpels* of a newly-opened flower are small and of delicate tints, and the points, or *stigmas*, are so close together as to be scarcely distinguishable one from another, whilst those of more mature flowers are larger, deeper in colour, and the stigmas have become elongated, recurved, and *open*, showing a whitish lining. The first form—and this only—can be made in one piece as now described :—A strip of white wax, a little wider than the length of the carpels, is

23

turned over about one-third of its width along one edge, and, with the doubled edge at the base and the fold *inside*, sufficient is rolled around the prepared end of a piece of wire to make the carpels. The remainder of the strip is cut off, and that piece upon the wire is moulded with the fingers, and trimmed, until it assumes the shape of the combined carpels, when the divisions may be marked with any angular tool. To reproduce

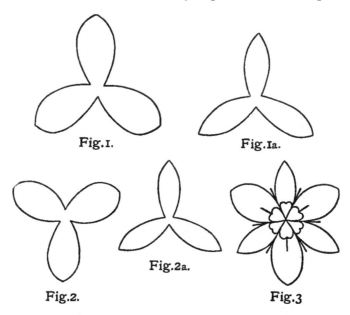

Fig.1.   Fig.1a.

Fig.2a.

Fig.2.   Fig.3

the later developments, it is necessary to cut out one of the natural segments, and, with this as a guide, roll a strip of wax (either white or pale pink), turned over as before, but in this instance without a wire, and mould and trim it into the form of the natural segment, and unless each one is modelled with extreme accuracy, it will be impossible to fit them together into a semblance of the living pattern. Having prepared six segments, the next step is to attach them by pressure around the end of a wire, turned over and tipped with wax, and, to make way for this small knob, it is sometimes necessary to cut out a particle of wax from the middle of the interior angle of each segment. When arranged in position, their largest portion should present the contour shown by Fig. 3, which also indicates the positions to be subsequently occupied by the stamens.

The *stamens* are cut from white fabric faced with wax, one of the natural stamens being used as a pattern. The anthers are made separately, and attached afterwards thus :—The long, light red, ribbed anther of the newly-opened flower is made by cutting two narrow strips of wax the length of the natural pattern, pressing them together with the extreme point of the stamen between, moulding with the fingers, and impressing the four longitudinal furrows with a fine pin or needle. The golden anther of the more advanced blossom is cut as a minute disc from double or treble wax, or wax and fabric, snipped half way across with the points of the scissors, thus making an open incision for the reception of the point of the stamen, the two being then welded together by pressure with the fingers, assisted by any convenient tool, and, unless this welding is thoroughly done, the anther is certain to fall off during the process of colouring.

All the parts of the flower being ready for colouring, first rub arrowroot on both sides of the inner whorl, and use the thinnest possible wash *inside* of rose madder pan-colour, leaving the edge, however, uncoloured ; *outside*, a rather stronger wash of the same, with a minute proportion of scarlet vermilion, leaving a somewhat broader margin untinted ; the inner half of this broad margin must be tinted with the most delicate wash —hardly perceptible—of aureolin. When dry, wash the centre with a stronger tint of rose madder, increasing the strength towards the base ; when dry again, superimpose a stronger line of the same colour in the centre. Note that it is very important that none of these colours form streaks towards the margin of each "petal" (*i.e.* segment of the whorl); and if this should happen, it must be restored by washing from the edge, with the slightest possible wash of cobalt; and, indeed, a very little of this colour washed within the margin is an improvement, and gives delicacy and atmospheric purity. At the very base of, and for some distance up, the median brighter line, put over it a very little Rubens madder.

Or, better plan, brush *dry* pink madder into the centre of the outer surface of each segment of the inner whorl, until of the lightest tint of the natural flower. The inside, being much paler, may be rubbed with the same brush without taking more colour upon it; but if this should have the effect of polishing the fabric, arrowroot may be rubbed on to dull it. Turning again to the outer surface, it will be seen that, bordering the median line—which is itself much deeper—there is a second shade, and this is given by rubbing in dry madder carmine by means of a small common camel-hair brush, mounted in tin, cut down to a stub. The central line, being slightly more purple, may be added in the same manner by rubbing in dry cobalt mixed with double the quantity of rose madder; and the extreme base, having a brownish tint, may be finished by brushing in a little dry Rubens madder. All the colours will show through to the inside of the segments, but probably the median line will require strengthening, and this may be done by brushing in dry pink madder with a *very* fine brush, cut down as before described.

The outer whorl may be managed in the same manner, but, being darker, requires a greater quantity of the Rubens madder, and the centre must be still further strengthened by brushing in dry brown madder. Finally, the base appears as though shot with green, and this effect may be imparted by brushing in a little dry oxide of chromium. On being turned over, it will be found necessary to remove any colour which may have accidentally got underneath, and also to give a little more brightness, and this may be done by means of the dry brush first used for the pink madder, and if this should polish the surface too much, it can be remedied as before by rubbing on arrowroot.

Where the pedicels have a reddish tinge, the effect can be reproduced by brushing in a little dry madder carmine mixed with the smallest possible proportion of pure scarlet.

This method of dry colouring, which is supposed to be practised only at present by the writer and his friend, is, if known, not taught by professionals, owing probably to certain difficulties which have to be overcome. There is no comparison, however, between the dry and the wet process, and all flowers may be managed as described, the result being not only greater purity of colouring when looking down upon the flower, but also possessing the incalculable advantage of allowing the transmission of light through the petals, when viewed against the light, and thus vying with the natural flower in that most important particular.

In some instances, fine lines, etc., of moist colour may be introduced without detriment, and they enhance the general effect ; but caution is needed not to overdo this. Indeed, every flower and leaf now made for the Leicester Museum is not only botanically correct, but undergoes the extreme test of being mixed with the natural flowers at the time of modelling, and is not passed as correct until it deceives the eye in every particular, and at close range.

The colouring of the carpels depends so entirely upon the variations of the natural blossoms—ranging from the most delicate pinks, etc., in new flowers, to deep purple in those fully matured—that this must be left to the judgment of the modeller ; it is merely suggested, therefore, that the colours should be rubbed in as *dry* as possible.   For tinting the stamens, a little pink or rose madder usually suffices, and during its application the ends of the stamens should be protected, or they will not adhere when wanted.   The early form of the anther may be coloured with a combination of the pink and light red powder-colours, which give the best results ; and the later forms may be first moistened with a light yellow pan-colour, then dipped into finely-pulverised yellows, mixed to suit the tint of the pollen at various stages ; and, finally, the *edge* of the anther should be *finely* marked around with red or crimson.

When all the parts are coloured satisfactorily, commence the putting-together by fixing the stamens as in nature (and indicated in Fig. 3), and then model the little knob which is seen at the junction of the stem and the perianth.   Next lay the inner whorl upon the palm of the hand, and model with a pin until it assumes the natural concavity and curvature ; pierce the centre with a point of the scissors, and cut minute slits in the form of a star ; slip upon the wire, and attach by pressure to the base of the carpels, taking care to arrange the " petals " in their correct position in relation to the parts which they surround (see Fig. 3).   Now model the outer whorl and affix it in like manner, arranging the " petals "—whose points should be pinched—between those of the inner whorl.   The pedicel merely requires the wire, and the little enlargement at the top, smoothly covering with a narrow strip of green wax, and may be rendered perfectly smooth and even by rolling between two pieces of glass with bevelled edges.

Buds are made by folding down one-third of a strip of white wax (the width determined by the size of the bud), rolling it around a prepared wire, and cutting, moulding, and tooling it to the required size and shape—a by-no-means easy matter. Large buds may have the outer whorl, cut in single segments, attached with the edges overlapping but not closely appressed.

The bracts are better cut separately, from brownish art fabric or from white coloured to nature, and they may be scratched, tooled, twisted, and stretched, to give the requisite creases, etc.

No definite instructions can be given for the arrangement of the flowers in the umbel, although an examination of a number of plants shows that the earliest blossom to open is usually that in the centre ; in *large* umbels, however, this becomes displaced by the growth of sets of flowers, these " sets " consisting almost always of *three*, of equal growth, arranged at regular intervals around the centre—three flowers or advanced buds on long pedicels alternating with three small buds on short pedicels, and the number seldom (or never) varies except occasionally when there are six in a set.

A modelled umbel, whose execution is in greater part due to the genius of Miss Squires, is shown on the right of Plate XVIII.

The Stem.—Take ordinary galvanised wire, gauge No. 13, three feet or more in length, but determined by the natural stem. Next take the softest of the modelling-waxes (Formula 74), and flatten it into strips or cut shavings from it. Commencing at two inches from the top of the wire, rub it for some distance down with a piece of the wax until somewhat sticky, and then take one of the strips or shavings, and knead it firmly around the wire, rolling it between the hands until it roughly assumes the shape of the natural stem, but is thinner. Having thus treated some six inches or more, lay it upon a stone slab, and roll with the hand until quite smooth. Probably this class of wax will stick a little to the slab, in which case dust the latter very lightly with powdered whiting, plaster, or flour. Proceed down the wire in like manner, gradually increasing the thickness toward the base. When shaped to nature, lay it upon the slab again and roll with a piece of board, oiled occasionally, and, commencing at one end, roll it until quite smooth and even throughout its entire length. Next take a piece of Mintorn art fabric, as long as possible, and of a little lighter green than in nature, lay the covered wire upon it, and cut it of such a width, and so graduated, that the edges will just join around the stem when pulled tightly together. Work one edge of the strip for its whole length firmly upon the wax—leaving, however, a small piece at the upper extremity uncovered—using a piece of flat bone or ivory, and then, holding it firmly upon the table, pull the strip tightly around until the edges meet without leaving any bagginess in any part, and examine the underneath from time to time, and, when all comes well together, the edges should be worked down closely with the stem of a large modelling-pin until the seam is no longer visible. Place another strip now to follow the first, and this cross joint, being much more difficult to hide, must be tooled with greater care. When all is smoothly covered and united, roll it again upon the board, supporting one end in the hand ; this will probably dull its lustre, and the stem must therefore be rubbed with the hand, and with a rag dipped in oil, superfluous oil being removed with another rag. Any imperfections, such as slight cracks, may be made up with a little very thin sheet-wax tooled carefully in, and the stem finally rubbed and polished with the hand and with a rag until smooth and bright as it is in nature. It must be borne in mind, however, that unless the foundation of common wax be made perfectly smooth and even, the irregularities will show through the outer covering, and spoil the shape of the whole.

To fix the umbel upon the flower-stem, cut off, half an inch below the bracts, all the wires except four outer ones, which should be two and a half inches in length. Make up the first half inch by folding sheet-wax around, then bind the four wires longitudinally upon the uncovered portion of the long stem, make up to the proper thickness with modelling-wax, and cover with fabric as neatly as possible.

The Leaves.—Probably the uninitiated would suppose, when viewing the simple radical leaves of this plant, that, although of great length, nothing could be easier to reproduce. After a little reflection, however, they may not be surprised to learn, that here they are face to face with a problem which, up to the present, has been unsolved. True it is that strips of fabric have been tooled into the semblance of "flags," etc., but even these have not been a success, and blades 4 feet and more in length, three-edged or bayonet-shaped, have not been attempted even by professionals. From attempts to weld fabric and wax, together or separately, into the shape required, it was evident that some entirely different method, probably outside the resources of the flower-modeller, would have to be invented, and various experiments made in the Leicester Museum have resulted in the following satisfactory method of reproducing such objects. These lengthy leaves, although apparently three-sided and fluted as a rapier, reveal under examination that one side is much flatter than the other two, and consequently not so deeply fluted ; this is the side, therefore, which will be undermost when casting, and to do this properly it will be necessary to be provided with a smooth board, about 4 feet in length by 1 foot in breadth, free from joints and large knots. This should be placed upon the modelling-table and covered with strong brown paper, unless, indeed, the board is smoothly planed, which is better. Upon this board place the longest leaf, with its flattest side, as explained before, downwards, the sharp keel being uppermost ; through this keel drive rather short, fairly stout pins into the board, following the curvature of the leaf, but being sure that each pin is sufficiently near its fellow to ensure the leaf lying perfectly appressed, throughout its whole length, to the board, with no risings nor elevations under which the plaster, when poured on, can creep. Another leaf should now be pinned down in a similar manner, just outside the other, with, say, an interval of an inch between ; this, with an inch outside each, will give a space of about 6 inches in width by 2 or 3 inches longer than the length of the leaf to be boxed in ; but before doing this be careful to cut off the pins close to the keel of the leaf, otherwise they will not draw through the leaf afterwards. Wet the leaves and board sufficiently, and, having boxed in the space in the usual manner, pour on the plaster of the proper consistence. When sufficiently set, the moulds may be turned over, but, being long and narrow and rather thin, they should have a strip of wood held on their backs whilst this operation is performed, the wood acting as a strengthening backbone. It will be seen by the above that only two sides are cast, leaving that side pinned down uncast ; probably, however, it would be better if this were done, and, although extremely difficult to allow much curvature in a leaf 4 feet in length, yet this can be done by packing underneath with sand or clay as described before. By keying and oiling the mould, therefore, and pouring plaster over both the leaf and mould, and, when dry, tapping gently with the mallet, the halves will separate, and, if all has been correctly managed, the leaves should, by being laid hold of at one end, slip out readily from the mould, leaving a sharp concave impression. After some days drying, the mould should be oiled as usual, and a supply of paper pulp (Formula 93) should be provided. This is, by means of the fingers and any suitable modelling-tool from amongst those figured, well pressed into the mould, and tooled into the deep channel which represents the sharp edge of the leaf, care being taken, however, that the pulp is spread on as thinly as possible, for the reasons given at p. 265. Afterwards back with muslin in the manner detailed at the same page, and let it dry as usual. In a day or so lift cautiously and examine for imperfections—which should not, however, be present if proper care has been exercised in laying down.

The imperfections, if any, being made good, replace the blade within the mould, and within the hollow of the model introduce a galvanised wire, gauge No. 13—although No. 12 may be required for leaves larger or longer than 4 feet. Let this wire, of whatever gauge, reach two-thirds or more from the bottom of the leaf ; follow this with a thinner wire just overlapping the other an inch or so ; follow this second wire with another still thinner, and so on, until a very fine one is required near the tip, as all of these wires, although passing one another in their sequence, must lie within the modelled leaf, and not show through it when finished.

The wires are now fixed in their proper positions by pasting muslin over them, and, when set and dry, rough paper is well pressed into the more hollow, or lower, parts of the leaf, followed by paper pulp if no mould of the other surface of the leaf has been made. This pulp is smoothed down, kept flat at the apex, and gradually hollowed by tools (Nos. 36 and 37) toward the base. When done, weights must be laid at intervals over the model until dry, to prevent it from rising out of the mould. In a day or so, remove it from the mould and trim the waste edges with a sharp knife until the model assumes the condition of the natural leaf, and afterwards use sandpaper to remove all unnecessary roughness, and also to smooth the trimmed edges. In cases where the under face has been made, —and this, as pointed out before, makes the only correct leaf,— the edges are joined together as practised for fungi (see p. 375), and are no more difficult to manage than is the filling of the hollows, as in the other method, by paper pulp. Otherwise,— and this is the better method,—after the most concave half has been properly wired, the two halves are joined together by good paste (Formula 90), and, where necessary, pasted tissue-paper is inserted in any hollows.   The waste edges are then sewn closely over, so that the front and back edges of the actual model come exactly together, which is easily tested by running the point of the needle through both parts close to the outline of the leaf; and, when finished, the whole is suspended by the wire at the base until dry, after which the waste edges are cut off, following the impression of the mould of the actual leaf.   The trimmed edges, if too thick, are filed and sand-papered to render them of the thinness apparent in the natural leaf.

In either event, after trimming and sandpapering, there results a strong paper leaf, smooth, and of the shape of the original ; and now comes the finishing process, which is to heat wax (Formula 98), coloured to the natural green, in one of the vessels mentioned at p. 211, warm the modelled leaf slightly in front of the fire, and paint it rapidly over with the coloured wax, putting on a sufficient body to give quality, but not, of course, to thicken or obscure the sharp keel.   Here and there the wax, put on with a soft brush, may have another coat, and, if the wax be properly hot, no joins will show, but only a little lumpiness, which can be removed by *coarse* sandpaper rubbed *along* (*not across*) the wax ; and here comes in an interesting " dodge "——the coarse sandpaper giving the exact texture of the natural leaf.   Any extra colouring is managed by rubbing in dry pigments with stiff brushes (see Fig. F, Plate II.), and, if skilfully done, nothing can be nearer nature than the green wax, delicately tinted in parts, showing over a white underground ; and thus this difficult leaf, when made according to the above instructions, amply repays all the trouble it has cost to execute.   If the leaf has a decided reddish or yellowish cast at the base, it may be tinted with coloured waxes direct, as mentioned for the bills of birds (see p. 210).

The Lily of the Valley, Convallaria majalis, *Linn.*

This lovely flower, so highly appreciated for its exquisite scent and delicate beauty, is so much better known as a cultivated than as a wild flower, that it is only introduced here as being easily procured to model from, and as a guide to the making-up of commoner wild flowers, such as the harebell campanula, *Campanula rotundifolia*, Linn., and other similarly bell-shaped flowers, useful as accessories to the advanced taxidermist or the economic entomologist.

In modelling the bells or perianths of this flower it is necessary to use the tool, Fig. K, Plate II., or larger, according to the size of the bell to be copied. Cut "on the cross" a strip of white art fabric, wider than the depth of the bell, and wind it once around the thin end of the tool, which should first be moistened in the mouth, allowing rather more of the fabric to extend beyond the end than appears to be requisite for uniting. Join the overlapping edges, and mould the upper margin upon the extremity of the tool, carefully cutting away any superfluous fabric. When modelled so that no joins are visible, slip the bell off the tool and cut it, at the open end, to the depth required, holding it lightly between the left thumb and fore-finger, and cutting at one snip with a pair of small sharp scissors. This, it will be seen, compresses the mouth of the bell, and, as six small notches have next to be cut around the edge, this compression is of service, the *ends* of the mouth indicating the position of two of the notches, and thus assisting to equalise the space for the remaining four. Now, with the head of a modelling-pin inside the bell, roll it about upon the finger until the upper part of the bell expands and takes the natural form. Replace the bell upon the tool as before ; thin the edges by rolling with a pin, and rub it over lightly with arrowroot. Then select a piece of very fine wire, prepare the end as usual, tip it with delicate green wax, and proceed to make the pistil and stamens by folding together about three thicknesses of pale cream sheet-wax ; cut seven short narrow strips or threads, and, having fixed one for the pistil, place the others around it, and tip them with a little yellow and white powder-colour. Prick a small hole in the dome of the bell, slip the wire through, fix carefully, and make the stem or pedicel by covering thinly with wax of the palest and most delicate green.

To make the unopened buds, roll a small folded strip of wax around the end of the wire ; mould into the natural shape with the fingers, mark the divisions by pressing with a pin, and whiten with arrowroot or tint slightly with green, as the case may be.

The Stem

The flower-stem or peduncle is made bit by bit from the top in the following manner : Select a bud, and having covered the stem very thinly, as before directed, to where the first bract appears, cut as many of these as may be required, taking a strip, half an inch wide, of the thinnest and palest green fabric, and cutting it thus—

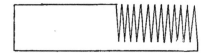

then, by cutting straight along the base of the cut portion, the points become separated, and, after being placed upon the finger and rolled once with a modelling-pin, are ready for use. Now proceed with the making-up by fixing a *small* bract to the stem of the top bud, and complete the stem to where the next bud or flower springs from it, but leaving a piece of wire uncovered to which to attach the flower. The stem of the latter, being already prepared, is merely pressed upon the wire at the termination of the wax covering, a bract is attached as before, the stem is made down to the next flower, and this is repeated until sufficient buds and flowers have been fixed, when the stem is completed by folding around the wire a strip of wax *graduated* in width, so that the stem will become gradually thicker towards the root.

The Leaves

The leaves being rather thick, and the venations extremely fine, it is better to cast them by pouring hot wax upon the plaster moulds, and for this purpose the latter should *not* be boiled in borax as usual. To make a leaf, therefore, saturate the plaster mould in hot water, take it out and pour over it hot wax of a delicate green tint. Leave this on the mould, and, having placed the " rib " in position, cover the back with pale green fabric, pressing and uniting it well to the wax. Remove from the mould, trim according to the impression shown by the latter, and thin the edges in the usual manner.

Bluebell, Scilla verna (*Huds.*)

This pretty flower, one of the few blue flowers the artist will find of value, is commenced by preparing a fine wire about 3 inches in length. Cut a small strip of white art fabric, turn down a very narrow edge, cut six stamens as finely as possible, colour the anthers with powder-colour as dry as can be used, and fix the stamens around the end of the wire. Take a strip of white wax about three-quarters of an inch in width and fold it lengthwise, bringing the lower edge to within the eighth of an inch or so of the upper ; now fold the double portion again, bringing the folded edge a little lower than the second single one, and wind it around the wire, the folds *inside* and at the base forming a bulbous foundation for the perianth, and the uppermost single edge just catching and binding the base of the stamens. Model into shape with the thumb and finger, and then proceed to cut, out of thick white fabric, six segments, taking as a pattern one of the segments from the flower to be copied. Put on the underground of powder-colour, leaving the *inside* of the lower portion of each segment uncoloured, or they will not adhere to the foundation. Thin the edges by rolling upon the left forefinger with the head of a modelling-pin, allowing the head to come well over the edge, and rolling up and down until quite thin. Now model the segments upon the palm of the hand with the same, or perhaps a smaller-headed pin, until the inner surface becomes concave as in nature, and tool the narrow portion on both sides with a blanket-pin to give it the proper channels and curves. Cover the foundation with the perianth by affixing the three inner segments first, and then the three outer ones, pressing all well at the base, and uniting the edges, where necessary, by rolling with the stem of a modelling-pin. Next add the darker streaks of colour with a fine soft brush, and then proceed to make the calyx, which, consisting of three long, narrow, pointed sepals, is cut from a straight strip of brown art fabric (or of green, afterwards coloured to nature) as shown by the diagram on p. 366, but of two-thirds of the width, and arranged around the wire close underneath the base of the flower, so that the sepals spread out to equal distances. Make the pedicel by covering just sufficient of the wire with a narrow strip of very pale green wax.

For buds, make the foundation in the same manner, but without stamens. Cut *three* segments similar to those for the open flower, but smaller, especially in the upper portion. Colour the outside only, and model each segment into a concave form, but do not curve the tip outwardly, and affix in such a manner as to completely enclose the foundation. Buds may be varied, not only in size, but also by making some of the larger ones slightly open, just revealing a glimpse of the foundation, which may be faintly tinted to represent the inner segments.

Having made sufficient flowers and buds for one raceme, cut a bract for each one out of pale art fabric, impart the natural curves by means of a blanket-pin, and proceed to make up the raceme.

Commence with a small bud, and, at the base of the pedicel, attach a bract of suitable size by pressing it upon the wax. Now select a sheet of light green wax, as nearly as possible of the tint of the natural stem, but rather lighter than darker, and cut a strip *lengthwise* from the sheet. Double the strip and roll it around the wire—adding another wire if necessary—until the stem is of the proper thickness, and then tear or cut off any surplus. Roll the stem between the thumb and finger until smooth, and then add another bud and bracts, and so continue until the raceme is complete, taking care to arrange the buds, flowers, and bracts in natural positions, and gradually increase the thickness of the stem (see p. 316). Steel " tails " will be found useful for the lower part of the stem, and can be added as occasion requires.

The leaves may either be cast (see p. 312) or made with four or five thicknesses of fabric, each succeeding one a little smaller than its predecessor, superimposed one upon another, and the edges well rubbed down upon a smooth damp board with the knob of a bone tool similar to Fig. J, Plate II., but with a point at one end instead of a knob, the point being used to make the centre channel along the leaf. No wire is required, but a small piece of loosely-rolled fabric may be inserted at the base.

Grasses

These are of various degrees of difficulty to imitate, the easiest being the sheep's fescue grass, which is made of thin

24

wire finely waxed by drawing it many times through a piece
of green wax doubled up, and afterwards thickening it gradually at the bottom.

Small meadow-grass is, when intended to underlie other
foliage, fairly well imitated by taking a strip of fabric and
cutting it somewhat to this shape—

which gives three blades to one half and two to the other, and
these, being tooled and twisted, make a respectable imitation.

The next is made by taking two thicknesses of fabric and
inserting between them a wire, which in some cases needs to
be covered or made like a leaf-rib. Each blade of this is
tooled, and scratched with the set needles (Fig. Q, Plate II.),
and this form leads up to the more elaborate grasses which
throw out several blades from one stem, and which require
to be put together in the same manner as more highly
organised plants. Such grasses are, it will be readily observed,
of a different colour at front and back of the blade, and
the dead blades may be successfully imitated by using brown,
yellowish-brown, or red-brown thin fabric, and scratching it
with the set needles.

Equisetum

To imitate any species of this genus satisfactorily, the
greatest possible delicacy of manipulation is necessary, as,
although the construction is by no means so complicated as
might be supposed, yet there is a certain lightness and transparency which would be quite lost if attempted by any but
the most skilful fingers. Cut a piece of fine wire rather
longer than one of the branches, cover lightly with delicate
green wax, graduating the thickness very slightly ; now

place a sheet of this wax upon green fabric, and cut a *very* narrow strip, commencing as a mere point, and increasing the width gradually as it proceeds; lay this upon the covered wire, fabric outwards, and delicately unite the two from the point to where the first joint should occur; to make this, fold the strip into a minute pleat or notch, which must not be tightly pressed, and then proceed as before until of the requisite length. The lower or thicker portion will require similar treatment on both sides of the wire.

Casting and modelling Fruits

The modelling of fruits which may be required as accessories is described in a work written by the late Mr. J. H. Mintorn.[1] He does not appear, however, to have described the best method of casting fruits which will not " draw " easily from their moulds, *i.e.* the method previously described in some of these pages for piece-casting ; but the reproduction of such objects is simple when viewed by the light of the instructions given for the execution of more difficult objects, such as the sepia (see pp. 286-289). The " paper mould " mentioned by him is simply a ring of stiff paper surrounding the fruit to be cast, and into which the plaster is poured.

Casting and modelling Fungi

Such fungi as the ordinary mushroom, and some " toadstools " which assume a close pyramidal form like the common yet delicately-flavoured "toadstool," *Coprinus comatus*, are, when young, much easier to cast from than when opened out in age, or when they resemble the shapes of others of the same genus.

Assuming that one or more specimens of this edible toadstool are procured, a small casting-box, formed by two zinc

---

[1] *Lessons in Flower and Fruit Modelling in Wax*, pp. 103-111.

strips and two pieces of wood with saw-cuts as detailed at p. 341, must be laid upon a piece of well-wetted glass or slate, and plaster, mixed in the ordinary manner, poured in to half its depth, and into this—as with fruits—gently drop and press the pyramidal fungus, with stalk attached, until one half lies embedded. Let the plaster set, and on each side of, and at some little distance from the fungus, scoop out a small concavity with the point of a knife; oil all over, and then mix and pour plaster over the uncovered half of the fungus; let it set sufficiently, and take away the walls of the casting-box, and, when a little drier, tap along the edges with a wooden mallet (not a hammer), and rock it about on the table, which should be solid, and the halves will part along the joint, and the fungus will often come out so perfect as to admit of another mould being taken if needful. The use of the concavities or scooped-out holes in the lower half is now evident, for in the upper half there are two pegs, as it were, of plaster, which serve to keep the halves exactly in line, in case a hollow wax model, like fruit models, should be required.

The ordinary mushroom, however large, is the next easiest to cast to the close pyramidal form, but first the stalk, which usually enters an inner ring on the under surface, must be removed by carefully cutting it away just at its apparent insertion within the ring. Now lay the mushroom underside uppermost on a wetted glass or board, and, if the upper surface is much twisted, spaces will be seen here and there where the edge does not touch the board; these must, of course, be filled in, otherwise the plaster, which must, as usual, be thin, will run underneath, with the risk of spoiling the specimen. Putty is, perhaps, as good as anything for packing with, but if putty cannot be readily obtained, clay will do, or, failing this, a piece of ordinary flour dough will be found to answer very well, and may be patted into position with the fingers, if the precaution be taken to dip them into flour. When all is satisfactorily "sleeked down," surround the fungus, leaving, say, an eighth- or quarter-of-an-inch margin, with either of the casting-boxes described ; into this, and of course over the underside of the fungus, pour thin and well-mixed plaster ; let it set a few minutes, remove the zinc, and tap the mould gently from the board. Only the top of the fungus is now visible ; remove all the putty or clay, and, if sticky, by washing with a soft brush and water. Cut two little channels or keys, and oil all that surface of plaster which shows, and possibly the top of the fungus itself. Put it on the board, top side uppermost, and, adjusting the box around in the same manner as before, pour thin and well-mixed plaster over all ; allow it to set, when, by jolting or tapping gently, and by pulling with the fingers, the moulds will come apart at the oiled line of division ; the fungus can then be picked out, and a perfect cast of the under and upper surface results.

The stem is now to be laid upon the board and built up half-way, along its entire length and at the ends, with the putty, etc., and one piece of zinc, bent into an oblong shape and retained at the free end by one piece of wood with saw-cuts, put around the stem, and plaster poured over ; this makes a half, longitudinal mould. Turn over and repeat the oiling and casting to make the other half, and so complete the stem.

If the fungus is of an open pyramidal or deep umbrella shape—which is the most difficult form,—the stalk should be carefully pulled out, and the inside should be cast into first to preserve the shape ; for this purpose, turn it that way up in a box deep enough to hold it, placing wool at the bottom to save the apex of the fungus from injury, and around the sides, letting it rise *above the edges* of the fungus, to prevent the plaster from running down on the outside, and also for another purpose which follows. When all is ready, pour the plaster gently into the cup-shaped or umbrella-shaped part, and before it sets bend a stout wire thus Ω as a loop, and thrust it half-way into the plaster ; when set, reverse the fungus, still with the plaster inside the umbrella, and, letting the wire loop rest in the wool in the box, proceed to wet the fungus slightly, and then pour plaster over the outside to a sufficient thickness, or until bounded by the sides of the casting-box ; when set, remove as before, and now the fungus is entirely out of sight. Pare the edges up to the insertion of the wire loop, all around, taking care not to reach the edges of the fungus ; then hold the wire loop, and, by pulling on this and tapping gently with the mallet, the centre will come out, leaving, probably, the fungus in the outer mould ; this is then easily removed, and there remain, if properly executed, moulds of the outside and inside of the umbrella-shaped fungus. The stalk, ranging from a couple of inches to sometimes a foot in length, is to be cast in the same manner as detailed for the casting of the others.

Some fungi are in form somewhat like a reversed umbrella ; from these also remove the stalk, and cast into the under surface first, and the upper surface and stalk follow as directed above.

The moulds, having been dried in the oven or on the top of a closed stove, should be treated as previously directed, and finally oiled with colza-oil.

The casts or models from the moulds can be made in a variety of ways, either by the direct plaster method, which is not recommended, by the direct paper process, by paper pulp, by glue-composition, or by wax, according as their nature suggests ; but numbers of them—in fact, the greater proportion—may be made by the direct paper process, and all mush-rooms, whether large or small, will require four thicknesses of tissue-paper, and two of "cap" paper to follow and finish. The paper should be cut V shaped, and pasted down, radiating from the centre, to obviate any tendency to wrinkle, which would otherwise happen, even in a small fungus, if put on in a piece. Each layer should be well pasted, brushed well into the crevices, and laid down with care.

A day or two in a warm room will set them, and, if the overlapping edges of paper are cut around, the models, if not quite loose, may be set before a not too fierce fire for a few minutes to hasten their drying, and may be gently lifted or "wriggled" out. The model fungus is now in two pieces if cast in vertical halves, or in three, if cast with upper and lower surfaces and with a separate stalk. This latter is the easiest to join together, as, after the superfluous paper has been cut from around the edges (best done with a sharp knife whilst the model lies upon a strip of glass), the upper and under portions are well pasted on their inner or plain surfaces, and joined together by the intervention of some wadding, also pasted, the edges, if "gaping," being made up with minute pieces of well-pasted tissue-paper and tooled to meet each other. "Wrapping-cotton" should be wound loosely around them during the time they are drying. If any uncertainty exists as to the exact relative position of the upper and under halves, place each in its mould and press the two together, which will give the correct fit. The stalk is joined on by the same method, or supplemented by wood within each half.

The putting-together of the two vertical halves is not so easy, especially if the stalk is closed at the base, as happens when the fungus has been pulled up, or is wanted as a botanical specimen and not as an accessory. If open at the base, some pasted wadding or tissue-paper can be gently pressed in ; this will partially unite the edges, whilst an elastic band or thread holds it in position. The edges will doubtless gape a little here and there, and must be united by plugging with small rolled slips of pasted tissue-paper, and, when dry, making up any further imperfections by the paper pulp, or by a little uncoloured modelling-wax (see Formula 73), which, if it shows, or indeed in any case, should be covered with small strips of pasted tissue-paper, which do not take out any of the underlying details if carefully managed, and effectually hide all imperfections. If cleverly done, the join should not be apparent even by close scrutiny, and the yellow "cap" paper, showing through the tissue, gives so close an imitation of the texture and colour of some dryish-looking fungi that but a very little colouring is necessary to perfect them.

When, however, the extreme base of the stalk is bulbous and to be shown thus closed, some wadding or tissue-paper must be smeared with paste and put into each half to fill up ; the edges must be smeared and united by tissue-paper, and made up, when dry, as before described. If necessary, glue may be used in certain contingencies to close the edges, but pasted paper or wadding is better. Glue is often preferable, however, to unite the stalk to the pileus or cap, and in heavy specimens it is advisable to introduce into the hollow stem a piece of soft wood on to which the cap is glued, a pin being driven through to hold all in place. For small, delicate fungi, and for larger ones showing much detail, the best medium in which to execute them is the pulp (Formula 93), which works and joins easily, and can be backed with muslin as usual.

The more fleshy fungi are often best executed in one of the glue-compositions (Formula 96 or 97 being admirably adapted for this purpose), and, when well managed, make beautiful objects. For very many of the self-coloured forms, such as the reds, oranges, and greens, the composition should be coloured by stirring in a *little* of the tube oil-colour most nearly approaching the ground-colour of the natural specimen, and the models can be tinted afterwards where required. The practice in the Leicester Museum has been to brush the hot

composition into both upper and under moulds, bring them
rapidly together, and place a weight upon them to press out
any superfluous composition, in order to make the edges of the
models as thin as possible. This method, however, often
resulted in the destruction of the mould, the composition being
so immovably set within, that, although the top sometimes
relieved satisfactorily, yet the part representing the gills held
with such extreme tenacity, that the least damage resulting was
the breaking of that part of the mould, if not the whole. The
plan now adopted, therefore, is to fill the lower half and nearly
fill the upper, and let them set ; then to relieve each half, but
leave it attached at one point as small in extent as possible,
and, turning it back without entirely removing it from the
mould, to trim the edges. The two halves are then replaced,
and the upper portion is filled with hot composition—not, however, in such volume as to melt the part already set, nor yet to
thicken the edge too much—whilst a hot tool is rapidly passed
around the edge of the lower half, or else a *very* little hot composition is run around the edge (which has, however, a tendency
to thicken it), and the lower half in its mould is turned upon
the upper half, the moulds fitting by their keys, and the edges
of the half models being brought together with great accuracy.
It is then placed under a weight, and, having been left for a
short time to set, a very little force suffices to part the moulds,
and the half models are found to be united. The complete
model is now trimmed as usual, and, should the edges be too
thick at any point, or not sufficiently joined, they are rounded
off or united by means of a moderately hot tool, which, should
the edges gape, is slipped between, and the edges quickly
pressed together with the fingers.

Stalks may be made in like manner, and, if thin, a slightly
heated wire should be thrust up from the base ; but, if large,
they should be scooped out from the base, and a piece of wood,

wrapped with tow and smeared with the same modelling-composition, hot, should be inserted, and, if the pileus be large and heavy, should extend within it for its support.   Stalks may also be made with paper, as before described, to support a glue pileus.

A curious thing about most of the glue compositions is, that where the joining of the edges is not quite satisfactorily hidden, or where any roughness is left by the hot tool, they may be *filed down* and *sandpapered* with the most perfect results ; neither the file nor sandpaper, however, must be too coarse.

When the fungus is executed in any of the paper media, it should be coloured in water-colours from a fresh specimen, which will probably show the apex slightly brownish, and will no doubt require delicate tints of brown umber, yellow ochre, and blue to get it exact.   The gills or lower half will show probably a peach-like bloom, and this can be managed by tints of light red, permanent mauve, Vandyke brown, yellow ochre, and a little permanent blue ; this latter probably in the deepest hollows and near the base.   The stalk requires blue, Vandyke brown, yellow ochre, and, at the base, brown umber, etc., but the tones are so delicate and subtle that no exact rule of colouring can be laid down, and the artist must be guided by what he sees and knows in the interpretation of these hues. Sometimes a little paper-varnish or slight stippling with Roberson's medium here and there over the colours may help the effect, but requires to be done with skill and judgment.

In some species, however, the use of water-colours will not give a sufficient " quality " to the surface of the fungus, and as oil-colours, on the other hand, are too " heavy," some modification is necessary, such as using turpentine as a vehicle for tube oil-colours, the colours to be floated on in the thinnest possible coat with a full body of turpentine and some flake white, which bears out the various tints, and often gives a satiny

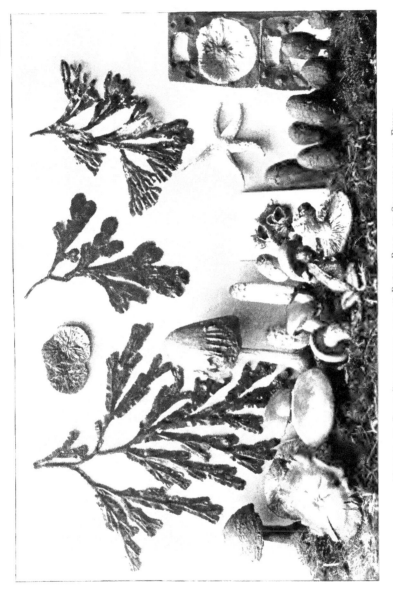

XIX

MODELS, IN GLUE COMPOSITION AND IN PAPER PULP, OF SEAWEEDS AND FUNGI.

lustre, if properly managed and contrasted, without appearing at all "painty." Indeed, it is often difficult to determine the real from the model when skilfully managed.

When executed in glue-composition or in wax, fungi should, as stated before, be coloured either by the introduction of oil-colour into the composition, or by subsequent treatment with oil-pigments.

Models of various fungi are represented on Plate XIX. On the right-hand side, at the bottom, are shown the upper and under moulds of a *Tricholoma personatus*, an edible fungus, and the group of six rounded ones by the frog, in the centre foreground, some of them showing their under surfaces, are models of the same species executed in glue-composition (Formula 96) and *coloured*. The seven dark, closely-pyramidal fungi on the extreme right, in front of the mould and starfish, are glue models (Formula 96), *uncoloured*, of that delicious fungus *Coprinus comatus*, whilst the three light-coloured, similarly-shaped fungi in the centre at the back are models of the same species executed in paper and *coloured*, and the tall campanulate one to the left and above them is a model, also in paper, of *Coprinus atratus*. The four small cup-shaped fungi shown on the tablet in the background near the starfish are executed in wax and *coloured*. Three fungi on the left are: the sweetbread, *Orcella deliciosus*, at the front; another at the back of that, and, on the extreme left, a rough, dome-shaped, common species often found in gardens, and these three are *uncoloured*. Above, between two fronds of seaweed, are shown the under surfaces or gills of two conjoined fungi, *Collybia velutipes*, executed in *coloured* glue (Formula 97).

ADDITIONAL LITERATURE UPON FLOWER-MAKING

REDOUTÉ.—*Fleuriste artificiel et Feuillagiste.* Illustrated.
SOURDON, MLLE.—*Fleuriste artificiel simplifié.*

CHAPTER X

THE MOUNTING OF ANIMALS IN AN ARTISTIC MANNER, WITH MODELLED ROCKWORK, TREES, ETC., NATURAL GRASSES, FERNS, MOSSES, SEAWEEDS, ETC., AND MODELLED FOLIAGE

DIVISION I

THE MAKING OF ROCKWORK, TREES, ETC., BY VARIOUS METHODS

HITHERTO the reader has been initiated into the mysteries of skinning, preserving, " setting-up," and modelling the various specimens treated of in these pages, and nothing has as yet been said upon the necessary " mounting "—mounting being a distinct performance calling for the exercise of some considerable artistic ability. It is, in fine, the arrangement of a specimen or specimens with appropriate surroundings, to be ultimately enshrined in a suitable receptacle or case.

The simplest form of mounting is that which the birdstuffers supply—a block of sanded or mossed wood, on which the bird stands ; the most elaborate, the introduction of natural accessories with modelled rocks and foliage into a study of bird life, and called a " mounted group." Between these extremes there are numberless stages.

Simple as sanding a board appears, there are certain rules to be observed ; one is, that ordinary fine or red sand does not do very well. What is wanted is a coarse, sharp sand or grit, such as may be got from the beds of large rivers. In the Midlands, the Trent sand is celebrated for this quality, and some marine sands may also be used, but they must be washed in fresh water and dried many times to free them from every trace of salt, as, indeed, must all marine shells, weeds, pieces of wrack, or the like, introduced into cases. The sand is retained, whether upon wood or rockwork, by means of thin glue, and, should there be any difficulty in getting the first coat to cover, the sand must be well rubbed in, or otherwise another coat of glue and sand must follow the first when dry. In some instances, where an irregular thickening of the surface is of no consequence, or where wanted, the glue-brush may be dipped into the dry sand and worked upon the object until it is covered, and this, followed by throwing on sand with some little violence, will often effectually complete the work.

Artificial " rockwork" may be roughly divided into two distinct classes—" fancy" and natural,—and each class is divisible into two or more varieties.

The " fancy" rockwork is that which usually obtains in the " stuffing" world and in most old museums, and is simply brown paper crumpled up into unnatural folds and shapes, and glued and sanded. This variety of the first (and worst) class stands a silent witness to the astounding simplicity of its manufacturer, who thinks that it can, by any stretch of the imagination, be considered anything else but very badly— indeed inartistically—wrinkled brown paper. Sometimes this " rockwork," or " rocking," as it is more frequently called, is coloured.

Another variety is embellished with the heads of dyed " everlasting" flowers, cut off short and stuck about the " rocking" where they are likely to do the most harm ; and yet another is lined out, wherever it touches the back of the case in which it is placed, with lines of pulverised pyrites or brass-filings, and sometimes outside that again another streak of glittering galena.   That such curiosities are found in museums is attested by the fact that in the Leicester Museum is a collection of British birds, nine-tenths of them exquisitely set up, but all mounted on sanded brown paper picked out with lines of brass-filings and galena.   The folly of accepting any donation tied by certain restrictions is exemplified here.   The beautiful birds, bequeathed in 1865, may not be rearranged, and therefore take up space, and, by their mounting, outrage the sensibilities of artists day by day.

Another and better variety of the same fancy rockwork occurs, when the artist sees a piece of living rock which he would like to imitate, and, by sketches and by memory, attempts to perpetuate it, or else when he gets as large a piece as possible and, with this before him, attempts to reconcile his lines with those of the rock.

In either instance, supposing the design aimed at to be a large wall case to hold several animals in various positions, a convenient foundation is made by putting together some boards to make a false bottom for the case ; at the back of this false bottom are nailed several uprights of, say, 3 inches by $\frac{3}{4}$ inch board, and of the various heights which the rockwork will subsequently attain.   Pieces of various lengths of half-inch or, if the specimens are weighty, thicker board are nailed on end to the back supports at any height required, and may have a cross-piece nailed on to them or from one to the other as an extra support where necessary.

From the back and over the supports, effectually hiding them, are nailed pieces of old cardboard, milliners' boxes, hat-boxes, paper boxes of all kinds broken up into suitable pieces, and assimilating roughly to the shape or character of the rock which is to be copied.   When the whole is covered with cardboard, brown paper is glued over all, and where there are rounded edges to be shown, these are either made up with pieces of card laid on and paper pasted over, or with pieces of crumpled newspaper glued on roughly and covered with pasted paper, or with wool pasted or glued. Where speedy drying is an object, glued paper is used instead of pasted, but where a sufficient time can be given for the layers to dry, paste is better on the score of economy, rapidity of working, and the nicer manner in which pasted paper behaves in rounding corners.

No wrinkles should show in the finished rockwork, and when any are seen they should either be filled in with pasted or glued wadding, or, if large, cut out and pasted over again. Often two or three coverings of paper are necessary to ensure sufficient hardness and stability, and, when satisfactory, the whole is glued and sanded as directed at the commencement of this chapter.

The section of such a piece of rockwork shows a false bottom, upright pieces nailed on the bottom and back of that, and supporting pieces for the ledges on which the animals are to rest, whilst outside all are the lines of the finished rockwork which, of course, masks all the wooden skeleton. If carefully done, and with some regard to the copy in general details, the effect is by no means bad ; indeed, its substratum of truth gives it an air of reality to any one—but a geologist.

By far and away the better plan is, however, to take nature entirely as the guide, and by this means achieve a real success. Let a large flint of good shape, or a fair-sized rock of any other kind be taken, and there are two ways of making a copy from it.

The first and simplest method is, after having well oiled it, to decide which of its surfaces is the least suited for the purpose for which the model is intended, and let that surface be the bottom. Now take rather thin but tough brown paper and paste it on one side ; lay the pasted side upon the stone, getting out all unnatural creases and wrinkles, at the same time well moulding the paper into every depression and cranny of the stone, and so go all over it except underneath ; follow this by other layers until the paper is thick enough— probably six will be sufficient, and there is no need to put more on than will prevent the model collapsing when dry, for not only does excess of paper increase the weight, but it takes out much of the detail, which in this case lies *underneath*, and can only be exhibited through a thin superposition of paper. When dry, the stone is easily removable, sometimes a little better before complete dryness, and, as there is nothing to spoil or crack by this method, the stone and its paper envelope may go in front of the fire or in the oven to help the drying. If the whole of the stone, perhaps a very rounded one, is required to be modelled, it can be covered entirely, but in this case the only way to get the stone out when the model is finished is to cut the paper around, and make up the cut edges with pasted paper. By this means very large rocks can be modelled over, and will come out excellently in shape, even if a trifle faulty in small details.

The other and more scientific method exactly conforms to nature, and is managed by taking moulds of rocks in plaster of Paris. It will be almost needless to observe, that there are hardly any rocks save very flat or slightly curved ones which can be cast in one piece ; nearly all require piece-casting (as detailed for other objects in previous pages), but many will not need more than two or three pieces to get their curves and depressions correctly. When the mould is dried and oiled and the parts tied together, paste the paper inside the mould in the manner described for the direct paper process for large fishes, etc., and although there is no need to add weight by piling layer upon layer, yet a little more thickness here and there will not matter, for now, be it observed, the imprint is upon the surface, and all erosions or striæ upon the original stone are faithfully reproduced upon the paper one. In some cases, where it may not be convenient, owing to the size or shape of the mould, to tie all the pieces together, they may be papered separately and their edges united afterwards to build up the entire stone, the joinings or ridges, when quite dry, being carefully sandpapered. These models must be more carefully dried, otherwise the moulds will split, as stated in previous pages.

In representing rocks which are supposed to give the exact appearance of the original, one must be careful not to do as was recently done at South Kensington, where, in a large case containing a group of Accipitres at the end of the bird-gallery, a double error was perpetrated, for, with a laudable desire to get as near to nature as possible, pieces of the rocks amongst which these birds nested were brought from Scotland, and moulds were taken from them, but unfortunately the resultant models were made in plaster as thin slabs, whose edges were laboriously joined together to produce one model, instead of the rocks being cast as just described, and modelled in strong yet light paper in one piece, or, at all events, with fewer and invisible joinings. The most unfortunate thing, however, about these models is, that the rock specimens or patterns brought with such care from Scotland were nearly all newly-fractured pieces, and that, therefore, the models of their sharply angular *inside* faces are now doing duty for what should be quite a different exposure, viz. a weathered rock-face, and the idea, which was good, is entirely spoiled by want of forethought and technical knowledge.

Afterwards, both properly-modelled and fancy rocks are to be glued and sanded if the originals have a sandy or rough texture, and in this event the colouring is best managed by

25

staining them in tints of common powder-colours (see list at pp. 90-92) well thinned with linseed-oil and turpentine, or with turpentine alone, and in some cases, where a little more body is required, by adding flake white and a little varnish.

In some instances, the finished colouring—if not done by tube-colours—is to be executed by thin washes of colour in turpentine (or benzoline, which is even a better "flatter," but trying to the lungs and dangerous to use at night), and all finishing must be done with the original, if possible, as a model.

No definite instructions for colouring can be given, but as a slight guide it may be stated that, if the rock represents a certain sandstone, the most prominent parts may be very lightly stained with a pale pinkish yellow only just past white, the hollows with blue black or ivory black and Vandyke, and, when dry, the tops and edges, where lichens would grow, touched up with tube colours as greys and greens, perhaps a little gold here and there, and the hollows and some other parts just floated over again ("glazed") with greenish; but the great thing is to copy the hues and tints of the rock itself, and sometimes another piece must be procured, as the over-modelling or casting from the original piece may have taken away some of its ancient surface colour.

If, however, the rocks are smooth, they must not be glued nor sanded when dried, but brushed over with—

101.—Preparation for Rockwork

Powdered whiting	.	.	.	1 part
Plaster of Paris	.	.	.	1 „

Sufficient thin flour-paste and water to make the above into a paint.

Any hue or tint in common dry powder-colours may be used as a ground for the darker rocks, but usually a white underground, as in a canvas, gives greater brilliancy and purity of colouring. The whiting has a slight tendency to show a network of small cracks, especially if much paste be used, which is often a valuable effect gained. Should the stones, however, be of a very smooth waterworn character, such as are often found upon beaches, dry flake white should be substituted for the whiting, and this preparation will not crack, or, should it do so, must be rubbed down with sandpaper until smooth ; sometimes it will be found expedient to leave out the plaster altogether.

The making of artificial trees falls into the same category of modelling by the eye and from the mould. The first or fancy tree is a hollow irregular cylinder of paper pasted upon cardboard as before directed, and fixed upon a base at any angle, and upon this the bark is made, either with other pieces of rough cardboard or paper, or both, if the model is intended to have a fairly smooth bark, or with long strips of wadding pasted or glued upon the cylinder to represent rough bark. Afterwards such trees should be glued and sanded, and subsequently coloured dark in the crevices of the bark, and grey or greenish grey with warm colouring here and there on the highest points ; this helps the light and shade of the model, and with touchings up of warm reddish ochre in the hollows and so on to represent decayed wood, makes a fairly respectable imitation—when no natural trees are brought near it. Another and much better method is to take nature for the guide, and with the bole of a small tree, say a birch, as a pattern, proceed to copy it carefully. Here, after the first rough cylinder is made, tissue-paper is used to imitate the bark, and, with careful colouring from the actual object, a fairly correct imitation may be made. The actually correct model is made in paper, as are the rocks, from a plaster of Paris mould—usually in two pieces—taken of the tree trunk itself ; this is undeniably correct in form, and the remainder depends upon the aptitude of the artist. Water-colours may be used in some instances to get effects both on rock and tree models, and they may either stand alone or be supplemented by oils flatted as much as possible; indeed, it does not matter *how* the effect is produced if it be managed successfully.

On no account let natural trunks and branches of trees be introduced into cases; they inevitably produce disaster, for sooner or later beetles or other insects make their appearance, and a beetle which emerges from the trees, and whose larva bores the woodwork of the cases, or gets out into the museum to bore into something else, is not a foe to be despised. Such an instance has happened several times in the history of the Leicester Museum. In the Bickley Collection, previously mentioned, beetles made their appearance after a lapse of thirty years, and in a collection of New Guinea birds, in which a natural stump was very prettily though wrongly arranged, they appeared after a lapse of twenty years, boring through the cases in both instances.

Birch is a sure harbour for these beetles, and all the birch furniture in the museum was destroyed by them, or their larvæ, as it is being destroyed elsewhere. The presence of these little-recognised museum pests may be known by a fine yellowish dust which drops. When they have reduced the inside to powder, they escape by the minute holes—"worm-holes"—to destroy something else.

Birch bark is so easily stripped from the trees, that it possesses a certain fascination in suggesting its use for covering the paper cylinder instead of by the laborious method of super-imposing layer upon layer of torn tissue-paper; but its use is dangerous, and unless it were steeped in the bichloride of mercury preparation (Formula 11), it would be impossible to answer for it, and although, no doubt, the trees and twigs which hid destroyers for twenty and thirty years had not been well dressed, yet the appearance of one of the stumps indicated that an abundance of turpentine and paint had been used upon it.

DIVISION II

GRASSES, FERNS, MOSSES, SEAWEED, SHELLS, ETC.

After the preparation of the groundwork or rock and the trees, the consideration of the collection and preparation of the mosses and grasses takes the next place. The mosses most suitable are those found in woods and damp meadows, but those which are very fine and "ferny" will not do at all, the coarser, more golden-green kinds being the best, especially those from old walls, rocks, and the boles of trees. They are well known, and cover quite large areas, and may be lifted up as flat masses, their under surfaces having but little soil attached. They are coarse in texture and wavy, and of a golden-green or reddish-golden colour. Gathered in dry weather they require but little extra drying, and, the dirt having been tapped out of them, they must be plunged into a bath of turpentine to kill insects, and especially the larvæ of a destructive *Tinea*, which, curiously enough, harbours amongst moss, no doubt finding a few feathers to feed upon, left by perching birds. Other plants exceedingly valuable as accessories are those known as the club mosses, such as the common one found in elevated or rocky districts, and in marshes. *Sphagnum* or bog moss, holding water like a sponge, is extremely pretty, often pink-tipped when growing, but when dried it is difficult to handle, and does not do itself justice unless damped again, placed in position, dried again, and tinted to nature. Very beautiful lichens, red, crimson, yellow, golden, purple, liver-coloured, grey, greenish, and of nearly every colour, are to be found on rocks and trees, chiefly in mountainous or humid districts, and these are most valuable for attaching to the modelled rocks and trees. They should be carefully stripped from their attachments by a thin-bladed knife, and carried in a flat tin until they can be brought in to be dried and put through turpentine or benzoline. What little loss of colour attaches to these is made up by subsequent tinting ; indeed, most of them lose colour by exposure to light, and, therefore, if they can be tinted naturally they should be, but beware of bright yellow " painty " lichen, and bright green " painty," or dark green *dyed* moss— all are abominations to be avoided.

Some grasses there are which dry and colour well, and, as a rule, those which are the most useful are the thinnest or most wiry in habit. The sheep's fescue, *Festuca ovina ;* several of the brome grasses, *Bromus* sp. ; the wall and sea barleys, *Hordeum murinum* and *marinum,* and many other stiff kinds of grasses dry without much shrivelling, and take colour well.

The short wiry grasses which grow upon walls, and those which carpet woods, upland slopes, or rocky districts (fescue and " hair " grasses), are the most valuable, and should be collected systematically ; they, with mosses, form the groundwork of nearly every mounted group, and, when burned dry and yellow and red by the heat of summer, will take colour readily, or may be used as they are, to give variety and colour to what would otherwise be a uniform green expanse of groundwork. It will usually be found that broad-leaved grasses, sedges, etc., do not dry, but shrivel and curl until they are entirely transformed and quite unlike what they were in growth. It is, of course, possible to iron such broad-leaved grasses and make them passably correct, but, unless recurled, there is a stiffness (and brittleness) about them not desirable, and such objects are better modelled (see p. 370), although *Carex panicea*—" carnation grass "—and *Carex flacca,* both found commonly in moist situations, are fairly amenable to treatment.

The colouring must be very delicately applied, and whatever oil-colour is used must be well thinned with the turpentine and varnish (Formula 84), and the varnish, if at all in evidence, must be let down with more turpentine, so that the grass may have a certain "nature," but not be "shiny." Often such grasses are crimson and pink or yellowish at their bases, and there may be greys at their tips or other parts, and all of these effects must be looked for and, when recognised, imitated as skilfully as may be. White is in nearly all cases present, and may be mixed with the pigments to get certain tints.

Other grasses, reeds, and carexes there are of which the "seed" (panicle) may be used, as in many species it dries well and retains its place. Leaving out the usual sedges and bulrushes—which are of no value, and are distinctly out of place in any other situation than in a case tall enough to hold the whole height of the plant,—the very pretty wood melick, *Melica uniflora*, is extremely elegant in its panicle of drooping flowers rising above a tuft of rather broad blades of grass. These iron very well, and, with a little care and the introduction of a few modelled leaf-blades, the result is very natural. The seed-vessels of the toad-rush, *Juncus bufonius*, and, indeed, the whole plant, dry and colour remarkably well, and there are various other rushes, including the great wood - rush, *Luzula maxima*, and the hairy wood-rush, *Luzula forsteri*, very valuable for mounting, and some others which come in handily.

It may be stated that, as a rule, there are no tree nor other leaves with which anything can be done ; a little reflection will show that such leaves must be dried and pressed, and that both processes deprive them of their natural succulency and shapes, and they must therefore be reproduced by modelling, as directed in Chapter IX.

Ferns, which are so very taking in a landscape, are, with few exceptions, too weak to take colour, and must be pressed also. The exceptions are the polypody, *Polypodium vulgare*, hart's tongue, *Scolopendrium vulgare*, and, best of all, the common brake or bracken, *Pteris aquilina*, of the heath or woodland ; this, if picked in the autumn, dries beautifully, and, with a little care, can be made to do so almost naturally. It takes colour finely, and, as it is often found with the chlorophyll partly discharged and of a fine yellow, red, or crimson-red, it can be used when in this stage without any colouring, and forms an agreeable contrast to the greens and greys of the remainder of the group.

The colouring of this fern is by no means all green, as it appears to the unaided judgment, and nothing is more grievous than the generally adopted plan of getting a bundle of bracken, a pot of dark green paint, and a labourer to daub the colour on. Examine a fern with critically artistic judgment, and observe the change from the yellowish-green tip to the other greens, blues, and greys of the remainder, then the yellows, oranges, crimsons, dull reds, purples, greyish blues, and olives of others. Instead of one colour, and that dark green, the palette needs to be set with all the pigments, including white and black, as if a picture were to be painted ; and it *is* a picture to be painted, which, instead of taking one half minute to do, may take several minutes, but the effect is that approaching nature, and is not a dull, lustreless, or shiny daub of dark green paint. Formula 84 will be found the most useful vehicle with which to thin the colours, and by thinning the colours is meant just the dipping of the hoghair brushes now and then into the medium to distribute the colours properly and to blend them, and, as before noted for the grasses, there must be body, but not an unnatural gloss.

This roughly summarises the dried plants which, either with or without modelled foliage, are available in the mounting of animals as single specimens or in groups, and thus dismisses those of the heath, moor, wood, and mountain, and leads to a consideration of the available plants of the sea coasts.

Sea-coast and marine plants which can be dried and used

for mounting are not many in number. The sea-holly, *Eryngium maritimum*, and a few other similarly harsh-leaved plants dry well, and also some sedges and rushes and number-less stunted grasses, but the Maram grass, *Ammophila arundi-nacea*, so lovely with its blue-green spears, and so suggestive of the sea, twists and curls into any other shape than its own, and so must be modelled, as likewise the beautiful yellow sea-poppy, *Glaucium flavum*, the handsome sea-rocket, *Cakile maritima*, and a host of other things. Of truly marine plants—" Sea-weeds "—there is, indeed, a wealth, and very lovely they are, but with the exception of a very few which do not dry very satisfactorily for mounting purposes, they are not useful. The great oar-weeds, bladder-wracks, and other large weeds are most valuable, but cannot be dried, and so until lately were not used, or, if used, were wetted, glued, and varnished, but always looked what they were—dried weeds without transparency or fulness. In the Leicester Museum, the first departure which gave a better result was the imitation of some of these by tissue-paper, coloured or stained and varnished, but this has since given way to a process which gives the exact texture, quality, and transparency, and in some cases the colour, namely, the casting of the bladder-wracks and other fucoids, and their repro-duction in the glue-compositions.

The casting of such objects will be found quite simple after the somewhat complicated processes before described in these pages. First the, say, bladder-wrack is well wetted, and laid out as flat as may be on a bed of sand, and, where any curves or folds are naturally present, sand is packed under them with any of the tools Nos. 29 to 36, as explained for leaf-modelling (see p. 309). Where there is any obstinate tendency to rise up, pins with their heads cut off are used to keep the plant down, and the casting-box being built around the weed, plaster is poured on in the usual manner. When the wrack is removed, the mould is dried, oiled, and filled (by brushing) with the Formula 96 glue - composition, which, when dry, is trimmed at the edges to the exact shape of the original wrack, and is then so like the natural object in some instances as to be almost indistinguishable from it, but usually it should be coloured.

On Plate XVI. (Fig. 6) is shown a mould of the common *Fucus serratus*, and on the left upper portion of Plate XIX. is shown a model from the same executed in glue-composition (Formula 96), whilst two other fronds in this material are exhibited on the same plate.

Lichens such as the lung-worts, *Sticta* sp., which do not dry properly, may also be cast and modelled in the same material.

The various corallines found upon the coast, such as the sea-mat, *Flustra foliacea*, the sea-fir, *Sertularia abietina*, and its allies, which, though really the productions of invertebrate animals, are popularly confounded with seaweeds, are often of extreme beauty, and valuable in mounting. They should be thoroughly and often rinsed in fresh water and dried before use. Many of them should be "twiddled" before the fire whilst just damp after the last washing, and will dry expanded, and, as many of them take colour well, their natural hues may be restored afterwards; beware, however, of *aniline* dyes, which, beautiful and natural-looking at first, will change under the influence of light to drabs or dirty browns. If no "fast" dye is at hand, let them be stained with light washes of water- or oil-colour.

Many sponges, dredged or cast up by the sea, are often of equal value. Sea-urchins (*Echinus*, *Spatangus*, etc.) are available for mounting, and, after having the insides removed and being well washed and dipped in the solution, Formula 33, may be tinted to nature, but not with aniline dyes nor loaded with crude masses of colour, as is done by some who ought to know better.

Star-fishes, when well bleached by exposure for a length of time upon the shores, are useful to throw down upon an artificial beach, but should first be well washed and plunged into Formula 11 or 33.   When, however, they are to be represented as if freshly thrown up by the sea, and with their natural colours, there is no plan whatever which will compare for one instant with taking a mould of the animal in plaster, and reproducing it in glue-composition, Formula 96 or 97, to be afterwards coloured to nature.

On Plate XIX. is shown, on the right-hand side, between the seaweed and fungi, an *uncoloured* model of the common *Aster rubens* executed in the light-coloured glue-composition (Formula 97).

Other invertebrata there are, such as land and marine worms, often useful to introduce as the food of birds, and these are only to be reproduced by the same methods.

Sea-shells are, of course, most useful either for breaking up to make a shelly beach or to be used whole.   The commonest shells are usually the best, as being the most frequently found in positions haunted by sea-birds, and amongst these the cockle, pectens, mussels, "tops," periwinkles, and some others are especially valuable ; but a few words of warning as to incongruities in mounting may not be misplaced, and the indiscriminate sticking of all species of molluscs, corallines, and seaweeds about modelled rocks is to be strenuously avoided. Remember, therefore, that sponges, corallines, and seaweeds do not grow above high-water mark, and be guided accordingly in the choice of a subject ; and although it is perfectly legitimate to place gulls, curlews, cormorants, and other birds upon a wet rock covered with growing bladder-wracks, mussels, periwinkles, and limpets, it would be ridiculous if in close proximity to a nest of ringed plovers or terns, for, although these nest upon the shore, yet it is always—if only just—beyond high-water mark, and what seaweeds or shells are scattered around are dead and dry, and have been brought there by winds or exceptionally high tides, and must not be represented as if *growing*. It is quite true that a coralline is often found erect in the sand or shingle, but its base will be found attached to a stone, and, if this is made evident, there is no objection to one or two (not more) being shown in an erect position so long as the stone is shown which keeps it upright. The plastering of rocks with molluscs which are inhabitants of sand or mud is just as untrue to nature, and absurd. Cockles, razor-shells, and others do not attach themselves to rocks, and so must be shown as dead and càst up by the sea.

Limpet, mussel, and periwinkle shells are found in all positions attached to rocks, posts, old iron, etc., and the shells, when cleared of their inmates and well washed, are fixed upon the models of such objects by means of glued wadding inserted within the shells and pressed upon the models. In the case of mussels, after being cleared, the shells should be closed again by glued wadding, and attached in strings as they are found. Such things as periwinkles may have the animal modelled and a few shown crawling. All of these carefully modelled invertebrates and seaweeds, be it remarked, although useful for mounting, are primarily museum objects, and should be shown in the biological or index collections.

DIVISION III

PICTORIAL GROUPS OF MAMMALS, BIRDS, ETC.

The pictorial mounting of mammals has not been much attempted in this country, and probably the Leicester Museum is the only one in which a long range of wall-cases, 80 feet in length and of some height and depth, is devoted to this purpose, and includes such large mammals as various deer, zebra, bears, lions, and other large carnivora. The case of fighting tigers previously mentioned and figured may, perhaps, be considered somewhat sensational and out of place as a museum object, but it was primarily executed to show that such things could be set up, not on weighty "mannikins" loaded with clay, but on light paper models, and also with some material (*not* putty and paint) which should faithfully and naturally imitate the flesh of the inside of the mouth.

In America, however, the Government Museums are in advance of ours, for the bisons in the National Museum are mounted in a large case, with all accessories, as detailed by Mr. Harry P. Godwin.[1]

Having warned the pupil not to commit errors of judgment, it may be stated that instances sometimes occur of apparent incongruity, which, though perfectly natural and often exceedingly beautiful, require some courage and a great deal of technical skill to reproduce with anything like an air of reality. Such objects as thrift or sea-rockets in flower, with dead seaweeds and shells, around a group of ringed plover are common enough, but even these are to be handled cautiously, for what is apparently a small space out of doors is a very large space indeed within the walls of a museum. What will be said, however, of tall and handsome flowering plants, associated in our minds with inland gardens, in close proximity to living seaweeds and sea-molluscs, and tenanted by numberless birds of many species?

Such a scene as this may be found in many parts along the east coast, and a description of one such scene in Lincolnshire, observed by the writer, may be interesting to those who are advanced enough to copy the idea now being carried out in the Leicester Museum.

---

[1] *Washington Star*, 10th March 1888, also *Smithsonian Report* for 1887, pp. 546, 547.

It was early in September, 1894, that, putting up at a
village within easy distance, he journeyed to a well-known
marsh on the Lincolnshire Wash.   The day was perfect ; a
slight breeze, bearing upon its wings the life-giving breath of
the sea, tempered the heat of the morning sun.   Above, the
few fleecy clouds moved lazily, scarce throwing a shadow over
the marsh pools.   Far away beyond the sea-bank, winding inter-
minably, stretched a yellowish line, and beyond that again a blue,
and now and then a blue-green streak.   Somewhere in that
direction lay the great marsh, creeping sinuously between land
and sea.   Piloted by two or three gaunt trees in the far
distance, and ever looking for the fast-receding sea, the marsh
was reached at last, a few birds being picked up on the way.
Here was a sight which inland dwellers might well open their
eyes to see—miles upon miles of marsh gleaming green and
gold and lilac between the inland bank and the sandy flats by
the sea.   Under the steep bank—the only protection afforded
to hundreds of square miles of flat, rich, cultivated land against
the inroads of the devouring sea—waved as a fringe the pale
grey sea-artemisia, laved in high tides by the salt waves it loves.
Farther out a dense carpet of the shrubby stems and glaucous
leaves of the sea-purslane, *Atriplex portulacoides*, mixed with the
glassy, transparent stems of the *Salicornia* or salt-wort.   Yet
nearer the sea, now retreating lazily with many a sigh and gurgle,
appears the green and gold and lilac.   What is it ?   Michaelmas
daisies, by all that is wonderful !   Yes, knee-deep, and more, rise
the lovely flowers, pale purple-lilac with eyes of rich deep gold,
set in dense masses above fleshy green leaves shrouded in coarse
grasses and *Salicornia*, the little mud-pools surrounding them
filled with the retreating salt wave, and tenanted by scuttling
crabs and minute fishes.   Small, deep creeks, mud-lined and
paved with dead shells, intersect these sea-gardens in every
conceivable direction.   Stumps and stems of small trees mark

the waterway of the deeper, larger creeks, and harbour stores of mussels, sea-wrack, and green "flannel-weed," and here and there the gaunt timbers of some poor wreck lie athwart the shell-inhabited ooze ; but on the edges of all flourishes the green and gold and lilac.

Here, where the garden is thickest, and the treacherous ooze with slimy weeds lets the foot slip to the shelly bottom a foot or more below, and where clear runnels course over ropes upon ropes of mussels and other living things, dart upwards, with lightning speed and with many a weird sharp whistle, two or three greyish birds. Bang, bang, clatters out the choke-bore ; a right and left. Good! both down ; and as a fresh cartridge is being inserted, a larger, browner bird crosses behind, bound for the sea-sands, which he never reaches, for again the gun rings out, and he falls dead at quite a long range. Certainly the first three shots—two redshanks and a whimbrel —in the flower-garden by the sea are encouraging, and so the bag swells, for beyond, where the mussels are thickest and the garden grows thin, flaps up on whirring wing a teal ; again a greenshank ; more redshanks—several of these decoyed near the concealed gun by an imitation of their notes, and brought headlong out of the sky. So with the curlews, which otherwise rise exasperatingly well out of range, and whistle their bold defiance, setting everything else in the marsh in commotion.

Far on the sands pipe the pretty ringed plovers, their note far softer and more melodious than the hurried shrill whistle of the redshanks, and as they rise at the sound of some big punt-gun, they gleam, as do the stints, silvery white against the darker clouds, only by the next waft of their wings to show dusky ; and so in dense flocks, alternately gleaming argent and sable, they wing their way along the edge of the waters, and again pipe their mellow note resonant of the sea and its wonders. Anon come, from high in the sparkling air, liquid piccolo-like notes, almost a warble, and looking, there is seen a quickly-flying bird far beyond gun-shot, and as he flies so does he utter his musical changing whistle; it is the green sandpiper seeking some inland pool or brook. Now the gulls come flying past, the tide has turned, and the oyster-catchers and curlews and other shore-birds are restless, and soon the sea will run in stealthily up some big creek, and no man's help can save the gunner who lingers, for the larger creeks fill rapidly, and he may run hither and thither, and see no sign of danger from the seaward side, but between him and the land there stretches some sinuous creek running in faster and faster, lapping in the runlets, and hastening with undreamed-of speed to join another and yet another creek, and so cut him off from safety. Follow the ebbing tide, but beware of the turn should be the marsh-fowler's motto, if he wants such a varied bag and the enjoyment of such a glorious scene without peril.

This brief recital of what really happened, and is to be seen any September, will suggest numberless studies by which the skill of the advanced taxidermist and modeller may be tried, but, as may be gathered, no one need attempt such a combination of many different processes until he has had a large experience in modelling plants, seaweeds, and mounting all his specimens with—brains.

Some of the groups at South Kensington are very suggestive and pretty, but, as stated before, the mounting is unequal in character. The large case of terns may be instanced as an example. There the idea of space and atmosphere is gained by a large case all glass, excepting, of course, its base and the light framework, and although the groundwork of flowering thrift, *Armeria vulgaris*, is very elegant, the birds themselves are ill managed and badly set up, and look what they are—"stuffed."

Indeed, the trouble seems to have been, that although many

of the birds appeared at first to be well done, yet in a short time they shrank in various parts and got out of shape, owing to faulty modelling and a disregard for the tight clay or composition packing insisted upon in Chapter VI.

Other subjects which the advanced modeller might be tempted to reproduce are :—

Whinchats, male and female, bringing food, and perched upon plant-stems just above their nest, containing seven young ones, almost hidden under a dense tuft of meadow-grass backed by modelled flowering buttercups, *Ranunculus acris* (Leicester Museum).

Robins' nest and eggs in a tussock of grass, surrounded by woodland leaves, lichen-covered twigs, moss, and well-modelled clumps of flowering primroses ; the hen bird just leaving the nest, and the male sitting singing on a twig near by (Leicester Museum).

Whitethroats, *Sylvia cinerea*, and their nest and young in a bramble bush of modelled leaves and flowers (Leicester Museum).

What would make a sweetly pretty group is one already projected, but not yet completed, for the Leicester Museum ; the subject, a nest of the reed-warbler, *Acrocephalus streperus*, found in an old-world spot—the Castle reed-bed, Leicester—now built upon.

To show how important it is to take exact notes of the surroundings of such nests, it will only be necessary to quote from memoranda made at the time—" The nest itself was suspended in the centre of three reeds, *Phragmitis communis*, growing in shallow water and surrounded by a fine-leaved sedge, and ' mare's-tails,' *Equisetum fluviatile ;* just beside it, on comparatively dry ground, were growing masses of meadow-sweet, *Spiræa ulmaria*, and meadow-rue, *Thalictrum flavum*, in blossom. At some little distance, between this nest and another (with young), were some yellow iris, *Iris pseudacorus*, in bloom."

The mounting of such a group as this, it will be seen, would tax the utmost resources of the modeller, but when accomplished would be a dream of beauty.

Perhaps the best group in the Leicester Museum is that of the herons, the account of whose capture may be interesting.[1]

On 5th May, 1884, I went over to Stapleford Park, by permission of the late Rev. B. Sherard Kennedy, to see the heronry, and, if possible, procure a pair of old birds with the nest and young for the Museum. The heronry had increased since Harley's time, from forty to fifty nests being built in high elms and firs on an island in the lake, to which the keeper rowed me. Nests and birds were so plentiful, and the latter doing so much damage to the fishery, that the keeper asked me to shoot several, and so, being provided, he with a 12-bore C.F. and I with a ·320 rook-rifle, we took up our position within sixty yards or so of a nest, which he believed to be tenanted by "chicks." Soon afterwards something stirred, and, thinking it must be the old bird, I fired and evidently struck it, as it then stood up, and slightly raising its wings, subsided again into the nest. Lucas, the keeper, at once said, "He's hit," and began to climb the tree, but, when near the top, out scuttled the bird, rising amongst the thick twigs and soaring overhead, and showing that the ball had cut some of the primaries away, and, in spite of perhaps a flesh wound, the bird—a fine example—made its escape. Moving to another part of the wood, we lay in ambush within about seventy yards of a large and high elm-tree, on the topmost branches of which were placed no less than five nests. Half an hour's watch brought what appeared to be—by one of the gleams of sunshine with which we were favoured—an adult bird slowly sailing around high up in the air. He saw no danger and lowered his flight, and, just as he poised himself with outstretched wings on the edge of one of the nests, I fired, cutting him headlong into it. Great was the jubilation! for, as he fell, we imagined we could see the black and white plumage, and the long plumes, of a

---

[1] *The Vertebrate Animals of Leicestershire and Rutland*, by Montagu Browne, pp. 121-123.

fully mature bird. Now for the best climber! Lucas ran to the tree and began to ascend, but, as he did so, the wounded bird rose upright in the nest, and I, fearing he was but slightly hit and would get away like the first, fired again from the same spot, and this time he lay lifeless, half in and half out of the nest, and, as his head depended, we could see his beautiful white neck plumes and long black crest. Manfully struggling upward, taking advantage of every twig and every hollow for the foot, the keeper got along bravely, until met midway by a huge boss which, jutting out, barred his progress. In vain he tried to get around it, and, coming down, confessed himself beaten. I then tried myself, with less success, and, disregarding his protestations that the feat of getting either bird or nest out of the tree was impossible, sent him off for a long rope and more string. He was away for about an hour and a half, and during that time a bird, which appeared to be a female, came to the next nest to that from which the first bird had been lost, and settled. Again the rifle rang out, and brought it to bag—this bird, a young female, falling dead out of the tree to the ground. Its mouth was full of loach, and, whilst warm, I noted the colour of the eyes and soft parts, and then covered it up with my overcoat, to protect it from the rain which was falling, and making things so uncomfortable that it was a relief when Lucas brought the lunch. After this we essayed to throw the rope over a limb of the tree just above the boss, but after a few trials Lucas tired of this, and was more than willing to give it up, but having by this time tied two of his cartridges to a length of string, I managed, at the sixteenth throw, to lodge it over the limb, and by careful manipulation got the end to the ground. The rope being tied to this was drawn back slowly over the limb above the boss. All was now easy climbing; both ends of the rope being made fast to the trunk close to the ground, Lucas went up hand over hand, and gradually wriggled himself over the boss, and rested on the fork. Here another difficulty presented itself. Just above were three other limbs, jutting out so awkwardly as to obstruct his passage, but by dint of coaxing and chaffing he was persuaded to persevere, and managed, by propping himself with his back to the trunk, to throw the rope, loosened from below, over the limbs above, and so progressed another stage. At this juncture I sent him up a little refreshment, by the aid of the weighted string he carried in his pocket. So he ascended, vowing at every step he could get no higher, and proclaiming his rooted objection to "such hard work as this." At last, when quite near the nest, made nervous perhaps by the thinness of the branches, he sang out, " I zay, zur, I can't go no furder, this 'ere is too 'ard work for me." "Lucas," I shouted up, "you MUST, and directly the nest reaches the ground, you shall have a sovereign." At this juncture he touched his forehead with thanks, and I, fearing for his safety, directed him to get above the nest, lie close to the trunk, and cut off the branch on which the nest rested; this he did by means of the saw passed up to him by the string he carried. Some time was occupied in sawing away lesser branches, until the main one was attacked. As it cracked, two great birds nearly as large as the parent ran out along the branches, and had to be brought to earth by the rifle. At last the bough with the great nest swayed, broke off, turned over in the air, righted itself, and finally fell upright supported by the underwood; with it came the old bird, a magnificent and fully adult male, with lengthy plumes and crests, together with the half of a large eel, which he had brought to his young. Two balls had passed right through the centre of his body, within two inches of each other, either of which would have been fatal. The nest—an enormous structure, four feet across, and two feet thick, built of sticks, and afterwards filling a cart—had not sustained the slightest injury, and was not even jolted out of the forks in which it was built. Lucas came down as he went up, assisted by the rope, and the getting of the nest, from the time of the bird being shot, occupied between four and five hours. Needless to say, he had not a minute to wait for his well-earned reward, and soon commenced to climb the tree from whence I had shot the female, and, to my delight, procured from her nest four small "chicks," which, by their charmingly-quaint hair-like crests and downy plumage, to say nothing of their size, were in striking contrast to the other two young birds. Soon after this we found an unbroken, quite fresh, egg lying on the ground at the foot of a tree, deposited, probably, by a gravid bird.

Four more adult birds were brought down, and thus, firing altogether nine rifle-shots, I bagged eight birds, five of which, viz. the male and his two young, another male, and the female—with the latter's four chicks, the two nests, the eel, and the egg—are in the

XX

GROUP OF HERONS WITH NESTS AND YOUNG.

Museum, mounted in a plate-glass case, six feet cube, the nests being embellished with the leaves and buds of the elm carefully reproduced by modelling on the natural twigs.

An odd thing in connection with this case, and one specially flattering to the artist, is that few people realise that the elm-leaves are modelled, and frequent questions have been addressed to the attendant as to where the water is kept in which the stumps are presumably placed to keep the leaves green, whilst one or two visitors have gone a step further, and inquired if it is the heat of the room which has caused the stumps or twigs to throw out leaves! The reproduction of a photograph (Plate XX.) gives as good an idea of the group as such reproductions usually do.

A group in the Leicester Museum which appears to attract some attention is far easier to manage. The scene represents a section of the interior of a cow-house—to the exact scale of the original—in which are swallows, *Hirundo rustica*, Linn., in all stages, just as they were taken. First there are the old male and female flitting past the nest, with four eggs, built upon a ledge; above this is a nest containing four young only a few days old; farther along, under the rafters, is another nest, with young birds some two weeks old; and yet another nest with young birds, fully fledged and with square tails, sitting outside it, they being just at that age when the young are able to fly from their nest in the day to return to it at night. The "bricks" and "mortar" are modelled, but are not so light as in the next group.

This represents the roof of an old Leicester house, such as may be seen in the older quarters of the town, and is covered with small Swithland or local slates, usually of very fine and varied colours, differing entirely from the Welsh roofing-slates, which are generally purple. At one end is an old chimney-stack without a pot, built of red bricks. Moulds of the slates were taken in plaster of Paris in the usual way, and, these moulds being oiled, paper was pressed into them by the direct process, care being taken that the edges of the paper models should represent the thickness of the original slates. The bricks and ridge-tiles were, however, made in a different manner. A number of bricks were procured—the older the better,—and, when oiled, their surfaces were pasted over, except on one side, with paper, which, being made of sufficient thickness, was allowed to dry, and the brick withdrawn from that side left open, the corners at one end being slit where necessary, to facilitate its removal; the open part was then made up by pasting paper over it. In some cases, however, the bricks had paper pasted over the whole of their surfaces, and the corners at one end of the model were slit to extract the brick. The ridge-tiles were treated in the same way, with the exception that their under surfaces were left open, the paper being brought over their edges to the underneath to show their thickness. When the models were coloured from the actual specimens the effect was very good—all looking solid and weighty, although really of extreme lightness. Around and about the model were perched eighteen starlings in various attitudes, and in the model, as representing part of a very old house, spaces were left here and there where the slates were disarranged, to allow for the apparent passage of birds into the roof to their nests.

The Frontispiece has been casually mentioned at p. 78, but, beyond stating the fact of the modelling of the grotesque face in glued wool, nothing has been said concerning the remainder of the model, the substructure of which is composed merely of a strip or two of thin wood, over which cardboard and brown paper have been tacked and glued, the mouldings and other parts of the " stonework," etc., being modelled with glued wool, the whole heavily sanded, glued and sanded again, coloured when dry, and finally pieces of short grasses and mosses, such as grow upon old ruins, being fixed thereon.

In all of these groups the modelling of the mouths of the young birds has been managed with wax, as described at p. 210.

Fishes, as previously stated (see Chap. VII.), are not usually mounted with any taste, and the time-honoured and orthodox system appears to be the cutting-up of the blades of reeds into small spears about 3 or 4 inches in length, colouring them deeply, darkly (but not beautifully) green, and dotting them in little clumps, at carefully measured intervals, along the bottom of a nicely sanded case. It seems to be important that these precise little spears should be so sharp as to give rise to the doubt whether the mummy sailing above with imploring eyes, or, rather, with eyes which the French call *fleur de tête*, would not be more comfortable if the spear points refrained from pricking his stomach.

There is no reason why such a system should endure, for, given a fish modelled by one of the paper or glue processes, water-plants might be modelled, and, when the fish is in a case, be depicted as growing both above and below the fish. It is possible to enhance the illusion of the fish in water by painting the back of the case in two tints to represent above and below water, or by placing a sheet of waved glass above the fish, and, where the edge of this touches the front glass, colouring it and a little below as if there were a floating mass of "flannel-weed"; the difficulty being that this represents a *section* of water—an obvious impossibility except when seen in a tank or aquarium.

Acting on this idea of an aquarium, the Leicester Museum has, with more or less success, attempted a large scene—a wall-case 15 feet in length by 9 in height—in which sea-fishes are represented as if swimming, with a background of rocks, over which crawl various molluscs, lobsters, crabs, and so forth, and on which are seated modelled sea-anemones, sponges, corallines, and seaweeds, all well varnished to give the idea of wetness. Beyond, on the back of the case, is painted a representation of other rocks, blending with the modelled ones, to give distance ; there are representations of swimming fishes, octopods, and Medusæ as if in the distance, and the top of the case, being of glass, is painted with representations of floating seaweeds. The front glass is a difficulty, and whether it should be quite plain or varnished and streaked is not quite evident.

It is very badly done, however, and might be much improved, and as for the specimens included, they are painfully and grotesquely ill-stuffed, being old " heirlooms," and are being replaced by properly modelled fishes.

Perhaps the most realistic manner of mounting fishes is placing them either singly or in groups upon a shore of sand, seaweed, and shells, if marine fishes, or upon a meadow-bank as though just caught, if fresh-water fishes. In either case opportunity is given to introduce modelled seaweeds or the ordinary meadow-flowers, and, if the fishes and the plant-accessories are well modelled and coloured, a fine result is brought about.

The mounting of the invertebrata is somewhat restricted in range, and probably, after mounting a few slugs and snails on the various plants suitable, the pupil will wish to devote his attention to the larvæ of the Lepidoptera, and here a wide field of charming work is opened out. Larvæ modelled by any of the methods described on pp. 291-294 may be arranged upon their various food-plants, and although it is somewhat of an anachronism to represent imagines, pupæ, larvæ, and ova together on the food-plant, yet it is valuable for museum purposes as bringing the various stages of the insect and the food-plant within a small compass for easy reference.

A very beautiful object is the lime, *Tilia europæ*, to exhibit as the food-plant of the lime hawk-moth, *Smerinthus tiliæ;* and, so far as is known, the lime-branch in flower, now in the Leicester Museum, is the first one executed in which size and detail are so great.

Another is the larva of the goat-moth, *Cossus ligniperda*, executed in the same materials, and this may be displayed on a stump (modelled) of elm or willow—the latter being the prettiest—and showing a few twigs with leaves. The caterpillar may be placed crawling on the wood, whilst another is just emerging from a hole ; the pupa-case may be shown projecting from another hole, and the moth itself may be suspended as if drying its wings, whilst another is in full flight. Hundreds of other instances might be given, but these few will, no doubt, suggest others to the ingenious modeller.

The mounting of a group of exotic butterflies, say those of the genus Morpho, with characteristic South American orchids and other plants is by no means a new idea, having been executed by Mr. Ashmead, the London taxidermist, and is one which museums might well copy. What South Kensington has done in this way is the very valuable case standing in the entrance-hall and depicting mimicry, where the Indian butterflies, *Kallima inachis*, at rest upon dead leaves, so exactly simulate the latter in the general colour of their under surfaces and in their pattern, as to be discovered with difficulty. Other cases are in preparation, and will no doubt be as well managed.

Many others of the insecta, and, indeed, of the invertebrata, can be mounted with a due regard to their natural surroundings, but probably the foregoing list is full enough, and will bring the pupil to a consideration of the cases and mounts in general use, and of others designed to meet special requirements, with a view to the selection of the most suitable receptacle for the finished specimen or group.

DIVISION IV

CASES AND MOUNTS FOR ENCLOSING SPECIMENS

The first "case" is the "box." It requires no description. Its demerits speak for themselves, and all that can be said in its favour is, that one will stack above another, like bricks, and so save space. The next form is the "canted-corner" case, which gives more glass and looks lighter.

The case proper is one which has a light framework of wood or metal, enclosing front and sides, and sometimes top, of glass, and with a wooden back. In the Leicester Museum the old "Bickley Collection" is contained in shallow "boxes," which stack up as formally as the birds are stacked within. Many of the new cases, however, have glass all around (four sides) and on the top, whilst others have a tinted background, either of wood covered with calico and paper, or of canvas backed by a board. In some instances these backgrounds are tinted in distemper, and in others in oil kept very flat; some represent a warm sky ranging from primrose through pink to greenish blue; others are simply grey, and one is painted as a seascape with rocks and a wreck, kept low in tone, and, although the all-round glass cases look a little the lightest, and should give the idea of greater space and atmosphere, yet it must be recollected that in a museum, or, indeed, in any room, the objects on the other side of the case from the spectator are plainly visible, be they other groups, furniture, or other spectators, and therefore the attention cannot be concentrated upon any particular group, but is constantly distracted by other stationary or moving objects. Then again, the object of the all-round case is defeated if placed back to back with another, and therefore the idea would now seem to be what is being tried, or rather re-tried, in the Leicester Museum, namely, cases with glass front, sides, and top, and a wooden back, over which is strained paper of a delicate grey tint, similar to that used for tablets for specimens in every department. This seems to confine the attention to the object to be observed, does not interfere with the colours of the specimens or of the modelled foliage, rather enhancing the effect, indeed, and when the cases are deep, as all should be, the grey seems to fade into nothingness, and the eye is only conscious of a sense of restfulness. Another very great advantage, where space is a consideration, is that one can back the other, and, standing on a table or " stand," will accommodate two sets of observers—one on each side. Probably, unless they are placed lengthwise with the wall-cases, they may not give the room such an airy aspect.

Cases for fishes have often a " sprung " or bowed glass fitted to the front, and this style renders glass ends unnecessary, whilst giving a somewhat more " dressy " appearance.

Glass shades, round, oval, and square, to be procured at certain glass-dealers, are much more expensive than cases, especially if of any size. They are mainly used by professional taxidermists, and suit many objects very well, but, unless very large and of a square shape, are entirely out of place in a museum. When very large, however, their prices are cumulative and very high, and must seriously affect the profits of professionals ; and to give some idea of this phase of the question, there is, or was, a large group of birds of paradise in Riber Castle, the glass shade for which alone cost £18.

The ordinary "mounts" are of several varieties. First there is the round, which is often evolved from a glass shade which has been broken lower down, and so cut to save the top. Again, there are large convex clock-glasses, and yet again "rings," which are cut of varying depths from shades, and on which are cemented flat plates of glass cut to their

sizes and shapes by a turn-table and diamond. These are the
three varieties of " rounds " usually to be seen, but there are
" sprung " ovals and squares. All, however, have the same
principle underlying their construction ; they are intended to
possess a wooden back, which retains the glass and allows the
mount to be hung by a ring upon a wall. They have the
advantage of appearing light and pretty in a room, but are
not, unless square, of utility in a museum.

A few words of caution are necessary : the backs in the
round varieties being usually of wood with a groove turned
in them to receive the glass, this should be calculated so that
the greatest width is *outside* the glass, as there is a constant
danger of it tumbling out unless securely fastened. If fastened
with putty, glue, glued strips, white lead, red lead, plaster of
Paris, or, indeed, any material which sets hard and unyielding,
there is a certainty of the glass cracking, sooner or later, by
changes of temperature affecting the wood or the holding
material, and accordingly the best plan has been found to cut
small pieces of cork the size of the groove outside the glass,
glue them at bottom, and press them tightly into the groove
when the glass rim is within it, and over all to *paste* strips
of strong paper, well fitted over the pieces of cork into
the groove, and coming a little way up the glass. This,
when dry, securely holds the glass in its groove, and prevents
subsequent breakages. Half a dozen small pieces of cork will
usually be sufficient, and if the groove be shallow and the
paper should rise above and show on the inside, black, grey, or
gilt paper must be pasted first around the bottom of the glass
rim, *coloured surface to show inside the glass,* and then the brown
paper, coming afterwards outside that, does not show through.
Another advantage which papering-in possesses over putty or
anything else containing oil is, that the backs may be coloured
in oil or distemper, without any grease appearing over the

XXI

A carved and enriched Case suitable for a Hall or Large Room.

tinted " sky " inside. Velvet or chenille laid around the groove outside the glass completes the mount if necessary.

" Mounts " can also be made with a carved wood or gilt frame of some considerable depth, and of any shape, with a groove around the edge, into which is fitted a sheet of glass, either plain or " sprung." When " sprung," however, the *raison d'être* for the depth of the frame vanishes, especially as flat glass usually shows up included specimens better, and can be fitted with a carved border laid over it. These mounts, which, if large, are better oval in shape, can be hung up or used on a standard as a " screen."

Another style of " screen " is presumably useful to place in front of the fire, but, as it is seldom or never used for such a purpose, the name is somewhat of a misnomer, and screen-mount would perhaps express it better. It is made in all materials, from bamboo and fancy woods to deal, gilded or black, and consists of two sheets of glass enclosed in a framework of turned and carved wood, with a handle on the top, and stands upon the floor upon splayed or carved feet. It usually contains brilliantly-plumaged exotic birds, or butterflies, seaweeds, pressed ferns, or other objects, and although very suitable for a room, especially when it can be used as a fire-screen, for which it is not difficult to arrange, it is quite unsuitable for anything but decorative purposes.

For purely decorative purposes, as furniture for, say, some private entrance-hall, the work of the case and of the stand itself may be, and probably should be, much more elaborate, and such a case is shown on Plate XXI., which represents one designed, and enclosing various water - fowl, for a certain well-known philanthropist of Birmingham.

Another elegant pattern, which may be called the picture-frame mount, and which is far superior to the ordinary round or oval mounts, is, when enriched by gilt or carved mouldings, eminently suitable for the walls of almost any room. This has been in use in England and on the Continent for some years, and of late the Americans seem to have taken it up, as it is mentioned in many of their books upon Taxidermy, but according to *The Oölogist*,[1] Messrs. F. H. Lattin and Company exhibited, at the World's Columbian Exposition, 1893, " A group of Bob-Whites, *Colinus virginianus*, Linn., under oval convex glass," and this, enclosing seven birds, apparently with foliage, and with a painted scene as a background, was surrounded by an elaborate oblong frame—whether of carved wood or of gilt the photographic process-block does not tell.

Perhaps an improvement on any previous modification of this kind of mount was a pair made in Leicester for the Chicago Exhibition, but which remained after all in England ; one of them enclosed a group of specially selected humming-birds, and the other contained exotic Lepidoptera, arranged as a harmony in blue, metallic green, and gold, which gave excellent results by a certain scheme of arrangement. Each case was, taking the frame-measurement, nearly 4 feet in height by 3 feet in breadth, but was kept to 5 or 6 inches in depth, to give it the appearance of a picture when hanging up. The framework, which was a long octagon, was formed of oak—afterwards gilded—rebated to receive glass all around, and was surrounded with a handsomely enriched and gilded frame, the back of which was ploughed out to receive the background, and upon which the light framework holding the glass was secured (see Plate XXII.)

Museum cases vary quite as much as do museums and curators themselves, and beginning, as nearly all did, in the cucumber-frame style of architecture for the " table-cases," and with small-paned fronts for the wall-cases, they have now become quite important articles of furniture, and a really well made and fitted museum wall-case or centre case for

---

[1] Albion, N.Y., April, 1894, vol. xi. No. 4, Whole No. 102.

XXII.

A Picture-frame Mount (containing Exotic Lepidoptera)
suitable for a Large Room.

the reception of valuable specimens will, if properly dust-proof and of any size, range in price from thirty to a hundred guineas, or even more. Descriptions of the various cases and their peculiarities in the various museums at home and abroad would take up too great a space, but may be found some day in a projected work upon "Museums and Museum Management." It may be stated at once, however, that a cut-and-dried formula for one particular case which will suit every museum—such as some persons, who endeavour also to introduce a universal label, would have us to believe possible—is a delusion.

The cases at South Kensington are each adapted, as they should be, to suit particular departments and certain spaces, and those who run may read ; the cases at Leicester are modifications of these and some other patterns, and are made of best oak, polished " dead," without any colouring matter.

It may be here stated that all glasses, in any frames whatsoever, should be *pasted* in all round with strips of brown paper.

" Distemper " colouring is simply powdered whiting (or, better, powdered flake white) mixed with a little very weak hot size, or even thin paste, to which water and various powder-colours are added to the tints desired, and of the consistence of thin cream. Professionals have usually a palette of three powder-colours only — chrome yellow, vermilion, and ultramarine—for their skies, but see pp. 88-93. It is important that a good body of white be used, or the colours will not " bear out " and give a clean and luminous appearance as they should do. Distemper colour upon a papered background is not available where putty or anything oily is in contact, as anything of a greasy nature rapidly spreads and spoils its appearance ; this may be seen even when the wooden back of the case is of resinous deal papered over, and undoubtedly the best plan is to cover the backboard by pasting common calico upon it, and follow with paper. The calico also pre-vents the back from splitting and carrying the paper with it, but a frame like those used for oil canvases, on which calico or sheeting is stretched and coloured in distemper, inserted in a rebate at the back of the case, and finally covered with a thin backboard, is the best for large cases.

Shields for the backing of horned or other heads are, when not diamond-shaped, usually either oval or, more frequently, cut to a pattern which is some modification of the conventional heart. It is so extremely easy to double a piece of stiff paper and cut a pattern to suit individual tastes, that there is no necessity for giving figures of such shapes. Of what wood they should be made is also a matter of individual taste, but oak appears to suit most things, and is to be relied upon for strength and durability. The edges are better bevelled, and the wood oiled or slightly polished ; the edges, however, and the border around the head, are sometimes carved or otherwise enriched.

A slot, longer than broad, should be chiselled out of the substance of the wood at the back, but need not, except in instances of very weighty heads or horns, penetrate the entire thickness. The upper half of the slot should be protected by a plate of metal screwed across, and the width of this, and of the uncovered half, and the depth also of the latter, must be determined by the thickness and length of the angle of the hook to be driven into the wall to hold it. Hooks for weighty heads should be of considerable length and thickness, and made of *wrought* iron, and sometimes the slot should be cut right through to the front to get more hold.

When the slot has been cut and the iron or brass plate arranged, the head is fixed to the shield by countersunk screws passing through it into the oval neck-board previously described, but when, as is sometimes the case, horns only are to be affixed to a shield, the screws should pass through the V-shaped bone from the front, the heads of the screws being *countersunk* into the bone, and covered with the most suitable of the modelling-compositions. Shed horns, or those without bone attached, are mounted upon a piece of hard wood carved to the shape shown by Figs. 6 and 7, Plate VII., which represent the under and upper surfaces of such an artificial frontal or V-shaped piece. The horns are fastened to this by screwed rod-iron, fixed firmly into their bases, and attached securely to the chevron-shaped piece by nuts screwed on at the back where the drill-holes are shown on Fig. 6.

To represent Blood and Torn Flesh

Sometimes it is necessary, say in the instance of a tiger or panther tearing its prey, or of a hawk tearing open another bird, to represent the appearance of fresh blood, and this has usually been poorly accomplished by sealing-wax, and but slightly better by vermilion or red lead mixed with varnish or glue, and thickly daubed upon the fur or feathers of the victim. Such effects are, however, better represented by gradations of tone, as it must be recollected that the hue of blood is not that of lacerated flesh, and that both differ from that of congealed blood ; hence it will be found that beeswax made hot and coloured with tube oil-pigments in different tints of vermilion, alizarin crimson, Rubens madder, and perhaps a little grey here and there, painted on with a brush, will admirably render the natural effect. In some cases it may be well to slightly touch up the wax afterwards with colour.

The internal organs of any animal may be represented by casting in the ordinary manner, and reproducing them in any of the wax- or glue-compositions treated upon in these pages, and finally by colouring.

27

To represent Frost, Ice, and Snow

The appearances of these are difficult to produce satisfactorily, and the usual method of rendering them, by means of a substratum of fine plaster of Paris over which " glass frosting " (to be procured at the glass-blower's or artificial-eye maker's) is sprinkled more or less thickly, fails to give the effect desired, for, although the powdered glass scales do very well to represent ice, yet the dead and unnatural whiteness of the plaster is but a poor substitute for the original " beautiful snow," and there is no doubt that roughly-pounded lump sugar as a substratum, thickly sprinkled with " glass frosting," gives the best results for small studies ; but where expense is an object, a combination of plaster of Paris as an underground, with sugar and glass sprinkled over, must suffice. Alum roughly pounded or put on hot and allowed to recrystallise, borax, and various other substances are sometimes used, but in all cases where the " snow " or " ice " is required to adhere to twigs, boles of trees, or rocks, no glue must be used, and paper-varnish, which is, perhaps, the best to use for this purpose, turns yellow and stains the " snow " at the time of using, or if not then, it does so ultimately.

An instance of this tendency can be seen in the ice-block upon which a polar bear stands in the Leicester Museum. This block was made of thin greenish glass in fairly large pieces, put together and covered here and there with thin tissue-paper subsequently varnished ; " snow " was strewn over the upper surface, and " icicles " modelled in glass depended therefrom, and the whole, when finished, looked as satisfactory as may be, but the varnish, having now been on some years, has turned everything of a yellowish hue, and the transparency of the ice is completely lost, the whole looking as if under the influence of a very dirty thaw.

At present, the best thing to fix the frost and snow on twigs, etc., appears to be clean flour paste.

The Americans have apparently been successful in using paraffin poured hot over glass or wood to represent ice, and have used powdered starch and white blotting-paper pulped and dried, together with plaster of Paris, to represent snow.

The most successful imitation of water is made by tinting, streaking, and varnishing " hammered " glass until the desired hue is obtained. To represent birds as though swimming, the best method is to cut the glass for the reception of the body; but this being an extremely difficult operation, frequently resulting in the breaking of the glass, the birds may be cut through, and their upper and lower halves attached to the upper and under surfaces of the glass either by glue or by shellac (Formula 78). Herons or similar long-legged birds may be represented as standing mid-leg in water by drilling holes in the glass, and this may also be done for aquatic plants to pass through. In the instance of the bird, however, the leg must be severed just above the foot, and this part replaced upon the wire after the leg has been passed through the orifice, the glass being supported meanwhile in any manner most convenient.

BIBLIOGRAPHY OF WORKS TREATING WHOLLY OR IN PART UPON TAXIDERMY, OR UPON THE PRESERVATION OF VARIOUS NATURAL OBJECTS.[1]

The following Bibliography has been in greater part abbreviated, corrected, and rearranged from articles in the Second and Third Reports of the Society of American Taxidermists, furnished by Messrs. F. A. Lucas and L. M. M'Cormick, to the former of whom the writer's thanks are due for kindly sending copies of the Reports which were not otherwise obtainable; readers of the present work will, however, confer a great benefit by the notification of any additions or errors.

The earliest work upon these subjects appears to be that by Bolnest (1672); the latest is, of course, that by the present writer.

Adams, A. "Directions for Collecting and Preserving Objects of Natural History," *Manual of Natural History*, by A. Adams, W. B. Baikie, and C. Barron. Part IV. pp. 623-693. London, 1854.

Adams, L. E. "Preserving Crustacea," *Science Gossip*, 1880, p. 138. London.

Aeby, Chr. "Ueber die Conservirung von Durchschnitten gefrorner Körpertheile," *Medic. Centralbl.* 13. Jahrg. (1875), No. 10, p. 150.

Alléon, Amédée. "Nouveaux Procédés de Taxidermie." Paris, 1889. (Illustrated.)

Altum, B. "Planmässiges Sammeln der Vögel und planmässiges

---

[1] The literature upon the preparation and preservation of insects is so vast, that it has been necessarily, although reluctantly, omitted from the present bibliography.

Ausstopfen und Stellen derselben." (Illustrated.) *Naumannia*, 5. Jahrg. (1855), pp. 29-38. Dessau and Leipzig.

Altum, B. " Ueber Ausstopfen und Stellen der Vögel in Allgemeinen," *Naumannia*, 5. Jahrg. (1855), pp. 301-307. Dessau and Leipzig.

———— " Aphoristische Bemerkungen für Ausstopfer." (Illustrated.) *Naumannia*, 6. Jahrg. (1856), pp. 35-40. Dessau and Leipzig.

Andés, L. E. "Das Conserviren von Thierbälgen, Pflanzen, und allen Natur- und Kunstproducten. Prakt. Anleitung zum Ausstopfen, Präpariren, Conserviren, Skeletiren, etc." Vienna, 1894. (Illustrated.)

Avis, Richard (pseudonym). "Bird Preserving, Bird Mounting, and the Preservation of Birds' Eggs, with Bird Catching." London, 1870. (Illustrated.)

Babington, Charles C. "Report of the Committee for the Preservation of Animal and Vegetable Substances," *Rep. Brit. Ass. Adv. Sci.* 12th meeting (1842), pp. 40, 41. London, 1843.

Bachmann, Otto. "Eine neue Conservirungsflüssigkeit für Mollusken," *Nachrichtsbl. d. deutsch. Malak. Ges.* 12. Jahrg. (1880), pp. 74-79.

Bailey, J. W. "On a Mode of giving Permanent Flexibility to Brittle Specimens in Botany and Zoology," *Sillim Amer. Journ.* ser. 2. vol. xviii. New Haven, 1854.

Baird, Spencer Fullerton. "Hints for Preserving Objects of Natural History." Carlisle, U.S.A., 1846.

———— "General Directions for Collecting and Preserving Objects of Natural History." Published by the Smithsonian Institution. Washington, 1850.

———— "Directions for Making Collections in Natural History," prepared for the use of parties engaged in the exploration of a route for the Pacific Railroad along the 49th parallel. Washington, 1853.

———— "Directions for Collecting, Preserving, and Transporting Specimens of Natural History," *Eleventh Ann. Rep. Smithsonian Institution* (1856), pp. 235-253. Washington, 1857.

———— "Smithsonian Collections. Directions for Collecting, Preserving, and Transporting Specimens of Natural History." Washington, first edition, 1852 ; third edition, March 1859.

Forming Art. VII. of Vol. II. of the series, but oftener found separate.

Balden, Felix. "Das Ausstopfen und Aufstellen höherer Thiere," *Isis* (Russ.), 1. Jahrg. (1876). Berlin.

Bartholomael. "Die Wissenschaft Vögel aufzulegen." Marburg, 1815.

Batizfavi, Samu. "Utasitás madarak embösök hüllök és halak börének lefejtérése, kitömése és fenntarására." Pesth, 1858.

Batty, Joseph H. "How to Stuff Birds," *Forest and Stream*, vol. i. p. 217. New York, 1873.

————— "Notes on Taxidermy," *Forest and Stream*, vol. iv. p. 181. New York, 1873.

Criticised by "Pickel" on p. 215, and this is answered by Batty on p. 247.

————— "Mounting Birds with Closed Wings; some Hints on the Art of Taxidermy," *Forest and Stream*, vol. i. p. 390. New York, 1875.

————— "Practical Taxidermy and Home Decoration, together with General Information for Sportsmen." New York, 1880. (Illustrated.)

Bauer. (See anonymous at end: "Die Kunst," etc.)

Bécœur, Jean Baptiste. "Mémoire instructif sur la manière d'arranger les différents animaux," etc. (from *Journ. Encyclopédique*). Liège.

Belknap, Rev. Jeremy. "Circular Letter of the Massachusetts Historical Society, respectfully addressed, in 1794, by Rev. Jeremy Belknap, D.D., then Corresponding Secretary, to every Gentleman of Science in the Continent and Islands of America," *Collections of the Massachusetts Hist. Society*, 2nd ser. i. pp. 14-26. Boston, 1814.

Bendall, Howard. "Note on a New Method of Preserving the Colours of Tissues," *Journ. of Anat. and Physiol.* vol. xiv. (1880), pp. 511, 512. London and Cambridge.

Beneden, Éd. van. "Note sur la conservation des animaux inférieurs," *Bull. de l'acad. roy. de Belgique*, 2. sér. tom. xxxii. (1871), pp. 179-181. Brussels. *Ann. Soc. Ent. Belg.* tom. xv. (1871-72). *Compt. Rend.* pp. 8, 9.

Berling, Dr. "Der praktische Thier-Ausstopfer." Berlin, 1861. (Illustrated.)

Bidwell, Edward. "Observations on Egg-Blowing." (Illustrated.) *Zoologist*, 3rd ser. vol. i. pp. 164-167. London, 1877.

Bird, W. F. W. "Moths in Bird Skins," *Zoologist*, vii. p. 2494. London, 1849.

Blakey, R. "On the Preservation of Birds for Stuffing," *Manual of Shooting*. London, 1854.

Bobierre, A. "Nuevos procedimientos de conservacion de las substancias animales," etc. Madrid, 1853.

Bocage, J. V. Barboza du. "Instrucções praticas sobre o modo de colligir, preparar e remetter productos zoologicos para o Museu de Lisboa." Lisbon, 1862.

Bock, Georg. "Notiz für Ausstopfer," *Journal für Ornithologie*, v. pp. 376, 377. Cassel, 1857.

Boisduval, A. (See Lecocq.)

Boitard, Pierre. "Le cabinet d'histoire naturelle, formé des productions du pays même que l'on habite, avec la méthode de classement, l'art d'empailler les animaux et de conserver les plantes et les insectes." Two vols. Paris, 1821. (Illustrated.)

——— "Manuel du Naturaliste Préparateur." Paris, 1825. (Illustrated.)

——— "Nouveau Manuel Complet du Naturaliste Préparateur." Paris, 1852. (Illustrated.)

——— "Nouveau Manuel Complet du Naturaliste Préparateur." Nouvelle edition. Paris, 1859 and 1868. (Illustrated.)

——— "Nouveau Manuel Complet du Naturaliste Préparateur." Première Partie. Paris, 1881. (Illustrated.)

——— "Nouveau Manuel Complet du Naturaliste Préparateur," Deuxième Partie, Taxidermie. (New edition entirely re-cast and completed by M. Maigne.) Paris, 1890. (Illustrated.)

Bolnest, Edward. "A Rational Way of Preparing Animals," etc. London, 1672.

Bordazzi, D. "Ueber die Anwendung des Chlorhydrat zur Conservirung von anatomischen Präparaten," *Lo Sperimentale*, tom. xxxix. (1877), p. 368.

Bossart, Joh. Jac. "Anweis. wie Naturalien zu sammeln u. zu verschicken sind." Leipzig, 1779.

Boswell, P. "Art of Taxidermy." London, 1841.

Boucard, A. "How to gain from Eighty to Two Hundred Pounds Sterling a year by Instructive and Amusing Means; or, Instructions for Collecting, Preserving, and Sending Collections of Natural History." London, 1871.

Boudet, ... "Procédé de conservation des pièces anatomiques," *Bull. Soc. anatomique*, pp. 186-191. Paris, 1877.

Bouvier, A. "De la conservation des fossiles fragiles et friables." (Procédés de MM. A. von Kœnen et G. Dewalque.) *Guide du Naturaliste* (Bouvier), 1. année (1879), p. 136. Paris.

——— "Nouveau piège pour petits Mammifères, Reptiles, Mollusques, et Insects." (D'après M. E. Carrière.) *Guide du Naturaliste* (Bouvier), 1. année (1879), p. 28. Paris.

——— "De la solidification des fossiles friables." (Procédé Stahl.) *Guide du Naturaliste* (Bouvier), 1. année (1879), p. 112. Paris.

Brady, George S. "On the Method of Collecting and Preserving Entomostraca and other Microzoa," *Nature*, vol. viii. (1873), pp. 68, 69. London and New York.

Brassart, J. G. "Anweisung zum Abbalgen, Ausstopfen und Conserviren der Vögel und Säugethiere." Bonn, 1827.

Braun, M. "Ueber die trockene Conservation von anatomischen Präparaten der Mollusken." *Zoolog. Anzeiger*. 1. Jahrg. (1878), pp. 56, 57. Leipzig. *Nachrichtsbl. d. deutsch. Malak. Ges.* 10. Jahrg. (1878), pp. 49-52.

——— "De la conservation sèche des préparations anatomiques des Mollusques." (Traduct.) *Guide du Natural.* (Bouvier.) 1. année (1879), p. 112. Paris. (*Zool. Anzeiger.*)

——— "Trockene Präparate von Meeres-Anneliden," *Tagebl. d. 52. Vers. deutsch. Naturf.* (1879), p. 229. Baden-Baden.

Bree, C. R. "Preservation of Organic Matter by Exclusion of Atmospheric Air," *Zoologist*, 2nd ser. vol. i. (1866), p. 435. (*Field*, 25th August, 1866.) London.

Brehm, Christian Ludwig. "Das Ausstopfen der Vögel," *Oken's Isis*, Bd. xx. (1827), pp. 147-168, and Bd. xxi. (1828), pp. 1244-1267. Jena.

——— "Die Kunst, Vögel als Bälge zu bereiten, aufzustopfen, aufzustellen und aufzubewahren." Weimar, first edition, 1842;

second edition, 1860; third edition in Martin (P. L.), *Die Praxis der Naturgeschichte*, etc., Weimar, 1869-82.

Free translation of Evans' "L'art de Préparer," 1841.

Breton. "On a Mode of Preserving Bird Skins in the Absence of the Ordinary Means," *Proceedings Zoological Society*, ii. p. 21. London, 1834.

Broderip, W. J. "Hints for Collecting Animals and their Products." London, 1832.

Bronn, H. G. "Gedrängte Anleit. zum Sammeln, Zubereiten und Ver-packen von Thieren, Pflanzen und Mineralien für naturhistor. Museen." Heidelberg, 1838.

Brösike, G. "Eine neue Anwendungsmethode der Wickerheimer'schen Conservirungsflüssigkeit," *Medic. Centralbl.* 18. Jahrg. (1880), No. 2, pp. 17-19.

——— [Ueber Wickersheimer'sche Präparationsmethode], *Tagebl.* d. 53. Versamml. deutsch. Naturf. (1880), p. 87. Danzig.

Brown, T. "The Taxidermist's Manual." Glasgow, 1833. (Printed since without the alteration of a single line up to last reprint.) London and Edinburgh, ? 1885. (Illustrated.)

There are three or four American reprints.

——— "Zoologist's Text-Book," 2 vols. Glasgow, 1833.

——— "The Taxidermist's Manual." American revised edition. New York, G. P. Putnam's Sons, 1870. (Illustrated.) Twenty-third edition, 1875.

——— Twenty-third edition. Boston, Little, B. and Co., 1872.

——— American revised edition from twentieth English edition. New York ? 1878. (Illustrated.)

——— American revised edition. New York, Orange Judd Pub. Co. ? 1880. (Illustrated.)

Browne, Montagu. "Practical Taxidermy," pp. 150. London, 1878. (Illustrated.)

——— Second edition (revised and enlarged up to pp. 344, with additional illustrations). London, 1884, followed by numerous reprints without date.

——— Article "Taxidermy," *Encyclopædia Britannica*, ninth edition, vol. xxiii. pp. 89, 90. Edinburgh.

Brunn, M. von. "Beitrag zur Museumstechnik." Hamburg, 1895. (Illustrated.)

Bullock, W. "A Concise and Easy Method of Preserving Subjects of Natural History." London, first edition, 1817 ; second edition, 1818.

Burgin, G. B. "A Comic Naturalist." (Illustrated.) *The Idler*, vol. vi. pp. 559-573. London, 1894.

Cabot, S. "Note on the Ravages of Dermestes and Anthreni in Specimens of Birds," *Proceedings Boston Soci. Nat. Hist.* vii. Boston, U.S.A., 1859.

Campiglio, Stefan. "Cenni sulle preparazioni zoologiche." Milan, 1837.

Capus, G. "Guide du Naturaliste Préparateur." Paris, 1879. (Illustrated.)

———— "Guide du Naturaliste Préparateur et du Voyageur Scientifique." 2nd edition, entièrement refondu par le Dr. A. T. de Rochebrune. Paris, 1883. (Illustrated.)

Carrière, E. (See Bouvier. "Nouveau piège," etc.)

Cathcart. *Trans. of the Edinburgh Med.-Chirurg. Soc.* No. 19. November, 1885.

Coal, W. E. (See anonymous works at end : "Directions," etc.)

Collett, Robert. "Taxidermi." Christiania, 1863.

Costes, A. "Méthode de conservation des Infusoires." (Extrait.) *Guide du Naturaliste* (Bouvier), 1. année (1879), p. 40. Paris.

Coues, Elliott. "Field Ornithology." New York and Boston, 1874.

———— "A Useful Hint," *The American Sportsman,* vol. iv. p. 3 1874.

———— "To Prevent Grease from Injuring the Plumage of Birds," *Amer. Nat.* xiii. p. 456. Philadelphia, 1879.

> Covering a letter on the subject from A. H. Stevens, Clinton, Conn., who used vegetable fibre for that purpose in his Taxidermy.

Coultas, Harland. "The Home Naturalist." London, 1877.

"Dr. Cutler's Method of Preserving the Skins of Birds," *Appendix Coll. of the Mass. Hist. Society.* Boston, U.S.A., 1795.

Cunningham, J. T. (For title see footnote, p. 26.)

Danger, F. P. "Mémoire sur une nouvelle méthode de préparer et de rendre durables les collections d'œufs d'Oiseaux." (Illustrated.) *Ann. Scienc. natur.* vol. xv. pp. 338-347. Paris, 1828.

Daudin, François Marie. "Sur l'art de la Taxidermie considéré par rapport aux Oiseaux," *Traité Élémentaire et Complet d'Ornithologie*, vol. ii. pp. 439-462. Paris, 1800.

Davie, O. "The Naturalist's Manual." Columbus, Ohio, U.S.A., 1882. (Illustrated.)

———— "Methods in the Art of Taxidermy." London, and Columbus, O., U.S.A., 1894. (Illustrated.)

Davies, James B. "Naturalists' Guide." Edinburgh, 1853.

———— "The Practical Naturalist's Guide." Edinburgh, 1858.

———— "Notes on some Experiments recently made on the Preservation of certain Marine Radiata," *Proc. Roy. Phys. Soc. Edinburgh*, vol. i. (1854-58), pp. 464-466. Edinburgh, 1858.

———— "Practical Naturalist's Guide." New edition. Edinburgh, 1870 and 1872.

Davies, T. "A Letter from Captain Davies to John Ellis, Esq., F.R.S., on a Method of Preparing Birds for Preservation," *Philos. Trans.* for 1770, lx. pp. 184-187. London, 1771.

Dawson, G. A. R. "Indian Taxidermy," *Nilgiri Sporting Reminiscences.* Madras, 1880.

De Castellarnau. "La Estacion Zoolog. de Napoles." Madrid, 1885.

Demaison, Ch. "Liquide arsenical antiseptique." (Liquide conservateur.) *Feuill. d. jeun. natural.* 2. année (1871-72), pp. 79-81. Paris.

Dexter, N. "Instructions in Practical Taxidermy and Bird Skinning," *The American Sportsman*, vol. iii. p. 342. 1874.

———— "Skinning and Stuffing Heads," *American Sportsman*, vol. iv. p. 23. 1874.

Deyrolle, E. "La préparation des peaux," *Le Naturaliste*, 1. année (1879), No. 16, pp. 124, 125. Paris.

Diorio, P. "Sullo indurimento e conservazione indefinita dei corpi degli animali," *Atti Accad. Pontif. d. Nuov. Lincei*, tom. xviii. (1864-65), pp. 357-360. Rome, 1865.

Donovan, E. "Instructions for Collecting and Preserving Various Subjects of Natural History." London, 1794.

[Donovan, E.] "Anleit. alle Arten näturl. Körper, als Säugethiere,

Vögel, Amphibien, Fische, Pflanzen, etc., zusammeln und aufzubewahren." Zurich, 1797. (Illustrated.)

Free Translation of Donovan, 1794, by J. Jac. Römer.

Duff, J. "Moths in Bird Skins," *Zoologist*, vii. p. 2450. London, 1849.

Dufresne, L. "Taxidermie," *Dictionnaire d'Histoire Naturelle*, vol. xxxii. pp. 529-592. Paris, 1803, 1819.

—— "Taxidermie." Paris, 1820. Traité de Taxidermie," 1829.

Duhamel, du Monceau, H. L. "Avis pour le transport par mer des arbres des plantes vivaces des semences et de diverses autres curiosités d'histoire naturelle." Paris, 1752.

Duncker, H. C. J. "Einige Konservationserfolge," *Isis* (Russ.), 4. Jahrg. (1879), pp. 54-56. Berlin.

Dupont, aîné, Edouard. "Traité de Taxidermie." Paris, 1823. Second edition (revised and illustrated). Paris, 1827.

Eger, L. "Der Naturalien-Sammler." Vienna, 1876. (Illustrated.)

—— e M. Lessona. "Il raccoglitore naturalista." Turin, first edition, 1877; second edition, 1882. (Illustrated.)

Eiben, C. E. "Praktische Anweisung zum Ausstopfen der Vögel." Quedlinburg, 1882.

Éloffe, A. "Traité pratique du Naturaliste Préparateur." Paris, 1861. (Illustrated.)

Elwin, Edward Fentone. "Cleaning Skeletons," *Science Gossip* for 1872, p. 39. London, 1873.

—— "On Collecting and Preserving Osteological Specimens," *Science Gossip* for 1874, pp. 226, 227. London, 1875.

Emerton, J. H. "Life on the Seashore." Salem, U.S.A., 1880.

Engel, Arth. "Procédé de M. Westring, à Gothembourg, pour la conservation des araignées," *Feuille des jeunes Naturalistes*, 5. année (1874-75), pp. 79, 80. Paris.

Enys, J. D. "An Account of the Maori Manner of preserving the Skin of the Huia, Heteralocha acutirostris, Buller," *Trans. and Proc. New Zealand Inst.* vol. viii. (1875), pp. 204, 205. Wellington, 1876.

Evans, P. "L'art de préparer, monter et conserver les Oiseaux." Paris, 1841; second edition, 1850.

For German translation see Brehm.

Faccialà, Luigi. "Nuovo mezzo di preparare scheletri delicati." Messina, 1880.

Farez, ... "Emploi du silicate de potasse pour donner de la solidité aux ossements fossiles," *Compt. Rend.* tom. lxx. (1870), pp. 1094, 1095. Paris.

Fatio, P., "L'oomètre." (Illustrated.) *Bull. d. l. Soc. Ornith. Suisse,* tom. i. (1865-66), pp. 94-110.

Fauvel, Albert. "Méthodes de chasse. Préparation et conservation des collections," *Annuaire Entomol.* for 1873, pp. 99-103; for 1874, pp. 116-119; for 1875, pp. 112-116; for 1876, pp. 123, 124; for 1877, pp. 119-123; for 1878, pp. 109-113; for 1879, pp. 108-115; for 1880, pp. 116, 117.

Feddersen, A. "Vejledning til at samle og præparere Naturgjenstande." Copenhagen, 1865.

Flemyng, William W. "Observations on Egg-blowing," *Zoologist,* 3rd ser. vol. iii. (1879), pp. 178, 179. London.

Flower, William Henry. "On the Preparation of Skeletons for Museum Purposes," *Zoologist,* 3rd ser. vol. i. (1877), pp. 465-468. London.

Forster, J. R. "Short Directions for Collecting, Preserving, and Transporting all Kinds of Natural History Curiosities," *Catalogue of the Animals of North America.* London, 1771.

Fredericq, Léon. "Communication préalable sur quelques procédés nouveaux de préparation des pièces anatomiques sèches," *Bull.de l'acad. roy. de Belgique,* 2. sér. tom. xli. (1876), pp. 1319-1325. Brussels.

Fürnrohr, Aug. Emil. "Anleitung zum Anlegen von Naturaliensammlungen für Anfänger." Augsburg, 1852.

Gallenstein, Meinrad von. "Kurze Anleitung für Studirende zum Sammeln und Conserviren der verschiedenartigen Naturalien behufs der Anlegung kleiner Sammlungen." Klagenfurt, 1854.

Gannal, J. N. "Histoire des embaumemens et de la préparation des pièces d'anatomie normale," etc. Paris, 1841.

Gardner, James. "Taxidermy." London, first edition, N.D. [? 1865]; fourth edition (enlarged), 1870. (Illustrated.)

——— "Taxidermy." (Champion Handbooks.) London, 1869.

Geire, Johann Daniel. "De vernice ad conservanda insecta animalia," *Miscell. Acad. Nat. Curios.* annus viii. (Dec. 2, 1689), pp. 297, 298. Nuremberg, 1690.

Gentile, P. "Taxidermie," *Dictionnaire Pittoresque Naturelle*, vol. ix. pp. 271-288. Paris, 1830-1839.

Geoffroy St. Hilaire, Isidore. "Zoological Instructions of the Royal Academy of Sciences, Paris, for the Scientific Expedition to the North of Europe," *New Phil. Journ.* xxviii. pp. 53-72. Edinburgh and London, 1840.

Gérardin, de M. Seb. "Tableau élémentaire d'Ornithologie." Paris, first edition, 1806; second edition, 1821. (Illustrated.)

Gerlach, Leo. "Ueber die Herstellung anatomischer Präparate nach der van Vetter'schen Glycerinmethode," *Sitzungsber. d. phys.-medic. Societ. Erlangen.* 11. Hft. (1878-79), pp. 205-210. Erlangen, 1879.

Gestro, R. "Manuale dell' Imbalsamatore (Preparatore Tassidermista)." Milan, 1883. Second edition, 1892. (Illustrated.)

——— (See Issel, A.)

Giacomini, C. "Nuovo processo per la conservazione del cervello." Turin, 1878.

[Gill, C. T.] "On Preserving the Skins of Birds, Beasts, and other Animals, and the Bill of the Toucan." By C. Waterton (*i.e.* as practised by Waterton). *Technical Repository*, vol. v. pp. 250, 251. London, 1824.

Gissler, Carl F. "Salicylic Acid as a Preservative," *Psyche*, vol. i. No. 25 (1876), p. 168.

Glasl, Carl. "Excursionsbuch, oder Anleitung alle Körper der drei Naturreiche zu sammeln. Wien, Braumüller, 1863. (Illustrated.)

Glasl, ... "Ueber das Anlegen von Naturaliensammlungen als Hilfsmittel bei dem Unterrichte in der Naturgeschichte," *Schulprogramm der Ober-Realschule am Schottenfeld.* Vienna, 1855.

——— "Ueber Präpariren der Amphibien und ueber Schmetterlingsabdrücke," *Schulprogramm der Ober-Realschule am Schottenfeld.* Vienna, 1863.

Goadby, Hnr. "On the Preservation of Animal Substances," *Proc. Amer. Assoc. Adv. Sc.* 6th Meeting (1851). Washington, 1852.

Godwin, Harry P. "A Scene from Montana" (a mounted group of Bisons in the U.S. National Museum), *The Star.* Washington, 10th March, 1888. (See also *Report Smithsonian Institution*.)

Gordack, Walter. "Ein Wink für die Einrichtung einer Eiersammlung," *Isis* (Russ.), 3. Jahrg. (1878), pp. 125, 126. Berlin.

Granger, Albert. "De la préparation et de la conservation des coquilles," *Naturaliste*, No. 13 (1879), pp. 102, 103. Paris.
—————— "Manuel du Naturaliste." Paris. (Illustrated.)
Graves, George. "Instructions for Preserving Mammals and Birds." (Illustrated.) *The Naturalist's Pocket Book or Tourist's Companion.* London, 1818.

> Collecting mammals, pp. 43-56; birds, pp. 128-135.

—————— "The Naturalist's Companion." London, 1824. (Illustrated.)
Green, Wm. "Remarks upon the Preservation of Animals," *Trans. Tyneside Nat. Field Club*, vol. v. (part 2, 1861), pp. 104-110. Newcastle-upon-Tyne, 1863.
Greenwood, F. "On the Preservation of the Bodies of the larger Animals for Dissection," *Report 45th Meeting British Assoc. Adv. Sc.* (1875), Notic. pp. 167-169. London, 1876.
Gronov, Joh. Fried. "A Method of Preparing Specimens of Fish, by Drying their Skins," *Philos. Trans.* 1742, p. 57. London.
Grotrian, R. "Prakt. Anweisung zum Ausstopfen von Vögeln und Säugethieren." Leipzig, first edition, 1886 ; fourth edition, 1892. (Illustrated.)
Guerne, Jules de. "Conservation des Limaces," *Feuill. d. jeun. natural.* 2. année (1871-72), p. 72. Paris.
Günther, Dr. Albert. "British Birds and their Nests." (Illustrated.) *Good Words*, April 1891, pp. 251-259, and June, pp. 383-391. London.
Hahn, C. W. "Gründl. Anweis. Krustenthiere, Vielfüsse, Asseln, Arachniden, und Insecten . . . zu sammeln, zu präpariren," etc. Nuremberg, first edition, 1834 ; second edition, 1854.
Hallock, C. "Backwoods Taxidermy," *Sportsman's Gazetteer*, pp. 652-656. New York, 1877.
Hamilton, D. J. "A Text-book of Pathology," pp. 43-76, 715-719. London and New York, 1889. (Illustrated.)
Hammargren, T. "Om foglarnas uppstoppning och förvarande," *Inledning till Foglarnes Natural Historia.* Stockholm, 1859.
Harding, S. "Amateur Taxidermy," *Amateur Trapper and Trapmakers' Guide.* New York, 1875.
Harrach, Aug. "Das Fangen, Tödten und Aufbewahren der Reptilien und Amphibien," *Isis* (Russ.), 4. Jahrg. (1879), pp. 4, 5, 47, 48, 94, 95, 143, 144, 150-152. Berlin.

Harting, J. E. "Hints on Shore Shooting." London, 1871. (Illustrated.)

Haupt, H. "Hints upon the Preparation of Zoological Specimens," *Literary Record and Journal, Linnæan Association of Penn. College*, i. pp. 38-41. Pennsylvania, U.S.A., 1845.

Hazelhurst, H. H. (See anonymous work at end : "Directions," etc.)

Held, A. "Demonstrative Naturgeschichte." Stuttgart, 1845. (Illustrated.)

Hénon, —, et Mouton-Fontenille [J. P.] "Observations et Expériences sur l'art d'empailler et de conserver les Oiseaux." Lyons, 1801. Second edition, 1802.

Hermann, Johann Gotthelf, and Reichel, Johann Daniel. "De modo cavendæ corruptionis corporum naturalium in museis." Leipzig, 1766.

Héron-Royer. "Préparation de petits squelettes," *Feuill. d. jeun. natural.* 7. année (1876-77), p. 23. Paris.

Hesse, Paul. "Das Konserviren der kaltblütigen Wirbelthiere," *Isis* (Russ.), 4. Jahrg. (1879), pp. 190-192. Berlin.

Higgins, H. H. "Life-History Groups," *Report Museums Assoc.* (England), pp. 49-56. York and Sheffield, 1891.

Holder, J. B. "Taxidermy," *Johnson's Universal Cyclopædia*, iv. p. 741. New York, 1878.

———— "Address," *Third Annual Report Soc. of Amer. Taxidermists* (1882-83), pp. 39-51. Washington, U.S.A., 1884.

———— R. H. "Taxidermy." (Illustrated.) *Trans. Ill. Nat. History Society*, vol. i. (1861), pp. 69-75. Springfield, 1862.

Embodied also in *Trans. Ill. State Agriculture Society*, iv., for 1859-1860.

Hornaday, William Temple. "How to Skin a Bird," *Western Farm Journal*. Des Moines, Iowa, 1874.

———— "Directions for Preparing Skins for Museum Specimens." 1877.

Issued for private circulation by Battle Creek College, Mich., 1877.

H.[ornaday], W. T. "Ten Commandments for the Hunter Naturalist," *Ward's Nat. Sci. Bull.* No. 1. Rochester, U.S.A., 1881.

———— "On the Uses of Clay as a Filling Material," *Second Annual Report Soc. of Amer. Taxidermists* (1881-1882), pp. 31-34. Rochester, U.S.A., 1882.

Hornaday, W. T. "A New and Easy Method of Mounting Fish Medallions," *Second Annual Report Soc. of Amer. Taxidermists* (1881-1882), pp. 38-41. Rochester, U.S.A., 1882. (Illustrated.)

"W. T. H." [ornaday]. "Fifteen Commandments for the Taxidermist. Applying to Mammals," *Ward's Natural Science Bull.* No. 2. Rochester, U.S.A., 1882.

Hornaday, W. T. "The Cambridge Elephant," *Ward's Natural Science Bull.* No. 2. Rochester, U.S.A., 1882.

"W. T. H." [ornaday]. "How to Soften Dry Bird Skins," *Ward's Natural Science Bull.* No. 2. Rochester, U.S.A., 1882.

Hornaday, W. T. "Every Boy His Own Taxidermist," *Mastery*, vol. i. eight chapters, pp. 131, 147, 167, 185, 337, 353, 369, 387. New York, 1883. (Illustrated.)

——— "Brief Directions for Removing and Preserving the Skins of Mammals." Appendix No. 22, *Proceedings U.S. Nat. Museum*, for 1883. Washington. (Illustrated.)

——— "Common Faults in the Mounting of Quadrupeds," *Third Annual Report Soc. of Amer. Taxidermists* (1882-83), pp. 67-71. Washington, U.S.A., 1884.

——— "How to Collect Mammal Skins for Purposes of Study and for Mounting," *Report Smithsonian Institution* for 1886, Part II. Washington, 1889.

——— "Taxidermy and Zoological Collecting." London and New York, 1891. (Illustrated.)

Hough, Walter. "The Preservation of Museum Specimens from Insects and the Effects of Dampness," *Report Smithsonian Institution* for 1887, pp. 549-558. Washington, 1889.

Housman, Rev. Henry. "The Story of Our Museum." ("Bird-stuffing," chaps. iii. and iv.) London and New York, 1881. (Illustrated.)

Howse, H. G. ["Ueber Conservirung anatomischer Präparate"], *Guy's Hosp. Reports*, 3. sér. vol. xx. (1875), p. 569.

——— ["Ueber Anwendung des Chloral zur Conservirung anatomischer Präparate"], *Guy's Hosp. Reports*, 3. sér. vol. xxi. (1876), p. 429.

Hume, A. "The Indian Ornithological Collector's Vade Mecum." Calcutta and London, 1874.

Huxley, W. "How to Skin Mammals, Prepare Skins, and make Rough Skeletons, and How to Skin Birds," *New England Journal of Education.* Reprinted also in an issue, for private circulation, by Battle Creek College, Mich., 1877.

Ingpen, A. "Instructions for collecting," etc. London. First edition, 1827. Third edition, 1843.

Issel, A., and Gestro, R. "Manuale del Naturalista Viaggiatore." Milan, 1883. (Illustrated.)

Jager, Wolfgang. (See Turgot, 1761.)

[Jencks, F. T.] "Instructions for making Bird Skins." Southwick and Jencks' *Catalogue of Bird Skins and Eggs,* 1883.

[———] "Colour of Birds' Eyes." "How to Soften an Owl's Foot," *Random Notes on Natural History,* vol. i. p. 1. 1884.

[———] "Value of Steam in Taxidermy," *Random Notes on Nat. Hist.* Feb. 2, 1884.

[———] "The Uses of Poisons," *Random Notes,* No. 4, vol. i. April 1884.

Jenks, J. W. P. "Hints for Preserving Skins of Mammals and Birds," *Fourteen Weeks in Zoology,* J. D. Steele. New York, 1877.

Junker, F. C. "Dianassologie." Hanau, 1825 ; second edition, 1832. (Illustrated.)

Kaltbrunner, D. "Les collections d'Oiseaux et de Mammifères," *Manuel du Voyageur.* Frauenfeld, 1879.

——— "Aide-Mémoire du Voyageur," etc. Zurich, 1881.

Kammerer. "Aërophytaxie. Nouvelle méthode de conservation des animaux sans mutilation." Paris, 1845.

Kazbundn, Th. E. "Der kleine Naturfreund," etc. Jičin, 1855.

Kiesenwetter, H. v., u. Reibisch., Th. "Der Naturalien-Sammler." Leipzig, 1876.

King, H. "Directions for making Collections in Natural History." Washington, U.S.A., 1840.

Kingsley, J. S. "The Naturalist's Assistant." Boston, U.S.A., 1882. Last edition, 1892. (Illustrated.)

Kjaerbölling, N. "Fuglenes Taxidermie," *Skandinaviens Fugle.* Copenhagen (1875), 1877.

Klautsch, M. "Konservationserfolge." *Isis* (Russ.), 4. Jahrg. (1879), pp. 78, 79. Berlin.

——— "Zum Wickersheimer'schen Konservirungsverfahren." *Isis* (Russ.), 4. Jahrg. (1879), p. 374. Berlin.

Klener, G. A., Chr.   "Anleitung zum Ausstopfen und Aufbewahren der Vögel und Säugethiere."   Göttingen, 1832.

Koch, G.   "Die Stellungen der Vögel," *Cabanis' Journ. f. Ornith.* 19. Jahrg. (1871), pp. 152, 153.

———   "Die Stellungen der Vögel. Für Präparatoren, Ausstopfer und Freunde der Vögel."   Heidelberg, 1871.   (Illustrated.)

———   The same, Part II., 1872.   (Illustrated.)

Kuckahn, T. S.   Four Letters to the President and Members of the Royal Society, on the Preservation of Dead Birds, *Philos. Trans.* for 1770, lx. pp. 302-320.   London, 1771.

Lang, Arnold.   "Ueber Conservation der Planarien," *Zoolog. Anzeiger.* 1. Jahrg. (1878), pp. 14, 15.   Leipzig.—Auszug., *Zeitschr. f. Mikroskop.* (E. Kaiser), 1. Jahrg. 9. Hft. (1878), p. 286.   Berlin. Abstract: "Preservation of Planaria," *Journ. R. Microsc. Soc.* vol. i. (1878), pp. 256, 257.   London.

Larousse, P.   "Taxidermie," *Grand Dictionnaire Universelle du XIX. Siècle,* vol. xiv.   Paris, 1875.

Lataste, F.   "Préparation des squelettes délicats."   (Extrait.)   *Guide du Naturaliste* (Bouvier), 2. année (1880), pp. 31, 32.

———   "Procédé facile pour la préparation des squelettes délicats," *Act. Soc. Linn. d. Bordeaux,* tom. xxx. (3. sér. t. 10), 1875, pp. 166-170.   Paris and Bordeaux.

———   "Sur un procédé facile pour préparer les squelettes délicats." (Extrait du procès-verbal.)   *Assoc. franç. p. l'avanc. d. sc. Comp. Rend. de la 5 Sess.* (1876), p. 543.   Paris, 1877.   *Arch. Sc. phys. et nat. Genève,* nouv. période, tom. lviii. (1877), pp. 111, 112.

Lecocq, H., et Boisduval, A.   "Taxidermie."   Paris, 1826.   (Illustrated.)

Lee, Arthur Bolles.   "The Microtomist's Vade Mecum."   London, first edition, 1885; third edition, 1893.

Lee, Mrs. R.   "Taxidermy," sixth edition (revised and enlarged). London, 1843.
    See note to anonymous work [Dufresne, L.] at end: "Taxidermy," etc.

Lemaire, F., and Prévost, C. L.   "De la Chasse et de la Préparation des Oiseaux."   (Illustrated.)   "Histoire Naturelle des Oiseaux." Paris [1837].

Le Roye.   "Traité de Taxidermie."   Paris, 1879.   (Illustrated.)

Lesson, R. P.   "Manuel de Taxidermie," *Annales Maritimes et Coloniales.* Paris, 1819.

——— "Taxidermie," *Dictionnaire Classique d'Histoire Naturelle,* vol. xvi. pp. 78-807. Paris, 1830.

——— "Taxidermie," *Dictionnaire des Sciences Naturelles,* vol. lii. pp. 353-436. Strasbourg and Paris, 1828.

Lessona, M. (See Eger.)

Lettsom, John Coakley. "The Naturalist and Traveller's Companion." First edition, London, 1773; second (corrected and enlarged), 1774; third, 1799. (Illustrated.)

Translated into both French and German. Most of the Taxidermy (about four pages) is credited to Kuckahn's letters in the *Philos. Trans.* 1771.

——— "A Method of Preserving Birds and other Animals." From the *Philosophical Transactions,* recommended by Dr. Lettsom in his "Traveller's Companion," p. 13, *Appendix, Coll. Mass. Hist. Society.* Boston, U.S.A., 1795.

Leven, F. R. "Anweisung zum Abbalgen, Ausstopfen und Conserviren der Vögel, Säugethiere, Fische und Amphibien." Heidelberg, 1844.

Lewis, Elisha J. "Some Hints on Taxidermy," in "Hints to Sportsmen," by E. J. Lewis. Philadelphia, 1851; second edition, 1854. Also in "American Sportsman," p. 456. West Minden, Conn., and New York, 1855.

A short chapter on skinning birds credited to Lee's (*i.e.* Dufresne's) *Taxidermy.*

Linnæus. "Instructio Musei Rerum Naturalium." Upsal. 1753; second edition, 1787. Also in "Amœnit. Acad." vol. iii. 1756.

Llofrier, M. "Taxidermia. Manual práctico." Madrid, 1885.

Lo Bianco. (For title see footnote, p. 26.)

Lovén, ... "Conservirungsmethode für anatomische Präparate," *Hygiea,* xxxv. (1874), 2, 3, 4. *Svenska läkaresällsk. Förhandl.* 1873, s. 30, 33, 58.

Löwe [Johann Carl Christian]. "Vermischte naturhistorische Bemerkungen 1) 2) 3) 4) vom Aufbewahren der Vögel," *Naturforsch. Gesellschaft zu Halle,* B. 1, N. St. 21, 134. Halle, 1783.

Lucas, F. A. "A Critique on Museum Specimens," *Second Annual Report Soc. of Am. Taxidermists* (1881-82), pp. 34-37. Rochester, U.S.A., 1882.

"F. A. L" [ucas]. "Hints about Making Bird Skins," *Ward's Nat. Sci. Bull.* No. 2. Rochester, U.S.A., 1882.

Lucas, F. A. "How to Mount a Bird," *Sport with Rod and Gun.* New York, 1883.

—— "The Scope and Needs of Taxidermy," *Third Annual Report Soc. of Amer. Taxidermists* (1882-83), pp. 51-58. Washington, U.S.A., 1884.

—— "On the Mounting of Crustaceans," *Third Ann. Rep. Soc. Amer. Tax.* pp. 74-77. Washington, U.S.A., 1884.

—— "On the Mounting of Turtles," *Ibid.* pp. 84-90.

Macartney, J. "On the Means of preserving Animal and Vegetable Substances." *Rep. Brit. Ass. Adv. Sci.*, 6th Meeting (1836). London, 1837.

M'Intosh, W. C. "On the Preservation of Annelids," *Zoolog. Anzeiger.* 1. Jahrg. (1878), p. 179. Leipzig.

—— "Conservation des Annélides," *Bull. scientif. du départ. du Nord,* 2. sér. 2. année (1879), pp. 47, 48. Lille, 1880. (*Zoolog. Anzeiger.*)

—— "De la conservation des Annélides." (Extrait.) *Guide du Naturaliste* (Bouvier), 1. année (1879), p. 56. Paris.

M'Murrich, P. (For title see footnote, p. 26.)

Maigne. (See Boitard, 1890.)

Manesse, l'Abbé Den. Jos. "Traité sur la manière d'empailler et de conserver les animaux et les pelleteries." Paris, 1786.

Manton, W. P. "Taxidermy without a Teacher." Framingham and New York, 1876. (Illustrated.) Second edition (revised and enlarged), Boston, U.S.A., 1882.

Martin, Philipp Leopold. "Ueber gewerckmässiges Sammeln und Aufstellen von Thieren der höheren Klassen in Sammlungen," *Naumannia,* 6. Jahrgang (1856), pp. 485-500. Dessau and Leipzig, 1856.

—— "Conservirmittel für naturhistorische Gegenstände," *Cabanis' Journ. f. Ornith.* 11. Jahrg. (1863), pp. 137-144.

—— "Kurze Anleitung zum Sammeln naturhistorischer, vorzüglich zoologischer Gegenstände; in Uebereinstimmung mit H. Ploucquet bearbeitet (von L. Martin)." *Cabanis' Journ. f. Ornith.* 11. Jahrg. (1863), pp. 144-153.

Martin, Philipp Leopold. "Nöthige Vorkehrungen inbetreff der Ankunft neuangekaufter Thiere," *Isis* (Russ.), 3. Jahrg. (1878), pp. 107, 108, 115, 116. Berlin.

—— "Die Praxis der Naturgeschichte."
    1. Thl., "Taxidermie." (Illustrated.) Weimar, 1869 ; second edition, 1876 ; third edition (revised by Leopold and Paul Martin), Weimar, 1886. (With Atlas of Illustrations.)
    2. Thl., "Dermoplastik und Museologie." Weimar, 1870 ; second edition (revised and enlarged), 1880. (Illustrated.)

—— " Die Versendung frisch erlegter Vögel zur heissen Jahreszeit," *Ornith. Centralbl.* 1. Jahrg. 1876, pp. 21, 22.

—— "Die Anwendung des Arseniks und andrer Stoffe bei der Naturalien-Präparation in gesundheitlicher Beziehung," *Ornith. Centralbl.* 1879 (No. 5), pp. 33-35.

Maruye. "Méthode nécessaire aux marins et aux voyageurs, pour recueillir avec succès les curiosités de l'histoire naturelle." Paris, 1763. (Illustrated.)

Mauduyt, de la Varenne, Pierre Jean Etienne. "Mémoire sur la manière de se procurer les différentes espèces d'animaux." (Extr. du Journal de Physique de Rozier.) Paris, 1771. (Illustrated.)

—— "Mémoire sur la manière de preparer les Oiseaux morts," *Encyclopédie Méthodique, Histoire Naturelle des Oiseaux*, vol. cxvi. (1782), pp. 434-468. Paris and Liège.

Maunder, S. "A Syllabus of Practical Taxidermy," *The Treasury of Natural History, or a Popular Dictionary of Zoology*. London, 1858.

Mawe, John. "The Voyager's Companion." London, third edition, 1821 ; fourth edition, 1825. (Illustrated.)

Maynard, C. J. "The Naturalist's Guide." Boston, U.S.A., and London, 1870 ; second edition, 1884. (Illustrated.) Revised edition, Salem, Mass., 1877.

—— "A Manual of Taxidermy." Boston, U.S.A., 1883 ; second edition, 1884. (Illustrated.)

—— "Taxidermy for Beginners." Boston, 1883.

Méhu, Adolphe. "De la préparation des Limaces pour les collections d'histoire naturelle," *Feuill. d. jeun. natural.* 3. année (1872-73), pp. 25-27. Paris.

Melsheimer, ... "Ueber das Conserviren der Fische, Amphibien und Reptilien in Petroleum," *Verhandl. d. naturhist. Ver. d. preuss. Rheinl. u. Westphal.* 34. Jahrg. (4. Folg. 4 Jahrg.), 1877. Corrspbl. pp. 99, 100. Bonn.

Meyer, A. B. "Wickersheimersche Präparate," *Sitzungsber. d. Ges. f. Natur- u. Heilk.* Dresden (1879-80), 1880, p. 19.

Meyer [Joh. Carl Fried.] "Vom Nutzen des Salmiaks bei Ausstopfung der Vögel," *Beschäftigungen der Berliner Gef. Naturf. Fr.* B. i. (1775), S. 423.

Mojsisovics, A. "Leitfaden bei zool.-zoot. Präparirübungen." Leipzig, 1885.

Mörch, O. A. S. "Method for killing Terrestrial Pulmoniferous Mollusks for the Purposes of Anatomical Research." Translated in *Americ. Journ. Conchol.* vol. iv. (1868), p. 281.

——— "Procédé pour touer les Mollusques pulmonés terrestres dont on veut pratiquer l'anatomie," *Journ. de Conchyl.* tom. xvi. (1868), p. 350.

Morosoff, G. L. "Kurze Anleitung zur Präparation der Thiere für Sammlungen, oder Darstellung der Hilfsmittel zum Ausstopfen der Thiere, Herstellung von Skeletten u. Insektensammlungen." 2. Aufl.

Mouton-Fontenille, J. P. 1801. (See Hénon.)

——— "L'Art d'Empailler les Oiseaux." Lyons, 1811. (Illustrated.)

M[urr], C. G. v. "Von der besten Art, Vögel in Sammlungen aufzubehalten. Aus dem Gentleman's Magazin vom 1772," *Naturforscher*, i. pp. 262, 263. Halle, 1774.

Naumann, Joh. Fr. "Taxidermie." Halle, 1815; second edition, 1848. (Illustrated.)

Neumayr. "Anleitung zu wissenschaftlichen Beobachtungen auf Reisen." 2 Bde. Berlin, 1888.

Newman, Edward. "Birds-Nesting and Bird-Skinning." London, 1862; second edition, 1888. (Illustrated.)

Newton, Alfred. "Anweisung zur Anlegung von Eiersammlungen," *Cabanis' Journ. f. Ornith.* 8. Jahrg. (1860), pp. 447-459. Also separate, Cassel, 1861.

——— "Instructions aux collecteurs d'œufs d'oiseaux," *Rev. et Mag. zool.* 2. sér. tom. xiv. (1862), pp. 285-292, 319-331. Paris.

Newton, Alfred. "Suggestions for forming Collections of Birds' Eggs," *Zoologist*, vol. xviii. (1860), pp. 7189-7201. Also separate, London, 1860.

Nicolas, Pierre François. "Méthode de Préparer et Conserver les Animaux de toutes les classes." Paris, 1801. (Illustrated.)

North, Franklin H. "The Taxidermal Art" (illustrated), *The Century Illustrated Monthly Magazine*. London and New York, December 1882, pp. 230-239.

Oppermann. "Ausstopfen der Thiere," etc. Delmenhorst, 1835.

Oré, ... [Procédé pour la conservation du cerveau avec sa forme, son volume et sa couleur.] *Compt. Rend.* tom. lxxxv. (1877), pp. 1119, 1120. Paris.

Osiander, Friedr. Beng. "Abhandlung ueber das vortheilhafteste Aufbewahren thierischer Körper in Weingeist." Göttingen, 1793.

Osler, ... "Note on Giacomini's Method of Preserving the Brain," *Journ. of Anat. and Physiol.* vol. xiv. (1879), p. 144. London and Cambridge.

Owen, Sir Richard. "Instructions for Collecting and Preserving Invertebrate Animals," *Edinb. New Phil. Journ.* vol. xlvii. pp. 280-292. Edinburgh and London, 1849.

Pacius, G. F. "Zur vortheilhafte Arten Vögel und kleine vierfüssige Thiere auszustopfen," *Naturforscher*, ii. (1774), pp. 87-89. Halle.

Pagenstecher, H. Alex. "Ueber Aufstellung der Quallen in den Museen," *Zeitschr. f. wiss. Zool.* 17. Bd. Hft. 2. (1867), pp. 379, 380. Leipzig.

—— "Demonstration eines neuen Verfahrens zur Aufbewahrung zarter zoologischer Gegenstände und Präparate in konservirenden Flüssigkeiten," *Verh. d. naturhist.-medicin. Ver. Heidelberg*, 4 Bd. (1865-68), p. 202. Heidelberg, 1868.

Pagliari. "Nouveau procédé pour la conservation, à l'air libre, des substances animales," *Compt. Rend.* tom. lviii. (1864), p. 258; tom. lix. (1864), p. 32. Paris.

Patti, Mario Zuccarello. "Metodo facile per formare gli occhi artificiali di cristello," *Atti Accad. Gioenia*, ser. 2, vol. viii. p. 111. Catania, 1853.

—— "Su varii metodi di preservazione per l'impagliamento degli Uccelli," *Atti Accad. Gioenia*, ser. 2, viii. 141. Catania, 1853.

Pearson, J. T. "Hints for the Preservation of Objects of Natural History," *Jour. of the Asiat. Soc. of Bengal,* vol. iv. pp. 462-471. Calcutta, 1835.

Peck, Wm. D. "Mr. Peck's Method of Preserving Animals and their Skins," *Appendix, Coll. Mass. Hist. Society.* Boston, U.S.A., 1795.

Pidsley, W. E. H. "Collecting and Preserving Birds." Birmingham, 1891.

Pinel, Phil. "Mémoire sur les moyens de préparer et de conserver les quadrupèdes et les oiseaux destinés à former des collections, etc.," *Journal de Physique,* tome xxxix. Paris, 1791.

—— "Les Préparations Ornithologiques." Paris, 1793.

Pistorius, Geo. [Geo. Bekker]. "Anleit. zum Ausstopfen und Aufbewahren der Vögel und Säugethiere." Darmstadt, 1799.

Plateau, F. "Note sur un procédé pour donner ou pour rendre leur couleur rouge aux muscles conservés dans l'alcool." Bruxelles, Hayez, 1874. (? Extrait.)

Plessis, G. du. "Note sur l'emploi du permanganate et du bichromate de potasse pour préparer et conserver des animaux marins délicats," *Bull. Soc. Vaud. Sc. nat. Lausanne,* tom. xv. No. 79, (1878), pp. 278, 280. Lausanne. Trans. by W. H. Dalton in *Science Gossip,* 1879, No. 171. London.

—— "Nouvelle méthode pour injecter facilement certains animaux inférieurs," *Bull. Soc. Vaudoise Sc. nat.,* vol. xi. (1871-73), pp. 212-214. Lausanne, 1874.

Plœm, J. C. "Mededeeling over eene vloeistof uitgevonden door Wickersheimer voor het conserveeren van voorwerpen uit het planten- en dierenrijk," *Natuurk. Tijdschr. Nederl. Indië,* 39 Deel (7. ser. g. D.), 1880, pp. 145-151. Batavia.

Power, Wilmot H. T. "Preservation of Objects of Natural History," *Ann. Mag. Nat. Hist.,* 4. ser. vol. i. 1868, p. 153. London.

Prévost, Florent, et Lemaire, C. L. "De la Chasse, et de la préparation des Oiseaux," *Histoire Naturelle des Oiseaux.* Paris, 1863.

Quimby, J. H. (See anonymous work at end: "Directions," etc.)

Race, H. T. Some Treatise upon Taxidermy, in Danish; title not discovered. 1842.

Rathbun, S. F. "How to make a good Bird Skin," *Third Annual Rep. Soc. Amer. Taxidermists* (1882-83), pp. 82-84. Washington, U.S.A., 1884.

Réaumur, René Antoine Ferchault de. " Divers means for preserving
from corruption dead birds intended to be sent to remote countries,
so that they may arrive there in good condition. Some of the
same means may be employed for preserving Quadrupeds, Reptiles,
Fishes, and Insects." Translated from the French by Phil.
Henry Zollman, Esq., F.R.S. *Philos. Trans.* xlv. 1748.

Relph, R. "Rise and Progress of Taxidermy." Read before the
Barrow Naturalists' Field Club and Lit. and Scient. Assoc., 16th
November 1885. *Ann. Rep.* 1883-1890, p. 27. Barrow-in-
Furness.

Report Smithsonian Institution, 1887. Mounted Group (of Bisons, etc.)
in the National Museum. (Illustrated, Plate I.), pp. 546-548.
Washington, 1889.

Richter, E. G. "Vögel auszustopfen nebst allen dazu erforderlichen
Hülfsmitteln." Mit Vorrede von Brehm. Jena, 1829.
(Illustrated.)

—— Dr. H. "Ueber die Anwendung der Schwefelblumen zum
Ausstopfen der Thiere," *Oken's Isis,* vol. xxx. (1837), pp. 520-522.
Jena.

[Versammlung der Naturforscher und Aerzte zu Jena. (Sechste Sitzung am 25
Sept. 1836).]

Ridgway, Robert. "Directions for Collecting Birds." (Illustrated.)
Part A, *Bulletin U.S. National Museum,* No. 39. Washington,
1891.

Riep, ... "Ueber das Conserviren der Thierbälge, *Isis* (Russ.),
3. Jahrg. (1878), pp. 28, 29, 44, 45. Berlin.

Rochebrune, Dr. A. T. de. (See Capus, 1883.)

Rolleston, ... "Note on the Preservation of Encephala by the
Zinc Chloride," *Journ. of Anat. and Physiol.* vol. xiii. (1879), pp.
232, 233. London and Cambridge.

Römer. (See [Donovan, E.].)

Round, O. S. "Bird-preserving." (Illustrated.) *Recreative Science,*
vol. i. (1860), pp. 117-120. London.

Roux, P. "d'Ornithologie Provençale suivie d'un Abrégé des chasses,
de quelques instructions de Taxidermie." Marseilles, 1825.

Schauenburg, ... "Eine Methode, zerbrochene Vogeleier für die

Sammlung zu repariren," *Verh. d. Ver. f. naturwiss. Unterhalt. Hamburg*, 4. Bd. (1876), p. 25. 1879.

Schilling, Dr. W. "Hand- und Lehrbuch für angehende Naturforscher und Naturaliensammler," 3. Bd. Weimar, 1860-1861.

Schmeling, C. "Das Ausstopfen und Conservieren der Vögel und Säugethiere." Berlin, first edition, 1871; twelfth edition, 1893. (Illustrated.)

Schmidt, Chs. Fr. "Versuch ueber die beste Einrichtung zur Aufstellung der verschiedener Naturkorper, etc." Gotha, 1818.

—— J. F. "Answer to the query in our last number on preserving birds and other subjects of natural history," *Technical Repository*, vol. v. pp. 166, 167. London, 1824.

Schultze, Christian Friedrich. "De sicca corporum animalium conservatione quædam exponit." Leipzig, 1741.

—— "De sicca corporum animalium conservatione." Leipzig, 1751.

Schulze, F. E. "Ueber Conservirung von Cœlenteraten," *Tagebl. d.* 44 *Vers. deutsch. Naturf.* 1871, pp. 53, 54. Rostock.

—— "Ueber das Präpariren von Quallen und Hydroidpolypen," *Arch. d. Ver. Freund. Naturgesch. Mecklenburg*, 26. Jahrg. (1873), pp. 107, 108.

Sharpe, R. Bowdler. "Ornithology at South Kensington." (Illustrated.) *The English Illustrated Magazine*, December 1887, pp. 165-175. London.

—— "The Young Collector's Handbook of British Birds." London. N.D. (Illustrated.)

Shufeldt, R. W. "Scientific Taxidermy for Museums." Report of the U.S. National Museum, *Report Smithsonian Institution* for 1892, pp. 369-436. Washington, 1893.

Sinclair, J. "Preserving of Birds," etc. *Edinb. Philos. Journ.* xi. (1824), p. 415.

Sömmering, Sam. Thom von. "Versuche u. Betrachtungen ueber die Verschiedenheit der Verdünstungen des Weingeistes durch Häute von Thieren, etc.," 3. Abhandl. *Denks. Bay. Acad. Wissens.* Bd. 3. Jahrg. 1811 and 1812. Munich, 1813-25.

Stables, Gordon. "The Boy's Own Museum," *The Boy's Own Paper*. London, 1881.

Stables, Gordon. "Reptiles and Fishes: How to Stuff and Set them Up," *The Boy's Own Paper*, 1883, pp. 139, 158, 159, 254, 255, 287, 288. London.

Stæbner, F. W. "Note on the Value of Animal Illustrations to Taxidermists," *Third Annual Report Soc. of Amer. Taxidermists*, (1882-83), pp. 72-74. Washington, U.S.A., 1884.

Stein, P. S. "Handbuch des Zubereitens und Aufbewahrens der Thiere." Frankfurt a. M. 1802. (Illustrated.)

Sterzel, T. "Ein Mittel, Amphibien zu conserviren," 6. *Bericht d. naturwiss. Ges. Chemnitz.* (1875-77), pp. 61, 62. Chemnitz, 1878.

Stetson, E. J. "Additions to Newton Dexter's Article," *American Sportsman*, iii. (1874), pp. 396.

Stevens, S. "Hints to Naturalists." *Wrinkles, or Hints to Sportsmen and Travellers*, by A. H. Levison. London, 1868.

The compilation of the chapter on preserving specimens and trophies is credited to Stevens by the author of the book.

Stieda, Ludw. "Ueber die Van Vetter'sche Methode zur Herstellung anatomischer Präparate," *Reichert u. Du Bois R.'s Arch. f. Anat.* 1872, pp. 503-508.

Stollas, M. B. "Instructions on the Manner of Preparing Objects of Natural History." Paris, 1752. (Illustrated.)

Stradling, Dr. "How to Skin, Stuff, and Mount a Bird in Five Minutes," *The Boy's Own Paper*, 1883, pp. 331, 332, London; and *Harper's Young People*, iv. p. 630. London, 1883.

———— "What to do with a Dead Snake," *The Boy's Own Paper*, 1883, pp. 334, 335, 351, 363. London.

Strenbel. "Der Konservator oder praktische Anweisung," etc. Berlin, 1845.

Suckow, Fried. Wilh. Ludw. "Vademecum für Naturaliensammler." Stuttgart, 1830. (Illustrated.)

———— "Das Naturalien-Cabinet." Stuttgart, 1832. (Illustrated.)

Swainson, William. "Instructions for Collecting and Preserving all Subjects of Natural History and Botany." (Privately printed.) Liverpool, 1808.

———— "The Naturalist's Guide for Collecting and Preserving all

Subjects of Natural History and Botany. Intended for the use of Students and Travellers." London, 1822. (Illustrated.)

Swainson, William. "A Treatise on Taxidermy," *Lardner's Cabinet Cyclopædia of Natural History*, vol. cxxvi. London, 1840.

———— "Taxidermy." London, 1851.

Sylvester, S. H. "The Taxidermist's Manual." Middleboro, Mass., U.S.A., 1865. Fourth edition, 1874. London, 1868.

Tampellini, G. "La zootecnia, sua essenza e suo scopo," *Annuar. Soc. Naturalisti in Modena*, 2. ser. anno 9 (1875), pp. 81-93. Modena.

Tate, Ralph. "Collecting and Preserving (No. xi.) Land and Fresh-water Shells," etc., *Science Gossip* (1872), pp. 265-268. London, 1873.

Taylor, J. E. "Notes on Collecting and Preserving Natural History Objects." London, 1876.

Thompson, E. P. "Softening the Skins of Birds" (in ans. to J. A. H.), *Loudon's Mag. Nat. Hist.* iii. (1830), pp. 192, 193. London.

Thon, Theod. (See note to anonymous work at end: "Handbuch," etc.)

Traill, T. S. "On the Preservation of Zoological Specimens from the Depredations of Insects," *Edinb. Philos. Journ.* xiv. (1825), pp. 135-138.

Turgot, Étienne François. "Avis pour le transport par mer . . . de diverses . . . curiosités d'histoire naturelle," 2. edition. Paris, 1783.

[Turgot, E. F.] "Mémoire Instructif sur la Manière de Rassembler, de Préparer, de Conserver, et d'Envoyer les diverses Curiosités d'Histoire Naturelle." Paris and Lyons, 1758. (Illustrated.)

[Turgot.] "Anweisung, wie die verschied. Seltenheiten der Natur-geschichte zu sammlen, zu zubereiten, zu erhalten und zu ver-schicken sind." Translated by Wolfgang Jager. Nuremburg, 1761. (Illustrated.)

Ussher, R. J. "Suggestions on Egg-blowing," *Zoologist*, 3rd ser. vol. iii. (1879), pp. 218, 219. London.

Verrill, A. E. "Glycerine for Preserving Natural Colours of Marine Animals," *Americ. Naturalist*, vol. iii. (1870), p. 156. Salem, Mass.

———— "New Fluid for Preserving Natural History Specimens," *Americ. Journ. Sc. and Arts*, 2nd ser. vol. xli. (1866), pp. 268-

270. New Haven. *Ann. Mag. Nat. Hist.* 3rd ser. vol. xvii. (1866), pp. 385, 386. London. *Canad. Naturalist*, new ser. vol. iii. (1866-68), pp. 76-79. Montreal.

Verrill, A. E. ["A New Preservative Solution as a Substitute for Alcohol in the Preservation of Natural History Specimens"], *Proc. Boston Soc. Nat. Hist.* vol. x. (1864-66), pp. 257-259. Boston and London, 1866.

———— "Preservation of Starfishes with Natural Colours," *Americ. Journ. Sc. and Arts*, 2nd ser. vol. xxxix. (1865), p. 228. New Haven. *Ann. Mag. Nat. Hist.* 3rd ser. vol. xv. (1865), p. 436. London.

Voigt, H. "Das Sammeln von Schnecken u. Muscheln," *Isis* (Russ.), 4. Jahrg. (1879). I. Die Landschnecken, pp. 236, 243 ; II. Die Süsswasserschnecken u. Muscheln, pp. 275, 276. Berlin.

Walchner. "Der praktische Naturforscher. Abtheilungen." Karlsruhe, 1843.

Walker, C. A. "Hints on Taxidermy," *American Naturalist*, vol. iii. Three chapters, pp. 136, 189, and 481. Salem, Mass., 1870.

Wallace, J. R. "Preservation of Specimens," *Science Gossip* for 1871, pp. 151, 152. London, 1872.

Ward, Henry A. "Directions for Skinning Mammals [beasts of all kinds] and preparing their skins for stuffing for museums. Rochester, N.Y., U.S.A., 1874. (Illustrated.)

————, R. "The Sportsman's Handbook." First edition, London, 1880. (Illustrated.) Second edition (with numerous additional illustrations). London, 1882. Seventh edition, 1894.

———— "The Sportsman's Handbook." *The American Field.* Vol. xxi. (1884), pp. 329, 330, 353-355, 376, 377 ; continued.

A reprint of Mr. Ward's work, as a serial article.

Waterton, C. "On Preserving Birds for Cabinets of Natural History." *Wanderings in South America.* By Charles Waterton.

First edition, 1825 ; fourth edition, 1828 ; eighth edition, 1877 ; and a cheap edition in 1882. London. Latest edition (edited by Rev. J. G. Wood). London and New York, 1893. (Illustrated.)

———— "Preservation of Birds for Cabinets of Natural History," *Technological and Microscopical Repository*, vol. v. (1830).

From *Wanderings in South America.*

Waterton, C.   "Preserving the Colour of the Legs and Bills of Stuffed Birds," *Loudon's Mag. Nat. Hist.* vi. (1833), pp. 183, 184. London.

———   "Museums," *Essays on Natural History.*   First edition in three series, London, 1838, 1844, and 1857, respectively.

There were several editions of this book.   One was edited by N. Moore, London, 1871 [*i.e.* 1870].

Webster, F. S.   "On the Placing and Winding of Birds' Feathers." (Illustrated.)   *Second Annual Report Soc. Am. Taxidermists,* (1881-82), pp. 41-46.   Rochester, U.S.A., 1882.

———   "Taxidermy as a Decorative Art," *Third Annual Report Soc. of Amer. Taxidermists* (1882-83), pp. 59-67.   Washington, U.S.A., 1884.

———   "How to clean Soiled Bird Skins," *Ibid.* pp. 77-82.

Whitlock, Nathaniel.   "Skinning and Mounting of Birds, Beasts, and Fishes.   London, 1831.

Wiepken, C. F.   "Herstellung der künstlichen Vogelkörper aus leichterem Torf (Moostorf)," *Bericht über d. XIII. Vers. d. deutsch. Ornith. Ges. Stuttgart,* 1860, pp. 94, 95.

Wiley, Prof. J. S.   "The Preparation and Preservation of Objects of Natural History," 1855.

Willich, C. M.   "Letter on M. Gannal's Method of Preserving Animal Substances," *Proceedings Zoological Society,* xi. pp. 135, 136.   London, 1843.

Wood, Rev. J. G.   "Home of a Naturalist," *Out of Doors,* pp. 290-318.   London, 1874.

Contains a critique on Waterton's *Collection and Methods of Taxidermy.*

———   "The Boy's Own Museum," *The Boy's Own Paper.* London, 1883, pp. 687, 699, 710, 735, 747, 763, 782, 799, 814.

———   "Taxidermy.",   (Illustrated.)   Waterton's *Wanderings in South America.*   London and New York, 1893, pp. 497-510.

Wood, Samuel.   "The British Bird-preserver."   London, 1877.   Reprinted until now with same date, but with an Appendix, pp. 129-141, which must be later.   (Illustrated.)

Wood, William.   "Preparation of Birds' Eggs, *American Naturalist,* vol. iii. (1870), pp. 106, 107.   Salem, Mass.

Wood, William. "Instructions for Preparing Birds' Eggs," *American Naturalist*, vol. vi. (1872), pp. 281, 282. Salem, Mass.

[Woodbridge, W. C.]. "Short Directions for the Preparation, Preservation, and also the Transportation of Mammiferous and Amphibious Animals, Birds, Fishes, etc." Issued by the Senkenberg Institution for Natural History in Germany. Translated by W. C. Woodbridge. *Sillim's Am. Journ. Sci.* xix. (1831), pp. 32-57. New Haven, Conn.

Wright, T. Strethill. "Note on the Preservation of Minute Animals in Acetic Acid," *Journ. of Anat. and Phys.* vol. iv. (1870), p. 259. London and Cambridge.

Zincke, G. Gtfr. "Die Kunst allerhand natürliche Körper zu sammeln, zu zubereiten für das Kabinet und sie vor Zerstörung feindlicher Insecten zu sichern," vi. 159. Jena, 1802.

Zollmann, P. H. (See Réaumur.)

ANONYMOUS

"Aanwijzing omtrent de bewaring van voorwerpen, uit het rijk der dieren, planten en delfstoffen," *Natuurk. Tijdschr. Nederl. Indië*, Deel. xxiii. 413-432. Batavia and Gravenhage, 1861.

"Anweisung wie Naturalien zu sammeln, zu zubereiten, zu verpacken u. weit verschicken sind." Leipzig, 1788.

"On the Art of Preserving the Bodies of Animals in Fluids of Different Kinds," *Edinb. New Phil. Mag.* vi. pp. 160-166. Edinb. and Lond. 1829.

"The Art of Stuffing," *Natural Science*, July, 1894, pp. 58-60. London and New York.

"On the Art of Taxidermy," *Gleanings in Science*, vol. ii. Calcutta, 1830.

"Ueber das Ausstopfen der Vögel" (Ungarisch geschr.), *Schulprogramm.* Pápa, 1855.

"Ausstopfen," "Dermoplastik," *Brockhaus Illustrirtem Haus und Familie Lexikon.* Leipzig, 1860-1865.

"Ueber das Ausstopfen von Thieren," *Ausland*, 34. Jahrg. (1861), pp. 791, 792.

"Das Ausstopfen der Vögel," *Isis* (Russ.), 2. Jahrg. (1877), pp. 208-210. Berlin.

29

"Ausstopfer, der, oder in kurzer Zeit gut und natürlich Vögel ausstopfen zu lernen." Veranlasst durch einen Freund von F. A. C. J. Querfurth. 1827.

" Birds' Nests and Eggs and Bird-stuffing " (Beeton's Country Books, No. 2). London, 1877. (Illustrated.)

" Compendio di Tassidermia." Two vols. Milan, 1834. (Illustrated.)

A Translation of Boitard.

" Conservation des chenilles et des Limaces," *Feuill. d. jeun. natural.* 2. année (1871-72), pp. 95, 96. Paris.

"Conservation des fossiles par la gélatine," *Feuill. d. jeun. natural.* 4. année (1873-74), p. 36. Paris.

"Conservirungsflüssigkeit von Wickersheimer," *Zeitschr. f. Mikrosk.* (Kaiser-Brandt.), 2. Jahrg. (1879-80), pp. 192-194. Berlin.

" Directions for Collecting and Preserving Objects of Natural History." Issued by the Maryland Academy of Science and Literature. *Trans. Maryland Acad. Sci. and Lit.* vol. i. pp. 148-154. Baltimore, 1837.

Not signed, but credited to W. E. Coal, J. H. Quimby, and H. H. Hazlehurst in *Trans. Nat. M. Inst. Prom. Science.*

" Directions for Collecting, Preserving, and Transporting Specimens of Natural History." Prepared for the use of the Smithsonian Institution. Third edition, 1859. *Smiths. Miscellan. Collect.* vol. ii. (1862), art. viii.

"Erhaltung ganzer Thiere." *Aus. d. Natur.* 53. Bd. (N. F., 41. Bd.), 1870, p. 480.

" Glycerine for Preserving the Natural Colours of Marine Animals," *Monthl. Microsc. Journ.* vol. i. (1869), p. 370. London.

(D. B.) " Gründliche Anweisung Vögel auszustopfen und besonders gut zu conserviren." Leipzig, 1788. (Illustrated.)

"Handbuch für Naturaliensammlungen." Ilmenau, 1827 (Weimar). (Illustrated.)

Free Translation by Thon, Theod. (C. G.), of Boitard's "Manuel du Naturaliste Préparateur." Paris, 1825.

" Hints to Travellers," etc., *Royal Geographical Society of London.*

" History of Embalming and of Preparations in Anatomy and Natural History." Philadelphia, 1891.

" How to preserve Spiders," *Canad. Entomologist*, vol. ii. (1870), pp. 100, 101. (Nature.)

"Ichthy-Taxidermy," *The American Angler*, vol. v. (1884), p. 71. New York. Copied from *The Chronicle*, Raleigh, N. C.

"Instructions relative to Botany . . . and Zoology for the Scientific Expedition to the Antarctic Regions, prepared by the President and Council of the Royal Society," *Ann. Nat. Hist.* iv. pp. 33-43. London, 1840.

"Instruction sur les recherches qui pourroient être faites dans les Colonies, sur les objets qu'il seroit possible d'y recueillir, et sur la manière de les conserver et de les transporter," *Mém. du Mus. d'Hist. Nat.* iv. pp. 193-239. Paris, 1818.
> A series of papers compiled by the officers of the Museum.

"Instructions pour les voyageurs . . . sur la manière de recueillir, de conserver . . . les objets d'histoire naturelle . . . rédigée par l'administration du Muséum d'Hist. Nat." Paris, 1829.

"Instructions in Zoology . . . for the British Antarctic Expedition," *Edinburgh New Phil. Journ.* vol. xxviii. pp. 72-76. London and Edinburgh, 1840.

"Jumbo, A Description of the Mounting of." (Illustrated.) *Ward's N. S. Bulletin*, May 1886, pp. 10, 11. Also scattered articles in various Nos. of the *Bulletin*. Rochester, U.S.A.

" Konservationserfolge," *Isis* (Russ.), 4. Jahrg. (1879), pp. 338-340.

" Die Kunst Thiere auszustopfen." Quedlinburg, 1835 and 1854. (Illustrated.)
> A Translation by Bauer of Boitard's " Manuel du Naturaliste Préparateur," 1825.

GREAT BRITAIN AND IRELAND.—*Admiralty*. A manual of scientific enquiry ; prepared for the use of Her Majesty's Navy, and travellers in general. Edited by Sir J. F. W. Herschel. London, 1849.

—— Second edition. London.

—— Third edition. London, 1859.

—— Fourth edition. London, 1871.

—— Fifth edition. London, 1886.

" Manual of the Natural History, etc., of Greenland, prepared for the use of the Arctic Expedition of 1875." Edited by T. R. Jones. London, 1875.

"Neue Methode, kleine Thiere aufzubewahren," *Natur* (Müller), N. F. 4. Bd. (1878), p. 123.

"Notes on Collecting and Preserving Land and Fresh-Water Shells," by G. H. H., *Science Gossip* (1873), p. 101. London, 1874.

"Un nouveau liquide conservateur (de Wickersheimer)," *Journ. de Micrograph.* 4. année (1880), p. 90.

"Nouveau procédé pour la préparation de petits squelettes" (par J. de G.), *Feuill. d. jeun. natural.* 6. année (1875-76), pp. 154, 155.

"Préparation des squelettes des petits animaux par les insectes," *Feuill. d. jeun. natural.* 6. année (1875-76), p. 90. Paris.

"Préparation des squelettes des petits animaux par les insectes et les têtards." (Extrait.) *Guide du Naturaliste* (Bouvier), 1. année (1879), p. 92. Paris.

"On the Preservation of Anatomical Preparations." (Abstract.) *Americ. Journ. Sc. and Arts*, 3. ser. vol. x. (1875), pp. 155-157. New Haven.

"Recettes pour conserver les objets d'histoire naturelle (liquide de Wickersheimer)," *Feuill. d. jeun. natural.* 10. année (1879-80), p. 83. Paris.

"Recollage et conservation des fossiles," *Feuill. d. jeun. natural.* 4. année (1873-74), p. 35. Paris.

"Short Directions for Collecting and Preserving," *Trans. and Proc. Roy. Soc.*, South Australia, vol. iii. (1879-80), pp. 185-191. 1880.

"Ueber das Skelettiren von Reptilien und Amphibien," *Isis* (Russ.), 5. Jahrg. (1880), pp. 414, 415. Berlin.

"To Soften the Skins of Birds" (by "A. Z."), *Loudon's Mag. Nat. Hist.* iii. (1830), p. 93. London.

"Softening the Skins of Birds" (by "H."), *Loudon's Mag. Nat. Hist.* iii. (1830), p. 93. London.

"A Syllabus of Practical Taxidermy," etc. New York. n. d.

"Taxidermi. Veiledning for den, som ville paatage sig Indsamling af naturvidenskabelige Gjenstande for Universitetet Samlinger," *Nyt Mag. f. Naturvid.* 12. Bd. (1863), pp. 356-369.

"Taxidermist's Guide." New York, Hurst.

"Taxidermist's Manual." New York, Haney.

"Taxidermy, or the Art of collecting, preparing, and mounting Objects of Natural History for the Use of Museums and Travellers." Fourth edition. London, 1829.

A Translation, by Mrs. Ed. Bowdich, of Dufresne's "Traité de Taxidermie."
(See Lee, Mrs.)

"Taxidermy Made Easy." New York, 1858.

"Taxidermy as a Fine Art." (Illustrated.) Special illustrated supplement to *Natural Science*, No. 30. London and New York, August 1894. This and the preceding are practically reviews of Shufeldt's *Scientific Taxidermy for Museums*.

"Taxidermy at Home." (Illustrated.) *Ward's Natural Science Bulletin*. Rochester, New York, January 1883, pp. 13, 14.

INDEX

THE END

Printed by R. & R. CLARK, LIMITED, *Edinburgh*